SUPERMAN

SUPERMAN

THE HIGH-FLYING HISTORY OF
AMERICA'S MOST ENDURING HERO

LARRY TYE

RANDOM HOUSE

NEW YORK

Copyright © 2012 by Larry Tye

All rights reserved.

Published in the United States by Random House, an imprint of The Random
House Publishing Group, a division of Random House, Inc., New York.

RANDOM HOUSE and colophon are registered trademarks of Random House, Inc.

Library of Congress Cataloging-in-Publication Data

Tye, Larry.
Superman : the high-flying history of America's most enduring hero / Larry Tye.
p.   cm.
ISBN 978-1-4000-6866-1
eBook ISBN 978-1-58836-918-5
1. Superman (Fictitious character)   I. Title.
PN6728.S9T94 2012
741.5'973—dc23   2011045280

Printed in the United States of America on acid-free paper

www.atrandom.com

2   4   6   8   9   7   5   3   1

First Edition

Book design by Christopher M. Zucker

To Lisa

Preface

ENDURANCE

THE MOST ENDURING AMERICAN HERO of the last century is someone who lived half his life in disguise and the other half as the world's most recognizable man. He is not Jack Kennedy or Joltin' Joe DiMaggio, Batman or Jerry Seinfeld, although all of them were inspired by him. It was on his muscle-bound back that the iconic comic book took flight and the very idea of the superhero was born. He appeared on more radio broadcasts than Ellery Queen and in more movies than Marlon Brando, who once pretended to be his father. He helped give America the backbone to wage war against the Nazis, the Great Depression, and the Red Menace. He remains an intimate to kids from Boston to Belgrade and has adult devotees who, like Talmudic scholars, parse his every utterance. And he has done it all with an innocence and confidence that allowed him to appear publicly wearing underpants over full-body tights, and to assume an alter ego who kept pursuing the prettiest girl in town even though he seldom got her.

The most enduring American hero is an alien from outer space who, once he reached Earth, traded in his foreign-sounding name Kal-El for a singularly American handle: Superman.

Ah, you say, the Man of Steel—I know him! But do you really? Do you know the wrenching story of his birth and nurturing at the hands of a parade of young creators yearning for their own absent fathers? The first was the youngest child of Lithuanian immigrants who was devastated when his dad died during a robbery. While there was no bringing back his father and role model, Jerry Siegel did bring to life a hero able not just to run fast and jump high but, as we see early on, to fend off a robber. Who would publish this fanciful tale? How about Jack Liebowitz, a hardheaded comic book entrepreneur whose own dad had died just after he was born and who needed a champion? Whitney Ellsworth, the man who wrote, edited, and produced nearly all the episodes of the 1950s TV show that introduced many baby boomers to this costumed hero, was just fourteen when he lost his forty-five-year-old father to a heart attack. George Reeves, TV's original Clark Kent and Superman, didn't even know who his real father was until he was in his twenties. Who better to create the ultimate childhood fantasy figure than men whose childhoods had been stolen from them?

Not just Superman but his rivals, too, were more than they seemed—and more than just fantasy. Many of them were real-world menaces, which made the Superman stories timely and authentic. Superman stood up to Hitler and Stalin before America did. The Metropolis Marvel used his radio broadcast to expose the savagery of the Ku Klux Klan, and in his comic books he upended slumlords and wife-beaters. Lex Luthor, Superman's most persistent foe, likely came from Jerry Siegel's boyhood. The day after Jerry's father died, his hometown newspaper published a letter denouncing the kind of vigilante justice that would become Superman's early signature. The letter writer: A. L. Luther.

The superhero never revealed how he voted, but during the Great Depression he was a New Dealer hell-bent on truth and justice, and during the Reagan Revolution he was a patriot trumpeting the American way. His sex life underwent an even more drastic about-face: from celibate to satisfied husband. There is one more thing that even his most fervent fans may not know about the Man of Steel: He is Jewish.

I have been captivated by Superman ever since I wrote my first book, the life story of the public relations pioneer and master manipulator Edward L. Bernays. Borrowing ideas from his uncle Sigmund Freud, Bernays single-handedly shaped many of our political and cultural appetites—from sweetening sour politicians like Calvin Coolidge to selling America on the European tenor Enrico Caruso. Negro Leagues strikeout king Leroy "Satchel" Paige, the subject of my most recent book, borrowed Bernays's techniques in crafting his own eye-popping legend. Paige and Bernays got me wondering: Why does America embrace the heroes it does? What do our choices say about them and, more important, about us? There's no better way to understand modern-day heroes than to look at Superman, the super-hero who tapped into the American psyche more effectively than anyone else and, as a result, has lasted longer than all of them.

Clearly there was a serious story here, but for me the other appeal of writing this book was getting to be ten again. I had grown up reading Superman comics and watching nearly all 104 episodes of *Adventures of Superman* on TV. I sat mesmerized by his movies and pondered: What would it feel like to actually take flight? Superman was comfort food for my spirit, and writing this book let me partake of that comfort all over again. It also let me imagine what Superman did between adventures, when he doffed his cape and sprawled out on the couch.

Okay, so I still cared about Superman, but did anyone else? Sure, he was a big deal when I was coming of age in the 1960s, but I assumed he was passé in the virtual realities of the new millennium. Then I started paying attention. My four-year-old nephew showed up one night wearing a Superman shirt. My sixteen-year-old step-daughter told me how, when she was four, she had trick-or-treated dressed not as Supergirl but as Superman. My oldest friend's fourteen-year-old daughter showed me her DVD collection of *Smallville,* a show I had never heard of that, for ten seasons, has chronicled the adventures of a young Clark Kent. The final test came on Halloween, when merchants in my hometown of Lexington, Massachusetts, hand out candy all afternoon, packing sidewalks with costumed kids who provide the perfect sampling with which to judge who's hot in the world of heroes. Spider-Man did well, with half a dozen children dressed in webbed costumes, but the hands-down winner was the blue tights, red cape, and bright yellow *S* of Superman.

I still had doubts, but they had changed from whether anyone cared to why. Why did Senator Barack Obama pose in front of a Superman statue and later, just before his election as president, joke that he, too, came from Krypton? Surely he understood better than anyone the value of bonding to such a symbol of strength and honor. Why is the Man of Steel as popular today as he was in my boyhood and in every era back to his begetting in the 1930s? That is more than we can say for Jim Thorpe or Dwight Eisenhower, the Phantom, the Lone Ranger, or Tarzan the Ape Man. By the time of his death, even a brilliant pitcher and consummate character like Satchel Paige had become a vague if nostalgic memory for most. Heroes, understandably, are woven into their time and seldom last far beyond it. How had Superman broken the mold?

To answer those questions, I did what any journalist would: I asked smart people who ought to know. I did more than two hundred interviews, starting with historians, clerics, and psychologists who have written and lectured about Superman's godlike attributes, his corrupting influences, and why children and their grandparents continue to embrace him. I spoke with writers and artists who brought Superman to life in comic books, comic strips, novels, and graphic novels, as well as on radio, TV, film, and animation. Ninety-two-year-old ghostwriter Alvin Schwartz told me that he wasn't supposed to tell anyone that he was the man behind the newspaper strip, but then *The New York Times* outed him. Jack Larson and Noel Neill explained why they initially did all they could to escape their Jimmy Olsen and Lois Lane personas from the wildly popular *Adventures of Superman,* but now—like Superman's other aging midwives—they relish the attention the connection still brings. Aaron Smolinski recounted the way kids teased him for appearing naked as baby Clark in *Superman: The Movie* and the way people still ask, "How did you lift the truck?" "I say, 'I'm Superman.'"

I visited Superman's publisher in New York. I went to his movie studio in California and his hometown of Cleveland. I talked to fanatic fans and casual ones, adolescents and octogenarians, here and abroad. They all agreed with Donald Wurzelbacher of Cincinnati that Superman is "the godfather of superheroes . . . the original, first, and greatest."

I listened to hour after hour of Superman's old radio broadcasts and watched his early and recent TV shows, cartoons, and films. I read everything I could find about him in books, magazines, and newspapers, where columnists loved to quote him in the financial and editorial sections as well as in the comics, in tabloids like the *New York Post* and high-minded broadsheets like *The New York Times.* I pored over thousands of pages of public records, and others that have never been released, from the ongoing lawsuit against Superman's publisher by his creators' heirs. I read the unpublished memoirs of Jerry Siegel and Jack Liebowitz, Superman's originator and patron, and talked to their friends and relatives. I reviewed yellowing police files and coroner's reports on George Reeves, the TV Man of Steel, with forensic experts and researchers who have spent a lifetime looking into his death. I began by worrying whether, given all that has been written on Superman, I would have anything new to say. I ended by worrying how to fit into a single manuscript all I have to say on this unambiguous hero who is as much a part of our communal DNA as Paul Bunyan or Huckleberry Finn.

So how has Superman managed to thrive for nearly seventy-five years?

It starts with the intrinsic simplicity of his story. Little Orphan Annie and Oliver Twist remind us how compelling a foundling's tale can be, and Superman, the sole survivor of a doomed planet, is a super-foundling. The love triangle connecting Clark Kent, Lois Lane, and Superman has a side for everyone, whether you are the boy who can't get the girl, the girl pursued by the wrong boy, or the conflicted hero. His secret identity might have been annoying if we hadn't been let in on the joke, and if we didn't each have a hero hidden within ourselves. He was not just any hero, but one with the very powers we would like to have: the strength to lift boulders and planets, the speed to outrun a locomotive or a bullet, and, coolest on anyone's fantasy list, the gift of flight.

Superpowers are just half the equation. More essential is knowing what to do with them, and nobody has a more instinctual sense than Superman of right and wrong. He is an archetype of mankind at its pinnacle. Like John Wayne, he sweeps in to solve our problems. No thank-you needed. Like Jesus Christ, he descended from the heavens to help us discover our humanity. He is neither cynical, like Batman, nor fraught, like Spider-Man. For the religious, he can reinforce whatever faith they profess; for nonbelievers, he is a secular messiah. The more jaded the era, the more we have been lured back to his clunky familiarity. The outcome of his adventures may be as predictable as those of Sherlock Holmes—the good guy never loses—but that too is reassuring.

So is his uniform. His tights and cape, in radiant primary colors, make Superman as instantly recognizable as Santa Claus—and as comforting. That familiarity helped his handlers move him from the printed page to the airwaves, then from the small screen to the big. No need to explain who he was; everyone knew as soon as they saw him. A costume could also be electrifying, the more so when it didn't come with a mask. Just ask Robin Hood and Elvis Presley.

That does not mean he hasn't changed with the times. Superman has evolved more than the fruit fly. In the 1930s he was just the crime fighter we needed to take on Al Capone and the robber barons. In the 1940s he defended the home front while brave GIs battled overseas. Early in the Cold War he stood taller than ever for his adopted country, while in its waning days he tried single-handedly to eliminate nuclear stockpiles. For each era he zeroed in on the threats that scared us most, using powers that grew or diminished depending on the need. So did his spectacles, hairstyle, even his job title. Each generation got the Superman it needed and deserved. Each change offered a Rorschach test of that time and its dreams. Superman, always a beacon of light, was a work in progress.

Over the years, comics, too, have been transformed—from childhood entertainment to art form to mythology—and Superman helped drive that transformation. The comic book and its leading man could only have taken root in America. What could be more U.S.A. than an orphaned outsider who arrives in this land of immigrants, reinvents himself, and reminds us that we can reach for the sky? Yet today this flying Uncle Sam is global in his reach, having written himself into the national folklore from Beirut to Buenos Aires. It is that constancy and purity—knowing that he is not merely the oldest of our superheroes but the most transcendent—that has reeled back aging devotees like me and drawn in new ones like my stepdaughter and nephew. It is what makes the Man of Tomorrow timeless as well as ageless.

Contents

SUPERMAN

CHAPTER 1

Giving Birth

LEGEND HAS IT THAT SUPERMAN was born under a fiery red sun on the futuristic planet of Krypton, in a crystal tower overlooking the Jewel Mountains and the Scarlet Jungle. But the legend has it wrong. In fact, Superman was born under a hazy yellow sun in a gritty Jewish precinct of Cleveland, two blocks from the Hebrew Orthodox Old Age Home and down the street from Glenville High. Just ask Jerry Siegel. He's the one who brought him to life there in the throes of the Great Depression.

Jerry Siegel happened to have been born in a gritty Jewish precinct of Cleveland, too, in 1914. And being Jerry never was easy. His trouble began in first grade. The stubby six-year-old had proudly memorized the rules for asking to pee: You raised your hand, and the teacher acknowledged you and said it was okay to go to the bathroom. The boy behind him did it. A pigtailed girl followed. But there was no reply when Jerry raised his hand. Finally the teacher turned his way: "What do *you* want?" He told her. "No," she said. Maybe she thought he was faking. Maybe it was that he was short, shy, wore glasses, and was the child not of refined German Jews but of unwashed immigrants from Eastern Europe. Whatever the reason, his bladder swelled and a puddle formed under his seat. With other children pointing, the teacher descended: "You are a bad, bad, bad, bad boy! Bad and disgusting! Leave the room, this very instant! Go home!" "At an early age," Jerry recalled decades later, "I got a taste of how it feels to be victimized."

That sensation became a pattern. On Valentine's Day, classmates addressed cards to one another; the teacher handed them out as the students waited anxiously. The first year Jerry got just one, from his sympathetic teacher. The next year he secretly inscribed a card to himself. Jerome the Loner, he thought. Jerome the Pariah. Jerome the Outcast. Schoolwork was equally problematic. The semester started with smiles and anticipation. "Happiness," he would say, "vibrated all over the place. But then, when the grim business of cramming knowledge into one's skull got down to business, interest in arithmetic, geography, etc. just slid off my brain, and oozed into a crack in the floor, where it gradually evaporated." He got used to Ds and Fs—and to summers repeating the failed subjects, which "was even more dismal. While other kids enjoyed summer vacation, I had my nose rubbed into education."

Recess, too, was a trial and oftentimes a terror for him. Tormenters were everywhere. Some tripped him as he tried to escape, others punched. His very name became a source of ridicule. "Siegel, Seagull, bird of an Eagle!" they would chant. If only he really could fly away. If only the girls hadn't heard. He was too bashful to say a word to pretty ones like Lois Amster, the girl he had a crush on, but even the homely ones showed zero interest. "I hadn't asked for the face or physique I was born with," he wrote. "I had not sculpted my nose, or fashioned my chin, or decided how broad my shoulders would be, or how tall I would become. I looked searchingly into the mirror for a clue. The mirror refused to commit itself." Doubts like those are part of growing up. Most kids outrun or outgrow them. Jerry's stuck like a mark of Cain from grammar school all the way through high school, where he would often turn up late, with his hair flying off in different directions and his pajamas just visible under his pant cuffs and over his shirt collar.

With the real world offering no solace, he created one built around fantasies. Mornings, he stood in the schoolyard until his classmates disappeared indoors, then he headed to the public library. Pulling his favorites from the tall stacks of books, he was transported into the dime-novel worlds of master detective Nick Carter, collegiate crime

buster Frank Merriwell, and adventurers closer to his age and circum-
stance like the Rover Boys. Fred Rover and his cousins Jack, Andy,
and Randy may have been in military school, but that never kept
them from exploring wrecked submarines or prospecting for pirates'
gold. On weekends, Jerry went to matinees at the motion picture
theater. Western megastar Tom Mix made 336 films and Jerry saw all
that his allowance would allow. He also was an insatiable consumer of
movies starring Douglas Fairbanks, Sr., as Zorro, Robin Hood, and
the thief of Baghdad. And watching was not enough. Convinced he
could replicate Mix's and Fairbanks's derring-do, Jerry darted in and
out of traffic on the narrow roads of his Glenville neighborhood.
"Those furious humans driving the cars, who yammered and glared
insanely at me," he said, "were mere mortals. But I . . . I was a leaping, twirling, gleeful phenomenon!" Back at home, with his hip
healed after one of those glaring drivers sideswiped him, he climbed
onto the roof of the garage holding an umbrella. "I opened the umbrella and leapt. Look out world, here I come! . . . I did this over and
over again. Unexpectedly, the umbrella suddenly turned inside-out as
I descended. I banged a knee, when I hit the ground. Just as I had
abandoned berserkly dodging in and out between moving automobiles, I gave up jumping off the top of my garage."

As freeing as it felt to mimic his idols, better still was concocting
narratives starring Jerry Siegel—not the shunned, tongue-tied adolescent the kids in the schoolyard saw, but the real Jerry, fearless and
stalwart. The setting, too, was of his own making, leaving behind
Glenville's twenty-five Orthodox shuls and row after row of faded
up-and-down duplexes. Crawling into bed at night with pencil and
paper, he imagined faraway galaxies full of mad scientists and defiant
champions. He loved parody, too, inventing characters like Goober
the Mighty, a broken-down knockoff of Tarzan. He went on day-
dreaming in the classroom, and his writing found its way into the
high school newspaper, the *Glenville Torch,* and onto the pages of his
own *Cosmic Stories,* America's first science fiction magazine produced
by and for fans.

Jerry wasn't popular, he wasn't strong, but one thing he knew: He
was inventive. Pointing to an empty Coke bottle, he told his cousin,
"I could make up a story about that." He even tried an autobio-

graphical novel but flushed it down the toilet after a friend suggested that perhaps not all his experiences were worthy of the label "ecstasy." No theme stuck for long, he confessed in a later-life autobiography. And he still couldn't decide whether good guys or bad made better protagonists.

Clarity came on the wings of his own tragedy. It happened on an overcast evening in June 1932, just after eight o'clock, in a downtrodden strip of Cleveland's black ghetto known as Cedar-Central. Michel Siegel was ready to head home to his family when three men whom police would describe as "colored" entered his secondhand clothing store, one of the few Jewish businesses left in a neighborhood populated by barber shops, billiard parlors, and greasy spoons. One man asked to see a suit, then walked out with it without paying; another blocked the owner's path. Michel, a slight man whose heart muscle was weaker than even he knew, fell to the floor. A month shy of his sixtieth birthday, he stopped breathing before medics could get him to the hospital. His wife, Sarah, was a widow now, on her own with three girls, three boys, and next to no savings. Jerry, her youngest, took the loss of his father the hardest. The boy who had been bullied was bereft. Sitting on his dad's knee and being rocked up and down had been one of Jerry's few safe havens. "Bliss," he called it later. "Supreme rapture." Now his father was gone.

The world of make-believe seemed more alluring than ever to Jerry, who was not quite eighteen. What had been a series of disparate characters with no focus or purpose now merged into a single figure who became a preoccupation. He called him "The Super-Man." Jerry's first story, written shortly after his father's death, envisioned the figure as endowed with exceptional strength, telescopic vision, the capacity to read minds, and a resolve to rule the universe. Over the months that followed, this character would drop "the" and the hyphen, along with his evil inclinations, becoming simply Superman— a bulletproof avenger who beat back bullies, won the hearts of girls, and used his superpowers to help those most in need. And who, in the only artwork that survives from that first imagining, soars to the rescue of a middle-aged man being held up by a robber.

.   .   .

SUPERMAN MAY HAVE BEEN A product of the 1930s and Jerry Siegel's teenage imagination, but his DNA traces back twenty-five hundred years to the age of the Tanakh, the Hebrew Bible. The evidence is there in the Book of Judges and the parable of its last and most exalted jurist, Samson. With the Israelites desperate to free themselves from forty years of enslavement by the Philistines, God offered up a strongman who killed a lion with his bare hands and then, using nothing more than the jawbone of an ass, slew a thousand enemy soldiers. The Philistines managed to capture this extraordinary being, gouging out his eyes and bringing him to their shrine in shackles to dance before them, humiliated. But in an act of self-sacrifice and backbone that would set a yardstick for every super-being who came after, Samson brought the enemy's temple crashing down around them as he proclaimed, "Let me die with the Philistines!"

Masterful as the Hebrews were at fashioning powerful and noble warriors, no one outdid the Hellenists. The very word "hero" comes from the Greek *heros,* meaning "protector" or "defender." The Greek pantheon of demigods began with Perseus, famous for slaying monsters from the sea and the land. There was Jason, who led the heroic Argonauts on a quest for the golden fleece; Euphemus, who could walk on water; Caeneus, who was invulnerable to swords, spears, or any weapon known in his day; and Hermes, speediest and cagiest of the gods. The ultimate exemplar of the Greek ideal of heroism was Herakles, the defender against evil and tamer of beasts, whom the Romans would adopt and rebrand as Hercules. Like Superman, Herakles signaled his special powers in infancy, grabbing by their necks a pair of deadly serpents that had crawled into his cradle and squeezing the life from them. And like Superman, Herakles devoted his days to rescuing ladies in distress, battling a shifting cast of villains, and searing a place in the public imagination as an embodiment of virtue.

Each era that followed produced its own mythic figures that reflected its peculiar dreams and dreads. In 1752, Voltaire anticipated the genre of science fiction and poked fun at contemporary dogmas in his tale of Micromegas, a 120,000-foot-tall super-genius who traveled here from a far-distant planet. Micromegas rendered his verdict on Earth: It's not nearly as special as its inhabitants think. Half a century on, nineteen-year-old Mary Shelley gave us Victor Frankenstein, who tapped his collection of dead body parts to build an eight-foot monster with yellowing skin. More even than Voltaire, Shelley reflected the tremendous leap from Hebrew and Greek legends built on superstition to a more modern reliance on science as the wellspring for fantastic literature. Likewise, her monster foreshadowed Jerry Siegel's early vacillation between Super-Man and Superman. Should his standard-bearer be a contemptible villain, an unwavering hero, or something more ambiguous like Dr. Frankenstein?

History's most infamously ambiguous blueprint for the hero was the German philosopher Friedrich Nietzsche's *Übermensch,* which translates literally as "overman" and colloquially as "superman." With God dead, Nietzsche argued, man would be tempted to look for salvation in an afterlife or from a society that was naively egalitarian. The real place to look, he said, was among mankind's talented few—its Caesars and Napoleons—who were ready to rule decisively and efficiently. "What is the ape to man?" Nietzsche asked in 1883. "A laughingstock or a painful embarrassment. And man shall be just that for the overman." Some interpreted Nietzsche's answer as a Buddha-like call for humans to reach for an enlightened state; others saw a clearheaded if cold assessment of the unequal allocation of human talents. Adolf Hitler used Nietzsche's argument to bolster not just his theory of a master race of Aryan supermen, but also his obsession with rooting out Jews, Gypsies, gays, and others he saw as subhuman. Whether Hitler appropriated Nietzsche's message or perverted it, the lesson for all hero-framers who followed was clear: Be careful. Whatever your intent, madmen can fuse their nightmares onto your dreams. Fairly or not, history will hold you accountable.

That prehistory was especially resonant in 1932, the year Michel Siegel died and The Super-Man was conceived. America's flirtation with science fiction had, by then, mushroomed into a craze. The only medium that mattered was the written one, with AM radio still in its chaotic early era, FM a year away, and network television but a gleam in its designers' eyes. Action and adventure were still essential, but better still was a story that drew on pseudoscience and a hero endowed with superpowers. Popeye the Sailor Man had both, which let him chase Bluto and Sea Hag all over the planet, popping open a can of spinach whenever he needed to recharge his muscles or fend off bullets or aliens. Buck Rogers's oyster was outer space, where his swashbuckling was such a hit that he spawned an interplanetary imitator: Flash Gordon. Alley Oop started out in the Stone Age, in the kingdom of Moo, and ended up in a time-traveling machine. And when it came to brainwashing there were no rivals: Ask any teenager in the 1930s, "Who knows what evil lurks in the hearts of men?" and they answered as one: "The Shadow knows."

The Shadow, an avenger with the power to cloud men's minds so they couldn't see him, was born on the radio and would catch fire everywhere, from magazines, cartoon strips, and comic books to TV, film, and graphic novels. A more typical launching pad was the funny pages, where tens of millions of readers followed Popeye, Tarzan, and their chums every day in black-and-white, and on Sunday in full color. The adventure strip was taking off in 1932, which was just the right moment given what readers were seeing in the rest of the newspaper.

Who wouldn't want to escape his circumstances, if not his planet, with the world economy in free fall? One in four Americans had no job. The British had just tossed into jail the conscience of the world, Mahatma Gandhi. Millions of Soviets were starving to death. Almost as unsettling was the human-scale drama of a twenty-month-old toddler: Charles Augustus Lindbergh, Jr., son of America's beloved aviator-inventor, was discovered missing from his crib the evening of March 1. The "crime of the century" riveted the nation, as a note from kidnappers told the Lindberghs to "have $50,000 redy" and assured them that "the child is in gut care." Gangster Al Capone promised that if he was let out of jail he would crack the case, while President Herbert Hoover vowed to "move Heaven and Earth" to find the infant. It was truck driver William Allen who actually did, two months after the abduction. Stopping to relieve himself in a grove of trees five miles from the Lindbergh home, he discovered the remains of a baby. The skull was fractured. The left leg was gone, along with both hands, and the torso had been gnawed on by animals. But the overlapping toes of the right foot and a shirt stitched by his nursemaid identified the body as the Lindbergh boy.

Escape indeed. Some kids chose dance marathons—known as "corn and callus carnivals"—to blot out the news and test whether they could keep fox-trotting or waltzing for twelve, twenty-four, or even thirty hours. An easier way to take flight during that decade of despair was through science fiction, and especially through a new trio of mythmakers. Each understood that while Herakles suited the needs of ancient Greece, and Frankenstein was monster enough for the 1800s, the twentieth century's expanding horizons of technology, medicine, and cognition required a paladin who was more expansive, more imaginative, more *today*. Each saw his hero not as a gift from God but as a triumph of fantastic science. All three could claim to be Superman's patron saint if not his progenitor.

First on the scene was Tarzan creator Edgar Rice Burroughs. His protagonist, John Carter of Mars, was actually from Earth, and more precisely Virginia. Carter had served in the Confederate Army and then struck gold in Arizona, but before he could spend it he was killed by Apaches. Instead of in heaven, however, he ended up on the red planet, or rather on its fantastic double that Burroughs dubbed Barsoom, where he stayed forever young and strong enough to defend his new planet from beastly villains. Burroughs introduced Carter to the world in the 1912 novel *A Princess of Mars,* which foreshadowed Superman in ways substantial and small. John Carter traveled in space and was invulnerable. His strength on Mars came from the planet's having less gravity than Earth, the flip side of what would happen to Superman when he reached Earth from Krypton. And the name Krypton came from the same line of the periodic table of the elements from which Burroughs plucked the name Helium, one of the empires on Barsoom.

In 1930, two years after Burroughs came out with his sixth Mars-Barsoom novel, Philip Wylie published a book called *Gladiator* with a hero named Hugo Danner. Danner's father, biology professor Abednego Danner, concocted a serum so effective in turning tame animals into ogres that he could not resist trying it on humans. The easiest subject at hand was his pregnant wife. It worked, and she delivered a son with the strength of Samson, the speed of Hermes, and skin, like Caeneus's, that was impervious to injury—a package similar to the one Siegel would unwrap eight years later. Hugo's powers were hinted at in the crib, as Superman's would be; both were cautioned by their fathers to use their gifts judiciously; and the two authors settled on the same superlative to describe their creations: "superhuman" for Wylie, "superman" for Siegel.

The last in the triumvirate of early-twentieth-century science fiction exemplars was Clark Savage, Jr., known to the world as "Doc." His first tale hit the newsstands in February 1933, just as the Depression was reaching its nadir, President Franklin Roosevelt was about to declare a holiday that would close every bank in America, and Jerry Siegel was putting the finishing touches on a superhero he would nickname the Man of Steel. It helped to have as a model Doc Savage, a.k.a. the Man of Bronze. Savage's name rightfully suggested brute strength, but he also was endowed with the deductive skills of Sherlock Holmes, the tree-swinging grace of Tarzan, the scientific-sleuthing acumen of Dick Tracy, and the morals of Abraham Lincoln. Doc crafted a hero's code of conduct that would offer a prototype for Superman and his crime-fighting cohorts: Do not kill your enemy if you can help it. Do not get entangled with women. Do find a remote getaway—he and Superman both picked the Arctic, and both called their getaways the Fortress of Solitude—where you can take a break from saving the world.

On the eve of his birth, then, Superman's world was awash in heroes. So keen was the ferment and the determination to be noticed that the word the Greeks had given us no longer was enough. Now authors and publishers were beating the drums for their champions by inflating their adjectives—*thrilling, marvelous, amazing,* and soon, the most singular and separating descriptive of them all: *super,* short for superlative. This new breed of hero started out with the models of strength and courage from the past, then added twists—interplanetary adventure, space-age gadgets, time travel—to spark the imaginations of readers reared in a world of automobiles, airplanes, and skyscrapers. Most had followings measured in the hundreds of thousands or even millions. None—not the buff Doc Savage or the brooding Hugo Danner, the soaring John Carter or the elusive Shadow—had whatever alchemy was needed to separate them from the crowd. As saturated as the market seemed, America was readier than it knew for a hero sized to the age of the metropolis.

· · ·

JEROME THE LONER GOT IT. He may not have been much of a student at Glenville High, where it took him five years to graduate, but Jerry Siegel was a scholar of science fiction and pop culture. He saw the lightning in the air and was determined to bottle it. Being in Cleveland put him far enough away from Oz that the only place to realize his dreams was in his imagination and his writings. Being a loner, with few friends and no girlfriend, let him be single-minded in those pursuits. Being a kid gave him just the right vantage point.

As early as junior high he was poring over the pulps, the ten-cent magazines that were the successors to Britain's aptly titled penny dreadfuls and forerunners to the comic book. Pulps took their name from the coarse paper they were printed on, and they took stories from just about anyone. A few were long-lived gems like *The Maltese Falcon* and *The Shadow,* which ran the length of a novel and had heroic narratives; more were trashy tales of sex and mayhem. The earliest pulps had appeared in the 1890s, and by the 1920s some were selling a million copies an issue to working stiffs anxious to escape their vanilla lives or kids with an extra dime and an appetite for wars and westerns. Jerry brought his everywhere, including study hall, which earned him a visit to the principal and a warning to "never, never, never again transgress in this unspeakable manner . . . or else." But the message he was getting from trade magazines was more persuasive, with announcements that authors nearly as young as he were being published in the pulps, while *Reader's Digest* trumpeted the big money that comic strip writers were making.

High school was the ideal testing ground for Jerry's fevered imagination. The *Torch* dubbed him the "master of deduction" and ran stories by him that aped his favorite writer, Edgar Rice Burroughs. He sent handwritten features and letters to the *Sunday Buffalo Times* and at least one was published, a piece titled "Monsters of the Moon." He corresponded with other wannabe writers. Over time he got bolder, launching The Fantastic Fiction Publishing Company, naming himself president, and putting out a typewritten journal called *Cosmic Stories.* He had but one writer, himself, although in what would become a pattern he took on a pen name, Charles McEvoy. Jerry's explanation for this: "Jerome Siegel did not seem very literary to me." A more likely explanation: A boy who saw himself as a pariah wanted to shield himself from brickbats, and perhaps from anti-Semitism.

Guests of the Earth was his next publication. He printed it after hours on the high school mimeograph machine and published it under an equally Waspy pseudonym: Hugh Langley. When an English teacher saw it, she demanded, "Jerome, why do you write these kinds of stories, when there are so many more worthwhile things you could write about?" His science teacher didn't bother to ask, dismissing Jerry's pamphlets as "junk" and "foolishness." His parents loved their last-born but were equally unimpressed with his scribbling. Michel merely shrugged. Sarah considered Jerry's dream of becoming a writer "a wild, erratic notion and that nothing would really come of it," Jerry remembered later. "She told me that of all her children, she worried the most about me."

No matter. Like his fellow science fiction aficionados, Jerry was not writing for his parents or their peers. His audience was youngsters like himself. So he wrote what he dreamed about—messages from the planet Mars, bullied boys who got even, an ape-man named Goober who was raised by lions. Neither the characters nor the writing was especially persuasive, not with lines like these: " 'Goober!' he shouted, 'Don't you recognize your old pal? It's me—Izzy the Ape! I've changed my name, that's all. Nobody knew the difference in Cleveland, I look so much like the people there.' " But the school paper published it for just that reason: It was not overthought. The language and plots were precisely right for kids like Jerry, kids with outsize imaginations and visions of a world beyond Cleveland, and who had peed in their pants or worried they might.

What did matter to Jerry was money. His dad, a tailor from Lithuania, had squeezed out a living selling and altering suits and other secondhand clothes. Sarah helped out behind the counter. At its best the shop's revenues were barely enough to sustain a family of eight, and during the Depression sales and profits were even lower. After Michel died, the Siegels were destitute. Harry, Jerry's oldest brother, kept them housed and fed with money he earned as a mailman. Others kicked in what they could, even Jerome, Sarah's baby and pet. That meant working after school as a delivery boy for a print shop, where he earned the royal rate of four dollars a week and dreamed of hitting the jackpot with his writing. It also meant sharing a bed with his brother Leo.

Most of the stories he wrote were mailed back by publishers or were gone forever, so Jerry decided to try his hand once more at publishing. His new magazine had a title worthy of his lofty hopes: *Science Fiction: The Advance Guard of Future Civilization.* He was not the only writer this time; fellow Glenville High students chipped in. Jerry was, however, still the sole executive, holding the titles of owner, editor, secretary, treasurer, and office boy. He continued to rely on the school mimeograph machine, but he vowed that would change when ads he placed in more established science fiction publications swelled his magazine's circulation. His rates—fifteen cents a copy, or $1.50 a year—were no bargain, not when thick pulps could be had for a thin dime. And he continued to sign with a name not his own: Herbert S. Fine, which blended the name of his cousin Herbert Schwartz with his mother's maiden name, Fine. Looking back, there are two names that stand out even more in *Science Fiction:* its primary illustrator, Joe Shuster, and the main character in a story in its third issue, Super-Man.

Jerry's and Joe's names would become as conjoined and revered in the world of comics as those of Rodgers and Hammerstein in song and Tracy and Hepburn in cinema. Jerry and Joe met through Jerry's cousin Jerry Fine, who lived in another part of Cleveland. Fine wrote a column in junior high called "Jerry the Journalist," which Shuster illustrated. When Joe was about to enter ninth grade his family moved to Glenville, and Fine suggested he look up Jerry Siegel. The boys looked almost like brothers even though Jerry was four inches taller and forty pounds heavier, and they seemed fated to become a twosome. Both wore glasses, were petrified of girls, and preferred to stay indoors reading when everyone else their age was in the park playing ball, which made them two-for-one targets for schoolyard toughs. Both were the children of Jewish refugees, and Joe's dad, Julius, was a tailor like Michel Siegel. Both grew up poor, although the Shusters' cramped apartment made the Siegels' two-story home ten blocks away look like a mansion.

Julius Shuster was brilliant with a needle and thread but not with a ledger. He had sunk his meager inheritance into a tailor shop in To-

ronto's garment district, but the shop failed when he charged too
little for clothes that took too long to stitch. His family was accustomed to changing apartments on rent day, but this time they moved
all the way to Cleveland, for the promise of a job manufacturing
men's suits. Joe had always helped pay the family's bills with the meager wages he could get by peddling newspapers, hawking ice cream
cones, and apprenticing with a sign painter. Still, there were winter
days and sometimes entire seasons when the Shusters went without
coal for the furnace or enough food for three meals. Liabilities like
those were not disabling back then, not during the Depression and
certainly not to children like Jerry and Joe, whose parents were needy
immigrants. The firmest basis for their bond had always been the passion they shared for fantastic stories, which is the way each saw himself getting even with his bulliers and getting out of Glenville. The
very day they met, after Joe introduced himself to Jerry at the library,
they dashed off to Joe's apartment and got to work on their first project.

Joe Shuster had loved the comics since he was a toddler back in
Canada, when his dad would boost him onto his knee and read aloud
strips like *The Katzenjammer Kids, Happy Hooligan,* and Joe's favorite,
Little Nemo in Slumberland. He also loved drawing, and he used to go
on sketching even when the house was so cold he had to wrap up in
a pair of sweaters and gloves. Lacking money for a drawing board, he
improvised: the wooden slab his mother used to knead her Sabbath
challah worked almost as well. Instead of a sketch pad he made do
with butcher paper, discarded wallpaper, and the barren walls of their
rented apartment. A scholarship let him study at the Cleveland School
of Art and he bought himself more instruction, for ten cents a class,
at the John Huntington Polytechnic Institute. His artwork was inspired but never visionary. The simple lines and expressive faces got
across his message the same way Jerry's craftsmanlike words did—with
joy, without flair. They were a well-matched pair.

Joe's limits were a matter of optics as well as talent. Even as a boy
he had major eye troubles. "He was in a sight-seeing class," remembers his junior high classmate Jerry Fine. "They had sight-seeing
classes for those kids who couldn't see well. Joe was very, very
nearsighted. His drawing had to be two to three inches from his face."

Rosie Shuster, Joe's niece, describes his eyes as "rheumy and soft-focused. He had Coke-bottle glasses. His family didn't want him to draw in the first place."

Eyesight was only the most obvious way in which Jerry and Joe, for all they shared, were different. Next to most of his peers Jerry seemed reticent, but Joe was so sheepish and sweet he made Jerry look fiery and bossy. Jerry did most of the talking, then and later; Joe trusted that Jerry would represent his interests. Crazy Joey, as one adoring cousin called him, had a broader, deeper inner life than Jerry, with fewer bridges to the real world. That made it easier both to like Joe and to take advantage of him. Joe gave Jerry the two things he most wanted: images to bring his words to life, and the clear understanding that Jerry was in charge.

Their first big collaboration was an illustrated short story called "The Reign of the Super-Man," a twist on the Frankenstein fable that they completed in 1932 and published the next January. The protagonist was Professor Ernest Smalley, a megalomaniacal scientist who tested a mind-bending chemical on a homeless man named Bill Dunn. The experiment yielded a monster with the power not just to read people's thoughts but to control them. Before Smalley could put that power to use, Dunn killed him, then hatched his own plan to manipulate stocks, clean up at racetracks, and generate enough wealth to dominate the planet. At the last instant Dunn lost his powers, re-turning to the breadline from which Smalley had plucked him. As he did, he had a bout of conscience: "I see, now, how wrong I was. If I had worked for the good of humanity, my name would have gone down in history with a blessing—instead of a curse."

Phew. The world was saved from a monster and Jerry was saved from what he would soon realize was a bad idea. A planet as troubled as his needed a hero, not another villain. At the time, he and Joe were glad to have a full-blown science fiction story, one that filled nine pages of *Science Fiction*. And certain of its themes would stick: an outer-space origin for Smalley's chemicals and Dunn's powers, a newspaper writer as the Super-Man's sidekick, and a sense of whimsy that was pure Jerry. The young writer named his reporter Forrest Ackerman, after the young science fiction fan who would later invent the term *sci-fi*. The Super-Man visited a library where his deskmate was reading *Science Fiction.* He also misbehaved there in much the way Jerry had, with the same result: a reprimand from the librarian. Yet the most striking element in this first take on Superman was its indecision—not just about big matters like whether the central character should be good or evil, but over whether to spell his name with a hyphen (as in the title), as "Superman" (the way it was in the text of the story), or as SUPERMAN (as he contemplated here and switched to in his next rendering). "The Reign of the Super-Man," Jerry explained later, was composed when he was very young, and while the central character was callow, he also "was a giant step forward on: The Road to Superman."

Soon Jerry noticed on newsstands a publication called *Detective Dan,* a forerunner of the modern comic book that lasted only that single issue but made a mark on at least one of its young readers. He started imagining a comic book that featured him, or rather his Superman. The version he was drafting would again begin with a wild scientist empowering a normal human against his will, but this time the powers would be even more fantastic, and rather than becoming a criminal, the super-being would fight crime "with the fury of an outraged avenger." Jerry and Joe worked up the copy and drawings, scraping together their nickels to pay for the paper, the ink, and the postage to mail everything to the owners of *Detective Dan.* Although the first response was encouraging, the second made it clear that the comic book was so unprofitable that its publishers put on hold any future stories.

Jerry had thought highly enough of Joe's talents in those early years that he gave him the title of art director at *Science Fiction* and enlisted him as a partner on his cherished Superman project. But now, with that project going nowhere, he had his doubts about their prospects. At first he thought the problem was that since they were just teenagers potential employers might presume their work was just a quick bit of patchwork, so he had Joe re-letter the cover of their mock comic book, backdating its origin from 1933 to 1928 to look as if it had been years in the making. Then he dropped Joe and tried to enlist an older, more established artist.

Hal Foster, who drew the Sunday *Tarzan* strip, said he was too busy. Another *Tarzan* illustrator, J. Allen St. John, expressed interest in working with Jerry on a comic strip that Jerry called "Rex Carson of the Ether Patrol," but the strip and the collaboration both died. Next on the list was Leo O'Mealia, who drew the *Fu Manchu* comic and soon found in his mailbox Jerry's more fully developed script for Superman. This one was set in a future where the Earth was about to explode. Minutes before the blast, a super-powered scientist-adventurer used a time machine to transport himself to the present, where he became a crime-fighter. His character didn't have a Clark Kent secret identity yet, although Jerry later recalled that there probably was a Lois Lane–like character. And he didn't have a publisher, although O'Mealia and the Bell Syndicate, which published *Fu Manchu,* both showed a brief interest in the sketchy story.

The one measurable result of Jerry's efforts to enlist the help of O'Mealia came from the mild-mannered Joe Shuster. "When I told Joe of this, he unhappily destroyed the drawn-up pages of "THE SUPERMAN," burning them in the furnace of his apartment building," Jerry recalled. "At my request, he gave me as a gift the torn cover." The story of Joe setting fire to the artwork is part of comic book lore, and most tellings say he did it in frustration after publishers rejected "The Superman." In his memoir, Jerry set the record straight: Shuster was angry and depressed not just because publishers weren't interested in their idea but because his partner had been disloyal to him.

Jerry was unbowed by Joe's reaction. His next target for collaboration was Russell Keaton, who drew and wrote the *Skyroads* strip. They exchanged a series of letters during the summer of 1934, with Keaton going as far as submitting what Jerry thought was inspired artwork for a Superman comic strip. Jerry, meanwhile, was fleshing out his thinking on his hero. He would not just be a man of adventure but would offer "great possibilities for humor," a device that Jerry felt could disarm readers. Superman's backstory also was shifting to what is now familiar ground. The last man on Earth had catapulted his baby rather than himself back in a time machine. The infant was found by passing motorists Sam and Molly Kent, who first turned him over to an orphanage, then adopted him and named him Clark. At the end of the second week of Jerry's scripts, Sam said to his wife, "We've been blind, Molly. The lad's strength is a God-send! I see now that he's destined for wonderful things." The story resonated more this way, and Keaton helped bring it alive with his drawings. The artist was interested enough to set up a meeting with a publisher late in 1934, but then, for reasons Jerry never understood, Keaton told him that "the book is closed." Maybe the publisher wasn't interested. Maybe Keaton was shocked to discover how young and inexperienced Jerry was. Maybe Jerry was simply a pest. Keaton is no longer around to ask, but Denis Kitchen, a comics publisher who represents Keaton's estate, says the illustrator was "a professional in his mid-twenties communicating with a teenager with a wacky idea about a guy with superpowers. . . . I think Keaton was very surprised by Superman's eventual success, since he didn't have any faith in it."

He may have been betrayed, but Joe Shuster did have faith, still, in Superman and in Jerry Siegel. And while Jerry had no scruples about going back to his abandoned partner, first he needed to retool his superhero. That happened on what he said was a hot summer night of divine-like inspiration whose timing and circumstances swelled slightly each time he revisited them. His most considered version came in his unpublished memoir—a hundred-page document whose exuberance and visual prose give it the feel of a comic book—where he recalled all the telling details of what he had done and thought a half century earlier. Jerry decided his only hope lay in crafting a hero so super that no publisher could resist, one whose story was just unbelievable enough to be credible. He vowed to stay up as late as it took. His newest incarnation of Superman would come from a dying planet called Krypton, not a dying Earth. Clark Kent, the superhero's alter ego, would be a reporter, just the occupation to snoop around for trouble. Lois Lane was here, too—a Lois who "was ga-ga over super-powered Superman" and "had an antipathy toward meek, mild Clark." The premise was easy: His character would have everything Jerry wanted for himself—he would be able to run faster than a train, leap over skyscrapers, and be noticed by a pretty girl. What teenage boy wouldn't love to be able to do all that?

The spine of the story was done late that night before Jerry climbed into his and Leo's bed, leaving paper and pencil nearby. His sleep was fitful. Every time he woke he slipped into the bathroom, flipped on the light, and filled in another piece of the tale. "This went on until the wee hours of the morning," he wrote in his late-life reminiscence. "At dawn, I enthusiastically raced about a dozen blocks to Joe's apartment. I showed Joe the script and asked him if he would be interested in collaborating with me on this newest version of my Superman syndicate[d] comic strip project. He enthusiastically agreed, and got to work at once."

The loyal Joe, hunched barely an inch above the paper as he strained to see, started drawing. Jerry hovered over him. They stopped only to gulp down sandwiches. The reunited partners now saw Superman as their joint property, although they would later disagree on who originated what. "I conceived the character in my mind's eye to have a very, very colorful costume of a cape and, you know, very, very colorful tights and boots and the letter 'S' on his chest," Joe recounted. Jerry begged to differ: it was he who dressed the hero in bold colors and an athlete's tights, and he who came up with the *S,* along with a cape that "would whip around when the character was in action." They agreed that Superman had to be everything they were not: strapping and dashing, fearless yet composed. As for the superhero's second self—Clark Kent—wasn't it obvious? Like Jerry, Clark wore glasses, wilted at the sight of blood or a pretty girl, and spent his days penning articles for the newspaper. Both lost their fathers and had their childhoods interrupted. When Joe was unsure how Clark should look, Jerry would pose for him. When it came to Superman, Joe often posed himself, in front of a mirror—contorting his face to look enraged, beaming with self-satisfaction, and, most convincingly, making his hero look uncertain about what he was doing but ready to plow ahead.

Lois was harder to picture. Joe and Jerry wanted to get her right, but there was no model at hand. So they hired one, from a Situation Wanted ad in the Cleveland *Plain Dealer,* at the lavish rate of $1.50 an hour, which was more than either boy made in a day. Jolan Kovacs, a skinny kid whose only training was posing before her bedroom mirror, had advertised herself as an "attractive model" named Joanne Carter. At two in the afternoon on a frigid Saturday in January, the scared high school student showed up at Joe's apartment. "My heart was pounding," she remembered forty years later, by which time she had still another name: Mrs. Jerry Siegel. "I knocked on the door, and a boy my age, wearing glasses, opened the door a crack, and I said, 'I'm the model Mr. Shuster wrote to.' So he opened the door and he motioned me in. We hit it off right away. We started talking about movies, we were talking about everything, and I was thawing out. And a woman stuck her head out of the kitchen and said, 'Hello'—an older woman—and a little girl ran through the living room, chased by a little boy, and out again. And we were talking for the longest time, and finally I said, 'Does Mr. Shuster know I'm here?' And he said, '*I'm* Mr. Shuster.' . . .

"So I posed for him, and his mother would look in, and I was turning blue," Joanne confessed. "My sister's bathing suit was too big, so I pinned it in the back. And he said, 'Never mind. I'll put a little bit more here, a little bit more there.' But he used my face and my hairdo and my poses that just made me look more voluptuous—and older. I had to be older." Jerry remembered that day even more distinctly and fondly: "'Wow,' I thought. 'She's terrific!' But I was too meek and mild to let Joanne know how great I thought she was. She was a very attractive girl, and I was just a teenaged kid, with a giant sized inferiority complex, who had nothing but grandiose plans that seemed very far from materializing into actuality."

Just how far is clear in hindsight. There they were, two young men who had just turned twenty, with no prospects of any kind nearly a year after graduating from high school. Both were shy of the grades and money needed for college. Neither had a real job, nor a place to live other than where they always had: with their parents. Yet they were paying money they did not have, to a teenage model who was not a model, to play a voluptuous newswoman who existed only in their imaginations. So far those imaginations had come up short, producing four renderings of a superhero who remained a closely held secret, not by design but because Jerry could not find anyone to buy his manuscript or Joe Shuster's drawings. Now even they were having doubts. "I have a feeling of affection for those lost supermen of the comics into whom I tried to breathe life, but who never surfaced onto comics pages," Jerry said. "On paper, they were the mightiest men on Earth. But in real life they were very, very fragile."

. . .

MAJOR MALCOLM WHEELER-NICHOLSON's biography reads like a Jerry Siegel adventure strip. The son of an early suffragette, he grew up at the turn of the twentieth century in a household that counted Herbert Hoover's wife and Teddy Roosevelt's mother among its intimates. A horseman from boyhood, Wheeler-Nicholson attended a military academy and then enlisted in the cavalry. He was one of its youngest senior officers and led one of the African American units known as Buffalo Soldiers. In Texas, he operated under the command of General John J. Pershing and chased bandits back across the Mexican border. In the Philippines, his squad set a world speed record for assembling its tripod-mounted machine gun. In Siberia, he was an intelligence officer working out of the Japanese embassy. When he turned on the military, publicly denouncing the outmoded way it trained and promoted troops, he was court-martialed and became the target of what his family has reason to believe was an Army-orchestrated assassination attempt.

His life as a gadabout is just half the story of the man his children knew as the Old Man, his grandchildren called Nick, and the comic book world knows as the Major. One of the most prolific pulp fiction writers of his day, he published more than ninety novels, novellas, short stories, and serials, which turned up on shelves as far away as New Zealand. He was a historian and a visionary. He knew the long and fertile life that comics had enjoyed in U.S. newspapers, beginning in the late 1800s with the launch of strips such as *The Yellow Kid* and *The Katzenjammer Kids*. The titles made clear the young audience newspaper titans were going after, and Wheeler-Nicholson was fixated on attracting that audience, along with its parents, by blending the magazine form of pulps with the picture presentation of comic strips. What he really longed for was a graphic novel—the perfect way, this literary entrepreneur thought, to bring culture to the masses—but it would be another generation before anyone even imagined that format. Instead he settled for what was at hand, launching National Allied Magazines in 1934 and a year later publishing what many consider the prototype of today's comic magazine. Unlike its progenitors, *New Fun: The Big Comic Magazine* featured comic strips that hadn't already run in newspapers and it carried money-making advertisements. Its title was apt both because of its ground-breaking contents and because it measured a whopping ten by fifteen inches.

For America, *New Fun* helped kick-start the emerging medium of comic books. For Jerry Siegel and Joe Shuster, it was a career-launcher. The Major needed writers to produce his strips, ideally ones who came cheap. It was his shortage of funds as much as creative zeal that inspired him to include only original material in his books, rather than buying the expensive right to reprint what newspapers already had published. No matter that Jerry and Joe were young and un-tested, or that their heroes were an unlikely swordsman from seventeenth-century France and an even less likely private detective investigating the supernatural. The Major needed filler. The boys needed money. And so the October 1935 issue of *New Fun* featured two single-page Siegel and Shuster titles: "Henri Duval of France, Famed Soldier of Fortune" and "Doctor Occult, the Ghost Detec-tive," a story whose protagonist had not just Superman's cape but his face.

It seemed like manna from heaven. For eight months, Jerry and Joe had tried to peddle their revamped superhero but found no takers. The Publishers Syndicate of Chicago turned them down. Owners of the *Famous Funnies* comic book returned their package unopened, Jerry's knotted strings still intact. The Bell Syndicate wrote that "the drawings are well done and the idea is rather interesting, but we would not care to undertake the syndication." So low were their funds that Joe was hawking ice cream bars on the street, and the only way Jerry could afford a movie was by selling empty milk bottles back to storekeepers. They had even started cannibalizing their sacrosanct Superman, with Doctor Occult getting his face and Henri Duval his penchant for adventure. Now, thanks to the Major, Henri Duval and Doctor Occult were being sold on the streets of Cleveland, with a promise of more work. Wheeler-Nicholson asked Jerry and Joe to prepare a four-page strip about a rip-roaring FBI agent, to be called "Federal Men," which would run in one of the new comic books he was launching. He also had ideas for three new series—"Calling All Cars: Sandy Kean and the Radio Squad," "Spy," and "Slam Bradley," a hard-bitten private eye who seemed like a dry run for Superman. Finally, in a move the young artists had been waiting for forever,

Wheeler-Nicholson wrote that their idea for a Superman comic strip "stands a very good chance."

The Major kept his promise about publishing nearly everything Jerry and Joe sent in, but there were red flags. His launches of books like *Detective Comics* were delayed. Promises of 15 percent of profits and half of syndicate sales remained promises. Some checks that were due never came, and one bounced. Early in 1936, Wheeler-Nicholson sent Jerry a payment with this postscript: "Do not be alarmed over the legal phraseology on the back of the checks. Our lawyers made us put it on after we had a couple of unfortunate experiences with chiselers who tried to hold us up after we'd paid them in full." But the boys were alarmed, less by the request that they release their rights than by the mounting evidence that the Major was running out of money. So while they continued to write and draw for him, and to live off what payments they got, they determined not to trust him with their prize possession. Please, they asked him, give us back our Superman scripts.

The truth is that Wheeler-Nicholson really did believe in Superman. His was the kind of life the Major had lived, a freewheeling and crusading one, and he was convinced that Jerry and Joe were sitting on a gold mine. That is what the Old Man told his children over the dinner table, where, said his son Douglas, Superman "was a major subject of discussion." The truth also is that the Major's approach to money was a lot like Joe's father's: noble intentions, bungled execution. In another business and another era this literary entrepreneur might have squeezed by, but not in the middle of the worst economic downturn in U.S. history, nor in a fledgling industry populated by racketeers and sharks. Two with the sharpest teeth would swallow up Wheeler-Nicholson's publishing houses before he saw what was happening.

The first of that pair, Harry Donenfeld, was a survivor. Born in Romania in 1893 just as it was turning against Jews like him, he came to America with his parents and brother and made his way as a child on the pulsating streets of New York's Lower East Side as a barker—pulling customers into clothing stores or dance halls, or hawking Yiddish and Russian newspapers. Harry neither denied nor embraced his Yiddishkeit roots, but he was hungry to leave his Jewish ghetto and determined never to go back. Money was his way out, and he made his through magazines with titles like *Juicy Tales* and *Strange Suicides*. Harry couldn't write, edit, or draw. What he did better than anyone was the hard sell. "He could sell ice to the Eskimos," said the now ninety-nine-year-old Jack Adams, who worked for him back then. "Once he got an order from Hearst for nine million inserts for magazines after he entertained their buyer by getting him drunk and laid in Canada. . . . Harry didn't know from nothing except making money." Some of that money was from printing the publications at his family's shop, but over the years more came from distributing them to drugstores and newsstands. The delivery trucks and drivers were ones bootleggers had used to supply speakeasies with hooch during Prohibition. So were the whatever-it-takes tactics needed to build and sustain regional monopolies, of which Harry had plenty. They were what led him, by the early 1930s, to become a magazine publisher and owner. As long as people were buying, what went inside the publications didn't matter.

The indictments changed all that. New York's new no-nonsense mayor, Fiorello La Guardia, was cracking down on public indecency, and nothing met that era's definition so clearly as pictures Harry ran in *Pep!* that glimpsed a woman's privates. A grand jury in Kentucky was equally offended. Harry beat the second rap and convinced an underling to take the fall for the first (the favor was returned when Harry gave the patsy, Herbie Siegel, a job for life). One lesson Harry took away was that while smut was profitable enough to sometimes justify the risk, it was best not just to sell it from behind the counter but to be a silent partner to avoid any potential embarrassment or jail time. The other lesson was to diversify.

Jack Liebowitz was everything Harry Donenfeld wasn't. His roots were in the same Jewish ghetto, and both had ties to the rabble-rousing International Ladies' Garment Workers' Union, but while Harry merely printed the guild's brochures and took its money, Jack was an officer and true believer. What Jack remembers most from his boyhood was not really having one. He was born in Ukraine in 1900, the year his father died. In 1904 his mother disappeared to America, leaving him and his older brother behind with their grandparents. By the time she came back his brother had succumbed to diphtheria.

Five months before his tenth birthday, Jack, his mother, and his little sister stole across the border in the dead of night into Austria, then made their way to Holland and got tickets in steerage for the journey to America. In New York, Jack slept on the roof of his tenement to escape the summer heat and his stepfather. With other kids, he used trash can covers to fend off rival gangs. He never owned an overcoat, or slept in a bed he didn't share with three brothers.

While Harry came away from his hardscrabble upbringing as a joyful backslapper, Jack emerged hardheaded and glum. Harry always had an expensive cigar in his mouth; Jack smoked cigarettes he bummed from friends, which was his way of disciplining himself not to smoke too much and to save money. Harry was the bluffer who showed his cards only when he had to and generally walked away with the jackpot; Jack was the house, getting a cut of every bet and never trusting to chance. His soul, like his training, was that of an accountant.

Jack went to work for Harry in 1935 after the Depression killed his hopes of making it on his own. Newly unearthed home movie footage of the two from those early years attests to the awkward pair they were—Harry short and thick, Jack six inches taller, thirty pounds lighter, and blanching as a beaming Harry, knowing the reaction he will get, reaches up and presses his face against Jack's in a warm embrace. But their differences made them perfect partners. Jack worked out the details of deals Harry made with a handshake, turned down bribes Harry had trouble resisting, and tidied up Harry's messes. Seven years Harry's junior, Jack acted like his big brother. In the process, Jack Liebowitz made himself so indispensable that Harry Donenfeld promoted him from bookkeeper to second-in-command and then to partner, with Jack bringing little equity to the table and barely anyone noticing. Not even Jack noticed as his flirtation with socialism yielded to a fondness for money.

Neither Harry nor Jack cared about art or storytelling, but they did know more than the Major about how to make a buck, and they liked the idea of branching out from the smooshies and horrors to cleaner kids' stuff. Not only did they print and deliver *New Fun* and Wheeler-Nicholson's other comic books, they also loaned him the cash to publish them. And while the Major could stay a step ahead of his writers, artists, and process servers, Harry and Jack were pros at spotting a dodger. Harry had defied the Depression trend that was bankrupting other publishers, getting his financing from a quiet partner named Paul Sampliner and Paul's indulgent mother, and buying up other presses as they teetered. In 1937 Jack became an uninvited partner in Wheeler-Nicholson's publishing house; by the next spring, the whole show was Harry and Jack's. The Major walked away with his debts wiped clean, his wallet empty, and his heart broken. Harry and Jack had all three of the Major's books, all published under the Detective Comics banner. They now owned the trucks, the printing presses, and the actual magazines, which gave them a foothold in this new world of kids' literature along with the diversity Harry the pornographer had been seeking.

Were those shifts in ownership aboveboard? Absolutely, according to Jack Liebowitz, who in his unpublished memoir said it was a straightforward matter: Wheeler-Nicholson couldn't pay his artists or writers or pay back his loans, creditors pushed him into bankruptcy, and "I went down to court and bought the two magazines." What Jack doesn't say but his company's records show is that Harry had orchestrated everything. He bought up, for fifty cents on the dollar, debts the Major owed his printer and engraver, thus meeting the three-creditor standard needed to force Wheeler-Nicholson into bankruptcy. The backdrop was Dickensian. Harry and Jack feted the Major by sending him on vacation to Cuba, tried unsuccessfully to buy him out for seventy-five thousand dollars, then took him to debtors' court during Christmas week. Harry made it happen; Jack dotted the *i*'s and crossed the *t*'s. The Major, meanwhile, overcame bouts of booze and nerves and moved on. His wife, Elsa, never did. "She hated them," said Douglas Wheeler-Nicholson, referring to Harry and Jack. "Any time any mention of them came up, she would spit fire."

The upheaval in ownership touched Jerry, Joe, and Superman in two ways. It gave Wheeler-Nicholson's old companies new bosses who could pay their bills, and it put the boys on notice that Harry and Jack relished playing hardball. Jerry spent 1936 and 1937 the way he had the two previous years, pitching Superman to anyone he thought might listen. Getting heard was harder than ever. United Feature Syndicate called the whole Superman concept "a rather immature piece of work. It is attractive because of its freshness and naïveté, but this is likely to wear off after the feature runs for a while." The Ledger Syndicate was equally blunt: "We feel that editors and the public have had their fill for the time being of interplanetary and superhuman subjects." By the end of 1937, copies of Jerry and Joe's Superman comic strip could be found in the backs of filing cabinets and the bottoms of wastebaskets across the world of publishing.

One of those who received the strip years before and never forgot it was Maxwell Charles Gaines, a senior executive at the McClure Newspaper Syndicate. Gaines could not interest his bosses so he sent back the drawings. Three years later, in December 1937, Gaines was looking for new material and decided to take another shot at Superman. Jerry and Joe mailed him proposals for five strips—about a cowboy, an adventurer, a detective, a sports star, and a sci-fi scientist, all knockoffs of icons like the Lone Ranger and Jack Armstrong, the All-American Boy—along with their latest rendition of Superman. The sketches still were on Gaines's mind and in his office a few weeks later when he got a call from the new owners of Major Wheeler-Nicholson's publishing business.

Jack and Harry wanted to launch another book. They had a title, *Action Comics,* but no material. So, as Jack wrote in his memoir, he phoned his friend Charlie Gaines. "I said, do you have any material laying around. The newspaper syndicate usually had stuff laying around. Stuff that had been submitted to them which had been turned down. So he sent me over a pile of stuff. Among that pile of stuff was Superman which had been submitted by Siegel and Shuster to the syndicate which had turned it down like all other syndicates turned it down. It was six strips, daily strips, made for newspapers. Anyway, we liked it." Charlie and Jack called Jerry in Cleveland. Gaines said he had bad news and good: His syndicate was not interested in any of the comic strips, but Jack might be. Would it be okay, Gaines wanted to know, if he turned over to Jack the scripts—including Superman?

It was the question Jerry had been waiting five years to answer. No matter that to the accountant-turned-publisher, the work of the young writer's dreams was "a pile of stuff." Vin Sullivan, an editor who stayed on during the transition from Wheeler-Nicholson to Donenfeld-Liebowitz, called Jerry in January 1938 to make plans. The boys would have to cut and paste their newspaper-style format into material that would fit in a thirteen-page comic book. And they would have to do it fast, Sullivan said, since Superman was destined for the inaugural issue of *Action Comics*. After lying around lifeless for what seemed like half a lifetime, Superman was on the fast track.

The matter of money was settled almost as fast. On March 1, Jack mailed Jerry and Joe a check for $412—$282 for work that had been done for but not yet paid by the Major, and, almost as an after-thought, $130 for Superman. It was double what they were used to and a fair rate—$10 a page—for the era and their experience, so Jerry and Joe cashed it and split it down the middle. It also was a swindle on the order of the Dutch West India Company's 1626 purchase of Manhattan from the natives for $24, for Jack and Harry were buying not merely the thirteen pages of that first Superman comic, but the right to do what they would with the character. They could clip his powers or his hair, bring him to life in new media or kill him out-right, or do whatever else they wanted. Harry and Jack were the honchos now, the boys mere hirelings. Jerry and Joe's deal with the publishing house was for five years; Superman's was forever.

That $130 contract signaled the beginning not just of the Super-man character but of what would become a multibillion-dollar indus-try: comic book superheroes. It also was the defining narrative—the original sin—in the relationship between comic book creators and owners. Jerry and Joe may have brought to life their superhero, but that is not what mattered. What counted then and for decades after was who had the money to put that hero on the printed page and deliver those pages to the public. To the publishers went not just the profits but the power. Each writer or artist who took up that cause in the future would hark back to what Harry Donenfeld and Jack Lie-bowitz did to Jerry Siegel and Joe Shuster. As if to underline the point—to demonstrate that for $130 Jerry and Joe, like all comics

creators back then, were giving up everything—their Superman artwork was destroyed soon after it was used. There would be no chance
for them to sell it again or save it for posterity.

IT WAS APRIL 1938 and the world was holding its breath. The Führer's storm troopers had just occupied and annexed Austria and were
ready to steamroll into Czechoslovakia. Joseph Stalin had shown the
West and his countrymen that he was as ruthless as the Nazis by staging a show trial for Nikolai Bukharin, a champion of the revolution,
and then liquidating him. Franklin Roosevelt's New Deal was in full
motion, but one in three Americans remained ill-housed, ill-clad,
and ill-nourished, and 250,000 teenagers had taken to the road to
earn money to send home. Never had America so craved a hero, if
not a messiah. Never had a publisher so perfectly timed its release of
a new title.

The very cover of *Action Comics* No. 1 signaled how ground-
breaking—how uplifting—this Superman would be. There he was,
in bold primary colors: blue full-body tights, a yellow chest shield,
and candy-apple cape, booties, and briefs worn over his tights. He
looked every bit the circus acrobat, only stronger, more agile, ready
for action. No mask for this adventurer; he wanted the world to see
who he was. While it was left to the imagination just whom he was
fuming at, it was clear that no one would want to suffer the rage of a
being who could single-handedly lift a car into the air and smash it
against a rock. Hopefully he was on our side. The date printed on the
top of the page was a standard bit of misdirection: It said June when,
in a bid to ensure it would still look fresh if it sat unsold two months
later, it actually went on sale in April. There was little doubt that this
was a comic book that would justify its ten-cent price and deliver on
its name, *Action*.

The first inside page introduced readers to the handsome, brash
avenger that Jerry and Joe crafted during that sleepless night of writing and frenetic day of sketching three years earlier. A scientist on a
faraway planet placed his infant son in a spaceship headed to Earth
just before his planet died of old age. The child was found by a passing
motorist, who turned him over to an orphanage. Reaching maturity

in just the fourth panel of the comic, Superman was able to leap an eighth of a mile, vault a twenty-story building, and hoist tremendous weight. Nothing less than a bursting shell could penetrate his skin. How was that possible? The "scientific explanation" was there on page 1: He did it the same way a lowly ant supported weights hundreds of times its own, or a grasshopper leaped what to a man would be several city blocks. That was it: the entire birth, growth, and backstory of a breathtaking superhero laid out in a single comic book page measuring 7¾ by 10½ inches.

By page 2 he was a full-grown Superman, racing off on adventures that didn't stop until the story did, eleven pages later. Along the way he saved an innocent woman from electrocution, beat up a wife-beater, rescued Lois Lane from kidnappers, and intercepted a warmonger. No worries here about laws or social niceties. Bursting into the governor's house was the only way to stop an unjust execution? Barrel ahead. Dashing across live electrical wires could make a lobbyist see the evil of his ways? Up we go. This Superman was a hell-raiser and an insurrectionist. Half Huckleberry Finn, half Robin Hood, he had a technique as straightforward and a purpose as pure as those of his teenage truth-and-justice-seeking creators. His story accounted for just thirteen of *Action* No. 1's sixty-four pages, but those are the only pages the world remembers.

Literature's most gripping love triangle also was there from the first, or at least the hint of it. Clark Kent was smitten with Lois Lane, asking her out on a date on page 6. Lois agreed, but when he pressed to find out why she was avoiding him, she let him have it: "Please Clark! I've been scribbling 'sob stories' all day long. Don't ask me to dish out another." A page later, she walked out on her timid colleague after he let a thug cut in on their dance, explaining, "You asked me earlier in the evening why I avoid you. I'll tell you why now: because you're a spineless, unbearable *coward*!" Lois's time with Superman in this first story was too brief for her to fall in love, or for him to dodge. Not yet. Their newspaper already had a name, *The Daily Star,* but Clark and Lois's boss was identified only by the nameplate on his desk: EDITOR.

It did not take long for the buzz to begin. Just who was this costumed hero anyway? writers, artists, and publishers wanted to know.

And who were Jerry Siegel and Joe Shuster, the uncredited creators who were unknowns in both the old world of comic strips and the new one of comic books? Was their Superman an original or a knockoff? Would he sell? Would he last? Those questions still resonate seventy-five years later.

There was no question that Superman built on what came before. He was as strong as Samson, as fast as Hermes, and as brain-bendingly smart as Micromegas. Douglas Fairbanks, Sr., and Rudolph Valentino were his model swashbucklers. Popeye and Tarzan showed him how to be a strongman. Whom better to look to for guidance on foppish dual identities than the Scarlet Pimpernel and Zorro? The Shadow offered up an alter ego named Kent and a female sidekick named Lane. Jerry and Joe made no secret of any of their inspirations, just as they acknowledged being saps for the endless newspaper comics, dime novels, science fiction tales, and cliffhanger movies they took in as kids, from *Mutt and Jeff* to the Merriwell brothers.

When does influence became borrowing and borrowing become plagiarism? Doc Savage lent Superman some of his best stuff. In less heroic settings, Doc used his formal first name, Clark, a nod to film star Clark Gable. Superman picked the same name with the same nod to the King of Hollywood. Doc had superhuman strength and a moral compass that compelled him never to kill an enemy unless there was no other way; so would Superman. Doc's nickname was the Man of Bronze; Superman's was the Man of Steel. There was no room for dames in Doc's life, or in Supe's. The borrowing was not confined to general concepts: Gimmicks like putting bad guys to sleep by pressing a nerve in the neck were fair game, as were entire plot lines. Jerry Siegel acknowledged having read Doc "with fascination," but that was as far as he went. Comics historian Will Murray, who has documented the close connection between Doc and Superman, says Jerry may have stopped there for fear of being sued, but future Superman writers borrowed even more from Clark Savage, Jr.

The case for a connection with Philip Wylie's Hugo Danner was even stronger. Hugo hurdled across rivers, bounded into the air, raised a cannon skyward with one hand, and lifted an automobile by its bumper. Like Superman, Hugo was said to be as strong as steel, and both used their strength to take on evildoers ranging from arms mer-

chants to entire armies. How did Hugo get to be so strong? "Did you
ever watch an ant carry many times its weight? Or see a grasshopper
jump fifty times its length?" Professor Danner asked his son, invoking
the precise natural principles—even the very same insects—Jerry
would to explain Superman's prowess. Philip Wylie's whole approach
in *Gladiator,* blending science fiction with action lore, seemed state of
the art when he published his novel in 1930 and a bit less fresh when
Superman came along eight years later.

But was superhuman Hugo Danner actually Superman? Wylie
thought so. In their first two years of writing and drawing the character, Jerry and Joe "used dialogue and scenes from GLADIATOR,"
its author wrote a colleague in 1970. "I even consulted my lawyer to
see if I ought not to sue for plagerism [*sic*]. He agreed I'd possibly win
but found the 'creators' of 'Superman' were two young kids getting
$25 a week apiece, only, and that a corporation owned the strip so
recovery of damages would be costly, long, difficult and maybe fail
owing to that legal set-up." Wylie was right: He might have won had
he sued, much as Superman's publishers did later when they went
after his imitators. Doc Savage's creators—Lester Dent, John Na-
novic, and H. W. Ralston—might have as well, and even Edgar Rice
Burroughs. But as Wylie himself conceded later in his letter, "We all
borrow in ways from others, tho. The first Superman wasn't my
Gladiator but Hercules or Samson."

That was the point. Jerry and Joe did not cook up Superman from
scratch. They built on as well as borrowed from a long line of mythmakers and storytellers, the same way Burroughs borrowed from
Homer and Wylie from the ancient Hebrews. "Our concept," Joe
said, "would be to combine the best traits of all the heroes of history."
He and Jerry sometimes took more than they might have, with too
little paraphrasing or crediting. But Doc Savage was an earthling
whose hardest job was building his muscles and brainpower; Superman was an alien whose biggest challenge was deciding what to do
with the powers he was born with. Danner, too, was decidedly different, a dark presence done in by his worry that mankind could not
abide a superhuman such as him. Superman was a creature of light,
and it was that very optimism that America loved most. And although
Savage and Danner were human and Superman wasn't, his pairing

with Clark Kent gave him a groundedness and humanity Doc and Hugo couldn't match.

What the two Cleveland teenagers had done was inspired. They had reached into the melting pot of fantastic characters bubbling up in the 1930s, picking out the choicest features then carefully reformulating them. *Voilà:* a freshly minted Man of Tomorrow for a world not sure it had one. Superman was an alien shipped to Earth rather than an earthling exploring the universe, like Buck Rogers or Flash Gordon—and he had come to help. Superman was no mortal donning an exotic costume like Zorro or the Lone Ranger; just the opposite, this honest-to-God extraterrestrial walked and worked among mortals like us by disguising himself as a bumbling reporter. No wonder we adored him. Although his enemies included run-of-the-mill rogues tracked down by the likes of Dick Tracy and Sherlock Holmes, Superman also took on the demons of his day, from abusive husbands to war profiteers to a penal system that executed the innocent—all in the very first issue.

By his own admission, Joe's renderings of Superman, Lois, and all the rest of *Action* No. 1 lacked luster and gloss. But that was their genius. They were straightforward and unprettied, making them as easy to follow as an architect's blueprints. His skyscrapers were impressionistic shafts, his criminals had angular mugs and stiff features. Primitive, yes, but primal and even ethereal. Likewise, Jerry's stories had his superhero racing up the sides of buildings and jerking getaway cars off the road: just the thing for ten-year-olds and for a nation tortured by self-doubt. Their creation was brilliant, whether or not Jerry and Joe themselves were. Superman was the ideal character at the right moment, and the boys sensed it even if they couldn't foresee how long it all would last. Jerry and Joe simply wrote and drew what they knew—which is why Superman embraced the vigilante justice that Jerry longed to mete out to his father's robbers, why Lois and Clark's *Daily Star* was modeled not on a U.S. newspaper but on the *Toronto Star,* whose cartoons Joe's father had read to him, and why Superman's alter ego looked and acted so much like the young Messrs. Siegel and Shuster.

CHAPTER 2

A Hero for His Times

IT HAD TAKEN SIX YEARS for Jerry and Joe to bring Superman to life in a comic book, six years that seemed like an eternity. It took six weeks for Jack and Harry to send him hurtling onto the bestseller list, and it seemed like an instant.

Turning the newly minted hero into a blockbuster was not a matter of meticulous plotting or cagey strategizing. Neither Harry nor Jack had much clue what they were doing when they took *Action Comics* No. 1 out for sale in 1938. The partners, whose slicked-back hair and unctuous smiles made them look like the scoundrels in that first Superman story, were pros in printing and delivering magazines. To them, publishing meant pornography and pulps. What did they know of kids or comics? Comic books themselves were new enough never to have produced a runaway hit. The anxious entrepreneurs did print up twenty thousand promotional posters for the newsstands, pharmacies, corner stores, groceries, and bus and train stations that sold National Allied Magazines' comics. But so doubtful were they that their costumed hero would catch fire that they already had resolved to take Superman off the cover after that inaugural issue. They had also arranged for *Action* No. 1 to stay on store shelves for six weeks rather than the standard four, hoping that if it sat there long enough someone might notice.

Someone did. There were two ways publishers back then learned how a magazine was selling. Dealers counted the comics gone from the spinner racks and overhead displays, recorded their tally on a penny postcard left by the distributor, and dropped it in the mailbox. They did that fifteen days after the comics were delivered and again near the end of the month. Jack the accountant pored over every card that came through the mail slot, but he and Harry knew that system was hit-or-miss. Some shopkeepers didn't keep a precise count; others didn't even mail back the cards. A more exact tally would come at the start of the following month, when trucks delivering new issues would pick up unsold old ones. Yet by then it would be too late: All returns were fully refundable, and too many could put them out of business.

Each new postcard raised hopes. The publishers dispatched their agents around Manhattan to check demand at kiosks and druggists; sales seemed brisk, but New York was not America. What would Youngstown think? Miami? Jack and Harry had printed up 202,000 copies of *Action* No. 1 and were worried they had placed too much trust in a hero Harry himself had said was a long shot. Finally, with all the numbers in, the verdict was clear: They had guessed right. Vendors had sold 130,000 comic books, or 64 percent of the print run. Anything over 50 percent constituted a success and guaranteed a profit. To top that by 14 percentage points, on the first issue, barely a month after they had taken over from the Major, was more than they had let themselves dream. This new adventure could work after all. Superman just might fly.

To be sure, Harry and Jack ran a test. They wanted to know that it was Jerry and Joe's caped hero who had driven those sales, not "Zatara Master Magician," "Sticky-Mitt Stimson," or any of the eight other features in that first issue, so in *Action* No. 4, readers were asked to list in order of preference their five favorite stories. As an incentive to respond, twenty-five one-dollar prizes were offered for the best accompanying essay. The results dispelled any doubts: 404 of 542 respondents named Superman as tops, with 59 more listing him second. It did not take a master magician to figure out who was driving sales. The publishers were beside themselves. Even as he waited for the returns, Jack was looking to drive demand. He printed only 200,000 copies of the second and third issues of *Action,* knowing that would leave some shopkeepers with fewer than they wanted and hoping that would build interest, not resentment. He was rewarded with a cry from wholesalers to "give us more copies." Sales, meanwhile, continued to climb—to 136,000 for the second issue, 159,000 for the third, 190,000 for the fourth, and 197,000 for the fifth. *Action* No. 13, released on the first anniversary of the original, offered up 415,000 reasons to celebrate. National printed 725,000 copies of *Action* No. 16 and sold 625,000—an unheard-of success rate of 86 percent.

Who were the buyers? There were no sophisticated surveys, but the drift was clear. Most were schoolchildren. Boys outnumbered girls, but not by much. And they all loved their Superman. He had quickly become the big brother every kid needed, especially half-pints who were being bullied by playground toughs or babied by teachers and parents. TV wasn't around yet to seduce kids, and radios were oversized consoles shared with the family. The one thing youngsters had that was theirs was what they read, and now they read Superman at night, under the bedcovers, using a flashlight to illuminate the pages. They brought him to school, camouflaged in their Dick and Jane readers. No highfalutin dialogue in these books, or ambiguity over right and wrong, winners and losers. Superman should win and did, which is just how kids would have it. He was unadult enough to be appealing, and he was the right price—ten cents—for consumers whose only income was their modest allowance and the pennies they dug out of the sofa. Nine and ten-year-olds finally had a language and hero who was theirs alone. Libraries got the message, too: Children's rooms began promoting books by saying they had Superman's seal of approval, which carried more clout than a recommendation by a librarian or schoolmistress.

And it wasn't just kids. All-Star pitcher Lefty Gomez recalled walking down the street with his Yankees teammate and roommate Joe DiMaggio when "he suddenly turns to me and says, 'Lefty, you know what day today is?' I say, 'Yeah, Wednesday.' Then he says, 'No, no, today is the day the new *Superman* comes out' . . . So now he sees this newspaper stand and looks to see if they got comic books. He points to it and wants me to get it for him. He stands off to the side. Hell, he was Joe DiMaggio and if the newsstand guy saw him buy *Superman* comics it would be all over the world. I got one of those faces nobody could ever recognize so he wants me to buy it for him. 'Joe, is this what you want, the *Superman* comics?' He looks around at a couple of people there and he says, 'No, you know I wouldn't buy that.' Then I walk away and he motions again. I finally buy it for him and he stuffs it into his pocket. He spends the night with Superman."

Harry and Jack read the trend lines and responded. Superman was back on the *Action* cover for issue 7, and again for 10, 13, and 15. Nine months after his debut in comic books he was given his own daily newspaper strip, which was where Jerry and Joe had wanted him in the first place. It was the only time a comic hero had ever jumped from comic books to strips rather than the other way around. The *Houston Chronicle* was the first paper to sign up, followed by the *Milwaukee Journal* and *San Antonio Express;* by the end of 1939, sixty papers were running the daily feature and a Sunday strip was gearing up. That June his publishers had made Superman the first character to have an ongoing comic book named after him, although the plan at the time was for just one issue. The first press run of 500,000 sold out, as did subsequent ones of 250,000 and 150,000. The trial balloon quickly became a regular item, with *Superman* No. 2 selling all of its 850,000 copies, as well as a second run of 150,000, and *Action* continuing its record-setting pace.

No one had seen numbers like that since the pulps of the Roaring '20s. Superman was outpacing the girlie magazines, the horror titles, and all his comics challengers. There were a dozen other comic books on the racks, all selling about 200,000 copies. Superman's tally was five times that, a pace so far off the charts that competing publishers presumed it was an anomaly and took nearly a year to gin up their own imitations. The industry may have been at a loss, but Superman's owners weren't. They kept pushing. In October 1939 Jack set up Superman, Inc., to protect the trademark and develop new products. Five months later a new tagline showed up on *Action* covers, trumpeting its status as the "World's Largest Selling Comic Magazine."

If a pair of teenage scribblers from Cleveland had made all that possible, it was a pair of middle-aged fortune hunters from the Lower East Side who were making it happen. Now they were ready to claim credit. Jack, who generally was neither boastful nor sentimental, made an exception with Superman. "We liked it," he said looking back at

Jerry and Joe's first set of Superman scripts. "We put it together and made a 13 page story out of it." Who chose the artwork for that *Action* No. 1 cover? "I remember picking the first cover," he said. Who harmonized the distribution and marketing? "I just wanted to create a demand." What about adding new comic books? "Donenfeld thought it was too many magazines and he didn't want to put out any more." What did all that effort lead to? "That was the beginning of the comic industry as far as I was concerned."

As far as Harry was concerned, Superman had a different heritage. Jerry and Joe wrote and drew him, and Jack did the marketing, but what mattered most were the brains and the bankroll behind the birthing. Both were Harry's. He was the one who bought the story after every other publisher had turned it down. He had the artwork ready for issues 2 and 3 even before *Action* 1 hit the stands. Gambler that he was, he bet his stash on a dark horse and it came in. In 1940, Jerry and Harry appeared on Fred Allen's radio show to talk about Superman. This would be the only recorded comment Harry would ever offer about Superman, and while it was comedy, it was revealing. Allen asked Jerry whether he was the man behind the hero and, with atypical modesty, he said, "I'm just *one* of the men, Fred." Then came Harry, who shared the stage with a character the announcer called Superman. When Superman did not recognize him, Harry chided, "Why, I'm Harry Donenfeld, your boss. . . . I took you off a drawing board and made a man out of you! I splashed your name from coast to coast . . . and you've never heard of me!" In later years, as others forgot his role, Harry reminded them by showing off a life-size portrait of Superman that hung in his office lobby. He took to calling himself Harry Superman Donenfeld. And, ever the showman, Harry would wear a Superman T-shirt under his suits and even his tuxedo, waiting for the perfect moment to rip open his jacket and shirt and announce, "This looks like a job for *Superman*!"

IT IS NOT OFTEN that a child gets a name and an identity before its parents. That is the freedom of fiction and the reality of comic books, where stories play out in diminutive dialogue balloons and thin panel drawings that put a premium on each word and image. So it was with

Superman: Jerry Siegel and Joe Shuster had trouble enough conjuring up and getting published the basic biography of their superhero. The rest they filled in as they went along.

Action 1 referred to Superman's home only as a "distant planet" that "was destroyed by old age." No name or location. No mention of its culture, religion, history, or why advanced age spelled destruction. Just these small teases: Its "inhabitants' physical structure was millions of years advanced of our own," and "upon reaching maturity, the people of his race became gifted with titanic strength!" That April 1938 backstory got more interesting the following January, with the launch of the *Superman* newspaper comic strip. Word one on day one gave his home planet a name, Krypton, followed by an elaborated context. The distant world was "so far advanced in evolution that it bears a civilization of supermen—beings which represent the human race at its ultimate peak of perfect development!" On day five we learned that Krypton was dying not of old age but of an implosion caused by "an internal cataclysm." Five installments after that, Krypton was no more, having disintegrated into a million fragments. The first *Superman* comic book, published in the summer of 1939, added one last fact about Krypton that would help explain Superman's super-strength: It was bigger than Earth, which meant that gravity had greater pull on Superman's home planet than on his adopted one.

Superman's parents fared worse. In *Action* 1 his Kryptonian birth father went nameless, although we were told he was a scientist who placed his infant son "within a hastily devised space-ship, launching it toward earth!" Not a word about his mother, assuming the baby had one. The first series of comic strips, titled "Superman Comes to Earth," started filling in the blanks. Superman's father got a name, Jor-L, and he was crowned "Krypton's foremost scientist." But while he was smart enough to detect his planet's impending doom, he was not persuasive enough to get the ruling council to evacuate. We also met Superman's mom, Lora, who came up with the notion that safety lay in the distant stars and decided that if only one of them could be saved, it would be her overactive newborn. The last we heard of either parent was as the baby rocketed toward Earth: "An instant after their glorious, self-sacrificing gesture, Jor-L and Lora perish in the earth quake's awful grip!" Just the sort of stilted prose and unequivocal heroism that appealed to Joe DiMaggio and every other red-blooded American.

Baby Superman, like his parents, first got a name and a life on Krypton only in the newspapers. He was Kal-L, and he quickly showed himself to be a chip off his dad's strong-willed block by giving his doctor a black eye and leaping from his mother's arms. His existence on Krypton lasted mere months, but after a perilous journey he made it to Earth, where he was found by a passing motorist and left at an orphanage. That motorist had no further role in either the first comic book or the original comic strip, and Superman had neither parents on Earth nor an explanation for why he was called Clark Kent. In *Superman* No. 1 he got a father without a first name and a mother named Mary, who adopted him from the orphanage where they had deposited him. They lasted for ten panels, or not quite two pages— enough time to name the boy Clark Kent, watch him grow to manhood, see him discover his powers, and caution him to hide those gifts while using them to "assist humanity." Then the elderly Kent couple died, and Clark was off to keep his promise to them. "And so," the comic announced, "was created—SUPERMAN."

It was not the full-scale world-building that visitors to J.R.R. Tolkien's Middle-earth would come to expect—that detailed lore would begin taking shape for Superman in the mid-1940s—but it did give the caped hero a little more context and depth. The creeping pace was partly a matter of the form: It would have taken nearly thirty years, or 350 issues, for a title like *Action* to equal the word count of the *Lord of the Rings* trilogy. It also was a matter of serendipity. There was no master plan for the related but distinct storylines of the *Action* and *Superman* books and the *Superman* strip. No one had known that *Action* would catch on enough for the McClure Newspaper Syndicate, which had turned the strip down twice before, to come begging to bring Superman to the funny pages. Neither Harry nor Jack had planned for a separate *Superman* comic book, or for that to be ongoing. Having Superman's story play out across different venues presented a challenge for Jerry and the writers who came after him: Each installment needed to seem original yet part of a whole, stylistically and narratively.

Their solution, at the beginning, was to wing it, which presented its own opportunities. The first *Superman* book opened with six pages that provided a critical introduction to the character and his world missing from the inaugural issue of *Action*. The comic strip allowed for a different pacing, composed as it was of digestible four-panel dailies whose storylines could run for months when the plot justified it. The newspaper funnies also would have five times as many readers as the books, with stories every day rather than once a month. The multiple offerings meant a lot more money—for Jerry and Joe along with Harry and Jack—from rabid readers who *had* to follow every turn and twist.

Lois Lane was a fixture from the very start, although at first she was mainly a foil for Superman to rescue and Clark to pine over. *Action* 1 set the pattern: Kidnapped by three thugs, Lois was quickly whisked to safety by Superman and then laughed at by her editor, who, hearing her recount her unlikely adventure, inquired, "Are you sure it wasn't pink elephants you saw?" The editor had his own problems. It took more than a year for him to get a name (George Taylor), and while it was clear from the beginning that his paper was the *Daily Star,* in *Action* No. 2 it was inexplicably called the *Evening News* and situated in Jerry and Joe's Cleveland. The creators must have had Cleveland on the brain, and lax editing in the office, because the Ohio city turned up again as Superman's home in *Action* 11. Everyone got their geographic bearings three issues later, in September 1939, when the superhero and his newspaper were situated once and forever in Metropolis. It would take until later that fall, and the second issue of the *Superman* book, for Metropolis to be situated in New York State.

Superman was a man of the world, perennially on call and needing to dash to wherever Lois and others required his help. Flying would have made that easier, but the most he could manage in 1938 was leaping an eighth of a mile and outracing an express train. Two years later, after what must have been intense training, he could vault into and beyond the stratosphere, outrace an airplane, and run a mile in a scant second. By 1942, he could run at the speed of light and outpace an electric current—but still no take-off. There were hints it was coming in a single frame of a story in May 1943, when his jump looked like he might be taking flight, and he did, finally and irrefutably, that October in the *Action* story "Million-Dollar Marathon." "Let's see ya fly!" adoring boys at Children's Hospital yelled to Superman, and so he did, telling them, "I'll be back for a real visit pretty soon! Up—up—and away!"

Veteran comic book writer Don Cameron, not Jerry Siegel, described that maiden flight, and Joe Shuster's stand-in, Ed Dobrotka, did the artwork. But flying was something Joe had contemplated early on and Jerry had been dreaming about even before he climbed to the top of his garage roof. "To fly, to fly, to fly! What bliss!" he scribbled in his memoir, thinking back to when, as a boy, he climbed onto his father's leg and was hoisted into the air. While Superman wasn't the first comic book hero to fly—that honor belonged to Namor the Sub-Mariner—flight did become the Man of Steel's most defining and coveted feature. It was a dream made real for millions of earthbound readers.

Superman always had the eyes of an eagle and the hearing of an owl, but over time both got sharper still. Within a year he could see what was going on in a building across the street whether or not it had windows, and it wasn't long before he brought into focus objects millions of miles away on a pitch-black night. Only lead could obstruct his view. His glare alone was hot enough to melt metal, a power that would come in handy for trimming his own hair, which wouldn't yield to scissors or even pruning shears. His ears, meanwhile, became so sensitive that he could eavesdrop on police radio calls without a radio and hear an ant fall thousands of miles away.

Following those twists and turns meant paying attention, and his young fans were transfixed. It was not just their hero's possibilities they were piecing together but their own. They knew that Superman could hold his breath for hours underwater or douse a raging fire just by blowing on it. His million-decibel yell had enough intensity and pitch to topple tall buildings. What if a building fell on him? A tickle at most. His nostrils were super-acute. His typing was super-fast. Superman did age, but super-slowly. No need for the FBI to run a fingerprint search; Superman could find the match. Of all his strengths and skills, the most invaluable was his intellect. He had a photographic memory that let him draw an exact likeness of someone he hadn't seen since childhood. His gaze was intense enough to hypnotize a whole tribe of South American Indians at once. He could converse with a mermaid in her native tongue and beat a checkers expert his first time playing. All that was partly a matter of nature, but he nurtured his intellect by reading, which is easier when you can scan the full contents of a library in under five minutes.

The challenge was to keep him human. The Kryptonian superhero was alien enough with the powers he had when he landed on Earth, and every issue or two the voltage was amped up. Humor helped soften him, as when he hoisted a circus strongman in one hand and iron barbells in the other, wondering, "Which is the greatest dumb-bell?" Jerry's words made the point; Joe's drawings of a beaming Superman and a terrified muscleman ensured that no one missed it. Being an orphan twice over—having lost his parents on Krypton, then watched the Kents pass away—made the invulnerable Superman more empathetic. So did mild-mannered Clark Kent, although an alter ego could only go so far in warming up a gladiator who could blast boulders to dust and move mountains. Humility went further. The name "Superman," the hero pointed out, was not his idea. Neither was saving the world. Both conceits came from his parents, were fanned by reporters like Lois Lane, and made him uneasy. He was not just the most manly of superheroes but the most modest, which made his fans hold him even closer.

Themes like those made Siegel and Shuster seem wise if not old, yet other aspects of their writing and drawing reminded the reader how young and green they were. Their very first story, which they had had years to fine-tune, ended nearly every sentence with the most exuberant, least subtle punctuation mark: an exclamation point! Early issues were full of awkward or inappropriate phrasing. Describing how Clark's posture straightened when he changed into Superman, Jerry wrote, "His figure erects." As Superman got ready to burst in on a boyish gang's secret meeting, he said to himself, "The boys don't know it, but they're going to have another attendant at their meeting." And while a twenty-five-cent word like "sardonic" might have impressed Jerry's high school teachers, a ten-cent one like "smart-alecky" would have been an easier sell to Superman fans. The illustrations also were uneven. Sometimes the superhero had facial expressions that were easy to read; just as often, Joe's blocky depiction made it difficult even to make out his face. Thankfully, the audience that ripped through the dialogue and devoured the drawings was even younger than Jerry and Joe, and they were willing to suspend their judgment along with their belief.

Superman was a money machine from the get-go, but he also was a butt-kicking New Dealer. His coming-out party in comic books saw the callow hero tackling a wife beater and liberating an innocent man from death row. In subsequent issues he upended a munitions manufacturer, humiliated the commanders of warring armies, exposed an unscrupulous mine operator, and finished the career of a crooked college football coach. Those no-goodniks didn't deserve a Bill of Rights, and they wouldn't get one with Superman. His messages were simple and direct: Power corrupts. The average Joe deserves a super-powered friend and rich SOBs deserve a boot in the rear. There's a new sheriff in town. These were the very lessons that Depression-era America wanted to hear and that FDR preached in his fireside chats and legislative crusades. But where the president was soothingly patrician, Superman was neither kind nor gentle. A nearer and more apt role model for the new comic book hero was Eliot Ness, who after pursuing Al Capone's mob in Chicago was taking a broom to Cleveland's scandal-ridden police force. So it was that Superman gave the wife beater a thrashing of his own, in the process sounding a warning that applied to all his lowlife targets: "Tough is putting mildly the treatment you're going to get! You're not fighting a woman, now!"

No story better reflected Superman's take on the world's wrongs, and his faith that they could be set right, than *Action* No. 8's "Superman in the Slums." It opened with a neighborhood tough appearing before a judge and his mother pleading on his behalf. Covering the proceedings for his paper, Clark Kent thought, "The mother's right! But if I know the court of law . . . her plea hasn't a chance!" This was a cynical and tough Clark paired with a take-no-prisoners Man of Steel. The courts wouldn't deal the kid a fair hand? Superman would. He rescued the delinquents from their double-crossing adult handler and from the police, then gave them a lecture worthy of settlement house pioneer Jane Addams: "It's not entirely your fault that you're delinquent—it's these slums—your poor living conditions—if there

was only some way I could remedy it—!" There was. He simulated a
cyclone that left the shantytown in shambles. But it did not stay that
way for long: "During the next weeks, the wreckage is cleared. Emergency squads commence erecting huge apartment-projects . . . and in
time the slums are replaced by splendid housing conditions."

It was Superman at his do-gooder best. He had no faith that the
government would fix things on its own and no patience to wait and
see. So he tweaked the system while being careful not to upend it.
His means were more those of a rebellious teenager than an anarchist,
his ends more FDR reformer than Leninist revolutionary. "In the
eyes and mind and heart of Superman," Jerry explained later, "the
problems of a penniless tramp or other troubled soul was important.
Wealth meant nothing to a super-being who could have acquired all
the riches on Earth for himself if he did not have high ideals."

While Jerry and Superman never stopped caring about penniless
tramps, they did stop trying to enrich them, or pushing the government to do so. The law became more sacrosanct and Superman less
of an outlaw. Robin Hood was giving way to Prince Valiant, or maybe
as he saw more of this world Superman was switching from Democratic idealist to Republican realist. Truth, justice, and the status quo.
Lost in the transformation was some of his glee. The remake started
in the summer of 1939 and picked up steam as the decades turned.
The one-year anniversary issue of *Action* captured the shift. The story
started with the same lifelike premise as in earlier issues, with a criminal syndicate using deadly force to drive independent taxi owners
out of business. Superman took off his kid gloves and dispatched a
gangster to his leaping death. Four pages from the end, however, the
story took a science fiction twist: behind the gangsters was not a con-
niving capitalist or crooked pol, but a dastardly and masterful scientist
named the Ultra-Humanite.

It was a new era and he was a new villain—sort of. Jerry and Joe
actually were recycling the evil Super-Man from their high school
story "The Reign of the Super-Man." Same bald pate, roots in a
scientific laboratory, and hyphenated name. Same dream of dominat-
ing the world. The Ultra-Humanite's body might be crippled, but his
plots to do in Superman were as ingenious as his getaways. He was
Superman's first recurring enemy—a worthy successor to Super-Man

and an apt precursor to Lex Luthor, Mr. Mxyzptlk, the Puzzler, and other brilliant (and bald) foes to follow. But culling them from the world of fantasy rather than the headlines carried a price: It meant Jerry and Joe were giving a pass to the real-world bad guys.

The timing was right, as it always seemed to be with Superman. America was in a curious interregnum between the summer of 1939 and the end of 1941: Employment and incomes were climbing back, and while the world was at war, we weren't, not yet. When the nation was mired in economic doldrums it had needed a combative hero. Now that its economy and spirit were rebounding, the new attitude was a return to normalcy. For Superman, that meant toning down the violence and adhering to a stricter set of rules. No killing unless he had to, and then only with his bare hands. No destroying private property. No hint of sex. No alienating parents or teachers. Evil geniuses like the Ultra-Humanite were too otherworldly to give kids nightmares. They leveled the playing field for Superman, upped the action, and escalated the escapism. This was exactly what post-Depression, prewar America needed. The results could be measured at newsstands across the nation as Superman, just two years after his entry into the field, had surpassed in popularity three of the marquee names in comics: Little Orphan Annie, Dick Tracy, and Popeye.

SUPERMAN WAS NOT THE only one who was changing. After a prolonged adolescence, Jerry was growing up fast. A year after the first *Action* came out and just as the *Superman* book was launching, he married Bella Lifshitz, the daughter of a Russian-Jewish plumber whose home was catty-corner to Jerry's on Kimberly Avenue. She was eighteen and only a week out of high school; he was six years older but still living at home with his mother. They had known each other forever. It was a June wedding arranged by the Siegels and Lifshitzes and paid for by Superman. Three hundred guests came from as far away as Los Angeles, and the already elegant Hotel Sterling was made more so with candles, palms, and flowers. Leo, the brother Jerry had shared a bed with and who made the family swell with pride when he got his dentist's degree, was Jerry's best man. Their mother, Sarah, was beaming, through gritted teeth.

Sarah had never liked Bella. She knew the bride's mother, who could neither read nor write, and her father, who fixed broken toilets and unclogged sinks for a living. Sarah Siegel came from the same impoverished ghettos of Eastern Europe as Sam and Esther Lifshitz, and had experienced enough hardship in the New World to last two lifetimes. But she was a proud American Jew now—the kind who learned the language and how to get by, and who put on rouge, lipstick, and a hat to go to the grocer because you never knew who you'd run into—and she couldn't abide people like the Lifshitzes who hadn't adjusted. Though Sarah liked living with just Jerry after the other children moved out, she was ready to surrender him to the right woman. But now, when his childish dreams about Superman and being a writer finally were coming true, it was the broad-shouldered, buxom Liftshitz girl with whom he chose to share them. Bella looked matronly even at eighteen, with her black hair pinned back and braided in a way that reminded Sarah both of Bella's mother and of her own babushka. It only got worse when she visited the couple at their new apartment and saw for herself how little Bella knew about keeping house. It broke Sarah's heart.

Jerry and Bella were sure they were in love as they headed to the World's Fair in New York for their honeymoon, although she was too young to know what it was supposed to feel like and he was too green. Once they got back to Cleveland, there wasn't much time to learn. He had to deliver a story for the *Superman* strip every week and monthly ones for the *Action* and *Superman* books. And he still was doing "Slam Bradley," "Federal Men," "Spy," and "Radio Squad." The deadlines pumped him full of adrenaline and depleted him of energy and time for Bella. "I wrote, wrote, wrote no matter how I felt," he said looking back. "I found myself writing about terrific super-deeds, even if sometimes I felt like I could barely drag myself to the typewriter."

He still did much of his typing at home, only this time it was his own home, not his mom's, and he typed to the beat of Benny Goodman vinyl. For variety he would head into the office that he and Joe had rented for the bargain price of thirty dollars a month. That was enough for a reception nook where Jerry had his desk, with five more desks squeezed into the main room, but too little money for a telephone or to inscribe their names on the frosted-glass door panels. So what? Comics were Jerry's life then. They were what he talked about in the office and over lunch, which often was just a candy bar, and they were what he dreamed about at night, same as when he was a kid. Another legendary comic book writer, Stanley Martin Lieber, would masquerade as "Stan Lee," looking ahead to the day when he might give up this kiddy medium to write the great American novel. Not Jerry. This was all he had ever aspired to, and now all his Superman comics were written under the name that Michel and Sarah had given him. He invented the vernacular of Superman as he went along, with his hands moving so fast over the keyboard that it felt as if somebody else were dictating the dialogue.

As time went on, somebody was. Initially Harry, Jack, and the managers they hired to oversee their growing editorial empire had let Jerry do as he wished with the character, and what he did was craft a caped avenger who delighted youngsters with his vigilantism and became a poster child for the goo-goos trying to clean up the government. Once Superman became big business, however, plots had to be sent to New York for vetting. Not only did editors tell Jerry to cut out the guns and knives and cut back on social crusading, they started calling the shots on minute details of script and drawing. Superman must be in costume while using his superpowers. His forelocks couldn't be too curly, his arms should be shorter and less "ape-like," and Joe should get rid of his hero's "nice fat bottom." The latter especially made Superman look too "lah-de-dah," 1940s shorthand for shading toward gay. Lois, too, needed a makeover. Nix the "roly-poly hair-do." Stop accentuating her breasts or tummy in a way that made her look pregnant. "Murray suggests that you arrange for her to have an abortion or the baby and get it over with so that her figure can return to something a little more like the tasty dish she is supposed to be," editor Whitney Ellsworth advised in a letter to Jerry early in 1941. "She is much too stocky and much, *much* too unpleasantly sexy."

In one now-famous case, an entire 1940 storyline was shelved. It was a twenty-six-page tale about a strange substance called K-Metal. Like Superman himself, the metal floated to Earth from the dying planet Krypton, and even brief exposure to it could rob him of his powers. As the story proceeded, Superman was faced with an onerous decision: Should he rescue Lois from a mine disaster when doing so meant revealing his true identity as Superman? True to form, he saved Lois. The two then agreed to become partners in battling crime and villainy. "How foolish you were not to let me in on the secret! You should have known you could trust me!" she chided. Superman: "You're right! There were many times when I could have used the assistance of a confederate. Why didn't I think of it before?"

It was a plot that would have changed everything. K–Metal would become the once-unstoppable superhero's Achilles' heel. Superman would learn for the first time about his origin on Krypton. There would be no more secret identity, at least with Lois, and no love triangle. Jerry might have been in the mood for humanizing his hero by consummating the longtime flirtation, as he was doing in his own life, but it was more than his bosses could stomach. No one knows for sure who pulled the plug, but the reason seems self-evident: Never meddle with a proven success. A metal from Krypton that could melt the Man of Steel did enter the lore in the form of kryptonite, but that took another three years, and while Superman would eventually learn the full story of his interplanetary origins, it was not until 1949. As for the thick K–Metal script, which would have run twice as long as the normal Superman comic, it remained secreted away in the archives of Detective Comics until a curious young staffer stumbled upon a smudged carbon copy forty-eight years later.

The message to Jerry was clear: Superman no longer belonged just to him. And there was more, as his editors spelled out in an onslaught of letters. Hire assistants so you can meet your deadlines, and set aside "Slam Bradley" and other second-tier characters. Stop crying poor mouth and begging for raises. Don't talk to the press. Say goodbye to Cleveland and come to New York, where we can keep a closer eye on you. Grow up. When they really wanted to make their point, his bosses at Detective Comics had their boss, Jack Liebowitz, sign the letter. "Bear in mind," Jack wrote five months after *Action* was launched, "that we own the feature 'Superman' and that we can at any time replace you." He wrote again the following April: "You have the germ of a great idea in SUPERMAN but you need constant editorial supervision." By January 1940 Jack seemed at the end of his rope, growling, "From your promised five releases a month I'm down to one. For anyone to have fallen that badly, you are certainly a Superman in reverse."

Jerry had moved to New York in 1939, and he reined in his hero to look more like what Jack and his editors wanted. He took the abuse and toed the line not just because Jack had all the power, but because Jerry liked the money Superman was bringing him and loved the prestige. Just how rich he was is a matter of contention. *The Saturday Evening Post* reported that he and Joe split $75,000 in 1940; Jerry said they were sharing just over $38,000, counting revenues from the comic books and strips. Even at the lower figure he was earning $307,000 a year in today's dollars, or more than thirty times what he had made two years before. A year later, his share had increased to $29,000. That was enough for him and Bella to move back to Cleveland—or rather to the upscale suburb of University Heights— and buy a home with two and a half baths, a paneled rec room with a bar, silk draperies, and air-conditioning, which was a luxury then. He got Bella a mink coat and a diamond bracelet, and bought himself a hip-reducing gizmo in hopes of undoing the damage done by all those candy bars.

What mattered more than money, to a boy who grew up thinking he was a pariah and sharing a bed with his brother, was being a man-about-town—not just in Cleveland, where newspapers and adoring fans sang his praises, but in New York. His editors might have been trying to cut Jerry down to size, but on the streets of the Big Apple there was no denying his hero's rise to iconic stature. It was on full display at the 1940 Macy's Thanksgiving Day Parade, where the biggest balloon was an eighty-foot-high replica of the Man of Tomorrow, and at the World's Fair in Flushing Meadows, which staged a first-of-its-kind Superman Day. Best of all: America's best-read magazine, *The Saturday Evening Post,* ran a seven-page feature on Superman and his creators that included a picture of Jerry lying in an oversized bed reading a book with hard covers and no graphics.

Joe's picture in that article showed him not in bed but at the head of a bountiful Sabbath table with his mother, Ida; father, Julius; younger brother, Frank; and kid sister, Jean. It seemed designed to underline how differently he and Jerry had responded to Superman's success. Joe acknowledged early on that he could not handle the workload. His eyes were bad and getting worse, and his left hand was a problem, too. He had what he called a spastic condition that had started a year after Superman first appeared in print; it prevented him from drawing for long stretches, made him switch to his right hand for lettering, and eventually forced him to wear a leather brace that completely immobilized his bad hand. So he hired assistants, although their bylines never showed up on the comic book or comic strip, and at first even Jack and Harry were kept in the dark. There was just one to start, Paul Cassidy, who worked from his home in Milwaukee and helped with "Slam Bradley," "Spy," and other early Siegel and Shuster efforts. Once Superman got going, Cassidy moved to Cleveland and Joe hired three more artists, including Wayne Boring, who would keep on drawing and redefining Superman for two decades. By early 1939 Joe was lightly and sparingly sketching the scenes and leaving them to others to fill in and fine-tune; the one thing he insisted on keeping control over was Superman's head, which he felt defined his hero. When he moved to New York later that year he did even less, not showing up at the office for long stretches and frustrating his bosses as much as Jerry did. In Joe's case the complaints were less about his attitude than his health and work ethic.

Joe drew the same salary as Jerry but his assistants had to be paid out of his cut, which in 1941 meant that he earned about $29,000 and kept $14,500. That may not sound like much to live on in New York, but in today's terms it is $220,000. It was enough to let Joe move out of the YMCA and into a small apartment, then into a ten-room house. He needed something that big because his parents and siblings were with him again, and to ensure they got to enjoy their new surroundings he had a car waiting in the driveway and a maid who came in twice a week. Joe was spending more of his weeks holidaying in Pennsylvania's Pocono Mountains. When he was around, he headed to Barney Kofron's gym, hoisting 175-pound weights and trying to ensure that the body that stared back at him in the mirror really was a model for Superman. That, along with a T-bone steak and two quarts of milk a day, inflated his weight from

112 to 128 pounds. To lift his height, which was just five foot two, he wore elevator shoes.

Joe stayed single all through those years, but it was not for lack of interest in girls, or for lack of their reciprocation. The once-shy teenager had more confidence now that he was Superman's personal artist, and he started dating the showgirls he had always dreamed about. Not just anyone would do; they had to have a model's looks and they had to be tall. "He loved *shiksas*," recalled his sister, Jean. "They were always tall and slender blondes like his dream girl Lana Turner." He also double-dated a lot, with Jean and with Batman artist Jerry Robinson. Once, Robinson fixed him up with his cousin in Trenton, who was brilliant, pretty, and the same height as Joe. The four young people went out dancing and had what Robinson thought was a terrific time. "Afterwards I said, 'How'd you like Shirley?' He said, 'Oh, well she's great. But she's too short for me.'"

Bob Kane, Batman's creator, loved double-dating with Joe, if only so he could tell the girls they were dating Batman and Superman. One Saturday night in the winter of 1940 he and Joe were due to go out with a couple of girls in Miami Beach, but Joe never showed up. He had stopped on the street near his hotel to ogle an antique car, but with his myopic vision, he had to lean in too close for the comfort of two patrolmen who spotted him. At the station he told them who he was, yet all they could see was a would-be auto thief, which earned him a threat of thirty days in the slammer. Although he drew several sketches of Superman, the police remained skeptical. Luckily Harry Donenfeld was in town and bailed him out, though not before word leaked to the press. SUPERMAN RESCUES HIS CREATOR FROM FLORIDA JAIL, *The Washington Post* blared across its front page.

HARRY AND JACK HAD never had things so good. As always they had their pornography profits, and their book and magazine distribution firm was on the way to becoming the biggest in the country. A year after Superman they scored another hit with Batman, and two years after that Wonder Woman gave them a third cash cow. Still, it was Superman who made the most money and generated the most

attention for Donenfeld and Liebowitz's Detective Comics, Inc. They
acknowledged the debt by amending the company logo to read A
SUPERMAN-DC PUBLICATION. The profits from Superman comic books
were all theirs. Detective took a cut from the comic strip, too—by
1941 it was up to 10 percent, which was a quarter of what Jerry and
Joe were getting but a good deal for middlemen who bore almost no
costs. There was yet more money to be made from radio shows,
movie serials, merchandising, and a full-length novel, and Jack pushed
and pulled for every dollar.

Woe to those who tried to horn in. If Superman was a demon in
tracking down his enemies, his accountant and attorneys were even
more single-minded in protecting their franchise of super-powered
costumed heroes. The only question was whom to sue first. Jack
settled on Wonder Man, who had been tapped by a Tibetan yogi to
fight evil and was given a ring that endowed him with super powers
nearly identical to Superman's. No surprise there: Victor Fox, Wonder Man's owner, was Harry's former partner and had seen Detective's ledger sheets showing how much money Superman made. So
the cigar-chomping Fox, a nasty little man who would call himself
"king of the comics" but whose kingdom at the time was a single
astrology magazine, hired comics wunderkind Will Eisner to beget a
hero "with a red, tight-fitting costume, and a red cape." Fox had one
more instruction for Eisner: Lie about Wonder Man's parentage when
he was called to testify in Jack's lawsuit. Trial records show that Eisner
did what he was told, despite his later denials. It didn't matter, not
with the evidence there in cartoon panels for the judge to see. Wonder Man became a one-issue wonder and Jack had bragging rights in
the first-ever comics copyright lawsuit.

Next up was Captain Marvel, a far more formidable foe who flew
onto the comics scene early in 1940 with a chiseled face that looked
just like actor Fred MacMurray's. His costume was a stunning red,
with a white cape trimmed in yellow. His alter ego was Billy Batson,
a radio newsboy who had only to say the magic word "Shazam!" to
transform himself into the World's Mightiest Mortal. So compelling
were the storylines and illustrations that by mid-1943 Captain Marvel
would outsell even Superman. Jack perceived the threat early, and in
1941 he sued Fawcett Publications, alleging that it had stolen Super-

man's life, looks, and even his shawl. To Jerry it was a slam dunk: "A Mongoloid idiot would have come to the same conclusion, because they both did the same things. They both had super-strength, they both wore costumes, they both had similar identities." A judge agreed that Marvel had infringed on Superman, but in a ruling delivered a full ten years after the suit was filed, he added that Detective had failed to properly copyright its character and therefore had no case. A year later the esteemed jurist Learned Hand overturned the copyright part of the ruling and sent the case back to the lower court. By then Captain Marvel had lost his luster, and rather than pay for another expensive trial, Fawcett gave Jack and Harry four hundred thousand dollars and agreed to retire the Captain.

Jack had made his point. While the superheroes who followed continued to be Superman knockoffs (from Captain America to Plastic Man, Doll Man, and Minute-Man) or purposefully un-Superman-like (Spider-Man), their creators disguised and denied any ties. No one, least of all Jerry, acknowledged the chutzpah in Detective's claims of plagiarism in light of how close Philip Wylie had come to charging Superman with plagiarizing Hugo Danner and the strong case Lester Dent could have made on behalf of Doc Savage. Otto Binder, one of Superman's best scripters in the 1950s, claimed that it was he who in the 1930s had planted the seed with Jerry and Joe for an interplanetary, super-powered orphan, although he never talked about suing. Jerry himself would point an angry finger at surprising targets in 1947, charging that his bosses along with his friend Bob Kane had stolen their Batman brainchild from Superman, and that Wonder Woman was a rip-off of his idea for Superwoman. "It is perfectly clear to the youth of the nation that Batman is really Superman with a mask on," Jerry's lawyer told a judge. And it was not just Batman, but "twenty of these features, all of whom are like Superman." The truth is that Batman was as human and somber as Superman was infallible and uplifting. If the Dark Knight and his second self, Bruce Wayne, stole from anyone, it was from Jerry himself: The death of Bruce's father during a robbery was eerily like what happened to Michel Siegel, and Bruce and Jerry both spent a lifetime trying to get over their early losses.

Shoring up their superhero cartel made it easier for Harry and Jack to live in a manner that their Lower East Side upbringings had not accustomed them to, but had made them crave. How rich was Harry? Jack told *The Saturday Evening Post* in 1941 that his partner had paid income taxes the year before on "more than $100,000." Harry, according to the *Post,* "once told a reporter that he netted $500,000 from Superman alone." The low-end projection would be $1.5 million in today's terms, the high end $7.7 million. Both are likely conservative estimates, given all the commerce Harry conducted above the table and under it.

What is clear is that Harry had all the money he needed to keep his wife, Gussie, his son, Irwin, and his daughter, Peachy housed first in a seven-room apartment on Riverside Drive and later in a large duplex on the Upper West Side with a thirty-foot terrace facing Central Park. His and Gussie's last stop was 710 Park Avenue, one of the first apartment houses erected after World War II on America's most prestigious promenade. There was enough money left over to give jobs to nieces, nephews, and others who came looking during the Depression, and to keep his mistress, Sunny Paley, happily ensconced twenty blocks down Park Avenue in a suite at the Waldorf Astoria. He slept in George Pullman's plush hotels on wheels when he traveled for business, and when he arrived he stayed in the best accommodations in town, sometimes having Frank the chauffeur meet him there with his car. The excursions he preferred were purely pleasure—to Miami Beach, Havana, and the circuit of speakeasies and strip clubs of New York City. One hand would lay claim to Sunny's midriff, the other cradled a glass of scotch, but his gaze was planted on the minions gathered round waiting for him to tell a story or buy another round. No one listened harder than his old friend Frank Costello, whom reporters had taken to calling "Prime Minister of the Underworld" and whom soldiers in the Luciano crime family called boss.

Harry savored his contradictions: a mobbed-up publisher whose superhero was the mob's greatest nemesis, a family man whose wife and children accepted that he had a mistress living down the street, a purveyor of adult erotica and kiddy comics who read neither. "He was many things—a heavy drinker, a womanizer, he gambled and he knew Costello—but you're talking to a daughter who absolutely adored him," says Peachy. "He was a very generous, caring, loving man, and he was very progressive."

Holding together his dissolute life was easier with Jack there to mind the businesses and pick him up if he fell apart. Sometimes Jack would have to shout to be heard, telling Harry he couldn't go on spending, or drinking, the way he was. But he never forgot that it was Harry who had brought him into the business when he had nothing. Harry also helped him set up a partnership with Maxwell Gaines to launch All-American Comics, and later helped him buy out Gaines for what Jack said was a million dollars. Jack regularly reminded his kids what it had been like at the beginning, when he and Harry had four or five different companies but "very little cash in the till." They would take whatever there was from one firm to cover the debts from the rest. Now loot was flowing in from everywhere, and especially from Superman, who by 1942 was starring in three comic books with a combined circulation of one and a half million and an estimated readership of four and a half million. Twenty-five million more followed him in 285 newspapers nationwide. For Jack, that cash flow bought him the freedom to launch new companies in the morning and weigh in on how big to make Superman's fanny or Lois's breasts in the afternoon. In the evening, just before the long drive home, he always sat down with the boys from the office for a hand or two of his favorite game, gin rummy. Not a bad life for a boy from the shtetl.

Jack also made investments of his own, in the stock market and in the five-bedroom house he owned on Long Island. Rose and the girls lived the good life in Great Neck—prep schools, their own sitting rooms next to their bedrooms, as many as three servants to tend to their needs—but it hadn't always been that good. They were in the Bronx when Jack was getting started, then moved onto Long Island and up the ladder as he and Superman did—to Laurelton, then Lynbrook, then a smaller home in fashionable Great Neck, and finally to the mansion. Jack was a founder of the Jewish Federation and had a box at the opera. Uncle Harry drove out with Aunt Gussie for family gatherings and games of pinochle, like in the old days; ties between the families were cemented when Harry's only son married Jack's niece. But Jack handled Harry the same way you would any relative you loved but knew wasn't a good example for the kids. "My father was so refined, so un-Harry," recalls his daughter Joan. Jack, Joan adds, was intimidating enough that his family was as afraid of him as his workers were, but when she needed him he always was there. He also always was clear about his expectations for her and her sister, Linda: "A young matron doesn't go out of the house without a hat and gloves. And he wouldn't let us work, it was not what a refined young lady should be doing. If you worked it meant your father wasn't taking care of you."

EVERY KID IN AMERICA knew that Superman could win any war he fought in five minutes, which posed a conundrum when the United States went to war in December 1941. The nation's fleet was in ruins at Pearl Harbor. Germany was holding the line in Russia and pressing ahead in North Africa. Normally bullish Americans were not sure this was a war they belonged in or could win. Adults argued about strategy and tactics at work and over the dinner table, and stayed up nights fretting about their teenage sons who were being drafted to fight. Adolescents had a simpler question: Why not send in Superman?

It made sense. In the space of the first two issues of *Action Comics,* he had reformed an arms dealer and made peace between warring forces in the fictional South American republic of San Monte. The stories left no doubt that he had clout, or that the conflict in San Monte was a stand-in for the ongoing Spanish Civil War. The vision of all that he could accomplish had become clearer still in the February 27, 1940, issue of *Look* magazine, in a cartoon story by Jerry and Joe entitled "What If Superman Ended the War?" World War II was at an early stage then and America still was officially neutral, but that did not stop Superman from twisting Nazi cannons into useless metal, intercepting Japanese fighter planes, and hauling Hitler and Stalin before the League of Nations for judgment. "Adolf Hitler and Josef Stalin," the presiding minister announced, "we pronounce you guilty of modern history's greatest crime—unprovoked aggression against defenseless countries."

But once the war heated up and America was forced in, Superman stepped back. It was not for lack of patriotic role models. Hop Harrigan, comic book America's Ace of the Airwaves, took to the skies "to rap the Jap a slap on the yap that'll corrugate his map!" Another comic starred Blackhawk, a crackerjack Polish pilot who had been shot down in 1939 and was back in the cockpit exacting his revenge against the Nazis. Rip Carter and the Boy Commandos did comparable damage on the ground, alongside Captain America, Captain Marvel, the Sub-Mariner, and the Human Torch. So why was Superman, the monarch of American heroes, sitting out the war?

That was a question being asked not just by juvenile fans but by letter writers to *The Washington Post* and editors at *Time* magazine. Jerry and Joe were fretting as well, along with Jack and Harry. They knew they had created that expectation by fashioning a hero powerful enough to intervene and righteous enough to recognize that the Allies were the good guys. They also knew that all anyone expected from non-super-powered heroes like Blackhawk was to shoot down an enemy fighter. With Superman the bar would be infinitely higher. Once he entered the fray, readers would demand real-world results that no make-believe character could deliver. Even having him try would make him look like a paper tiger and could damage morale among American soldiers who were fighting for real. "As the mightiest, fightingest American," *Time* wrote in a story called "Superman's Dilemma," the Man of Steel "ought to join up. But he just can't. In the combat services he would lick the Japs and Nazis in a wink, and the war isn't going to end that soon. On the other hand, he can't afford to lose the respect of millions by failing to do his bit or by letting the war drag on."

The solution: Clark Kent tried to enlist in the Army in 1941, but during his eye exam he inadvertently read a chart in the adjoining room with his X-ray vision. "You're physically superb," the doctor told him, "except that you're obviously blind as a bat. . . . The Army *doesn't* want you." It was a remedy attributed to editor Murray Boltinoff, but it may have been cooked up in collaboration with Joe, who failed his own preinduction eye test and was declared unfit for duty. It got Superman off the spot in a way that satisfied everyone from youthful comic book readers to the editors of *Time*. But not Lois. "I might have known the Army would turn you down," she told Clark. "How you summon up enough strength even to peck at your typewriter keys is beyond me!"

He may have been out of the Army, but he was bent on helping. "The United States Army, Navy and Marines are capable of smashing their foes without the aid of a Superman!" he told readers in that same 1942 cartoon strip. "Perhaps I could be of more use to my country working right here at home, battling the saboteurs and fifth columnists who will undoubtedly attempt to wreck our production of vital war materials!" And so it was that his direct confrontations with Hitler, Hirohito, and what he called the Japanazis were confined to comic book covers, which were attention-grabbing but unrelated to the stories inside. The stories had him joining war drills, battling "Japoteurs," and standing up to "Mr. Schickelgruber" and his "so-called master race," making the case without having to say it that the real *Übermensch* was on our side.

The U.S. military knew that Superman was a flying Uncle Sam—an embodiment of the red, white, and blue virtues for which America was sacrificing its sons—and it used him to solicit blood donations, spur drives for scrap iron, and sell savings bonds. After just one radio appeal from their hero, 250,000 young patriots mailed in pledges to buy war stamps. The British Admiralty named its most powerful oceangoing tug *Superman*. U.S. servicemen had done the same with jeeps, tanks, landing craft, and the planes of the Air Corps Reserve's 33rd Bombardment Squadron. The Navy strove to end illiteracy within its ranks in part by having the dialogue in a Superman comic shaved to single or double syllables, then rolling out to its sailors 15,000 copies a month of the easy-to-read books. After D Day, an anxious infantry officer told war correspondents, "When I saw one of our boys in our landing craft nonchalantly reading a copy of *Superman,* I knew everything would be all right."

Superman's biggest contribution to the war effort was setting free the imaginations of America's warriors. They got all the blood and guts they needed on the battlefield, and all the run-ins with the Nazis and Japanese. Watching Superman battle with Lex Luthor and other fantastic villains let them escape. It offered them a way to feel like kids again and reminded them of the lives back home that they were fighting to protect. No gift could matter more.

How do we know that? At U.S. military bases, comic books out-sold *Reader's Digest, Life,* and *The Saturday Evening Post* combined. Estimates said 80 percent of the Army's reading matter was comics, and Superman was tops among the comics. It was a two-way street for the Man of Steel: He helped sell America on the war, and the war pumped up his sales. Kids who had grown up on him were heading overseas, and they brought the knight from Metropolis along as a security blanket. The Navy found Superman so soothing that it tucked his comic books into ration kits bound for the Marine garrison on embattled Midway Island. So concerned was Canada about Superman's influence on its troops that in 1940, when he convinced both sides in a comic strip war between Blitzen and Rutland to temporarily lay down their arms, censors ordered the *Toronto Star* to leave it out.

U.S. censors didn't step in there, but they were worried four years later when Superman got too close to the sensitive subject of an atom-smashing cyclotron. "The FBI came into the office," Superman editor Jack Schiff recalled years later. "They told us to change the syndicated Superman strip then running in order to eliminate a cyclotron that was featured. For reasons unknown to us then, this was a no-no. We really should have suspected what was happening: the A-Bomb was being developed and this was a possible leak." A 1945 document from the War Department, declassified after the war, downplayed the concern, saying that the very fact that the cyclotron story was playing out in the funny pages would ensure no one took it seriously. The war planners, however, had taken the matter seriously enough to mark their memo SECRET, and Harry's marketing team later used the crackdown to boast that "Superman readers had a comic strip preview of the world's most carefully guarded secret." Two other Superman stories—one with a cover of him watching an atomic bomb test, the other where Lex Luthor tries to use an A-bomb to do away with Superman—saw their publication postponed until after the war.

Superman's owners were good at keeping secrets. They made sure that no one knew that Jerry was not scripting the character at the time of the FBI visit in 1945 and hadn't been for two years, although his was the only writer's name on every story. Jerry had been drafted into the Army in the summer of 1943 and sworn in on July 4. Ghost-writers who had done an occasional story before now were writing nearly everything. Jerry's proxies and Joe's made a motley crew. There was Alvin Schwartz, a Trotskyite who loved debating over lunch with his editor, Jack Schiff, a Stalinist. Leo Nowak, a musician as well as an artist, had been sent Joe's way by a whiskey salesman he met in a bar. Paul Cassidy was a schoolteacher before he drew Superman, and afterward. Nearly everyone who joined up in Cleveland and later in New York backed FDR and the New Deal. Many were in their twenties—only slightly older or more worldly than their readers—and most didn't tell family or friends that they had fallen so low they were writing for the funny pages. They called it Hungry Money; once they had enough, they would find real jobs writing magazine stories, novels, or film scripts. Their tightly packed workspace was a cross between a newsroom and a sweatshop, with an unremitting stream of pages passing from pencillers to inkers, sandwiches sufficing for lunch and dinner, and deadline pressure intense enough to breed ulcers and nervous breakdowns.

Alvin Schwartz had been co-editing a literary magazine that published luminaries like William Carlos Williams and Ezra Pound, but the Depression upended that career. One day he tried to bum a quarter off an old friend; the friend, a comics artist, said there was writing work to be had in his field. Alvin penned his first Superman comic strip in 1944 and his last in 1952. In between he earned enough money to buy a house, even though he was making $250 for a strip that earned Jerry $800. And while he didn't get a byline, he did get a *New York Times* story revealing that he was one of Superman's writers. He also got to put his stamp on the hero: "I tried to change Superman from being a meathead who simply had a harder punch into something more human and philosophical."

To Jerry, ghostwriters like Alvin were mere seat warmers. After all, Superman was his brainchild, and he kept sending in ideas while he was serving his country in the Army. Although he wore the insignia of the infantry, as a minor celebrity he wasn't about to see real action. His special-assignment company in West Virginia was called DEML, for Detached Enlisted Men's List, but it was known throughout the Army as Damn Easy Military Life. In a 1944 letter, Jerry asked Jack whether he could pull strings to land him an even cushier job in Washington writing for the Army newspaper. And while he was at it, could he send Superman pins and secret codes to all of Jerry's fellow soldiers in DEML?

Jerry ended up not in Washington but in Alabama, then in Hawaii, where he was promoted to corporal and wrote a comic strip for the troops, the first time a member of the military had ever done that. It was called *Super G.I.* and its hero, Private Joe Droop, again was modeled after Jerry—a soldier who was "small, weak . . . timid." Every human being, Droop told himself, "is two persons. The person he is . . . and the person he'd like to be. It's all a matter of concentration and psychic conditions." While Jerry loved the attention he was getting in the Army, he was too obsessed to focus just on his military cartoon and his war. He worried that each check coming from Jack was too small, and that Detective was using his old idea for a *Superboy* comic book without giving him proper control or compensation. He complained less when Joe Shuster—who had been ceding increasing authority to his artistic assistants as his eyesight and work ethic frayed—was stripped of any remaining control over Superman's design.

Superboy wasn't the only new product to emerge from World War II for Detective Comics, and Joe wasn't the only one whose duties changed. Writers and artists were coming and going with the draft and other wartime demands, and Jack Liebowitz found new talent to replace them temporarily or forever. He discovered that a full-length novel worked as well as a thin comic book to tell Superman's story, and that George Lowther was as good a storyteller as Jerry Siegel. And he found all the paper he needed for his books and comics despite a shortage that had forced newspapers to shrink the Sunday strips. No one knew better than Harry Donenfeld and Jack Liebowitz how to dip into black markets and make cross-border deals with Canadian publishers. Beyond that all they had to do was count their money, with monthly sales of comic books doubling to twenty million between 1941 and 1944, dealer return rates plummeting to zero, and war-related prosperity generating a windfall for the whole comics industry. Superman caught the breeze, with thirty million Americans regularly reading his comic books or strips. Soldiers were loyal fans, but truer still were their kid brothers and sisters back home, who bought Superman stories, read and reread them, then traded them in schoolyards and backyards. As for Jerry's complaints that he was being shortchanged while he was in the Army, Jack said that in addition to commissions for stories others were writing, Jerry got a $5,000 bonus at the end of 1945. "You did not see fit to acknowledge [it]," Jack wrote, "though you did deposit it."

The riskiest business decision Jack Liebowitz made during the war—to keep Superman off the battlefield—was rewarded in spades afterward. Hop Harrigan, the Boy Commandos, and nearly all the other comic book heroes who were on the front lines saw their popularity fade, and many disappeared entirely. Finding a role for real warriors in peacetime was hard enough, but it was impossible for fantasy characters meant to provide an escape. Their association with a war America wanted to forget was too painful. Superman's shepherds had bet right, keeping him engaged as a cheerleader rather than a combatant. It was a lesson they would not forget.

An even more valuable lesson was one that Superman himself understood better than anyone. Over the course of World War II, the hero and his country went through a similar process of self-discovery. America learned that it had the world's most vibrant and malleable economy and used it to forge a military complex powerful enough to smash the Axis juggernaut. Superman found he could not just jump high but he could take flight, see through or topple buildings, and defeat any foe. The mightier the superpower and its superhero got, the more both realized that the challenge was to marshal their strength not merely to win battles but to stand for something worthy of the fight. Truth was a good starting point. And of course there was justice. As GIs sacrificed their blood everywhere from the Ardennes Mountains to Iwo Jima, the United States and Superman added another element to their moral code: They were fighting to advance not just universal rights but very particular ones, like life, liberty, and happiness, that they called the American way. The Man of Steel and the nation that loved him were, during the long years of war, growing up together in a way that made him more relevant than ever in postwar America.

CHAPTER 3

A Matter of Faith

HE DIDN'T LOOK JEWISH. Not with his perfect pug nose, electric blue eyes, and boyish spit curl that suggested Anglo as well as Saxon. No hint in his sleek movie-star name, Clark Kent, which could belong only to a gentile, probably one with a lifelong membership at the country club. His social circle didn't give it away either: Lois Lane, George Taylor, and even Lex Luthor were, like him, more Midwest mainstream than East Coast ethnic. The surest sign that Clark was no Semite came when the bespectacled everyman donned royal blue tights and a furling red cape to transform himself into a Superman with rippling muscles and expanding superpowers. Who ever heard of a Jewish strongman?

The evidence of his ethnic origin lay elsewhere, starting with Kal-El, his Kryptonian name. *El* is a suffix in Judaism's most cherished birthrights, from Isra-el to the prophets Samu-el and Dani-el. It means *God*. *Kal* is similar to the Hebrew words for *voice* and *vessel*. Together they suggest that the alien superbaby was not just a Jew but a very special one. Like Moses. Much as the baby prophet was floated in a reed basket by a mother desperate to spare him from an Egyptian Pharaoh's death warrant, so Kal-El's doomed parents, moments before their planet blew up, tucked him into a spaceship that rocketed him to the safety of Earth. Both babies were rescued by non-Jews and raised in foreign cultures—Moses by Pharaoh's daughter, Kal-El by

Kansas farmers named Kent—and the adoptive parents quickly learned how exceptional their foundlings were. The narratives of Krypton's birth and death borrowed the language of Genesis. Kal-El's escape to Earth was the story of Exodus.

Clues mounted from there. The three legs of the Superman myth—truth, justice, and the American way—are straight out of the Mishnah, the codification of Jewish oral traditions. "The world," it reads, "endures on three things: justice, truth, and peace." The explosion of Krypton conjures up images from the mystical Kabbalah, where the divine vessel was shattered and Jews were called on to perform *tikkun ha-olam* by repairing the vessel and the world. The destruction of Kal-El's planet and people also calls to mind the Nazi Holocaust that was brewing when Jerry and Joe were publishing their first comics, and it summons up as well the effort to save Jewish children through *Kindertransports*. Superman's lingering heartsickness was survivor's guilt. A last rule of thumb: When a name ends in "man," the bearer is Jewish, a superhero, or both.

If most of his admirers did not recognize Superman's Jewish roots, the Third Reich did. A 1940 article in *Das Schwarze Korps*, the newspaper of the SS, called Jerry Siegel "Siegellack," the "intellectually and physically circumcised chap who has his headquarters in New York." Superman, meanwhile, was a "pleasant guy with an overdeveloped body and underdeveloped mind." Creator and creation were stealthily working together, the Nazis concluded, to sow "hate, suspicion, evil, laziness, and criminality" in the hearts of American youth who "don't even notice the poison they swallow daily."

Superman had even stronger cultural ties to the faith of his founders. He started life as the consummate liberal, championing causes from disarmament to the welfare state. He was the ultimate foreigner, escaping to America from his intergalactic shtetl and shedding his Jewish name for Clark Kent, a pseudonym as transparently WASPish as the ones Jerry had chosen for himself. Clark and Jerry had something else in common: Both were classic nebbishes. Clark and Superman lived the way most newly arrived Jews did, torn between their Old and New World identities and their mild exteriors and rock-solid cores. That split personality was the only way he could survive, yet it gave him perpetual angst. You can't get more Jewish than that.

So compelling were those bonds that decades later TV's Jerry Seinfeld would refer to Superman as his Jewish brother-in-arms, and BBC Radio would air a debate entitled "Is Superman Jewish?" *The Jewish 100,* a book about the most influential Jews of all time, listed Jerry and Joe alongside Sigmund Freud, Albert Einstein, and Abraham. Jules Feiffer, an authority on cartoons and Jews, said the Last Son of Krypton was born not on Krypton but on "the planet Poland, from Lodz maybe, possibly Crakow, maybe Vilna." The alien superhero was, more than anything, "the striving Jewish boy's goyishe American dream."

Was that what Jerry and Joe had in mind? Neither was an observant Jew or attracted to organized Judaism. Some of Superman's Jewish touches—such as the spelling Kal-El, versus Jerry's more streamlined Kal-L—were added by later writers and editors, the preponderance of whom also were Jewish. But Jerry acknowledged in his memoir that his writing was strongly influenced by the anti-Semitism he saw and felt, and that Samson was a role model for Superman. He also was proud that his anti-Nazi superhero touched a nerve in Berlin. So, undoubtedly, were Harry Donenfeld and Jack Liebowitz, both of whom had experienced Jew-baiting up close in Eastern Europe and the Lower East Side. What Jerry did, as he said repeatedly, was write about his world, which was a Cleveland neighborhood that was 70 percent Jewish, where theaters and newspapers were in Yiddish as well as English, and there were two dozen Orthodox synagogues to choose from but only one place—Weinberger's—to buy your favorite pulp fiction. It was a setting and time where juvenile weaklings and whey-faces—especially Jewish ones, who were more likely to get sand kicked in their faces by Adolf Hitler and the bully down the block—dreamed that someday the world would see them for the superheroes they really were.

THE EVIDENCE THAT HE was a Jew did not stop other faiths from claiming Superman as theirs. Christian enthusiasts saw him as Jesus, the child dispatched to Earth by his omnipotent father to save mankind. No surprise that his Kryptonian name was Hebrew, since Jesus was a Jew, but the *Kal* in front of *El* suggested to Christians a presence beyond just God—a son, perhaps. The fact that Clark Kent's adoptive mother originally was called Mary added to their argument, as did Superman's cape, which can look like the wings of an angel. Superman's story reminds Jews of Old Testament heroes from Moses to Aaron and David; Catholics and Protestants find the holy saints when they read between the cartoons' lines.

The case for a Christian Superman was grounded in geography. It was not merely that he came from the heavens—but that he landed in Kansas. It was a state made up mainly of God-fearing Roman Catholics, Baptists, and Methodists. It fell just outside the Bible Belt but deep within the Grain Belt, thanks to its sorghum and wheat, soybeans and corn. It was the American heartland, with plainspoken rules about how to treat others and clear-cut values taken straight from the Ten Commandments. It gave Clark a grounding in right and wrong as he headed to the big Metropolis and gave Middle America a sense that he was one of them.

Symbols mattered, too, as always in religion and popular culture. Baby Kal-El's blanket brought to mind Jesus' swaddling clothes. Clark's Fortress of Solitude rose like a cathedral. His fellow reporters had as much trouble recognizing him as Superman as Jesus' fellow Nazarenes did seeing him as their savior. True believers also have attached meaning to names. *Krypton* is Greek for *hidden,* which is one way the New Testament described the kingdom of heaven, and in Kryptonese *Kal-El* means *Star-Child,* which could refer to the Star of Bethlehem, signal of the birth of Christ. *Lex Luthor* sounded and acted like *Lucifer. Clark* means *cleric,* in this case one whose middle name—Joseph—is perhaps a wink to the carpenter from Nazareth. These and other connections are laid out in Stephen Skelton's book *The Gospel According to the World's Greatest Superhero.* The dots became even easier to connect in later years. Comic books would kill off Superman, then resurrect him. In the movies, a godlike Marlon Brando would dispense to his son advice straight out of the Book of John to "show the way" to the earthlings who "lack the light" but have the "capacity for good." On stage in *Godspell,* Jesus would wear a Superman shirt. And a television show about an adolescent Superman would open with an episode showing a young Clark hung on a crucifix by a gang of football players.

While the search for religious meaning has yielded compelling nuggets, sometimes it seems strained. Is Jor-El, Superman's father, a play on Hebrew words for "God teaches"? Or is it, as Jerry insisted, Jor as in Jerome and El as in Siegel—making Jerry Siegel, rather than any deity, the true father of Superman?

The truth is that Superman's most Christ-like features have less to do with how he looks or sounds than how he behaves. He represents our best selves and highest aspirations. He intervenes where he can, as with the abusive husband and death row inmate, but recognizes that man must have free will even when it hurts, as in World War II. That sense of devotion and duty inspired Father John Cush to enter the priesthood, and it resonates with the high school students he teaches in Brooklyn. "Obviously," Cush explains, "as a Roman Catholic priest, I see Superman as a Christ figure." To some clerical leaders, that is apostasy. "The Word became flesh, not steel," said the Reverend Kenneth Reichley of New York's St. Peter's Lutheran Church. "Superman is magic. He manipulates fate and history . . . Jesus is not magic. He works within history." Not so, said the Reverend Andrew Greeley, Catholic scholar and author: "Superman, I've always thought, is an angel. Probably the angel stories found in all of the world's religions are traces of the work in our world of Superman and his relatives. Who is to say I'm wrong?"

Christians and Jews were not the only ones. Muslims, at least some of them, saw in the Superman creation story a reflection of their own origins, with Jor-El dispatching Kal-El as a messenger to mankind much the way God did Muhammad. Buddhists put in dibs, too, seeing the superhero as the Man of Zen. Superman knew how "to live entirely in the *now*," explained Alvin Schwartz, who was born Jewish, was long interested in metaphysics, and wrote Superman's comic strip when Jerry was in the Army. "He's totally fixed on a single point. His one defining act—his rescue mission. That's what he does . . . and that's why you can't have a Superman without a Clark Kent—because no one can live all the time at that level of experience. There has to be a retreat to ordinariness, to self-recollection."

Nonbelievers had a different take: Superman was a paragon, but he wasn't a Jew or a Christian, a Buddhist or a worshipper of the ancient gods of the sun that gave him his power. He was so strong he could truly move mountains and so pure he would neither litter nor jaywalk. He could crawl away from kryptonite but was undone by moral relativism. He never asked his followers to die in his name or to proclaim themselves the chosen ones. This vision of Superman as a secular messiah tapped into America's cultural myths and oral traditions—into its communal do's and don'ts—which is just the way agnostics, atheists, and spiritualists would have him. It also is just what Geoff Johns calls to mind when he writes Superman stories or edits them. "You can have spirituality and morality without religion," says Johns, today's chief creative officer at the company built by Jack and Harry. "Superman shows that is possible." Mark Waid—who collaborated with Alex Ross on the graphic novel *Kingdom Come,* the most spiritual Superman story ever—agrees that religion is not the point: "Superman is not a story about faith, it's about inspiration. It's a story about trying to move us into emulating, into being, into doing."

The early Superman did that not by preaching, or even explaining, but by letting his actions speak to his intent. The governor wouldn't pay attention to a prison superintendent who was abusing his inmates? No problem. Superman burst into the governor's mansion just as he had a year before to stop an execution, whisked the state leader to the prison, and let him see for himself the abuse. The superintendent wouldn't confess? Into the sweatbox he went, with the governor looking on and Superman vowing, "I'm going to plug the air-holes . . . You'll suffocate and die, just like your own victims did!" Superintendent: "No! No! Let me free! I swear I'll never torture the prisoners again!!"

By the time Waid wrote *Kingdom Come,* more than half a century later, the Man of Tomorrow had found his voice after abandoning—then dramatically reclaiming—his mantle as a superhero. "Years ago, I let those I swore to protect drive me away. We all did," Superman—speaking for Batman, Wonder Woman, and the other crusaders—explained to United Nations leaders. "We saw you as gods," said the UN secretary-general. Superman: "As we saw ourselves. And we both were wrong. But I no longer care about the mistakes of yesterday. I care about coping with tomorrow . . . together. The problems we face still exist. We're not going to solve them for you. . . . We're going to solve them with you . . . not by ruling above you . . . but by living among you. We will no longer impose our power on humanity. We will earn your trust."

Noble words, but can a comic book character actually move readers to change their behavior and lift their horizons? He can, says Emilio Ramos, Jr., if that character represents not just an abstract notion of good but the good in each of us, the way Superman does. Ramos grew up in the "slums and ghettos" of Holyoke, Massachusetts, with few men to model himself after. He got his first Superman comic at age six and was hooked. "I've never had alcohol, never smoked, never done a drug in my life. People are surprised with that because of the environment I was exposed to growing up. People are even more surprised when they asked how I turned out the way I am and I just say one word: 'Superman,'" says Ramos, who is twenty-nine now and training for a career in law enforcement. "Superman definitely drew me into that field." The Man of Steel taught Peter Lupus how to defend himself and others. "Up until I was fourteen everybody in the neighborhood beat me up for practice," recalls the seventy-nine-year-old actor who was the muscleman on TV's *Mission: Impossible* and later played Superman in commercials for the U.S. Army. "I started working out to overcome that bullying. Superman was my guy. I could equate with the Clark Kent–to–Superman transformation. I felt maybe I could go through life trying to help the underdog."

Superman changed Tom Maguire's life, too, especially his spiritual side. "I had what I considered to be too much religion in my life as a youngster. I found it confusing. Which was the true god, my grandmother's Armenian Orthodox god, my father's Irish Catholic god, my best friend Bobby Barwald's Jewish god, or my other friend Marty Pushkowicz's Catholic god? Was the true god the Muslim god, the Muslims that my Armenian grandmother escaped from at age 12 to come to America? It was all so confusing to me as a child growing up in the '60s. And then there was Superman, who provided an escape for me as a young reader. Superman didn't ask me to believe in a god," says Maguire, a fifty-six-year-old environmental regulator in Boston. "For 10 cents and later 12 cents an issue, Superman was an escape for me from those who asked me to believe in their god. Superman protected the oppressed and downtrodden and the poor, regardless of their religion or race. And my family was downtrodden at the time. I'm agnostic today, in part because of Superman."

AS WE EXPLORE SUPERMAN'S FAITH, it helps to consider what, if anything, he had in common with his vengeful crime-fighting compatriot Batman. What did Batman share with his archenemy the Joker? Was there anything other than superhero status that bound Superman and Batman to the Spirit, Green Lantern, Captain America, Spider-Man, the Incredible Hulk, the Fantastic Four, the X-Men, the Human Torch, and the Boy Commandos?

All were the products of fertile Jewish imaginations. The midwives to the biggest and boldest comic superheroes and supervillains were young men with names like Lieber, Eisner, Finkelstein, Kurtzberg, Katz, and the dynamic duo of Siegel and Shuster. These aspiring writers and artists went into comics for the same reason bright Jewish doctors in the early 1900s practiced at hospitals like Beth Israel and Mount Sinai: It was the only option open to them. Anti-Semitism barred Jews from advertising agencies, which were lily-white and mainly Protestant, while the lack of a college diploma kept many out of other lucrative careers in publishing. Desperate for an outlet to display their wares and pay their bills, they turned to the nascent comic book industry. Comic books were to the high-end magazines and newspapers of the day what the *shmatte,* or rag trade, was to high-style clothiers, but that didn't bother these young writers, most of whose parents or grandparents had been in *shmattes*. The comics offered a toehold and a paycheck. Jewish mothers may not have bragged about their son the cartoonist, but it was a way to earn a living and, in a surprising number of cases, fame and fortune.

History equipped them for the task. Jews have been fine-tuning their storytelling skills since the days of Abraham, four thousand years ago. They did it first and best in the Torah, which is the first five books of the Hebrew Bible. Biblical commentaries were collected in the Talmud, rabbis' sermons were published in the Midrash, and mystics' tales found their way into the Zohar. No wonder Muhammad called them the People of the Book. While much of that writing was on esoteric matters of religious practice and legal dictates, it was told with such flair and essence that the books have remained in print for thousands of years, and telling stories still is an esteemed calling for Jews.

Whimsy was another critical attribute for the cartoonist and another rich vein in Judaism. Jews have been cracking jokes for centuries. It was a way to stay sane in the face of repressive Spanish inquisitors, marauding Cossack horsemen, and all the other faces of despotism. Oftentimes the humor was self-mocking, as in the saying that any Jewish holiday can be summed up this way: "They tried to kill us. We won. Let's eat." Sometimes it teased the holy one, Yahweh, the way Moses supposedly did on Mount Sinai: "Let me get this straight. We cut off the tips of our penises and You promise to take care of us until the end of time. You better put that in writing." By one count in the 1970s, more than 80 percent of America's best-paid comics were Jewish, even though Jews made up less than 3 percent of the population.

Telling a good story and making people laugh were good starting points for writers of comic books. But stories about superheroes required prototypes, and there were slim pickings for those in a world of Jewish milquetoasts. Yes, there was Samson, yet it was his very singularity that fueled our interest and his legend. The key, it turned out, was knowing where to look, and a good place to start was with the Golem. A he-man shaped from clay, this mythic character emerged repeatedly throughout history to safeguard Jews from aggressors. In some incarnations he was dim-witted and turned on his creator; at other times he was eloquent and loving. Always, he was big, powerful, and just the thing for a people in trouble. So was Siegmund Breitbart, a flesh-and-blood Polish-Jewish circus performer known to his landsmen as Zishe and to everyone else as the Strongest Man in the World. He could pound nails into wood with his fists and pull a wagon full of people with his teeth. He was becoming famous across America at the very moment that the Jewish creators of Superman, Batman, and other heroes-to-be were coming of age and looking for role models.

Will Eisner was one of those creators. He went to the mainly Jewish, all-boys DeWitt Clinton High School in the Bronx, where his classmates in the 1930s included two teenagers who would invent

Batman and two more who would reshape Superman. Eisner was confident that comics could become his vocation based on his writing and drawing for the school newspaper, literary magazine, and yearbook. He also knew from an early age that organized Judaism meant nothing to him and that God was take it or leave it. He was right about the former: He dreamed up the quickly successful crime-busting comic strip *The Spirit,* inspired generations of comic artists and writers, and, at the ripe age of sixty-one, wrote his first graphic novel and a landmark of the form. As for Judaism, its God and heroes became the centerpiece of his novels and he became a standard-bearer for the American Jewish experience. "I write about the things I know," Eisner explained late in life. "I know about Jews."

Eisner was not the only comic book creator who was ambivalent about his Jewish identity. His fellow writers and artists were routinely reshaping their proud Russian and German Jewish names into monosyllabic, ethnically vanilla ones. So Stanley Martin Lieber became Stan Lee, Max Finkelstein was now Carl Burgos, and Jacob Kurtzberg rebranded himself as Jack Kirby, an appellation that suggested roots in Ireland, not Austria. Green Lantern artist Gil Kane lost not just his Latvian name, Eli Katz, but his arced nose; both changes were conditions his then-girlfriend set for marrying him. Eisner, meanwhile, wrote his early stories under four pen names—Willis B. Rensie, W. Morgan Thomas, Erwin Willis, Wm. Erwin—none of which sounded remotely Jewish. His sensitivity to ethnic appellations, like his compatriots', grew out of boyhood pain. Will's younger brother was named Julian—which neighborhood bullies sounded out as "Jewleen." Will tried fighting for his brother's honor, then settled for convincing Julian to become "Pete," arguing, "That's a better name for around here!"

Their names may not have sounded Semitic, but their writing did. Jack Kirby and his collaborator Joe Simon, also Jewish, created Captain America, the first major comic book hero to declare war on Hitler and the Nazis. Marvel Comics kingpin Stan Lee brought in imaginary characters like Willie Lumpkin and Irving Forbush, whose names were as unmistakably Jewish as Lee's had been. More to the point, he brought to life stars like Spider-Man, whose working-class beginnings, childhood persecution and alienation, and purposeful life mirrored the experiences of Romanian-Jewish immigrants like Celia and Jack Lieber, Stan's parents. Lee, however, resists reading too much into his characters or his own actions. He chose the name "Lee" to preserve "Lieber" for the Pulitzer Prize–winning novel he knew was in him, he says. As for suggestions that his characters came out of his past, "I never consciously added any Jewish qualities or elements."

Conscious or not, those elements were there in the adventures of one superhero after another. Who better to empathize with the fight for the underdog than Jews who had grown up reading signs saying NO NIGGERS, NO JEWS, NO DOGS? And who better to join that battle than the heroes they spawned, such as Lee and Kirby's Mighty Thor and Carl Burgos's Human Torch? The Jewish writers were outsiders by birth. They were conflicted, with one foot in their parents' shtetl and another in their brave new universe of opportunity. They gave life and shape to heroes whose very names, from Batman to Captain America, reflected their creators' reach for the otherworldly and the all-American. Yet the themes and the characters they brought to life grew out of the very past they were trying so hard to escape.

JERRY SIEGEL SHARED THE Old World Jewish heritage of his comic book comrades and he grew up in the same American ethnic melting pot. His father and mother met and married in Kovno, in southern Lithuania, and that is where they had their first two children, Rose and Minnie. The family name then was Sigalowitz; Jerry's dad was Michel, his mom was Sore. Michel took a ship to America in 1900, planting stakes in New York with guidance from his wife's brother, who had arrived earlier. Sore came with the girls two years later. In between, the family name got shortened to Segal; no one knows why, but it didn't happen at Ellis Island, where complicated names often were butchered, and it wasn't to whitewash their religion, since Segal was almost as transparently Jewish as Sigalowitz. The alteration likely arose from a Yiddish-speaking immigrant trying to avoid spelling a long name in a strange tongue. Whatever the motivation, the effect, as her ship's manifest indicates, is that Sore Sigalowitz was met at the dock by her husband M. Segal.

The continuing evolution of their names offers a window into their continuing adjustment to life in a very different land, where they tried their best to fit in and nearly managed to. Sore picked a name that worked better for an American and a Jew—Sarah—and she stuck with it. Michel changed both his names with each new census: from Moses Sigel in 1910 to Michael Siegel in 1920 to Michael Sigel in 1930. Dual death records and dueling obituaries went back and forth between Michel and Michael (although all agreed on Siegel); some stories since then have called him Mitchell. During their brief time in New York, Michel and Sarah had either one or two more children, depending on which census they filled out accurately. Then they headed to the Midwest the way lots of Jewish families were doing, pulled by family or pushed by the German-born Jews who ran the New York community and disdained the poor migrants from Eastern Europe.

The Shusters had more stops and fewer name changes on their way to Cleveland. Joe's father, Julius, was from Rotterdam, in Holland, where Julius's father was a successful hotelier catering to immigrants and where he met his wife, Ida, who was from Russia. The family was doubly blessed: Julius and his brother met Ida and her sister and the outcome was two weddings. All four young newlyweds ended up emigrating to Toronto, where they shared a flat and split their salaries right down the middle. Julius and his family couldn't have made it otherwise, given his difficulty finding work. Later, when his brother and sister-in-law moved with their kids to Niagara Falls, Julius, Ida, and their three kids followed. In May 1924 Julius headed to Cleveland, where a job was waiting. Ida and the children followed in August.

New York and Toronto had been thriving Jewish communities that more than matched in spirit and numbers those the Siegels and Shusters left behind in Europe, but neither family knew what lay ahead in Cleveland. They need not have worried. Cleveland back then had 85,000 Jews, which was more than 10 percent of the city's population, and nearly half of them lived in the Glenville area, where the Siegels started out and the Shusters moved later. Gentiles were a minority in the neighborhood, which was 70 percent Jewish, and they were even rarer at the high school, which had the highest median IQ in the city. Most dads were small businessmen like Julius and Michel.

Few moms were as active as Sarah, who volunteered with the Jewish Consumptive Relief Society, the Orthodox Orphan Home, the B'nai B'rith community service organization, the temple sisterhood, and the benevolent society. The Jewish Center, which was on its way to becoming the largest Conservative synagogue in America, had a basketball court and a huge swimming pool; neither Jerry nor Joe had much use for either. When the boys went outdoors it was Yiddish, not English, they heard from the ragman, the bread man, the iceman, and the fruit and vegetable men. When the boys said they didn't grow up very Jewish they meant they didn't go to synagogue much, but Glenville then was like Israel today: Just being there, breathing in the culture and street life, was living a Jewish life.

Just how fully they had absorbed that worldview became apparent in a comic book Jerry and Joe collaborated on in 1948. *Funnyman* was about, as historians Thomas Andrae and Mel Gordon tell us, "America's first Jewish superhero." Comedian Larry Davis battled mobsters and goons not with super-strength but with wisecracks, wit, and comedic contraptions, the way Jews had been doing for centuries. No carefully sculpted body or small, straight nose on this champion. In costume he wore a Jimmy Durante schnozzola to go with baggy polka-dot pants and blue plaid tails; in street clothes he was drawn to look like the carrot-topped Jewish comedian Danny Kaye. No need for these stories to be scrubbed of their ethnic flavor, which was part of their appeal. One episode centered on a pain-in-the-rump character with the Yiddish handle Noodnik Nogoodnik, while another featured a medieval magician named Schmerlin. In this series the unlucky, awkward schlemiel was no longer the hidden half of our protagonist but the hero himself. It was not just Larry Davis who was showing his true ethnic self, but Jerry Siegel and Joe Shuster.

Jerry says he dreamed up *Funnyman* when he was in the Army. Joe's sister says it was Joe's idea. The truth is that both had been hams at least since their boyhood days of imagining characters like Goober the Mighty. Jerry had gone so far as to co-write with Joe's brother a 134-page manual entitled *How to Be Funny: A Practical Course of Serious Study in Creative Humor* and to cook up the Siegel-Shuster School of Humor. By the time they created Funnyman, Joe and Jerry had learned their lesson on giving up control of their character to a corporation and were determined not to do that again. The postwar era, they reasoned, was the right moment for the country to laugh again and forget about being heroic. They were sure they could rebottle the magic of Superman. Unfortunately, they weren't as funny as they thought. Without backing from deep-pocketed publishers like Jack and Harry, the new comic book lasted just eight months, and the syndicated strip stopped the next year. It would be Jerry and Joe's last collaboration, but it was their most joyous.

The Jewish inflections in Funnyman were also there in Superman, although finding them meant looking closer, the way a Torah scholar might. Superman was a refugee who had escaped to America from a world about to explode, just as the Shusters and Siegels did in fleeing Europe before the Holocaust. His parents rocketed him to Earth in hopes he would find a new beginning. He adhered to ethical guide-posts as unbending as those of the *tzadik,* or righteous man, in the Old Testament tradition. Clark Kent was Superman trying to assimi-late. Superman was the real thing—as muscle-bound as Siegmund Breitbart, as indestructible as the Golem, and an inspiration to every Jewish schlump who knew there was a super-being inside him. Even kryptonite radiated with symbolism: It showed the influence his homeland still had over its Last Son, threatening to upend his life in the diaspora.

Joe and Jerry were living that immigrant experience alongside their hero. Joe had been hoisting weights for years, building up his body in hopes of snagging a girl. No worries if she wasn't Jewish, so long as she was tall and a dish. Jerry bought a big house, went to res-taurants that saved him their best table, and adopted pen names more white-bread than Clark Kent's. Joe and Jerry wanted to fit in, to be all-American big shots. They also wanted it both ways. What they were running away from was not their Judaism but their nebbishness. They hoped people would see that they had been special before they became famous.

One thing that made them special during the war years was the belief that Hitler himself was after them, even if that wasn't entirely true. The German American Bund did send Joe hate mail in the years leading up to the war, and its members picketed outside Detective Comics' headquarters. The SS newspaper did write a story attacking

Jerry and Superman after *Look* ran the Superman story in which he defeated the Führer. That was where the facts ended and the media frenzy began. Each time the story was reported in a newspaper or book it got ratcheted up: Now propaganda chief Joseph Goebbels was angrily attacking Jerry in the middle of a Reichstag meeting, and Adolf Hitler was threatening to exterminate him. Hitler and Goebbels didn't, but their ally Benito Mussolini did ban from Italy Superman, along with every American comic book with the exception of Mickey Mouse.

Those years on either side of World War II were ones in which Jerry and Joe evolved alongside their cartoon characters. Their confidence grew as they were celebrated for their work and sought out by other artists. That made it easier for them to experiment with formats like humor, which had always been there in Superman and took center stage in Funnyman. They did the same with their Jewishness, which became more pronounced when their hero was a comedian instead of a strongman. They had only been willing to reveal so much about Superman's ethnicity, but it was more than anyone else had done with an all-American superhero.

HARRY DONENFELD AND JACK LIEBOWITZ affirmed their Jewish roots in ways that made clear they were children of the shtetl. They believed you should never deny your heritage, and they kept intact names as manifestly Jewish as Liebowitz and Donenfeld. You gave to Jewish causes (both did, generously) and favored Jewish entertainers (Gussie Donenfeld said what she liked most about clarinetist Benny Goodman was "that he never changed his name"). You hired fellow Jews as often as possible, and with the exception of Italian American artists, the roster at Detective Comics and on Superman especially was mainly Jewish. It started with Siegel and Shuster and continued with editors, writers, and illustrators with surnames like Weisinger, Schiff, Joffe, Binder, Dorfman, and a pair of Schwartzes.

There was one more guidepost for children of the ghetto: You didn't let ethnic identity get in the way of making money. That was why Harry overruled himself and opted to call his company not Donenfeld Comics but Detective Comics. "Donenfeld," his daughter

Peachy remembers, "sounded too Jewish to him." He and Jack almost certainly would have intervened in the same way if they had felt that Superman, their number one moneymaker, was stepping too far into their Yiddishkeit world.

He never did. Superman's handlers from the beginning planted clues that Superman was Jewish, but that evidence was subtle and ambiguous enough that it convinced many readers that Superman was seriously Christian. Giving him a backstory straight out of the Bible also inoculated Superman against claims of being a false prophet, and those claims would have come, whether from priests, preachers, rabbis, monks, or imams. Presenting him as a moral man in a world of temptation made him compelling to people in search of ethical as well as religious direction. In the end, his appeal was his universality along with his particularity, which ensured his stories would live on the way most parables do. Here was an exemplar, one of the few, who was embraced with equal ardor by Jews and gentiles, believers and agnostics, and anyone else in search of a hero.

CHAPTER 4

The Speed of Sound

IT WAS HOW AMERICANS SPENT their evenings in the era before TV—chairs and sofas pulled around the two-foot-high Philco radio console, the brown Bakelite dial carefully tuned to *Fibber McGee and Molly, Ellery Queen, Amos 'n' Andy,* or, on sixteen history-making nights in June and July of 1946, *Adventures of Superman.* Listeners came ready to leap out of their corn-fed lives and into their superhero's fantastic one—his slugfests with atom men and mind games with leopard women—which was what had made the Man of Steel such a smash when he debuted on the airwaves two years before the war. What they heard instead during that first summer of peace was a tale of real-life, home-grown fiends who masked their ashen faces with white sheets, twisted their followers' minds with Nazi-like schemes of racial cleansing, and defied Superman or anyone else to try and stop them.

The series was called "Clan of the Fiery Cross" and it was not an easy story to tell. Not then, when professional baseball, public bathrooms, and even the Army and Navy still were divided into white and colored realms. It would be another year before ex–Negro Leaguer Jackie Robinson toppled the color bar when he joined the Brooklyn Dodgers, and another eight before the Supreme Court declared that racially separate schools could never be equal. Jews, Asians, and

Roman Catholics still saw signs saying they need not apply. The Ku Klux Klan wasn't as powerful as it once had been, but it didn't have to be. It already had planted doubts about anyone who looked or prayed differently; those who didn't heed its warnings could always be reminded with a flaming cross or lynching noose.

Robert Maxwell didn't care. He detested the Klan and had been given the keys to the Superman radio kingdom by Jack and Harry. The wordsmith turned pitchman turned radio producer knew he had to get to the kids before the haters did. He hired one of America's most trusted education experts to tell him how. They gathered all the intelligence they could on the Klan's passwords and rituals, its ways of corrupting politicians and its means of wrapping itself in the flag. They consulted psychologists, psychiatrists, and propaganda special-ists. They tested their approach with five weeks of broadcasts railing against a fictitious organization of anti-Semitic "hate mongers." Now was the time to ratchet up the moralizing and zero in on a real-life hate group. They even had a name for their bold enterprise: "Opera-tion Tolerance." Their secret weapon—the surest way to win over the children and take down the xenophobes—was to sic on them, at the speed of a radio wave, America's most trusted and ferocious do-gooder.

"Clan of the Fiery Cross" ran for sixteen episodes of fifteen min-utes each, built around a straightforward storyline. Tommy Lee, who was Chinese, rose to become the star pitcher on his youth baseball team, beating out a hot-headed white hurler named Chuck Riggs. Riggs took his beef to his Uncle Mac, who was secretly the grand scorpion of the Clan. The white-hooded Clansmen terrorized first Tommy and his family, then Jimmy Olsen and Perry White, whose newspaper had taken up Tommy's cause. Superman stepped in just as Mac and his crew were about to finish off Olsen and White.

Every chapter ended with a cliffhanger and most featured dueling sermons from the grand scorpion and Clark Kent. "We're a great society pledged to purify America—American for 100 percent Americans only. One race, one religion, one color," Mac told his nephew. "Are we going to stand idly by and see these scum weasel their way into our neighborhoods and our jobs. . . . We'll strike back, and the time is now, so get set for action. The fiery cross burns tonight." Not so fast, Kent shot back: "Intolerance is a filthy weed, Jim. I told you before—the only way you can get rid of it is by hunting out the roots and pulling them out of the ground."

Superman's political evolution on the airwaves was the reverse of what had happened in the comics. There, Jerry and Joe molded their avatar into an agitator only to have editors in New York reshape him into something tamer and less likely to offend. Robert Maxwell sprang from the same Eastern European Jewish roots as the boys from Cleveland and he was at least as idealistic, but he was older and wilier, and in those years he had almost complete editorial freedom. His radio Superman carefully picked his enemies: Nazi saboteurs, jewel thieves, witch doctors, and others unlikely to generate sympathy or controversy. He built his audience of kids, stay-at-home moms, and dads who got back home from the office or factory in time to catch the early evening broadcast. It was a full six years into his show when he finally turned Superman loose on the Klan. Even then, Maxwell's venom was directed not at the political corruption or corporate villainy that riled up Jerry and Joe, but rather at narrow-mindedness. The distinction was critical. The new focus might alienate listeners who identified with Mac Riggs, most notably the flesh-and-blood Klansmen who at that very moment were trying to recruit kids in New Jersey, just across the Hudson River from Superman's Manhattan studio. That only helped the cause. Maxwell used the threatening letter he got two days after the series started to stir up publicity. More to the point for his bosses, "Clan of the Fiery Cross" posed little risk of upsetting the advertisers who paid the bills, especially since the focus was prejudice against Asians rather than the more culturally condoned bias against blacks.

Kellogg's, the primary sponsor, was over the moon. Operation Tolerance had given *Superman* a bump in the ratings. With an audience of 4.5 million listeners it was the number one children's program in America, leaving in its wake old standbys like *Captain Midnight* and *Hop Harrigan*. The *Superman* shows also were a boon for Pep Whole Wheat Flakes, the breakfast cereal ballyhooed by the narrator at the beginning, middle, and end of each episode. "Tolerance is rampant in Battle Creek," Maxwell gloated to *Newsweek* after the airing of the hate mongers series. "Every bit of pep in Rice Krispies is tolerant." The magazine added its own hurrah: "Superman is the first children's program to develop a social consciousness."

The angle that gripped *The New Republic* was where Superman got his dope on the Klan. Newspaper reporter Stetson Kennedy had gone undercover in the hate group, the liberal journal reported, passing its "code words" to the Anti-Defamation League, which forwarded them to Maxwell. "As a result, Samuel Green, Grand Dragon of the KKK, had to spend part of his afternoon with his ear pressed against the radio. As soon as Superman used a KKK password, Green had to send out urgent orders for a new one. The Grand Dragon is said to have taken this reverse very badly." Kennedy picked up the story in his own book, saying he gave *Superman*'s producers "the Klan's current password, and promised to keep them informed every time it was changed." The scheme worked so well that kids invented a game they called "Superman Against the Klan," rattling off secret passwords "a mile a minute!" Thanks to his work and the Man of Steel's, Kennedy concluded, "I knew that the millions of kids who had listened to Superman were not likely to grow up to be Klansmen."

It was a seductive backstory, and much of it was true. Kennedy did provide invaluable intelligence on the Klan, although he embellished what he had done and blended his narrative with those of others. Did he pass secret passwords on to Superman? None that he cited were actually broadcast, and the only thing that came close to a code in all sixteen episodes of "Clan" is when "the robed figures solemnly placed their right hands over their hearts, crossing the first two fingers of their left hands," and muttered an "anti-democratic oath." Journalists and authors were so taken with Kennedy's version that no one fact-checked it against the radio script. But compelling though they were, the media accounts missed the point. The wizard hiding behind the studio curtain was not Stetson Kennedy, it was Robert Maxwell.

Siegel and Shuster's comic books and strips already had made Superman a hero on every playground across America; Maxwell's broadcasts made him one in boardrooms, too. The Veterans of Foreign Wars and American Veterans Committee awarded him special citations for leading the battle against bigots. The Mutual Broadcasting System said it was "prideful" to be Superman's station. Sharing that glow were the National Conference of Christians and Jews, the American Newspaper Guild, and the Calvin Newspaper Service, most of whose readers were black. (Apparently none of his progressive boosters minded that a dining-car porter speaking dialect was about the only black face in Superman stories, or that the most prominent mention of Asians was the reminder to wartime readers to "slap a Jap.") In New England, radio stations banded together to get permission to start their broadcasts fifteen minutes late, ensuring that young fans wouldn't miss their hero while their parents listened to coverage of that summer's pennant run by Ted Williams's Boston Red Sox. "We had been getting a lot of complaints about the blood and thunder stuff until we decided to put in these social episodes," said a spokesman for the advertising agency used by Kellogg's, which recognized early on the dividends that could be earned from a crusade for tolerance. "Now all the parents' organizations are congratulating us on the show. The psychologists tell us we're planting a 'thought egg' in the kids' minds."

Whether or not that egg actually hatched, it was clear that Superman and his handlers had staged another triumph. They had inoculated themselves against parents, teachers, and even psychoanalysts who worried about the impact of action heroes on young minds. Thirty-five million American homes had radios in 1946, and Superman was beaming into more of them than ever, entertaining entire families rather than just the kids who read comic books. At a time when nearly all the wartime superheroes were fighting for their lives, the Man of Steel was thriving. To Superman, Inc., crisis meant opportunity, just as it had during the war.

This latest victory was particularly sweet for an old socialist like Jack Liebowitz, who approved Maxwell's hiring and green-lighted Operation Tolerance. Jack had consciously assembled a team of artist-entrepreneurs who were youthful as well as inventive, with the audacity to presume they were shaping not just a fictional character but popular fiction itself. Jack understood that Superman's success in radio helped ensure a growing market for his comics, and vice versa.

He also understood that, as he had always said, if you were smart you could do good at the same time you were getting rich.

MAKING SUPERMAN BELIEVABLE ON PAPER was a relative cinch. Good eyes were all that was needed to see him leap and fly, defy bullets along with alien invaders, and metamorphose from buttoned-down Clark Kent in a double-breasted suit to a soaring superhero in a pajama-like uniform. Radio was different. There were no alleyways in which we could witness his makeover, no costumes or hairstyles to show us there had been a switch. Listeners had to visualize for themselves what he looked and acted like to make it work. The fact that it did—from the very first broadcast on February 12, 1940—was a tribute to the skills of the actors and producers and, at least as much, to the supple imaginations of young fans who wanted to believe.

The show's first challenge was finding one performer who could play Superman and another for Clark Kent. The solution was Clayton "Bud" Collyer. The choice seemed obvious to everyone but him. Collyer had trained to be a lawyer, like his dad, but he paid his way through law school by singing and acting on the radio, following in the show business footsteps of his mother and grandfather, sister and brother. After two years as a low-paid law clerk he was back performing—using his mother's maiden name of Collyer so he could preserve his birth name, Clayton J. Heermance, Jr., in case he ever resumed his legal career. By the time *Superman* was ready to air, Collyer was starring in two radio adventure series—*Renfrew of the Mounted* and *Terry and the Pirates*—along with a comedy, several soap operas, and three news features. That was more than enough. The idea of a comic strip on the radio was such a stretch that he made clear he didn't even want to audition. Maxwell tricked him into doing that, twice, but still Collyer tried to get out of it.

That he didn't was a stroke of luck for both Superman and Collyer, since they made a brilliant match for 2,008 radio shows and for thirty years in various media. Collyer drew on his training as a crooner to underscore the difference between Clark and Superman, playing the former in a tenor that oozed milquetoast, then dropping several pitches midsentence to a gravelly baritone that was just right for the world's strongest man, yet making clear that both voices came from the same man. That preserved the essential ego/alter-ego relationship and saved Maxwell from having to hire a second actor. Being the first to impersonate either character meant the only standard Collyer had to meet was the one he was setting. Performing on the radio, where no one could see him, meant he never ran the risk of growing too old for the role. It also reduced the possibility of his being typecast, which was a fear (and reality) that would later plague TV and film actors playing Superman. Even though they couldn't see what he looked like and there were no credits naming him, his voice was rousing enough for female listeners to flood the studio with mash notes addressed to Superman. They might have been disappointed to know that he had a wife and three children and that he taught Sunday school on Long Island. Portraying Superman "was the ultimate in unabashed corn," said Collyer, who would later become known to a generation of baby boomers as host of the TV game show *To Tell the Truth*. "So many people get the least bit embarrassed by fantasy when they're directing it or performing it and it loses all the great charm it could have, but if played honestly and whole-hog all the way, it's great."

Joan Alexander was Collyer's co-star and opposite. She needed the work playing Lois Lane at first to support herself and later to provide for her daughter after she left a troubled marriage. She got the role early on, lost it when Maxwell decided he didn't like her, then disguised herself in a wig and showed up at the audition for her replacement. "The producers hired her!" her daughter recalled sixty years later. "They were astonished to find out they had rehired the woman they'd just let go. This time she kept the part forever."

Jackie Kelk had nailed down the role of Jimmy Olsen by season two. Like Alexander, he needed the part, but like Collyer, he had to fit it around other acting jobs. The solution: Kelk's Jimmy was written into the action four days a week, while on day five—Thursdays, when Kelk was rehearsing with *The Aldrich Family*—Jimmy was AWOL and a character named Beanie Martin took over as copyboy.

As critical as those and other main characters were, the narrator was more so, especially after Jackson Beck took over the job. He saved Maxwell from needing to have his actors self-consciously stop the action to explain what they were doing or why. Beck set the scene and caught up listeners who had taken a bathroom break or sneaked into the kitchen for a snack. In between his narrations he played as many as four other roles in a single episode, from villains to Beanie the copyboy, which was even more impressive since most of the broadcasts were live. He also was an accomplished huckster, working with his sidekick, Dan McCullough, to weave into high-energy plots messages about Pep cereal, "the eighteen-karat breakfast dish that sparkles with sunny cheerfulness." For Kellogg's, those pitches were what the show was all about, and why they kept Beck around for some 1,600 broadcasts.

The maestro who assembled that extraordinary cast and launched Superman onto the airwaves was Robert Maxwell, the orchestrator of Operation Tolerance. Who better to reconfigure Superman for a new medium and to refresh radio by introducing its first superhero than a thirty-two-year-old artist-entrepreneur who had reinvented himself? Born Robert Maxwell Joffe, this oldest child of Russian-Jewish immigrants had taken the pen name Bob Maxwell to protect himself and his family when, in his early twenties, he wrote stories with titles like "He Had Push" for Harry Donenfeld's bawdy and bloody pulp magazines. The brashness of the tales and their author caught Harry's eye and he drafted Maxwell into Superman, Inc., first to oversee the licensing of toys and other products, then to bring the superhero into the world of broadcast. Before he hired writers or actors, Maxwell sat down with Harry and Jack's masterful press agent, Allen Ducovny, to put together audition discs that would sell the show to prospective sponsors. They couldn't have picked a better moment. Few families had television sets in the early 1940s and almost none had the money, gasoline, or motivation to go out. Radio was the era's hottest medium, with its comedies, harmonies, and mysteries helping to take people's minds off the lingering agony of the Depression.

A new show required another origin story. It had to be familiar enough to loyal comic book and strip readers that they wouldn't see it as tinkering with the legend, and it couldn't presume any preexisting knowledge of Superman lore, since part of the point of a new medium was to attract new fans. So whereas *Action* No. 1 described

Superman's home planet as distant and destroyed by old age and *Superman* No. 1 simply called it doomed, the inaugural radio show brought the action closer to home and gave more telling details. Krypton was in our own solar system—hidden from us by the sun— and it was that sun's gravitational pull that overpowered the planet and made it "explode like a giant bubble, destroying every living thing on it!" Superman grew up on his way to Earth and by the time he stepped out of his spaceship, in episode two, he was ready to save his adopted planet.

Superman's war against the Nazis also looked different on the radio. In the comics, he stayed in his civvies and fought on the home front. On the airwaves he was commissioned as an undercover Secret Service operative. He still lived by clearly delineated rules, just as he had in print, including doing all he could to spare the lives of his enemies. And he came into America's living rooms with an opening sequence that would become the signature of Superman on the radio and later on TV, even though it has been altered over time and the first paragraph was borrowed from the animated cartoons. So familiar was the refrain that children across the forty-eight states could recite it as readily as the Pledge of Allegiance:

"Faster than a speeding bullet," the narrator intoned. "More powerful than a locomotive. Able to leap tall buildings in a single bound!"

Man: "Look! Up in the Sky!"

Second man: "It's a Bird!"

Woman: "It's a Plane!"

First man: "It's Superman!"

Narrator: "Yes, it's Superman! Strange visitor from another world, who came to Earth with powers and abilities far beyond those of mortal men. Superman, who can change the course of mighty rivers, bend steel in his bare hands! And who, disguised as Clark Kent, mild-mannered reporter for a great metropolitan newspaper, fights a never-ending battle for truth, justice and the American way!"

The last four words, which were added in the summer of 1942 and became part of Superman's motto, were chosen with the help of a child psychologist to ensure they touched the right chords. Superman, of course, had always fought for patriotic principles, but it was only with the nation at war—and Americans thinking more than ever about why their country was worth fighting and dying for—that the idea of a distinctly American way of believing and acting took hold in the public mind and the Superman mythos. Yet again, Superman was reflecting and refracting his era in a way that helped define it.

But words alone wouldn't do. Listeners needed to visualize the action. So as the narrator talked about a speeding bullet, the radio audience heard a burst of machine-gun fire. Locomotive? Let's hear the roar of a passing train. The biggest challenge for the three sound effects men was Superman taking flight. At first a hand-cranked wind machine had to suffice, but the artifice grew more convincing with the addition of several recorded sounds: a wind tunnel playing in reverse, a plane diving with a deafening roar, and a newsreel of an artillery shell whizzing through air during the Spanish Civil War. For Superman's landing, the sound guys slowed by hand those recordings, the way disc jockeys do today. When the record stopped, listeners were assured that Superman was back on solid ground.

A radio writer's mission was different than Jerry Siegel's had been in the comics. Jerry aimed strictly at kids. Radio writers started with young people as the target, but their scripts also had to appeal to grown-ups, who made up more than a third of the listeners. The best way to reach both, advised the show's first director, was to assume the best in each. "Kids can detect the patronizing tone of an adult who tries to reach down to their mental age, and they resent it," said Jack Johnstone. "You've got to be perfectly natural." Another challenge: How to keep the pot boiling when everyone knows that nothing can hurt your hero. "A railroad train runs across his chest. It doesn't hurt him, it hurts the train! Where do you get the suspense from?" asked scriptwriter Edward Langley. "I was a young writer in my twenties. So I asked a guy I knew in his fifties. . . . He said: 'The one thing Superman can't do is strike a match on a cake of soap!' That was the kind of 'peg' that you used—to try to use what he can't do. . . . They were wide open to anything, as long as you could make it suspenseful and interesting. Topics didn't make a damn bit of difference."

That challenge got a bit easier in the spring of 1943, when Superman finally got a worthy adversary. It happened while Clark Kent was interviewing Dr. John Whistler at the Metropolis Museum. The scientist showed the journalist an unusual green meteorite that made

Kent suddenly feel "as if every ounce of strength had been drained out of me." The narrator explained the game-changing implications: "Superman for the first time in his life faces an enemy against which he is entirely powerless." That enemy, a radioactive fragment of the planet Krypton, prompted Superman to recall his birthplace, his parents, and how and why he had been sent to Earth. It was the first the world heard of kryptonite, although Jerry Siegel's twenty-six-page story on K-Metal was sitting on the library shelf at Detective Comics and could have been read by the radio scriptwriter. It would take another six years for the deadly metal to make its way into the comics and another two before a nation that was still at war, and understandably nervous about the mention of anything involving radiation, would hear much more on the radio about the glowing green element.

When kryptonite returned to the airwaves it became the centerpiece of an epic battle between Superman and the Atom Man. At seventy-seven episodes, this struggle was the longest in all of the Superman radio series. The face-off began in September 1945, less than two months after America dropped its "Little Boy" nuclear bomb on Hiroshima and the world was thrust into the Atomic Age. Perfect timing. The final story aired the following January, two days before the inaugural meeting of the United Nations. In between, the villainous Scarlet Widow stole from the Metropolis Museum the single known sample of kryptonite, only to see a Nazi scientist named Der Teufel (German for "the Devil") steal a chunk of it. Determined to "succeed where Hitler failed," Teufel fed his kryptonite to Heinrich Milch (a.k.a. Henry Miller), turning him into Atom Man, whose radioactive powers were too much even for Superman. Miller seemed unstoppable, as the narrator warned: "Superman is pitting all his strength and speed against the one force on earth which is mightier than he is—the force which twice brought him within the very shadow of death. Can he possibly win this time, when he fights for his very life, and for the lives of those he loves? Monday brings the smashing, dramatic climax of our story, fellows and girls—and a startling surprise, so don't miss it." When Superman triumphed the next evening, he told a grateful Metropolis police inspector, "You don't owe me anything. I'm fighting for the same things you are—the end of tyranny and intolerance—all the things that Miller and the Nazis stood for." Inspector: "Then I'll only say thank heaven that the worst threat America ever faced is over."

Ahh, but it wasn't over. Two more pieces of kryptonite were somewhere in the city, and to track them down, Superman had to enlist the help of Batman and Robin. That meant confessing to them his secret identity, the first time he had ever done that. Showing his full self would pave the way for Superman to forge with Batman his first true friendship, one based on an honesty he couldn't afford with anyone but his foster parents and the sharing that was possible only with a fellow superhero, who understood the anxiety and exhilaration that came with the job. So effective was this radio collaboration in defeating the Atom Man that the Dynamic Duo was back again for more than a dozen other guest appearances. Being able to rely on them as stand-ins proved particularly useful when Superman was taken out of the action by kryptonite—and when Bud Collyer wanted to go on vacation.

It was on the radio, too, that Superman learned to fly. He was aloft by the second episode in 1940, which was three and a half years earlier than his flying debut in the "Million-Dollar Marathon" story in *Action,* although in the early years of broadcast his power of flight waxed and waned from adventure to adventure. Radio's immediacy and Maxwell's brashness once again let Superman dive into a topic that comics writers would only slowly tease out. Kryptonite seemed like a good idea, so give it a try. Same with turning a high jump into full flight. What didn't change was Superman's boyish delight each time he tested his aerodynamic abilities, as he did in May 1943 when he was battling the Ku Klux Klan. "Up in my arms with you, Chuck," Superman said to the young ballplayer Chuck Riggs. "Are we going to fly?" Riggs asked. Superman: "We are. Hang on now." Riggs: "Oh boy—flying with Superman, I must be dreaming." Superman: "Here we go. Up, up, and away! Is that your house down there, Chuck?"

While some of the radio firsts involved expanding and curtailing his powers, others filled in what was quickly becoming the best supporting cast a superhero ever had. An intrepid copyboy showed up at Clark and Lois's newspaper as early as *Action Comics* No. 6 in November 1938. He was given a bow tie but not a name or an ongoing role; he would make three more cameo appearances through the end of 1939. Jimmy Olsen was introduced to the world in April 1940, on a radio episode called "Donelli's Protection Racket." He was a red-headed, freckle-faced boy who worked at the paper. His mother had run a candy store since his dad died three years before, and a local mobster named Donelli was trying to extract money from her. Jimmy turned to Clark and Superman for help. Over the next several episodes we learned more about Jimmy: He was a Boy Scout but couldn't find his way out of the woods; he perpetually annoyed his boss by calling him "chief" even as he asked to be promoted to real reporter; he reacted to everything good and bad by gasping "Holy smokes"; and he had a knack for getting into trouble and counting on Superman to bail him out.

Perry White, too, came alive on the radio, fencing with Jimmy from the start and eventually making his way into the comics. The editor was first identified as Paris White, but his first name evolved to one more suited to his gruff demeanor even as his newspaper was changing from the *Daily Flash* to the *Daily Planet*. Inspector Henderson—first called Charles, then William—was Clark's best source and Superman's closest ally at the Metropolis Police Department. He was made for the radio and was intended to reassure parents that Superman was a friend of the police and not the vigilante he started out as. It took seven episodes on the airwaves for Lois to appear, which was a long time compared to her debut in *Action* No.1, but she was the only adult female character on any afternoon action-adventure radio show.

There were actually several Superman radio series, not just one. They ranged from fifteen to thirty minutes, and aired three to five times a week. The shows were meant to be kid-friendly, although for thirteen weeks in 1949 a crime version aimed at adults ran on Saturday evenings. The Mutual Broadcasting System aired the program for most of its run and Kellogg's was by far the longest-lasting sponsor. The end came in March 1951, which was sooner than most fans wanted but more than a year later than for competing shows like *Captain Midnight* and *Tom Mix*. Because tapes of the old shows became available only recently, the radio *Adventures of Superman* hasn't gotten the attention from historians and fans that his exploits on TV and film have. But it was radio that lifted the hero from a devoted audience of comic book fans into a broadcast universe that reached nearly every corner of the nation. The radio series came onto the scene two months into 1940 and it wound down fifteen months after the decade did. In between it joined Kilroy and the Slinky, *Citizen Kane* and Rosie the Riveter, as hallmarks of 1940s America.

HIS SUCCESS IN OTHER MEDIA made it inevitable that Superman would find his way to the big screen. It was equally certain, as the 1930s came to a close, that America someday would produce an animated cartoon star who was not a funny, furry animal. The two trends collided in the Miami studios of a pair of Austrian-Jewish animation geniuses, the brothers Max and Dave Fleischer.

It wasn't the Fleischers' idea. They thought building a "realistic" cartoon around Superman was a lousy idea given the problems they had encountered the only other time they tried to do that, with *Gulliver's Travels*. What they did best was conspicuously unreal characters, like Betty Boop, Popeye, and Koko the Clown. So when they were approached by Paramount Pictures, which owned the screen rights to Superman, Max and Dave had to think about it. They told Paramount that they could produce the ten-minute movies, which theaters craved as lead-ins to feature films—but given the unusual animation requirements and special effects they would have to charge $100,000 per episode, or four times the going rate. "They thought that would be the end of the project—but it wasn't," said Richard Fleischer, Max's son. "Paramount said: 'Okay, go ahead.' "

The brothers were right: It wasn't easy. Special lights were needed to extend shadows and depths and create the right dramatic touch. They tried oblique angles, freeze-framing, double exposures, and other camera techniques that heretofore had been the domain of live-action films and the high-priced Walt Disney Studios. Rotoscoping—a technique the Fleischers had pioneered with Koko in which real-life figures were traced in ink, frame by frame, much as comic book artists sometimes did—made the animated figures believable. Max and Dave's composers knew what Superman, Lois, and the others should look like, thanks to model sheets provided by Joe Shuster. Their voices came from the world of radio, with Bud Collyer playing Superman and Joan Alexander reprising the role of Lois. Composer Sammy Timberg supplied the theme music. The plot lines—thieving robots, rampaging dinosaurs, and jingoistic Japanese saboteurs—were familiar to fans who knew Superman from comic books, comic strips, and the airwaves. So was the sound of an exploding Krypton, which was generated by amplifying the sound of an apple being ripped apart by hand. The films borrowed the expressionism of Orson Welles's *Citizen Kane* and the futurism of Fritz Lang's *Metropolis,* blended with the Fleischers' unique feel for scale and vision. To put together a single ten-minute cartoon took a full six months, or twice as long as the normal Fleischer production.

Did it work? *Time* magazine didn't think so, branding the Fleischer productions "the movie cartoon at its worst. Superman looks and acts like a wooden puppet. So do all his playmates." The *New York Times* film critic Janet Maslin, writing forty years later, was equally dismissive: "The Fleischers show so little aptitude for—or interest in— realistic animation." Both were right in their own way. There was precious little dialogue and the characters seemed as stiff as Joe's drawings. That was their genius. The Fleischers managed to bring into two dimensions and full motion the same simple strength that Joe had captured on paper, and it was that rendering that led animation historians to deliver a judgment decidedly different from that of newsprint reviewers. "These films are among the best fantasy cartoons ever produced," said Leonard Maltin. "SUPERMAN stands as one of the Fleischer studio's finest achievements." The Academy of Motion Picture Arts and Sciences agreed, nominating the first of the Fleischers' seventeen Superman films for an Academy Award as the Best Short Subject (Cartoon) in 1941. While it lost out to a Disney feature, the nomination sent a message to skeptical critics.

Whatever the experts said, the verdict from fans was boisterous and unanimous. "Some 20,000,000 Supermaniacs can hardly wait for Superman's ten-minute, one-reel cartoon to appear once a month in more than 7,000 U.S. movie houses," *Time* wrote in July 1942. "Supermania is the only word for their devotion to this irrepressible Citizen Fixit, who smacks death rays back into the cannon, restores toppling skyscrapers to their foundations, knits broken bridges together with his bare hands, and who has brought a new cry into the world: 'It's a bird! It's a plane! It's—SUPERMAN!'" While the films necessarily lacked suspense, with Superman always winning, "his idolators (of all ages) seem satisfied to see him flex his muscles. This vicarious satisfaction has made Superman Paramount's most popular and profitable short. . . . So popular is the muscular moron that 114 female artists at the Famous studio recently answered a questionnaire asking whether they would prefer Superman for a husband or a boy friend. All said: boy friend. Explained one: 'Trying to live with so super a husband might be awfully fatiguing.'"

Reactions like those earned the Superman cartoons an uncharacteristically prominent spot on theater marquees. But that was not enough to save the series or the Fleischer Studios. The Fleischers were deep in debt on other projects, and in mid-1942 Paramount took over their business and changed its name to Famous Studios. Budgets for the Superman cartoons were cut, quality suffered, and in 1943 Paramount killed the series.

That was not the end of the story. The Fleischer cartoons gave Superman some of his most famous catchphrases—from "faster than a speeding bullet" to "more powerful than a locomotive"—which made their way first to the ongoing radio series and later to TV. These short Superman films were so effective that they even turned up in the comic books: In *Superman* No. 19, Clark feigned a choking attack and kicked Lois's purse to distract her from a Fleischer cartoon that would have revealed his identity as Superman. Twentieth Century Fox and animators at Terrytoons were paying attention, too, drawing on Superman's cartoon success to create their own super-strong character who could fly and wore a blue costume and red cape. The costume eventually changed to yellow and the new cartoon hero's name went from Super Mouse to Mighty Mouse. One bit of Superman mythology that is never attributed to the Fleischer Studios but should be is the use of a telephone booth as a dressing room. The first time Clark Kent ducked into a phone box to change into Superman was in November 1941 in "The Mechanical Monsters," the second of the animation films. It proved convenient enough that he did it again on the radio, in the newspaper strip and comic books, on Broadway, and, most famously, in the movies. Pulling it off was easy when the booth was the old, heavy wooden box with a small window up front, but privacy would be tougher to come by in the newer, all-glass version.

The Superman animation series' most lasting legacy was in show-ing that the Man of Steel could conquer yet another medium. He was quickly becoming ubiquitous, succeeding not just in the worlds of comic books and free radio entertainment but on the silver screen. That was a lesson Hollywood would remember.

THE MOVIE SERIALS WERE Hollywood's stepchild, representative not of what the filmmakers could accomplish in their heyday in the 1940s but of what they could get away with. A serial was a short sub-ject that theaters showed alongside the featured movie, with a new chapter each week and a dozen or more chapters in all. The format was a carryover from serialized pulp fiction and a precursor to early TV, where the movie segments were rebroadcast at the rate of one a day. The storylines—westerns and science fiction, crime and espionage—were aimed squarely at youngsters, who never stopped relishing them, from the silent era in 1912 until TV made them ob-solete in the early 1950s. The writing was thin, with little love, no sex, and the beginning of each twenty-minute episode wasted re-counting the last one. Few came for the acting, either, which was slapdash, with escapes and chases routinely lifted from old films and producers hoping nobody would notice. The draw was the cliff-hanger, in which the hero (often literally) hung over a cliff as the villain gloated and fans were reminded to return the following week to see whether what came next was a death (almost never) or a rescue (count on it). Even when they flopped, which was often, studios could dub and resell the shorts in France, Italy, Turkey, China, and, most obliging of all, Spain and Latin America, where episodes were stitched back together for a single five-hour viewing.

"Jungle Sam" Katzman was the king of the serials, for better and worse. The producer and director was Jack Liebowitz's kind of guy, a penny-pincher and autocrat who had never lost money on a film. He started not with a story or idea, but with a wild and colorful title like *Flame of Calcutta*. From that he built a narrative of intrigue set in eighteenth-century India. His biggest earners were the *Jungle Jim* pic-tures, or at least they were until the Superman serials he made for Columbia Pictures in the late 1940s. To make sure the new films would be a hit with the adolescent fans who loved Superman in his other media incarnations, Katzman tested them on his fifteen-year-old son, Jerome, and his friends. "If they guess how the guy gets out of the predicament each week," Katzman said, "it goes out immediately and we rewrite until they can't guess." The other key, the producer knew, was a Superman in whom his son and millions of other kids could believe.

Kirk Alyn was an odd choice for the job. He was more a song-and-dance man than an actor, having studied ballet and performed in vaudeville and on Broadway in the 1930s and early forties. That's where he decided to trade in the name he was born with, John Feggo, Jr., for Kirk Alyn, which he felt was better suited to the stage. He appeared in chorus lines and in blackface, modeled for muscle magazines, and performed in TV murder mysteries in the days when only bars had TVs and only dead-end actors performed for the small screen. But he had experience in serials if not in superheroes, so when he got a call from Columbia in 1948 asking if he was interested in trying out for Superman, he jumped into his car and headed to the studio. Told to take off his shirt so the assembled executives could check out his build, the burly performer complied. Then Katzman instructed him to take off his pants. "I said, 'Wait a minute.' They said, 'We want to see if your legs are any good,'" he recalled forty years later. They were good enough, and fifteen minutes after he arrived, Alyn was hired as the first actor to play a Superman whom his fans could see as well as hear.

Alyn and his directors were smart enough not to try to reinvent the character Bud Collyer had introduced so effectively to the airwaves. "I visualized the guy I heard on the radio. That was a guy nothing could stop," Alyn said. "That's why I stood like this, with my chest out, and a look on my face saying, 'Shoot me.'" His demeanor said tough guy, but his wide eyes signaled approachability and mischievousness, just the way Jerry Siegel and Joe Shuster had imagined their Superman a decade before. Alyn understood much as Collyer had that kids like fifteen-year-old Jerome Katzman could spot a phony in an instant. If they didn't think Alyn was having fun—and that he believed in Superman—they wouldn't pay to see his movies. His young audience, after all, didn't just admire the Man of Steel. They loved him. Superman was not merely who they dreamed of becoming but who they were already, if only we could see. The good news for them was that Alyn was having fun, and he did believe in his character in a way that these preteens and teens appreciated even if movie reviewers wouldn't.

Columbia Pictures, too, had learned something from the *Superman* radio broadcasts: It pays to let children hold on to their fantasies. Sam Katzman announced at his first press briefing that he had despaired of finding an actor capable of portraying the mighty Man of Steel but thankfully had persuaded Superman to appear as himself. The credit lines continued the ruse, billing Kirk Alyn as playing just Clark Kent.

Superman's comic book colors—blue and red—would show little contrast in a black-and-white film, so Alyn wore gray and brown. Being the first live-action Superman meant making a series of adjustments, some of them painful. When it became clear that no stuntman could convincingly stand in for him Alyn performed his own stunts, or so he claimed, including one where he intercepted an electric current the Spider Lady had intended for Lois Lane. No one counted on the sparks catching on the metal of his Superman belt buckle. "I was saved from incineration only by the insulation on my boot soles," he said later, "but it scared the blazes out of me." Producers also promulgated rules about superpowers like X-ray vision. There were two things it shouldn't penetrate: lead, whose X-ray blocking power proved to be Superman's sole defense against the deadly radiation emitted by kryptonite, and clothing, which was Lois's only defense against prying eyes.

Making Superman fly was a more vexing problem. The technical crew strung cables from the studio ceiling to pull Alyn aloft and molded a steel breastplate to hold him there, and for twelve long hours he was filmed dipping, banking, and, yes, flying the way men had dreamed of since Daedalus built wings for Icarus. The flaw this time was the wiring: It was so painfully visible that the crew was fired and Superman was grounded. Filmgoers saw Alyn poised on the window's edge, but what flew away from the building or any other setting was an animated Superman. He always landed behind a bush or wall, from which his human counterpart could dash out and resume the role. The effect was cartoonish.

Parts of the radio Man of Steel were reprised on film, with Alyn self-consciously announcing, "This is a job for Superman!" before each rescue and shouting, "Up, up, and away!" every time his cartoon double took off. That made sense on radio, when listeners needed cues; it seemed like a parody when everyone could see that Superman was on the job and airborne. Equally jarring to observant fans was noticing that Clark went through the identical motions every time he changed into Superman in the *Daily Planet* storeroom, and that the rough airplane landing in the final episode looked an awful lot like one in the 1947 serial *Jack Armstrong.* Why were they using scavenged film? Surely it wasn't for lack of money: Columbia poured $350,000 into the filming, making *Superman* one of the most expensive serials ever. In the end, the fifteen–part film that aired in 1948 looked like what it was: a B movie sliced into fifteen disjointed parts.

But kids whose Saturday at the movies was the highlight of their week ate it up. These were the same youngsters who, even before they could read the words, had thumbed through their Superman comic books until the pages grew ragged. In later years the reward for finishing their homework, or the inducement to get started, was the chance to listen to Superman on the radio. Saturdays had meant Superman cartoons at the movie house downtown, while on Sunday he showed up in regal color in the funny pages. Now there was a new treat: their hero, in live action, as part of the weekend matinee. Their parents dropped them at the theater thinking the attraction was Charles Dickens's penniless orphan Oliver Twist, but the real reason they wanted to come was *Hurled to Destruction,* the Superman short that ran first. That explains not just why *Superman* played in seven thousand movie houses nationwide but why it took in more than a million dollars, which was three times what Katzman had invested and enough to make it the most successful serial of the time.

In 1950, two years after the first set of shorts, Katzman and Columbia released a fifteen-set sequel called *Atom Man vs. Superman.* The title was borrowed from the radio series that introduced kryptonite, but almost everything else was different. The enemy this time wasn't Der Teufel, the Nazi scientist, but the comic books' Lex Luthor, who slipped in and out of prison and banished Superman to outer space using a secret ray that "breaks down your atoms and reassembles them wherever I desire." Even as the hairless villain was re-writing the laws of physics and inventing flying saucers, his henchmen inexplicably continued pulling off low-tech capers like holding up shoe stores and laundries. *Atom Man* used a hybrid approach to flying that made it more convincing than in the first serials, though it still left a lot for the fans to wish for. Animated stand-ins were used again, but the transition from human to cartoon was smoothed by filming Alyn with his arms raised above his head, an electric fan blowing from above to simulate whooshing air, in front of blue staging that was supposed to look like sky. Other shots had him straddling an airplane and later a missile. The changes made *Atom Man* better than its predecessors, but there was no denying that these short Superman movies did not have the taut drama of the radio broadcasts of the same name.

The Superman serials launched the careers of several actors, some of whom, like Alyn, came and went with the short films while oth-ers, like Noel Neill, would be back later. Neill, a twenty-seven-year-old "sweater girl," became known to adoring fans as the sweet Lois Lane and to detractors as the saccharine one. Like Superman, Lois had a uniform for the first fifteen shorts: a wide-brimmed white hat, a wool business suit, and wavy black hair bouncing off her shoulders as she walked. In *Atom Man* her wardrobe expanded to three outfits and her hair was trimmed to well above the shoulder line. Katzman knew Neill from their earlier collaborations and thought she looked enough like the comic book Lois that he didn't require a tryout. The direc-tion he gave her during filming was clipped and pointed: Play your-self.

In an era when studios carefully managed the lives of actors, Co-lumbia was obsessed with keeping intact the illusion of Superman. Every aspect of the making of the serials was to be secret. Katzman banned outsiders from the set when scenes with Superman were being shot. He screened any personal appearances scheduled for Alyn, and told the actor that he "wasn't to appear on the studio lot wearing the 'uniform,'" which is the way his bosses insisted he refer to his costume. But the studio simply couldn't suppress Alyn's swaggering pride at the role he had been given to play. He loved it when Katzman would tease the maître d' at lunch by asking, "Do you know who this is?" then delightedly telling him, "This fellow is Superman!" When he was off the set Alyn refused to brush back his Superman spit curl, which clearly identified him with the character, and when he was on he gleefully told nonstop stories of derring-do. That identification came back to bite him: He was so widely viewed as an alien from outer space that it became difficult for him to get other roles. "Everyplace I'd go," he explained, "they'd say 'Hi ya, Superman!'" This would become a familiar complaint for future actors playing the role.

In the end the serials suffered the same fate as Superman on radio and in animation: they faded out as the spotlight moved elsewhere with changing American tastes and technologies. By 1948 America had four television networks, and in another three years their broadcasts would be beaming across the nation. TV didn't kill the movie business, as Hollywood had feared, but it did change the behavior of the American public, especially young fans like those Superman leaned on. The cabinet radio that had been the focus of family entertainment was replaced by a TV console, and kids who had flocked to Saturday matinees increasingly stayed home and watched for free.

The Man of Steel, though, was far too potent to fade away himself. Kirk Alyn, Noel Neill, and Sam Katzman had proved that their superhero could be wildly popular as live-action entertainment, and Jack and Harry already were lining up the talent and gadgetry to bring Superman into the era of the television.

BACK IN THE COMIC BOOKS, something curious had been happening to Superman: He was maturing and evolving. That had never been a consideration before, not when he went from infant to adult in a single page of *Action Comics* No. 1 and it was uncertain whether he would last beyond a few issues. No one had given any thought to how or even whether he should continue aging. Joe and his assistants had drawn the character as if he would stay thirty-something forever, even as they went from being young artists to middle-aged ones (editors would later explain his slow aging with the contrivance that he was born on February 29, the leap day, so he added a year only once every four years). Just as important, no one had scoped out which parts of his past readers would want to explore and how his present world should be enlarged. Now, as Superman was looking ahead to his third decade of stardom—and Jerry and Joe were reluctantly relinquishing control over him—a new lineup of artists and writers had begun scoping and enlarging.

Krypton was one of the first elements to take on added dimensions. All we knew to start was that the planet had exploded and Superman had escaped. That seemed like enough, since what mattered was his life with us on Earth. The newspaper strips and the radio show had begun to fill in details about Superman's parents and their world, but the comic books didn't catch up until the summer of 1948, and the first full-length origin story was written not by Superman's creator but by Batman's. Bill Finger's tale opened with this teaser: "Who is Superman? Where did he come from? How did he obtain his miraculous powers? Millions keep asking these and many other questions." The next nine pages took readers back to "the great planet Krypton," populated by "humans of high intelligence and magnificent physical perfection." A handsome, tall Kryptonian scientist wearing a green costume and yellow cape was trying to convince the ruling council that their planet was doomed. The uranium in its core had been quietly churning for ages to the point where "Krypton is one gigantic atomic bomb!" There could be no more hair-raising words for readers, even young ones, who just three years before had lived through the staggering news of what happened to Hiroshima and Nagasaki thanks to the nuclear bombs that ended World War II. Kryptonians' only salvation, Jor-El insisted, would be to build huge rocket ships and flee to Earth, a world with a similar atmosphere and far less gravity. When no one would listen, Jor-El and Lara sent their only child off in a tiny spaceship.

That enlightened readers about Krypton, but Superman himself still didn't know his planet's history or its fate. It took another fifteen months for Finger to bring the hero back to Krypton for the first time since he was an infant and for comic-book-only fans to get their first look at kryptonite. Superman encountered a meteorite infused with the metal in a jewelry store on Earth and, alarmed at how it wilted him, he followed it back through space and time to its source. Arriving on Krypton just as the planet was about to explode, he had a quiet look around. (He "is invisible to these people because he is not of their time and doesn't exist for them," an editor's note explained. "He can only view them as he would a silent movie, but he can read lips.") Following Jor-El and Lara's baby as he rocketed to Earth, Superman did not realize he was following himself until he saw the infant rescued by the Kents, his foster parents.

Going home humanized the Man of Steel. He knew now why the meteor from Krypton had weakened him and why his parents had abandoned him. But that understanding brought with it a loneliness that would never leave. He realized now what Jerry Siegel had confided in us from the beginning: Superman was an orphan and an alien. His planet's sole survivor, he was the last of a long-lived and majestic race. It was not an easy burden to shoulder. "Now I understand," he thought to himself, "why I'm different from Earthmen! I'm not really from Earth at all—I'm from another planet—the planet Jor-El called Krypton!!"

The character named Jimmy Olsen was another instance of comic books catching up with radio as well as with a changing world. While we were introduced to Jimmy and his mother in an April 1940 broadcast, it would take another nineteen months for the comics to give him a personality and a starring role. It took just four panels for the boy, who looked to be ten, to let editor Perry White know his dream: "I—I'd like to become a real reporter—like Clark Kent. And if you'd only give me a chance." White's reply hinted at the repartee the two would continue for decades: "Tell you what I'll do, kid. Come back again in five or ten years. . . . And I may give you a break." Too impatient to wait, Jimmy stowed away in Lois's car as she chased a story about the villainous Archer, then he helped Lois skedaddle into the woods when the Archer took aim at her. The story ended with Jimmy getting his first byline in the newspaper. It would be four more months before he got a last name, twelve years before he earned a promotion to cub reporter, and seventeen years before he settled in with his trademark blazing red hair after experiments with blond, honey blond, and light red.

As with most of the borrowing back and forth between comics and other media, Jimmy stuck because he tapped a nerve. Being a kid, he could share in Lois and Clark's zany adventures without feeling any of the responsibility that weighed on adults like them. Jimmy was a foil for everyone around him—letting Superman repeatedly sweep to his rescue, Perry snarl at and then warm to him, and Lois display her suppressed mothering instincts. Every ten-year-old who flipped through a Superman comic book and tuned in to the radio show identified with him—which is why, however tired his shtick sounded, Jimmy has lasted through thousands of radio and TV broadcasts and through seventy years and counting of comics.

Perry White was everyone's grandfather or favorite uncle—hard-boiled on the outside but soft as a yolk once you peeled back the shell. And while he, too, got his name and personality on the radio, he quickly came to play a major part in Superman's expanding comic book universe. Whereas Jimmy started out with just a first name, Perry, as befit his age and irascibility, at first had just a last one. Six months later he was humanized with a given name, although it was one that more commonly is a surname. His writers were novices when it came to newspapers, so it shouldn't be surprising that they couldn't decide just what rank he held, moving between editor, editor-in-chief, managing editor, and editor-publisher. The one constant was his championing no-holds-barred journalism.

Perry's most versatile reporter and Superman's most cherished and tormenting friend was Lois Lane, who came onto the scene just five pages after Superman did. Readers could follow her infatuation with Superman, which in 1949 looked as if it might end in marriage, and her exasperation with Clark, which Superman exploited to get out of marrying Lois in the 1949 story with the implausible title "Lois Lane Loves Clark Kent." She lived in unit 1705 at the Ritz Plaza Apartments, which was near Clark and filled with pictures of Superman. At the *Daily Star* and its successor, the *Daily Planet,* she held almost every job there was, from sob sister and columnist for the lovelorn to war correspondent, weather editor, question-and-answer editor, and head of the lost and found department. The story she most wanted to write in the early years but could never pin down was "that Clark Kent and Superman are one and the same." We learned that she had a bottomless collection of fashionable hats, a weekly show on radio station WCOD, and a pistol in her purse that she used to defend herself when Superman wasn't there to save her.

What fans couldn't see but did speculate on endlessly was who was the inspiration for America's most famous lady journalist. Was. it Margo Lane, girlfriend of one of Jerry Siegel and Joe Shuster's favorite pulp heroes, the Shadow? Perhaps it was Torchy Blaine, the fast-talking, crime-solving newspaper reporter who starred in a series of 1930s films and, in one, was played by actress and singer Lola Lane. That is what Jerry told relatives and friends over the years. Or was it Glenville High's Lois Long, Lois Ingram, Lois Peoples, Lois Donaldson, Bertha Lois Beller, or Lois Amster? Joe repeatedly singled out Amster, a class beauty and National Honor Society member whom he said he had a crush on. Jerry did, too, but he backtracked when that struck a nerve for his new wife, Jolan Kovacs, who had modeled for Joe when he was drawing Lois. A character named Amster also showed up in one of the first issues of Jerry and Joe's early collaboration "Doctor Occult." The real-life Lois Amster, reminiscing at age ninety-three, says she "never spoke to" Joe and Jerry, "never had anything to do with them. They weren't my type. . . . My type was more sophisticated than they were, more affluent than they were."

Easier to trace were Clark Kent's roots, at least the ones outside the comics. His first name came from Gable, the king of Hollywood and star of *Mutiny on the Bounty,* and his last name was borrowed from a less well known film star of that era, Kent Taylor. His reporting style was based partly on the kind of journalist Jerry had once fancied becoming himself, when he doubted his comics would sell. A better model was Wilson Hirschfeld, the crusading reporter and managing editor of *The Plain Dealer* in Cleveland and a high school classmate of Jerry and Joe's. The three had worked together on the *Torch,* and dreamed up stories together on the front porch of Wilson's home. Hirschfeld, who died in 1974, alternately confirmed and denied that he was Clark, although a warm condolence card from Jerry after Wilson's death helped settle the case for the Hirschfeld family.

Clark's parentage inside the comics remained more ambiguous through the 1930s and 1940s. The couple who found and raised him at first were simply called "the Kents." Ten years on, in a comic book published in the winter of 1948, his foster parents got first names: John and Mary, although those names appeared not in the text but on the Kents' gravestones. A year later Pa Kent would inexplicably become Silas, and it would take until the 1950s for the couple to settle in as Martha and Jonathan. From the first the Kents were big-hearted. They saved the baby boy who rocketed into their world, adopted and raised him as their own, and imbued him with a mission. "No man on Earth has the amazing powers you have. You can use them to become a powerful force for good!" John admonished from his deathbed. "There are evil men in this world . . . criminals and outlaws who prey on decent folk! You must fight them . . . in cooperation with the law! To fight those criminals best, you must hide your true identity! They must never know Clark Kent is a . . . super-man! Remember, because that's what you are . . . a Superman!"

Inspired though that message was, it was not original. Nearly identical passages had appeared six years earlier in yet another medium, the novel. It was written by George Lowther, a scriptwriter for the Superman radio show, and had the same title as that show: *The Adventures of Superman*. It was the first full-fledged book ever centered on a comic character, and Lowther was the first writer other than Jerry Siegel to get credit for writing a Superman tale. The comic strips' Jor-L and Lora became Jor-el and Lara in Lowther's book, and those spellings stuck although Jor-el became Jor-El. The Kents, too, got new names here: Sarah and Eben. Lowther fleshed out the worlds of Superman's parents on Krypton and his foster parents on Earth. His longest-lasting contribution to the mythos was having Clark slowly discover his powers during his teens, which made him more empathetic and believable. "It was not until his thirteenth year that the incident occurred that was to set him apart from ordinary humans," Lowther wrote. "Clark watched the teacher as she poked about in the desk drawer, and as he did so he became slowly aware that he was also looking at the inside of the desk, that his eyes had pierced the wood. . . . The simple truth was that he *had looked through the desk* as though the wood were transparent."

Such narratives about Superman's growing pains were captivating to adolescent readers who imagined themselves in Superman's place. The Superman legend had never waded into any of that. The Kents hid from him his otherworldly origins; he didn't don his Superman identity until he was an adult; and his childhood took up just eight panels in the first *Superman* comic book and two fewer in *Action* 1. Jerry Siegel realized what a rich trove he had glossed over and now proposed a comic focusing on the pranks of a noncostumed character he called Superboy. Detective picked up the idea—minus the whimsy and with a costume—while Jerry was in the Army, launching a feature that explored Superman's adventures growing up in the Midwest. It began in 1945 in *More Fun Comics,* a year later switched to *Adventure Comics,* and in 1949 Superboy got a comic book of his own. For the first time, readers learned how Martha Kent had stitched her adopted son's playsuit into a red-and-blue cape and tights, and how she used glass from his rocket ship to make Clark's special eyeglasses. The stories were not just about Superboy but about a *Saturday Evening Post* world of picket fences that needed painting and apple pies warming in brick ovens. Fans went wild—young ones new to the legend and their parents who had grown up with Superman and *The Saturday Evening Post*—making *Superboy* the most popular new title of 1949, a time when most superheroes were fading away.

If learning about his roots on Krypton had humanized Superman, learning what he was like as a boy softened him. To his young fans, girls as much as boys, he was more than ever one of them. Yet even as the new stories answered questions that kids had asked since the beginning, they raised concerns that would take years more for Superman's handlers to sort out: How could Superboy know about his origins long before Superman did? How could there even be a Superboy if, as the earliest *Action* and *Superman* stories made clear, Clark didn't acquire the Superman costume and identity until he was an adult?

Those questions mattered to readers and writers but not to Harry and Jack. By the mid-1940s they had a better fix on who was buying comic books. The most devoted audience was kids aged six to eleven, with 95 percent of boys and 91 percent of girls reading them regularly. The numbers slowly declined in successive age groups, but even at age thirty half of the men in America and about 40 percent of the women were poring over comic books occasionally, and many were still steady fans. That helped explain the 150 different titles that jockeyed for space on newsstand racks, accounting for record monthly sales of forty million. Detective now faced competition from Fawcett, Timely, Dell, Street & Smith, and a series of other publishers, while

Superman was going head-to-head with the likes of Batman, Flash, Green Lantern, and Bulletman. While they wanted to give kids the new Superboy stories they craved, Jack and Harry also wanted to satisfy adults who were devoted to the old Superman tales they'd been raised on. The solution: Reap profits from both old titles and new, contradictions be damned.

The adult Superman was getting a different sort of makeover. Joe Shuster had drawn a sticklike superhero whose skimpy facial expressions were difficult to see, not to mention read. By the late 1940s, Wayne Boring was setting the standard with a more muscular Man of Steel whose face was chiseled, whose jaw jutted onto the page, and who had more stature, bulk, and gravitas than his early incarnation. It was an image that fit with a Superman who had gone from leaping to flying and whose powers were perpetually expanding. Everything around him got bigger, too, from city skyscrapers to the *S* emblem on his chest. His world was now as outsized as his place in it.

Superman and those he treasured were not the only ones who were evolving. Those he loathed were, too. His first enemy to appear in a costume was the Archer, who, once Superman unmasked him as Quigley the big-game hunter, confessed that "I thought hunting human beings would prove more profitable!" Superman: "Any kid could tell you that crime doesn't pay, Mr. Quigley." The Prankster, the Toyman, the Puzzler, and J. Wilbur Wolfingham, a W. C. Fields lookalike, used tricks and gags instead of a bow and arrows in their bids to conquer Superman. For editors wary of controversy, 1940s villains like those were a way to avoid the sharp edges of the real world. For a nation weary of war, they offered a release. For Superman, the masters of disguise and the tricksters let him demonstrate that his wit was at least as potent as his fists in battling bad guys.

While none of those villains lasted long, Lex Luthor did. When he first turned up in the spring of 1940 he had a full mop of bright red hair. By that summer he was gray, and a year later he was as bald as the evil Super-Man of Jerry and Joe's high school imaginations. What didn't change was Luthor's determination to take down Superman on his way to mastering the universe. In their first encounter Superman confronted him, asking, "What sort of creature are you?" Luthor answered with candor if not modesty: "Just an ordinary man—but with th' brain of a super-genius! With scientific miracles at my fingertips, I'm preparing to make myself supreme master of th' world!"

It is true that you can judge a man by his enemies, and Luthor had a way of bringing out in Superman both his vulnerabilities and his invincibility. From that opening encounter Lex drew on the full mix of villainous tactics—zapping Superman with an all-powerful ray gun, fomenting war as part of his scheme to grab power, and kidnapping Lois Lane. He tested Superman's mettle and exploited his soft spot. But in the end the Man of Steel smashed to bits the ray gun, talked the warring parties into signing an armistice, and rescued Lois. Holding her in his arms, he announced, "And that's th' end of Luthor!" If only it were true. Having created the closest thing Superman would ever get to a nemesis, Jerry and Joe were not about to let him die.

Mr. Mxyztplk, a bald imp who wore a purple suit and derby, was a different sort of adversary: He had superpowers but no interest in world domination. That had been his goal when he arrived on Earth from the fifth dimension, but he decided it would be more fun to discombobulate Superman by playing pranks on him, the way Bugs Bunny did with Elmer Fudd. What he hadn't counted on was that the no-nonsense superhero could be as playful as he was. Superman learned he could send the little man back for at least a month to his home world of Zrfff if he could trick him into saying his name backward—Klptzyxm. So he came up with a different way to do it every time they met. "Let's test your eyesight," the Man of Steel teased his adversary in one such meeting, after convincing him he was losing his sight. "There are three small signs 20 miles from here! If you can read them off, fast . . ." Before he could finish, Mxyztplk was breezing through sign one, sign two, and finally: "It says, 'Oxygen! Hydrogen! Nitrogen! Klptzyxm—' Oops—I spoke the word that's sending me back to Zrfff!"

Jerry Siegel said he invented the elfin character to give Superman and his readers "a change of pace" after all the battles against deadly adversaries like Luthor. "I think it added something to the feature to show Superman tangling with a magical foe who enjoyed making the idol of millions uncomfortable on his super-pedestal." What made editors at Detective Comics uncomfortable was having to spell the Zrfffian's name. One time when they typed it wrong—Mxyzptlk instead of Mxyztplk—the misspelling somehow stuck.

Names already were an obsession for Detective's writers and artists, most of whom had transformed theirs for reasons of art or assimilation, so it is not surprising that they had fun with the names of their characters. With Superman their obsession was nicknames, the best gift you can give a friend. Man of Steel was the most used, but he also was known then or later as the Last Son of Krypton, Metropolis Marvel, Kryptonian, Citizen Fix-It, Wonder Worker, Man of Tomorrow, Champion of the Underdog, Champion of the Oppressed, Champion of Democracy, Champion of Justice, Colossus of Krypton, World's Mightiest Hero, World's Mightiest Citizen, Man of Might, Big Blue, Big Blue Boy Scout, Big Blue Cheese, Action Ace, Smallville, Strange Visitor, King of Speed, and, the simplest and most intimate, Supes.

The era that stretched from the late 1930s through the end of the 1940s became known as the Golden Age of comic books. It was a time when the comic book became an accepted art form and the superhero played a central role in American culture. Fans would look back longingly as comics hit a rough patch in the 1950s, with fewer heroes and plummeting sales. The dawn of the earlier, more hopeful era was marked by the birth of Superman. Its last important title was the *Superboy* comic launched in 1949. Who better to bookend comics' gilded age than its reigning monarch? And in Superman's case it wasn't just a Golden Age of comic books but of comic strips, dramatic radio broadcasts, pioneering animation, and wildly successful movie serials. Superman was jumping from medium to medium just as Americans were, responding to society's likes and dislikes and, just as often, shaping them.

CHAPTER 5

Superman, Inc.

THE COMICS HAD NEVER BEHELD a golden goose like him before. Superman was now the marquee attraction in four separate comic books and he shared top billing with Batman in a fifth. Each magazine brought in just ten cents, but a 1940s dime is today's dollar and 3.2 million dimes were rung up every month. True Man of Tomorrow addicts could get a daily dose in the funny pages. They were the newspapers' most fought-over feature, especially Sunday's four-color splash, and every Sunday Superman's strip was delivered to twenty-five million homes, each of which swelled his royalties. Ka-ching.

The cash value of stardom was even easier to measure outside the comics. The radio *Adventures of Superman* was a runaway hit, with every "Atom Man" or "Clan of the Fiery Cross" adventure bringing a fat check from sponsors such as the snap, crackle, and pop makers of Battle Creek. Superman cartoons and serials were selling out—at forty cents a ticket for a weekend matinee—at theaters from Boston and Baton Rouge to Barcelona, where moviegoers cheered their "El Hombre Supre." Even department stores were mining the gold. Starting in 1942 they bought up and gave away millions of *Superman-Tim* booklets, featuring cutout puzzles, heroic stories of Superman and his young pal Tim, and a reminder from everyone's favorite strongman not to "Be A Whoo-Shoo! He's The Boy Who

Gets This Magazine Every Month, But Never Buys Any Of His Clothes At The Superman-Tim Store! Gee!" Ka-ching.

Then there were the synergies, a newly minted term for the way Harry Donenfeld, Jack Liebowitz, and their apprentices were turning Superman into a product line. As early as 1941, buttons designating the wearer as a paid-up member of the Supermen of America Club were proudly worn by hundreds of thousands of youthful fans, including Mickey Rooney, Our Gang's Spanky, and half a dozen middies at the Naval Academy. Kids across America lathered peanut butter and jelly onto super-flavored Superman bread and, if they ate all the crust, they might get treated to a Superman lollypop or Superman chocolate bar. Their Superman suspenders held up Superman dungarees. They stored their money in Superman billfolds until they had enough to buy Superman bubble gum, squirt guns, lunch boxes, underpants, jammies, moccasins, horseshoes, and a Krypto-Raygun complete with bulb, battery, lenses, and seven strips of film that let them flash onto a wall images of their idol in twenty-eight action-packed poses. Ka-ching.

By 1949 the cash registers were ringing nonstop in Harry and Jack's offices at 480 Lexington Avenue. National Comics Publications, the new name for Detective Comics, had a bullpen of heroes from Batman and Wonder Woman to Hawkman, Flash, and Green Arrow. None could match Superman as a box office headliner or newsstand heavyweight. Nobody was consulted as faithfully by kids across America before they got dressed, decided which game to play, or picked a cereal for breakfast. It was on the Metropolis Marvel's muscled shoulders that Harry and Jack were constructing their empire in the 1940s and that they would withstand the comic book scare of the 1950s. Ka-ching had become the soundtrack for Superman, Inc., much the way "Up, up, and away" was for Superman himself.

The impact went well beyond comics and kids. Disney may have been the guru at building Mickey Mouse and its other four-legged celebrities into long-lasting brands, but Superman, Inc., was becoming master of the fad. It didn't have Disney's patience yet it knew how to bottle the zeitgeist while it was happening. From the five-and-dime to movie houses and corner newsstands, the Man of Steel had been welded into the American consciousness. That model would be applied later, by many of the same marketing whizzes, to clients ranging from James Bond and Dobie Gillis to Major League Baseball. For now, all eyes were on Superman.

There were pitfalls. Push too cavalierly to commercialize your hero and you might threaten his integrity and his moneymaking potential, much the way Aesop's greedy cottagers killed their golden goose. That almost happened with the serial movies, which lacked the radio show's creative scripting and technical wizardry. Thankfully, kids laughed with Superman's cartoonish bid to fly even as the critics laughed at it. Managing Superman across media posed its own challenges: On paper Superman merely leaped even as he was flying across the airwaves, while his super-fueled adolescence in one comic book contradicted his adult-onset power-up in another. Product placement posed a risk, too. It might have been visionary when cellphones, holograms, and even biological weapons turned up in the comics decades before they did in the real world. But what about when writers came up with a three-part series on why Superman needed a Super-mobile to promote a toy car the licensing people had dreamed up?

The line between art and merchantry got blurrier still in the case of the Krypto-Raygun. The new toy "looks exactly like the KRYPTO-RAYGUN used by SUPERMAN in his never-ending fight against crime . . . like the one SUPERMAN had made of KRYPTONITE—that amazing metal from SUPERMAN'S birthplace—the planet KRYPTON!" read an ad from the back cover of *Superman* 7 in 1940. It would have been an interesting tie-in to the comic book and radio stories except for one thing: Kryptonite wouldn't appear in comic books until 1949, or even on the radio until 1943. It *was* there on Detective's library shelves, in Jerry's never-used script, but he had called it K-Metal, not kryptonite. Was the ad part of an anticipated marketing campaign for K-Metal or kryptonite on the radio, in the comics, or both? Was it an instance of selling overtaking storytelling?

Jerry and Joe had fantasized from the first about Superman's merchandising potential for everything from box tops and T-shirts to billboards. This was an obvious way to extend his fame and inflate their incomes. But they were torn: Wouldn't commercializing their hero diminish him? They had sounded that alarm just five months after Superman's debut, in the November 1938 issue of *Action*. A fictional con man named Nick Williams claimed to be Superman's personal manager and used his "client" to sell movies and breakfast cereals, gasoline and physical fitness programs. All were items that Harry and Jack had Superman selling, or soon would. And so it was with glee that Jerry and Joe took a shot at the avarice of their bosses by not just exposing Williams and his henchman, but tossing them in a cartoon jail.

JERRY WAS HAVING LESS LUCK in the real world. His home movies offer a lens into his life in the 1940s. He filmed his excursion to the World's Fair in New York, and he filmed the Macy's parade, where he and Superman were treated like royalty. Jack and Harry were there, with Harry riding an elephant and afterward clowning with Jack, who was somber as ever, and both trying to pay attention to the boys from Cleveland. Other surviving tapes show Jerry and Joe in a crowd of kids and a harem of women, with Jerry looking thinner than he ever had and Joe loving being the center of attention. There are movies of Jerry and Bella, too—as newlyweds, then with their son Michael, who was born early in 1944. Jerry was in the Army but got a leave so he could be home for the birth of his baby, who came out weighing a robust nine pounds. He was home again to take movies of Michael's first few birthday parties, each showing the boy getting a bigger gift than he had the year before. There was Michael sitting on his big red truck, riding his scooter, dressed in an aviator's suit climbing aboard his chrome toy airplane, and trying on his dad's Army cap. Mostly it was Michael alone, looking overwhelmed. Jerry seemed equally awkward, more a visitor in Bella's home than a part of his son's life.

Michael never got to meet his grandma Sarah; she died three years before he was born. It happened on a Sunday at the family home on Kimberly Avenue, a place Jerry didn't visit much after his marriage to Bella and his success with Superman. The newspaper listed Sarah Siegel's cause of death as a sudden heart attack, but family members say her descent was more gradual and began the day Jerry announced his wedding plans. Seeing what their married life was like "led to her death," says Jerry Fine, the cousin who introduced Jerry to Joe.

Sarah was right about the marriage: It soured early. Jerry was absorbed in his work, what with all the deadlines for Superman and his other creations, celebrity appearances in New York and elsewhere, and his battles with his bosses. Then came the war, which took him away from Bella when she was four months pregnant—although Jerry's VIP status spared him any combat. The biggest blow came in 1946, when Michael was nearly three and Bella was getting ready to deliver their second child. "Bella went to the hospital a month earlier than expected," Jerry wrote Jack Liebowitz in November 1946. "The boy child that was born lived only eight hours, for somehow the cord had gotten about its throat and cut off its air supply." For Jerry, his son's death was like his father's: He never talked about the pain, not even in his memoir, where he chronicled his many turmoils, and he never got over the feelings of loss and anger.

Jerry's angst was made worse by his inability to bottle lightning again with any of his new comic characters. He had tried in 1940 with the Spectre, a murdered cop whose spirit returned to Earth to battle evil. That flopped, and he was back two years later with Robotman, who had the brain of a murdered scientist inside the body of a robot. In between came the Star-Spangled Kid, who reversed the usual formula by pairing a boy hero with an adult sidekick. Detective Comics rolled the Kid out with a four-page house ad ballyhooing the plotline and the fact that it was the brainchild of the creator of Superman. Instead of becoming Jerry's next big thing, the Kid was yet another ho-hum, spawning whispers that its author was a one-trick pony. *Funnyman* fueled the doubts. It wasn't nearly as funny as Jerry thought, and Detective wasn't about to grant him the ownership rights he demanded. "I never indicated that we would take your Funnyman feature," Jack wrote stiffly in February 1947, "but as long as your ego tells you that anything you do must be a preordained success, I would be interested, just for the record, in having you name one feature—other than Superman—out of the numerous ones you've developed, which has enjoyed even a modicum of success."

Even Superman was no longer his alone. It wasn't just that other writers were turning out many of the biggest stories now, but that the superhero had left behind his creator as he moved to other media. Jerry played little if any role when it came to writing scripts for the radio drama, the serials, the cartoons, or the endless promotions of the sort Jerry had been spinning out in his head since he dreamed up the character. Whether or not Superman's fans noticed Jerry Siegel's absence, Jerry himself did, and it hurt.

In the meantime, his relations with Joe were turning frosty. He had always resented Joe's wavering work ethic, and it got worse over the years, as Joe went from drawing his own sketches, to filling in with ink his assistants' pencil work, to supervising other artists and rendering just Superman's head, to doing what Jerry said was "practically none of the actual art." It was true that Joe wasn't nearly as diligent as Jerry, but what really ate at Jerry was the suspicion that his childhood buddy was conspiring with another writer on new comics and other creative works. No matter that Jerry himself had been working with other artists since they were kids and still was, collaborating with Hal Sherman on Star-Spangled Kid and with Bernard Baily on the Spectre. "In line with your negotiating increases for yourself alone on 'Superman,' and working on 'Superboy' without first consulting me if it was all right for you to work on my comic, you are now preparing to collaborate on comics with others," Jerry wrote Joe in September 1946. "In the past we've operated under a gentleman's agreement, with mutual trust, but in view of what has occurred since I went into the Army, and your apparent unwillingness to continue our association as it was, I'm afraid that continuing to work with you under just a gentleman's agreement, would be hazardous." To underline his point, Jerry added a postscript: "Since Detective Comics, Inc. is involved in this situation, I am mailing a copy of this letter to Jack Liebowitz."

Jerry likely did not know just how involved Jack and Harry were. They despaired of Jerry's increasingly angry tone with them, too—a rage that, according to Harry's children, saw Jerry and Bella picketing in front of Harry's Long Island home, following the kids around in their car, and writing neighbors to say how unfair Harry had been to Superman's creator. While Harry and Jack knew that Joe was no longer doing the work he was being paid for, they liked him more than they liked Jerry and felt it couldn't hurt to curry favor with him. Harry's son, Irwin, claimed that his father—apparently without Jerry's knowledge—paid for Joe to have an operation to help his failing eyesight, a terrible affliction for an artist. Harry also joined with Joe in an improbable partnership: In December 1946 they filed a certificate to do business as Shuster & Donenfeld in the hamlet of South Fallsburg in New York's Catskill Mountains. While there is no evidence that they actually launched a business, it is fun to wonder what a dreamy artist like Joe Shuster could have cooked up with a wheeler-dealer and pornographer like Harry Donenfeld.

Three months later Jerry and Joe were once again partners, this time for the purpose of suing Harry, Jack, and their Superman empire. Money was a central narrative in the more than one thousand pages of transcripts from the proceedings. Jerry forever regretted that he and Joe hadn't copyrighted Superman for themselves, believing—justifiably—that the oversight had cost them millions of dollars. Now their lawyers made the case that what Harry and Jack had bought for $130 was the ownership rights not to Superman but to the first thirteen-page story alone. Then there was Superboy. "No compensation has ever been paid for this. No permission has ever been secured for this," argued their attorney. "It was purely and simply an act of appropriation of this script." Ditto for Batman and other "union suit characters" who were mere knockoffs of Superman, for comics built around Wonder Woman, for George Lowther's book on Superman, and for the Superman radio show, animation, and accessories, a share of the profits for which had been promised (but never delivered) to Jerry and Joe. "While we are interested in being paid for these past misdeeds," the lawyer said, "the most important thing is this: to satisfy your Honor of the fact that we are entitled to be rid of these people once and for all, and of this contract which keeps these people from sleeping nights and keeps them from earning an honest living." Harry and Jack were the people the boys wanted to be rid of, Jerry and Joe the ones who couldn't sleep. What it would take to make it all better was a round $5 million.

The comic book company had a different take on the law and the numbers. Jerry and Joe weren't the aggrieved schlubs they made themselves out to be but thankless self-seekers. National, the company claimed, had turned over to them everything they were entitled to, which is what enabled them to live the high life. In the ten years from 1938, when the first *Action* was published, to the filing of the suit in 1947, Jerry and Joe were paid $162,627.08 for their work on comic books, $205,998.21 for comic strips, and $32,569.56 for other uses of the character they had dreamed up, for a total of $401,194.85. That was a king's ransom—more than $5 million in today's terms—even after they split it in half.

Whether or not that was enough wasn't something the Supreme Court of New York ever weighed in on. Its referee affirmed Harry and Jack's ownership of Superman but not Superboy. After further legal wrangling, Jerry and Joe signed an agreement in May 1948 selling the rights to Superboy and related characters to Harry and Jack for $94,013.16. Once the lawyers and broker took their shares, Joe and Jerry each walked away with $29,000—barely one one-hundredth of what they had hoped for. Even then there were onerous terms: The creators had to agree that Superman and Superboy—in all their forms and forever—belonged to Harry and Jack. Gone were Jerry and Joe's jobs writing and drawing the characters. Gone were the bylines indicating that the Man of Steel and Boy of Steel were theirs. Gone even was their right to claim a historic connection if it "may be likely to induce the belief that such past connection still exists."

The lawsuit had always been about Jerry's grievances—the ones he had been carrying around since Superman caught fire a decade earlier, along with the gripes that remained from his forlorn Valentine's Days in grammar school. The suit was never about Joe; although his life would be painfully reshaped by the outcome, he still let Jerry call the shots. In fact, this was the first in a series of lawsuits that would play out over the decades, none of which gave Jerry anything close to what he was after. He could have had more money if that had been all that mattered: Batman founder Bob Kane proved that when he renegotiated his deal with Jack instead of joining Jerry's lawsuit. What Jerry seemed to want was not only for Jack and Harry to give him the money he felt he deserved, but also the homage for having dreamed up the most successful hero in American history. What he couldn't grasp was this: He had already gotten more of everything than any of his peers in an era when comics writers got no bylines, no royalties, and nowhere near the kind of payouts that Jerry and Joe had been enjoying. Jerry, in fact, couldn't enjoy any of it. All that was left was the anger.

Jerry's biggest miscalculation was failing to understand who Jack was—a bean counter so hard-nosed that even his adoring daughter was afraid of him—and failing to deal with him on those terms. In a decade of letters between them, Jerry essentially dismissed his boss as a shyster and Jack branded his scriptsman an ingrate. But there also were heartbreaking moments in the exchanges, like when Jerry confided to Jack—as he might have to his father—news of the wrenching death of his newborn. Jerry's loss in the courtroom was Jack's enormous gain. He walked away with unfettered access to Superman and freedom from a writer who had become a dreadful nag. In the process Jack sent a message to the rest of his writers and artists: Beware. If I can fire the creator of the mighty Superman, any one of you who steps out of line could be next. But in the end Jack lost, too. The narrative had been written: Jerry was the martyr, Jack the bully. What he had done to Siegel and Shuster would remain part of Jack's legacy, as Al Capp, America's most read satirist, made clear in a *Li'l Abner* strip in 1947. Rockwell P. Squeezeblood, head of the corrupt Squeezeblood Comic Strip Syndicate, was a stand-in for Jack Liebowitz, head of the bare-knuckled National Comics Publications. Squeezeblood published a bestselling feature about a crime-fighting strongman named Jack Jawbreaker, whose creators even looked like Jerry and Joe. "Those boys created 'Jack Jawbreaker' in poverty!!" Squeezeblood told Abner. "Poverty is the greatest inspiration to creative genius!! I won't let all this wealth spoil those innocent boys!!"

Two months after Jerry settled with National Comics, Bella sued him for divorce. During their nine years of marriage, her complaint read, Jerry "absented himself from their home in Cleveland for long periods of time without giving any excuse or reason" and "during the short periods of time he was at home in Cleveland, he displayed a moody, quarrelsome and argumentative attitude toward the plaintiff." Jerry didn't respond. The marriage had been dying for years. Bella had a right to be mad, and he didn't want to fight. He just wanted out. The judge pronounced him guilty of "Gross Neglect of Duty" and said it was "impossible for them [any] longer to live together as husband and wife." Bella got her freedom, custody of their son, all the household furnishings, and 60 percent of their joint assets, which included the house in University Heights, $98,000 in cash and bonds, and a year-old Chrysler. Jerry got the remaining 40 percent, along with his typewriter and Dictaphone. He said he would pay alimony, child support, and 20 percent of his annual earnings once they hit $10,000, which was less likely now that he was jobless. He also said that, with help from Bella, he would pay the Internal Revenue Service $24,000 in back taxes along with whatever extra levy was owed for the settlement money he had just received from Jack.

Jerry would have agreed to anything. He was crazy about a woman he had rediscovered just months before at a Cartoonists Society costume ball at New York's Plaza Hotel. This wasn't just any woman: It was Lois Lane, or at least the young model Jerry and Joe had hired more than a dozen years ago to help them envision what Lois should look like. Joanne Carter was back in his orbit and he was smitten, the more so when she came to the ball dressed as the dreamboat comic strip showgirl Dixie Dugan. In the years since she had posed as Lois, Joanne had lived on both the East and West coasts and gotten married and divorced. It was Joe who fell for her first. He had tumbled more than a decade before, when she spent most of the winter posing for him. He had been corresponding with her ever since then and had invited her to the New York gala, even renting her an elegant gown. No matter. Once they got to the ball, she was drawn to Jerry and he to her. No surprise. With her slim figure, piercing dark eyes, and tightly coiled shoulder-length hair, she was far more attractive than the matronly Bella. Joanne, meanwhile, was eager for a second shot at love and life—not with an artist like Joe, whose type she was weary of after a frustrating career in modeling, but with a celebrity writer. "Jerry and I started dating," she recalled years after, "and a few months later, we were married."

The marriage couldn't happen fast enough. They filed their application on October 13, 1948, asking the state to waive the normal waiting period so they could have a "ceremony at once." Both were already living at the Commodore Hotel in Cleveland, and her marriage had been over for years. His divorce agreement was worked out three months before and accepted by the court on October 7. A justice of the peace married them at the hotel on October 14, and the Cleveland *Plain Dealer* ran a story the next day. Three days later national gossip columnist Walter Winchell wrote, " 'Superman' creator Jerry Siegel and model Joanne Carter had it sealed in Cleveland." But it wasn't quite sealed. For a reason neither ever talked about, Jerry and Joanne were back with a second marriage application three weeks after the first and were wed again that same day, November 3. Whatever the glitch, it was fixed. Jerry had turned thirty-four in the interval. Joanne told Jerry, *The Plain Dealer,* and the state of Ohio that she was twenty-five, which would have made her a cherubic twelve or thirteen when she modeled for Joe as a voluptuous Lois Lane. Her birth certificate clears up the confusion: She was, in fact, about to turn thirty-one when she married Jerry, which she must have worried was over-the-hill.

Joanne knew about Jerry and Joe's legal battles with National Comics, which is why she had changed her plan to come to the Plaza costume party as Lois Lane. She hadn't had it easy herself. After high school she had left Cleveland for Chicago, then Boston, when a young man who had spotted her ad in the newspaper invited her to join his skating act. She said she couldn't skate; he said he'd teach her. The act broke up before she had to perform the dangerous stunts he had planned for her, and she stayed for a while in Boston, where she "went to a local bar and began phoning artists listed in the yellow pages. As a result, I became a professional model instead of a professional skater."

Joanne came into Jerry's life just as he was losing his home, his car, his livelihood, and his superhero. His privations became her cause. She had never known high living, so didn't have to make the adjustments he did; having her there made it easier for him. So did being able to lash out at his old bosses in the only forum still open to him, the comics. Less than three weeks after his marriage to Joanne, he published a Sunday *Funnyman* newspaper strip about a writer (Jerkimer) who was ripped off by a chiseling business executive (Winston Lightfingers of Gypsum Music). The writer was saved through the intervention of Funnyman, the only superhero Jerry still could call his own.

EVEN AS JERRY AND JOE were parting company with Superman, their hero was showing up in places no one expected to find him. There he was in the dentist's office, in an eight-page thriller in which he rescued a U.S. pilot whose aching tooth crippled him in the middle of a dogfight, warning that "smart fellows take good care of their teeth and visit the dentist regularly." Department stores gave out a *Superman's Christmas Adventure* booklet, as well as *Superman-Tim,* which was published year-round and was half adventure story, half sales pitch. Superman adorned the backs of cereal boxes, the front of a holiday display at R. H. Macy & Co. that drew a hundred thousand visitors, and ads for Dr Pepper, sandwich spreads, and flour mills. The Man of Steel had gone viral and merchandisers wanted to go with him.

Sometimes the link-ups paid direct dividends to National Comics, as with *Superman-Tim:* A marketing firm bought the rights to produce the six-by-nine-inch booklets, then sold them to stores. The one million dental brochures that Jack and Harry printed, like the Superman balloon they entered in New York's Thanksgiving Day Parade, earned them nothing directly but built name recognition and trust for their hero. So complete was that trust that a corps of secretaries at National was kept busy answering moms' questions about how to make their kids stop biting their nails, eat egg yolks, and walk the dog. Mothers were learning the lesson librarians had years before: When Superman spoke, kids listened. As for name recognition, popular culture maven Harlan Ellison got it right when he observed that "the urchin in Irkutsk may never have heard of Hamlet; the peon in Pernambuco may not know who Raskolnikov is; the widow in Djakarta may stare blankly at the mention of Don Quixote or Micawber or Jay Gatsby. But every man, woman and child on the planet knows Mickey Mouse, Sherlock Holmes, Tarzan, Robin Hood . . . and Superman."

That celebrity let National license more Superman products—over one hundred in all—than were commissioned for Sherlock, Tarzan, or Robin Hood, although no one could touch Disney's Mickey. Superman, Inc., started licensing merchandise in 1940 and within months there were more than twenty items, from film viewers to military-style hairbrushes, which netted about one hundred thousand dollars for Harry and Jack. A year later, forty companies were making Superman toys, candies, games, and other items, with profits swelling. Jigsaw puzzles were an early favorite, with more than a dozen being produced in 1940 alone, from intricate five-hundred-piece ones showing him leaping to the rescue to box sets of six puzzles with forty-two pieces each. The first dolls had adjustable wooden joints and squinty eyes and cost just ninety-four cents (although today one in mint condition can fetch eight thousand dollars). For the action-oriented, the Turnover Tank let Superman flip the vehicle all the way over, no mean feat for a toy produced in 1940.

Superman, Inc., offered something for every taste and age. Fathers could drench their cereal in Superman milk, lather up with Superman shaving cream, add Superman hood ornaments to their cars, then drive away using high-octane Superman-certified gasoline. The latter made it especially clear that the only thing needed to make an association with the Man of Tomorrow was a client willing to pay today. Kids could trade seventy-two different Superman picture cards, just as they did baseball cards or comic books. Mothers could take the kids to the Macy's Christmas show, then fit them out in a blue broadcloth shirt, red broadcloth cape, and navy cotton twill pants—all for just ninety-eight cents. Anyone of any age interested in bulking up could try a Superman muscle-building set, with hand grippers, a jump rope, a measuring tape, and a chart to track their progress.

Public relations and advertising were in their adolescence as the 1930s were yielding to the 1940s, and both vocations were hell-bent on making every American a consummate consumer. It was a time before focus groups, when anything went, and Robert Maxwell fit in instantly. Even before his Superman radio show debuted, Maxwell was put in charge of Superman, Inc., where he was anxious to show how much money he could make for Harry and Jack. Some of the promotional deals he negotiated involved products that grew out of the hero and his exploits. Others added Superman's endorsement to items or services already on the market. "Let Superman be your Super-salesman," Maxwell's brochure pitched. "Superman has a tremendous, loyal fan following, a ready-made juvenile market that will respond by boosting your sales volume." It worked from the start and got even better when Maxwell brought it with him to the radio show he was launching. Laundries, dairies, and meat packers signed up as sponsors, then watched their profits shoot up. The Rochester, Minnesota, bottler of Dr Pepper and 7 Up offered an object lesson, its sales doubling after it started sponsoring the show on KROC.

While Superman, Inc., vanished as a corporate entity in the summer of 1946 when it was absorbed into National Comics, the mindset remained that he was a commodity that could be branded, packaged, sold, and incorporated. Neither National nor its predecessors had ever pretended to be a charity. They had always been focused on building a commercial success hand in hand with the Superman story, in whatever form that story might take. Making money was a way of ensuring that Superman would not suffer the fate of the Green Lantern, whose plummeting sales led to his being pulled from publication between 1949 and 1959, or of World War II aviation ace Hop Harrigan, who was grounded forever in 1948. But Maxwell, Liebowitz, and Donenfeld were smart enough to know they could push only so far before they threatened the integrity of their character, and they rarely tested those limits. They took care to associate their all-American hero with all-American products like piggy banks, coloring books, and sliced white bread. Keepers of the legacy from Superman comics would sit in on plotting sessions for his movies, and in-house censors pored over each printed word to ensure the Big Blue Boy Scout stayed true to his name.

That name defined not just one hero but the whole National Comics universe in its early years. Superman, Inc., managed Batman, Wonder Woman, and the rest of National's stable of heroes in the 1940s, none of whom had nearly the product line that Superman did or brought in nearly the revenues. The more success Superman had in one medium, the more others wanted him, with comic books leading to comic strips, radio, cartoons, and film. And the fans who read, listened, and watched couldn't get enough of Superman valentines, timepieces, and the Super-Babe dolls that Macy's introduced just in time for Christmas in 1947. "Superman turned baby by mysterious atomic rays," the ads explained, and for $5.59 ($56 today) kids could have their own fifteen-inch doll with latex rubber skin, moveable arms and legs, and eyes that opened and shut.

Kids were the key to National's strategy, and not just because they were Superman's most avid fans. Hooking them young could mean keeping them forever, and Superman was proving to be a gateway to get young people to try all kinds of other comics. Their parents might have worried about adult conceits like consumerism and commercialism, but kids had their own truth: the Superman they were reading in comic books, listening to on the radio, and watching at the movie house was as pure as ever, and he was theirs. Having Superman toys on the shelf and Superman food in the pantry brought their hero closer and made him more central than ever to their lives.

And it was not just in America. France and Italy imported the Man of Steel barely a year after his debut here, with kids in Paris calling him Yordi and ones in Rome preferring Ciclone, or "hurricane." South American children loved him, as did Germans before the Nazis started railing against his Jewish roots. He was America's most iconic export. Superman is a hero "for the whole universe," explains Vincent Maulandi, a lifelong fan in France. The Last Son of Krypton "had no more homeworld and the Earth would replace that home, not only America." As Superman's comics and films spread around the globe, so did the international flavor of his wares. From France would come a Superman towel rack, from Nepal a can of cooking oil with a large picture on the front of the Man of Steel, and from Mexico a papier-mâché piñata built to look like El Hombre Supre. Ka-ching.

CHAPTER 6

The Deadly Truth

SUPERMAN HAD AN IMAGE PROBLEM. During World War II, the Nazis had denounced him for being a pawn of the Jews and poisoning the minds of America's youth. In the Cold War that followed, a Jewish psychiatrist was accusing him of being a Nazi out to corrupt the adolescents of America. Either way, his detractors were sure that Superman was bad for the kids.

Now they had Melvin Leeland and Billy Becker to prove it. On a cool summer night in 1947, Melvin, a fourteen-year-old from Washington, D.C., was showing a friend how to play Russian roulette. He spun the loaded cylinder, raised the .22-caliber revolver to his right temple, and, as his mate watched in horror, blew a hole in his head. His mother told the police that he had read about the deadly game in a comic book. Two months later Billy, a twelve-year-old from Sewickley, Pennsylvania, tossed a clothesline over a rafter in his basement and hanged himself. Mrs. Becker said he was reenacting a scene from a comic book. "I burned every one I found," she told a coroner's jury, "but Billy always found ways of hiding them."

The common denominator in tragedies like these was "crime" comic books, Dr. Fredric Wertham explained. From Batman to Wonder Woman, Superboy too, all shared the blame for the scourge of juvenile delinquency sweeping the nation. They were "an invitation to illiteracy" and encouraged "criminal or sexually abnormal ideas." Batman and Robin were secret lovers. Wonder Woman was an overt lesbian. Most depraved of all was the Man of Steel, "with the big S on his uniform," Wertham wrote. "We should, I suppose, be thankful that it is not an S.S. . . . The very children whose unruly behavior I would want to prescribe psychotherapy in an anti-superman direction, have been nourished (or rather poisoned) by the endless repetition of Superman stories."

Looking back, Wertham's warnings read like the ravings of a quack, but he was an esteemed psychiatrist and he wasn't alone. In the spring of 1940, just two years after *Action Comics* No. 1, the literary editor of the *Chicago Daily News* leveled the first broadside. "Unless we want a coming generation even more ferocious than the present one, parents and teachers throughout America must band together to break the 'comic' magazine," Sterling North warned. The cure, he added, "can be found in any library or good bookstore. The parent who does not acquire that antidote for his child is guilty of criminal negligence." *Catholic World* weighed in next, asking, "What's Wrong with the 'Comics'?" Its answer: "The influence of these comics over the popular mind is one of the most striking—and disturbing— phenomena of the century." As for Superman, "in a vulgar way this fantastic character seems to personify the primitive religion expounded by Nietzsche's *Zarathustra*. 'Man alone is and must be our God,' says Zarathustra, very much in the style of a Nazi pamphleteer." The shrillest denunciation came from cultural critic Gershom Legman. "The Superman formula," he wrote in 1949, "is essentially lynching." The Man of Steel "is really peddling a philosophy of 'hooded justice' in no way distinguishable from that of Hitler and the Ku Klux Klan."

Could the cause-and-effect relationship between Melvin and Billy's reading habits and their deaths be that clear-cut? Scores of librarians, teachers, judges, and priests had been saying so for years, but the wider world wasn't buying it. Wertham tipped the debate. He had been taking detailed case histories from troubled youth at his mental health clinics in New York. "Comic-book reading," he concluded in a 1948 *Collier's* article headlined "Horror in the Nursery," was "a distinct influencing factor in the case of every single delinquent or disturbed child we studied." His findings carried the weight of science and of his résumé. He was the senior psychiatrist for the New York Department of Hospitals and former chief resident psychiatrist at Johns Hopkins University. Born in Nuremberg as Frederic Wertheimer, the Americanized Wertham was a friend of culture critic H. L. Mencken's, a collaborator of renowned criminal attorney Clarence Darrow's and syndicated columnist Walter Lippmann's, and a valued ally of the NAACP as it gathered evidence on the harms of racial segregation. He may not have been trained as a social scientist, but he was a social reformer and his judgment—rendered in repeated press interviews, then in a book with the unnerving title *Seduction of the Innocent*—was taken as gospel.

His timing couldn't have been better. Postwar America was feeling prosperous in ways it couldn't have imagined when its young men were overseas fighting and its economy was on a full military footing—but that prosperity brought changes that unsettled many Americans, especially ones who had grown up in a more austere and hidebound prewar world. Kids had more money to spend now and they spent more time away from home. Rock and roll was picking up the beat, with Jackie Brenston's Delta Cats and Bill Haley's Comets setting the tempo. Hot rods (cars with tuned-up engines and no hoods or fenders) were the bossest way to get to the passion pit (drive-in theater), and the kookiest films to see there were James Dean's *Rebel Without a Cause* and *East of Eden*. This new generation even spawned a term for itself—teenagers—and they brought with them a new fear: juvenile delinquency. The FBI said that kids under eighteen were responsible for half of America's car thefts and burglaries and a rising share of robberies and rapes. Gangs of working-class whites were facing off against poor Puerto Ricans on America's urban streets, or so the Broadway hit *West Side Story* told us. Years later, studies would demonstrate that the rise in youth crime was due to crackdowns by law enforcement and the way family life was disrupted when fathers shipped off to war and mothers took their places in the factories. But in the heat of the moment, parents, newspaper columnists, and crusading scientists like Wertham latched onto an easier target: the mass media, and especially the billion comic books American kids were buying each year.

The finger-pointing was understandable. It was what later generations would do in blaming television, video games, and social media for corrupting the youth of their eras. And it was what Americans in the 1950s were doing on the foreign front, where the Russians had an H-bomb to go with their A-bomb, the Reds in North Korea had invaded the democratic South, and G-man J. Edgar Hoover and Senator Joseph McCarthy were finding communists wherever they looked in Washington, Hollywood, and classrooms across the country. Just as domestic subversives were real and did pose a threat, so comic books were swelling in popularity and challenging more cultured reading habits for youngsters. But both threats also were overtaken by hysteria and overreaction. Borrowing from the term "Red Scare," as the crusade against communists was called, the campaign against Superman and Batman would come to be known as the Great Comic Book Scare. "We are dealing with the mental health of a generation," Wertham told 2.5 million *Collier's* subscribers, "the care of which we have left too long in the hands of unscrupulous persons whose only interest is greed and financial gain."

Here, finally, was not just a clear diagnosis of what was wrong but a remedy. Five months after the *Collier's* article, six hundred grade school children in Spencer, West Virginia, gathered to hold last rites for two thousand comic books they had rounded up. "Believing that comic books are mentally, physically and morally injurious to boys and girls, we propose to burn those in our possession," said thirteen-year-old David Mace before he ignited a copy of *Superman*. "We also pledge ourselves to try not to read any more." Additional burnings followed across the country, along with a police raid of a publishing house. More than a dozen states started regulating comic books, with New York dealing the harshest blow by banning any that depicted explicit sex, brutality, or criminal techniques as well as any that used in their titles the words *crime, terror, horror,* or *sex*. The National Parent Teacher Association pushed for a "national housecleaning" of comic books. The United States Senate held hearings under the leadership of the ever-ambitious Senator Estes Kefauver of Tennessee, who had his eye not just on Superman but on the White House. In Cleveland, which counted Superman among its favorite sons, the city council outlawed comics showing rape, arson, assault, kidnapping, burglary, mayhem, larceny, manslaughter, murder, prostitution, sodomy, or extortion. To show it meant business, the city assigned two policemen to the comic book beat. Comics had always operated around a generational divide between adoring kids and fretting parents. A Gallup poll showed that 70 percent of adults now believed that comic books were at least partly responsible for juvenile delinquency and 26 percent felt they deserved a "great deal" of blame. No one bothered to ask kids how they felt, but the pollster couldn't resist offering his surmise: "Older people are much more inclined to brand both comic books and TV-radio crime programs as factors contributing to juvenile delinquency than are young people."

Wertham and his allies conceded that not all comic books were menacing. It was easy to agree on the increasingly popular and macabre horror books, with titles like *Out of the Night* and *Weird Thrillers* and stories about a human head that doubled as a bowling ball and a wife roasting on a barbecue her husband's head, legs, hands, and feet. They had to go. But even ones that seemed harmless might not be, Wertham warned: "You find that what all the little animals are doing involves undue amounts of socking over the head and banging in the jaw, and that the toys that come to life at night sometimes put in the time strangling one another."

Superhero comics were a different animal entirely, focused not on the lurid but on the ennobling, and having aided the nation in its patriotic war against the Axis. To critics, however, that was a bygone era. What mattered now were the crimes depicted in these comic books, their heroes' resort to force, and the very notion of superpowers, which had the stench of fascism. Superman, as king of the superheroes, was especially reviled. He was one of four characters put on trial in 1949 by students at St. Mary's High School in Cape Girardeau, Missouri, no matter that the boy who played him in the mock tribunal had never read a comic book. The Colossus of Krypton was often the first onto the funeral pyre at comic book burnings and was singled out for special scorn at public hearings. He also was Wertham's favorite target. "I would like to point out to you one other crime comic book which we have found to be particularly injurious to the ethical development of children and those are the Superman comic books," the psychiatrist told members of Congress. "They arouse in children fantasies of sadistic joy in seeing other people punished over and over again while you yourself remain immune. We have called it the Superman complex."

THIS WAS NO TIME to launch another Superman experiment. Not in 1951, when the whole comic book world was running scared. Not when the medium into which he was being catapulted, television, was so callow that it was unclear whether it would succeed, and it was perfectly clear that actors with real promise would opt for Hollywood or Broadway. Not when Superman himself was being labeled a socio-path.

But that wasn't the way National Comics or Robert Maxwell thought. They knew that there were more children than ever in America, where soldiers had come home from Europe and made up for lost time by igniting an unprecedented boom in babies. They also knew that radio was dying as a venue for children's adventure and that movie serials wouldn't be far behind. While TV might be new and untested, so were comic books when Superman broke through in that medium. Now was precisely the time when the battered Super-man of the static page could use a lift onto the small screens that were turning up in America's dens and playrooms. For Superman's own-ers, the question wasn't whether but when to push ahead, and whom to sign up as the Man of Steel for this most up-close of media.

Maxwell and his director, Tommy Carr, screened nearly two hun-dred candidates. Most made their living as actors, although some were full-time musclemen. Nearly all, Carr said, "appeared to have a serious deficiency in their chromosome count." So thorough—and perhaps so frustrating—was their search that the executives stopped by the Mr. America bodybuilding contest in Los Angeles. One can-didate they never seriously considered, despite his later claims, was Kirk Alyn, who had done well enough in the serials but had neither the acting skills nor the looks around which to build a Superman TV series. The search ended the day a barrel-chested B-movie actor named George Reeves showed up on the studio lot.

Maxwell's co-producer, Bernard Luber, had recognized Reeves in a Los Angeles restaurant, seeming "rather forlorn," and suggested he come in for a tryout. He did, the next morning, and "from that moment on he was my first choice," said Tommy Carr. "He looked like Superman with that jaw of his. Kirk had the long neck and fine features, but although I like Kirk very much, he never looked the Superman Reeves did." His tough-guy demeanor was no put-on. Standing six foot two and carrying 195 pounds, Reeves had been a light-heavyweight boxing champ in college and could have gone further if he hadn't broken his nose seven times and his mother hadn't made him step out of the ring. It wasn't the first or the last time she would interfere. A headstrong and self-focused girl from Illinois, Helen Lescher had eloped with a pharmacist, Don Brewer, in Iowa in 1914 and within five months they had a son, George Keefer Brewer. The marriage didn't last long and George didn't learn about his real father or his real birthday until he was into his twenties. Helen altered his date of birth to make it look like she was married when he was conceived. She hid his father's fate, telling George he had committed suicide, until Brewer turned up one day. Helen's second marriage wouldn't last, either, nor would the second version of George's name, George Lescher Bessolo.

After giving up boxing George landed a job at the prestigious Pasadena Playhouse, which was more to his mother's liking. It was then that he learned to act and that nearby movie executives got to see what he could do. They liked him enough to give him the modest role of Stuart Tarleton, one of the Tarleton twins and a suitor of Scarlett O'Hara in the 1939 blockbuster *Gone with the Wind*. Even before the film came out, George had been signed by another studio, Warner Bros., where Jack Warner pushed him to change his name to one he felt would look better on movie theater marquees: Reeves. George didn't see his name in lights for anything but lesser films, but he did land minor roles alongside major actors. In the 1949 *Samson and Delilah,* Victor Mature was Samson and George was a wounded messenger, while that same year, in Bob Hope's *The Great Lover,* George was a gambler killed in the first three minutes. Between acting jobs, he dug cesspools at the rate of one hundred dollars a hole.

When the offer came in 1951 to play the TV Superman, George was torn. He had barely heard of the Man of Steel, knew that the six hundred dollars a week he was offered was a pittance, and realized that the chance of getting a real acting job would be harder once the movie studios saw him playing a comic book character or any role in a medium that Hollywood disdained. Yet he needed the money, and, as his agent advised, there was a slim chance that the new show would even be broadcast and a slimmer one that anyone in Hollywood would notice. Television, after all, was in its infancy, with the nation just witnessing the first-ever coast-to-coast broadcast in the form of a speech by President Harry Truman. "Take the money and run," George's agent said. Reluctantly, George did. "I've played about every part you can think of. Why not Superman?" he told a friend. To Phyllis Coates, the new Lois Lane, he confided the first time he met her, "Well, babe, this is it: the bottom of the barrel."

Like many in Hollywood and in the growing Superman family, Coates was using a pseudonym. In her case it sounded more like a real name than the one her parents gave her: Gypsie Ann Evarts Stell. The tall, slim brunette had gone from chorus girl on vaudeville to actress in second-tier movies. She was glad to land the role of Lois less because of the professional opportunity—"I'd never read Superman comics, never heard the radio show, never heard of the character"— than because of the paycheck, which she needed to pay doctors' and physical therapists' bills for a daughter born with a displaced hip. Getting the job was easy. Her agent called and told her, "Wear a suit and low-heeled shoes." The next morning at the RKO studio, "I met Bob Maxwell. . . . I read for him and he said, 'I think you're perfect for the part.' It was that simple: I didn't even get a call-back on it, they just decided that I was it. And there were a *lot* of good gals up for it."

The first production was a fifty-eight-minute movie called *Superman and the Mole Men* that was a way to tease as well as finance the TV series. The story was set in the small town of Silsby, where the National Oil Company had just drilled 32,740 feet to create the deepest well in the world. Up came not just petroleum but four small humanoid creatures whose home was in the center of the Earth. The residents of Silsby, stirred to a frenzy by a shotgun-carrying rabble-rouser named Luke Benson, assumed the worst about the subterranean beings and vowed to find and exterminate them. Luckily, Clark Kent was reporting on the oil drilling and did a quick change when he saw the gathering mob. "I'm going to give you all one last chance to stop

acting like Nazi storm troopers," Superman lectured the townspeo-
ple. When his words were unheeded, he disarmed Benson and the
others and helped the underground creatures return down the well. It
was exactly the sort of morality tale that Jerry Siegel and Joe Shuster
had brought to their early comics and that Maxwell tackled on the
radio. Having Superman take this stance was especially brave coming
just as Senator McCarthy—striking a pose like Luke Benson's—was
beginning his meteoric rise. It also sent a message to Dr. Wertham
and his followers: The real threat was the Nazi-like citizens of Silsby,
not the superhero roused to violence as a last resort.

Mole Men was a classic Superman enterprise—done on the cheap
but at full throttle. The original idea was for children to play the mole
men, but Maxwell and crew decided that dwarfs—two of whom had
played Munchkins in The Wizard of Oz—would be more believable.
Their heads were enlarged to make them scarier, they wore fuzzy
jumpsuits to ensure that kids wouldn't be too scared, and their laser
weapon was the handiest and cheapest the crew could come up with:
a handheld Electrolux vacuum cleaner. Maxwell tried to make the
"flying" more realistic than in Kirk Alyn's serials, with George Reeves
being hoisted with a harness and piano wire for takeoffs and landings.
On-screen, it was believable. Off-screen it was a near-disaster; the
wire broke early in the production and George crashed to the ground.
Maxwell's first reaction was to cry, "My God—the star!" He knew,
given a shoot of just eleven days, what it would mean to lose his Superman. "We went lickety-split," recalled Coates. "I took my money
and went home! It was nice working together and everybody liked
everybody, but in the final analysis it was a crock of crap!" Mole Men
opened in 1951 and for the next year and a half it appeared as a Saturday matinee in movie theaters across America and as far away as
Scotland, where a vacationing Coates was shocked to see her "crock
of crap" playing at a local movie house. The verdict for National
Comics was unequivocal: The movie pilot was a success, so upward
and onward to television.

The TV series opened the way every Superman project did, with
a creation story. It welcomed back old fans of the comics and radio
productions and introduced new ones to the narrative. The opening
narration was word-for-word the same as in the radio series, which

isn't surprising since Maxwell oversaw both. On Krypton, Jor-El tried and failed to convince the ruling council that its planet was about to be sucked into the sun, then he sent his infant son rocketing to Earth. Here, a young Clark watched his powers slowly surface the way they did in the *Superboy* comic books, and he heard his mother explain, when he was twelve, why he could see through rocks and do other things that set him apart. His adoptive parents were the Sarah and Eben Kent dreamed up by novelist George Lowther and brought back to life on the radio. The storyline was familiar, but TV added a decidedly new kick to the myth. Here was Superman in real life, and he was sturdier and more steadfast than kids had pictured from the cartoons, imagined on the radio, or seen in the big-screen serials. Here, finally, was a flesh-and-blood Superman worthy of Jerry and Joe's hero.

The pace of filming for TV was even more frenetic than it had been on *Mole Men,* with just twelve days to complete each batch of five half-hour episodes. That meant working from seven in the morning until dusk six days a week, with no time for retakes. The undertaking was saved by George's photographic mind, which let him memorize the twenty-four pages of dialogue that came his way every day. Scenes were shot in blocks. Monday might be *Daily Planet* sequences. Tuesday all eyes would be on the gangsters in their boxy suits and rumpled fedoras. It drove the actors mad, reading lines without knowing the context of the story, or even which story it was. The newspaper never had a newsroom—that would have required too many desks and extras—just cramped private offices. Other money-saving precepts: No need for more than two gangsters; limit crowd scenes to the opening, where everyone was looking skyward; and make sure the actors never changed clothes so stock scenes could be spliced in anywhere. Clark stayed in his gray double-breasted suit with padded shoulders. Jimmy wore out his sweater and bow tie. Lois had one hat, one suit, and one set of earrings. On Krypton, Jor-El used Buster Crabbe's old shirt from the *Flash Gordon* serial while other ruling council members recycled costumes from Captain Marvel and Captain America movies. So what if they were the competition? What mattered to the Superman team, as to most other TV

crews back then, was being on budget, which was just $18,500 per episode, or barely enough for a single set in a B picture.

Special effects also were done on the cheap. The bullets that bounced off George were blanks and the revolvers he bent were made of soft lead. With a mere $175 budgeted for each episode's flying sequences, it is not surprising that George took another spill. It was the pulley that gave way this time. "That's enough of that," he announced after he dusted himself off. "Peter Pan can fly with wires, but not Superman!" In another episode, George was set to burst into a room. The cast had rigged a door of balsa wood held up by two-by-fours, but they forgot to take out the extra lumber. "George came running up the stairs right into the frame," recalled Lee Sholem, who directed that show. "The balsa wood barely gave way because George bounced off the heavy wood, and fell to the floor—unconscious." George wasn't the only one taking his knocks. Playing Lois, Phyllis Coates, who prided herself on ad-libbing rather than following a script, moved closer than called for to a thug she was confronting and "he decked me! I was knocked out cold, and they sent me home—that left me a little black-and-blue, but I was back at work the next day." A knockout blow was no reason to stop filming; the director reshot the scene before Lois's face started to swell.

Just getting dressed was a challenge for Superman. George's costume came in two gray-and-brown wool pieces that he dubbed the "monkey suit." It had to be sewn into place on him every day, which meant standing still for an hour and suffering the indignity of having clothespins hold his suit together when the sewing didn't. "What is a man my age doing running around in my underwear?" he would mumble as his personal dresser worked on him. There was a silk cape, too, along with rubber latex padding that he wore under his shirt to lift his sloped shoulders and thrust out his chest. Altogether the outfit weighed twenty pounds, and the materials in it gave him a rash. Imagine effortlessly battling villains with that on, under hot studio lights, with no air-conditioning in the heat of a Los Angeles summer. No wonder he never smiled as Superman.

That also explains why, between takes, George would sit in front of blocks of ice with a wind machine aimed at them and him. The effort of shooting was enormous, so it was a blessed relief when the action came to a temporary halt at precisely four every afternoon and George would pour himself, Phyllis, and sometimes Robert Maxwell what he called "my olive"—a martini or, for a change, a brandy. "This drove the production office crazy, and George would say to them, 'Go shit in your hat!'" said Coates. "George's face was like a baby's butt—he never did show it when he would drink." Another way the actor let off steam was telling stories, which was especially entertaining when his audience included John Hamilton, the gruff white-haired actor who played Perry White. Hamilton liked his olive at least as much as George did, although he did his drinking after work at the Brown Derby. The off-camera scene that first year of filming was worthy of its own shoot: Superman holding court from a director's chair, a cocktail in one hand, a cigarette in a silver-and-black holder in the other, his cape tucked neatly behind his back.

All this was exhilarating to Jack Larson, who was just twenty-three when he signed up to play Jimmy Olsen. Reconnecting with Superman was a boyhood dream come true for Larson, who had adored the character back when he read *Action* comic books at Campbell's Drug Store in Los Angeles, slurping a cherry phosphate and hoping his parents would keep talking so he could keep reading. His real ambition was performing on the stage in New York. A short stint on the Superman TV show, for which he was offered $250 a week, seemed like the surest route to pay his way to Broadway. But doubts set in for poor Jack on day one, which he spent locked in a safe, sweating while he waited for Superman to rescue him. "This," he explains, "is not what I had been preparing to do in life. I was young and energetic and innocent and eager and dumb as could be. I didn't know that Clark Kent was Superman because he had on a pair of horn-rimmed glasses." Larson was six years older than the radio Jimmy, yet his version was more boyish and innocent. The straight-out comedy didn't come until later. In the first season he was mainly getting in trouble (he did most of his own stunt work, "which meant I sprained a lot of things"), getting wet ("they were always trying to drown me, and the water was cold and dirty"), and getting rescued (in the nick of time). On the radio and in the comics, Jimmy had been one in a series of supporting roles around Superman. Larson's

TV Jimmy connected so completely with viewers that the copyboy became a star—such a star that today his trademark bowtie is enshrined at the Smithsonian.

Robert Shayne was another regular in the cast, as Metropolis Police Inspector Bill Henderson. Maxwell had just one condition for hiring the fifty-year-old character actor: that he dye his hair gray so he would look older than George Reeves, who dyed his hair to *hide* the gray. The true test of Shayne's forbearance, and Maxwell's, came near the end of shooting for the first season, when real-life federal agents came onto the lot with a subpoena ordering Shayne to appear before the House Un-American Activities Committee. He was a self-described "rabid union man," but denied being a communist and surely wasn't a subversive. Reeves and the rest of the cast, along with Maxwell and the honchos at National Comics, stood behind Shayne when he came under fire, first from congressional inquisitors, then from the show's sponsor. They weren't in a position to take on Wertham and McCarthy, but they could stand up for a man they knew and liked.

Impressive as the supporting cast was, the TV show, like the other incarnations of the story, turned around Superman himself. Bud Collyer, the first flesh-and-blood Man of Steel, had set the standard. Collyer lowered and raised the timbre of his voice as he switched between Superman and Clark, making the changeover convincing. Maxwell's wife, Jessica, who was the dialogue director for the TV show, would follow George around the set urging him to do the same—but he just couldn't master the switch, and soon he stopped trying. The result: a Superman who sounded just like his alter ego. They both swallowed their words. They looked and acted alike. There was no attempt here to make Clark Kent into the klutz he was in the comics. No slouching, no shyness. George portrayed the newsman the way that he knew and that Jessica's husband told him to: hard-boiled and rough-edged, Superman in a business suit. As Clark Kent, George would shed his rubber muscles and add thick tortoiseshell glasses with no lenses— that was the sum total of the switch.

But it worked. It worked because fans wanted to be fooled, and because of the way George turned to the camera and made it clear he knew they knew his secret, even if Lois, Jimmy, and Perry didn't.

This Superman had a dignity and self-assurance that projected even better on an intimate TV screen than it had in the movies. George just had it, somehow. He called himself Honest George, the People's Friend—the same kind of homespun language Jerry and Joe used for their creation—and he suspended his own doubts just as he wanted viewers to. He looked like a guy who not only could make gangsters cringe but who believed in the righteousness of his hero's cause. His smile could melt an iceberg. His cold stare and puffed-out chest could bring a mob to its knees. Sure, his acting was workmanlike, but it won him generations of fans. Today, when those now grown-up fans call to mind their carefree youth, they think of his TV *Adventures of Superman,* and when they envision Superman himself, it is George Reeves they see.

In this first season on television, Superman's fans were not just kids but adults, who were now more of a focus for Maxwell than they had been with the radio show. That became especially apparent in the content of the first year's twenty-six episodes. Phyllis Coates's Lois was, as she said, "a ballsy broad" who never let up on Clark or on chasing down a story. The plots were film noir, with enough kidnappings, murders, suicides, and men slugging women to alarm not just parents but Maxwell's bosses. It was dicey to pull the leg braces off a crippled girl, the way heavies did in an episode called "The Birthday Letter," but gassing to death a cocker spaniel? Another episode tested the no-kill decree: Superman deposited two crooks who had learned his secret identity on the top of a snowcapped mountain and, just after he flew away, both fell to their deaths. In "The Evil Three," the most aptly named and nail-biting of the shows, Perry and Jimmy spent the night in the ramshackle Hotel Bayou. Its proprietor had already killed his uncle, and he tried to do the same to the editor and copyboy. That failed, but he did manage to viciously silence a wheelchair-bound old lady named Elsa by shoving her and her chair down a ramp to the basement. Splat.

The melodrama didn't win any fans at the PTA. A self-proclaimed watchdog group, the National Association for Better Radio and Television, listed *Superman* among seventeen children's series it found "objectionable," and that was before "The Evil Three" had aired. "Monitored programs," the group wrote, "included a demonstration

of how to cripple a wrestler, a doctor using drugs to hypnotize patients, torture, and the kidnapping of a child." Wertham would be
harsher still in *Seduction of the Innocent:* "Television has taken the worst
out of comic books, from sadism to Superman. . . . The television
Superman, looking like a mixture of an operatic tenor without his
armor and an amateur athlete out of a health-magazine advertise-
ment, does not only have 'superhuman powers,' but explicitly be-
longs to a 'super-race.'"

The brewing controversy didn't help in the search for a company
willing to underwrite the broadcast. It took just two and a half months
for the production team to shoot twenty-four new episodes, with the
Mole Men film cut into two parts and renamed "The Unknown People" to make a total of twenty-six. It took nearly two years to find a
sponsor. Flamingo Films, a firm made up of twenty-somethings,
bought the distribution rights early on from Harry Donenfeld, paying thirty million dollars for a thirty-one-year deal. Flamingo pitched
the production to Kellogg's, which remembered all it had earned
from Superman on the radio but, like other would-be sponsors, was
afraid of the new medium of television. Higher production expenses
meant that it cost ten times more to underwrite a show on TV than
on radio. The commercials also were much more expensive to make,
since film was needed in addition to audio. Most disquieting of all
was the worry that this new medium, with its more explicit format
and more intimate entry into people's home, would offend buyers of
breakfast cereal and anything else sponsors were peddling.

That last apprehension was especially daunting with *Adventures of
Superman,* which Kellogg's wanted to pitch to children but couldn't
with the kind of violence Maxwell was filming. The end result was a
painstakingly engineered compromise: Maxwell shortened the mountain death scene, eliminated drive-by shootings, and watered down
other elements that were especially offensive to the cereal maker. Elsa
and her wheelchair still made their way into the cellar, but it was left
to the imagination of viewers how they got there. Ads also had to be
shot, including one with George dressed as Clark and telling the children who flanked him about "that favorite new cereal of mine, Kellogg's Sugar Frosted Flakes." Finally, in September 1952, the show
aired on its first station, in Chicago. Small cities lined up after that,

with Los Angeles coming aboard the next February. By April, the show was airing in New York, the biggest market, along with fifty metropolitan broadcast areas, and it had become the gauge for measuring the success of adventure TV.

The press cheered. "At long last, *Superman!*" wrote the *Brooklyn Eagle,* with *Variety* agreeing that "this one's a natural for TV." Kellogg's signed on for two more years. The reaction on the street was even more bullish. Larson recalls that he couldn't walk down Madison Avenue without cabbies yelling, "Hey Jimmy, where's your buddy? Where's Superman?" One day Larson was in a restaurant on Eighty-second Street having lunch with a friend when he noticed that hundreds of kids had gathered outside, peering through the window. "The police came into the restaurant and apologized. They said I was creating a public nuisance and they had to get me out or something bad could happen. They gave me an escort into the Metropolitan Museum around the corner. I was followed by a mob of kids but the museum refused them entrance and I was given refuge. That's the first time I realized I was in a lot of trouble. I was the first TV teen idol."

Phyllis Coates realized her own newfound celebrity less than a week after the show started airing in Los Angeles. "I had to change the color of my hair! From auburn to blonde. And you know why? I couldn't go anywhere without being mobbed. Not only boys and girls but big, grown-up women. They'd spot me in the super-market or just taking a walk with Crinker," her two-and-a-half-year-old daughter, said Coates, who had grown up on a cattle ranch in Odessa, Texas. "The first thing they wanted to know was how it feels to be held in Superman's arms."

THE FIRST SEASON OF THE TV *Adventures of Superman* was Maxwell's last. Jack Liebowitz, ever the accountant, said the departure was a simple matter of money: Maxwell had promised to spend just fourteen thousand dollars on each episode, which would have ensured a substantial profit, but instead each ended up costing twenty-eight thousand, "so he was out as producer." Maxwell also could be dogmatic, which meant he burned bridges at National as well as on the

set, and he was ambitious, to the point that even as he was working
on Superman he was negotiating with another company to produce
a TV show about Lassie, the heroic Rough Collie. Yet what ultimately did him in, after four years as one of Superman's most influential movers and shakers, was a cultural shift into an era when
Americans liked Ike, hated Bolsheviks, and added "under God" to
the Pledge of Allegiance. The same way Jerry and Joe couldn't resist
their bosses' order to rein in their crusading Superman in the 1930s,
so Maxwell was fighting a battle he couldn't win against an
image-conscious Kellogg's and a public riled up by Fredric Wertham
and his allies. The consensus at National Comics was that it was time
for a kinder, gentler Man of Steel on TV and for a loyal company man
to handle him.

Whitney Ellsworth brought a fresh perspective and a Superman
pedigree even longer than Maxwell's. Ellsworth was the token goy in
the National brain trust, having grown up in the Congregational
Church, but he shared the Brooklyn background of many comics
pioneers and, like Jerry Siegel, he lost his dad as a teenager and it left
him bereft. Ellsworth was an editor for Major Wheeler-Nicholson for
nearly three years starting in 1935. Harry and Jack brought him back
in early 1940 as their first editorial director, a job that included overseeing the Superman books. He picked up some of the writing duties
when Jerry was in the Army, penning newspaper strips and the inaugural Superboy story, and helped oversee the Fleischer cartoons, the
Kirk Alyn serials, and the radio show. Then his bosses wanted him to
ride herd over Jerry and Joe. He did, pressing the creators to "de-sex"
Lois, downplay Superman's jockstrap, and generally understand
"what sort of censure we are always up against, and how careful we
must be."

That background made Ellsworth the perfect choice as Maxwell's
successor. He knew Superman. He knew Harry and Jack. He knew
what it would take to keep them off his back and Wertham off theirs.
He even knew about the televised *Adventures of Superman,* having
written, edited, or otherwise contributed to many of Maxwell's episodes. His budget was nearly 40 percent higher than Maxwell's, and
he had the kind of backing from Kellogg's that Maxwell never did.
He arrived with so many ideas, and drew up such detailed outlines of

how the stories should begin and end, that, as he said, "We never had a writer who had to come in with his own idea." There also was less pressure on the production by the time he moved to Los Angeles. It had proven it could be a blockbuster, the actors knew their roles and their lines, and Superman was the number one reason to turn on the TV for millions of American kids and their parents.

From the start, Ellsworth's shows differed from his predecessor's in ways that were easy to measure. The storylines were ripped more from the comics, which is what Ellsworth knew best. Humor mattered now as much as dark drama. So did science fiction. There were more feel-good plots, like "Around the World with Superman," where, in thirty minutes, the Man of Tomorrow helped a blind girl regain her sight, patched up her parents' shattered marriage, and flew the wide-eyed child around the world. Ellsworth's Superman could make himself invisible and split into two. Crooks had fewer shootouts and wrestling matches with him and were more likely to run into each other or a wall. "Maxwell's first twenty-six shows were a lot more violent than my shows," Ellsworth said looking back. "My concept was that the enemy should be played, for the most part, as semi-comic—and a little bit stupid. . . . I think the kids liked this better."

More than any episode of his five years, "Panic in the Sky" was Ellsworth at his best. Superman lost his memory trying to stop an asteroid rocketing toward Earth in this show, the last of the 1953 broadcasts. It wasn't the plot that grabbed his audience but the subplots. With Clark not remembering he was Superman, his everyman persona took center stage and the fans loved it. Their hero was manly as always, but also tender and vulnerable. Less alien and more human— more like us. The threat, meanwhile, was not just a bank being robbed but the world being destroyed, an increasingly plausible fear in an era of intercontinental missiles, hydrogen bombs, and flying-saucer sightings. Pint-sized viewers yelled at their TV screens: "I know who you are, Mr. Kent, you're Superman and the world needs you." The show, the most expensive of the 104-episode series, was probably based on a recent comic book and the program's popularity would inspire another comic book forty years later, along with a future TV show and cartoon. Even Superman groupie Jerry Seinfeld would count this episode as his all-time favorite. The key to all that acclaim was simple, says Jackson Gillis, who wrote the script: "Pure fantasy," which was "what I thought the show should be."

Popular, yes, but "Panic" had more than the normal flaws. If you listened closely you could hear the hollow sound of Metropolis residents lumbering down the sidewalk with plywood underfoot, not concrete. Tune your ears when Superman landed on the streaking meteor and you could make out birds chirping. Clark showed himself to Jimmy, Lois, and Perry without his glasses, the centerpiece of his disguise, and without any of these inquiring journalists wondering why Superman disappeared at the very moment Clark had amnesia. Had they been in a mood to question, they might also have asked how viewers were supposed to trust newspeople like them who never carried a notebook. Or how Clark could head for the newspaper storeroom with no hat in sight but be wearing one when he arrived.

One premise that got more credible as the series went on was that a man could fly. After the early mishaps, a mechanical arm was rigged up and Superman lay on an attached Plexiglas pan that had been fitted to his chest and thighs. The tray could be turned and tilted, with twenty stagehands pulling to lift and lower the lumbering arm and the camera following it on a hydraulic dolly. There were no more wires, although there still was a wind machine and compressed air to give the feel of Superman whooshing through the air when really it was the filmed background that was moving. George was skeptical. "I had to get in first, then my helper, and still one other guy to make sure it held," said Thol Simonson, who was brought in to manage the special effects. The aerial action happened now in three phases: George got a running start, jumped on a springboard positioned out of sight below a window, and dove head-first through the opening and onto a pile of wrestling mats. Then came film of the mechanical arm moving him through the air. The last sequence showed him hitting the ground feet-first as if he were landing. This all-human, no-animation approach made more convincing not just the flying but the science fiction itself.

Spicing up the fantasy, upgrading the aeronautics, and toning down the violence weren't the only changes Ellsworth wrought. The action was shot in color starting in 1954, although high costs meant that it

would be several years before the color film was aired and it wouldn't
be until the 1960s—when color TVs began to proliferate—that most
viewers actually saw Superman in his new blue and red costume. The
actors were evolving, too, because they felt more comfortable in their
roles and because the new producer and his team insisted on it. Perry
White was less grizzly and more teddy bear, showing his young journalists how to do their jobs rather than just yelling at them. Inspector
Henderson was more relaxed. As for Jimmy, "I loved and admired the
first twenty-six shows under Maxwell, but when they lightened up
they turned me loose and I got to do comedy," says Larson. "That is
exactly what I wanted to do."

The biggest transformation in the cast was a new Lois. Phyllis
Coates left after the first season, despite what she said was an offer
from Ellsworth to pay her five times what she had been earning. She
had the chance to co-star in a new show and was concerned about
being typecast as Lois Lane. She also worried about all the drinking
on the Superman set, especially by George, and given her family history of alcoholism she felt staying could have a "devastating effect."
Looking back, she also had no doubts about what the transition from
Maxwell to Ellsworth meant for the show: "I've had people write to
me to say that as kids they watched those early shows where the heroes were clear, the bad guys got it. Superman was really Superman. . . . The new gang came in and turned it all to pudding!"

Her successor, Noel Neill, was a lot like Ellsworth, softer-edged
but steeped in the Superman tradition. Daughter of a chorus girl and
a journalist, the Minneapolis native had acting in her blood and newspapers in her home. Her résumé included singing for Bing Crosby,
playing in westerns and bobby-socks movies, and sharing an agent
with Jack Larson. A leg-art poster of her in a bathing suit leaning
seductively against a rock ledge was a favorite for GIs. But what really
caught Ellsworth's eye was that she had been the first live-action Lois,
alongside Kirk Alyn in the serials. She hadn't read Superman growing
up—"comic books in those days were a boy thing"—but as soon as
she landed the serial role "I rushed out and bought a book to see
what Lois Lane looked like. I wanted to see what she wore, how her
hair was, this and that."

When Ellsworth called to offer her the role, Neill was ecstatic even though all he was paying was $185 per episode, or half what Coates said she got. The perks were even fewer than in the serials. She had to dress her own hair, bring her own shoes and socks, and shoot scenes in such quick succession that she had no time to learn her lines or to socialize. She got no royalties when the shows were rebroadcast. She was never invited to appear in the commercials for Frosted Flakes, which more than doubled Jack and George's salaries. Kellogg's, she says, worried about how scandalous it would look if she turned up at the breakfast table with Jack or George. Teenager rock and rollers surely would have been delighted, but not their priggish parents.

Neill found it troubling enough to have bosses who were "very, very, very, very cheap," and worse to have a director, Tommy Carr, who gave her a hard time from day one. He didn't like the way she said her hallmark line, "Gee, Superman, am I ever glad to see you!" and had her repeat it until she started to cry. That's when Superman stepped in. "George saw what was happening and immediately asked for a break. He walked over to Tommy and calmly said, 'Why don't you give the kid a break?'" Neill remembered. "After George intervened, he eased up and let me do it my way."

Neill's Lois reflected more than anyone the change from Maxwell to Ellsworth. She was easier on Clark than Coates had been and more dazzled by Superman's rescues. It is no accident that none of Coates's pictures show her smiling, whereas Neill is smiling in every shot. It also is understandable that they didn't like one another. Neill denied ever meeting Coates, whom she called "whatshername." Coates said George introduced them and that Neill told her, "I *hate* you!" Which Lois was the better fit and whether the show headed downhill after Maxwell's first season are matters still hotly contested. The truth is that the Neill-Ellsworth version had less punch but more warmth than the Coates-Maxwell episodes. Take your pick.

Lost in all those arguments is all that remained the same. Superman still took on third-rail issues like atomic power and political corruption, as he had in the comics, radio shows, and Maxwell TV shows, and he still got skewered by the National Association for Better Radio and Television. Ellsworth had to do the same dance that Maxwell had on the phone every week with Jack Liebowitz. Ellsworth: "Jack, I got no money." Liebowitz: "Well how much do you need?" Ellsworth: "I need $25,000 this week." Liebowitz: "So much?" Ellsworth: "Well yes, so much. Maybe a little more." Kidnappings still were part of *Adventures of Superman* plots, along with hauntings and rough times for ladies and dogs. There were even killings. What was different with Ellsworth producing the shows is that the dogs survived. In the one Ellsworth episode in which the villains didn't, their deaths happened off-screen. The show knew whom it wanted to reach—kids—and it aimed squarely at them with fare designed to placate their parents and Ellsworth's sponsors.

That same kid-friendly ethic was being applied in the Superman comic books, and for the same reason. Wertham had the entire industry running scared. In just two years, from 1954 to 1956, the number of comic book titles published in America plunged from 650 to 250. It was "like the plague," observed longtime comics artist Carmine Infantino. "If you said you drew comic books, it was like saying you were a child molester." Editor Al Feldstein worried that "the industry's dying, the comics industry. All they need is a spade to bury it." By the fall of 1955, a Comics Code Authority had been set up, and its black-and-white seal appeared in the upper right corner of every book it had approved. Without a seal, most distributors wouldn't carry the comic. Winning the Code Authority's approval meant scrubbing titles and stories of horror and terror, along with anything that could be seen as disrespectful of police, parents, and government. No vampires or werewolves, references to physical afflictions, or exaggerations of the female anatomy. Illicit sex couldn't be hinted at and characters could not be divorced. No ads for liquor, tobacco, fireworks, or weapons. It was the kind of self-policing the motion picture industry had been practicing for twenty-five years, only more so. These restrictions were less severe than the outright bans Wertham and other critics wanted, but they meant much more censorship than printed publications, with their First Amendment protections, usually agreed to. It was a strategy of self-preservation, which made sense given that a dozen publishers had already been forced to shutter their doors and more than eight hundred comic book artists and writers were looking for work.

No publisher pressed the stay-pure strategy on more fronts than Harry and Jack did. They distanced themselves from the "mercenary minority" who were producing most of the violent and vulgar material. They established a "Distinguished Advisory Board" of child behavior experts who gathered the latest evidence of how comic books were helping kids read, helping teachers teach, and, as one panel member told *Time,* offering "the same type of mental catharsis to their readers that Aristotle claimed was an attribute of the drama." Harry and Jack adopted their own standards of editorial purity, as spelled out in a memo from Ellsworth when he was editorial director, that went even further than the Comics Code. The inclusion of females in Superman stories was discouraged. "Expressions having reference to the Deity" were forbidden, and so were bloodletting and killing, even of killers. "The use of chains, whips, or other such devices is forbidden. Anything having a sexual or sadistic implication is forbidden," the guidelines said. "HEROES SHOULD ACT WITHIN THE LAW, AND *FOR* THE LAW." Ellsworth had to sanitize his productions even further, banishing killings even off-screen, dumbing down the bad guys, and steering clear of controversial social issues. There was one last move Jack and Harry made in the mid-1950s that Wertham would have found interesting had he known: They quietly acquired the distribution rights to America's sexiest magazine, *Playboy.*

Stories of kids who tried to take wing and fly, as Jerry Siegel had as a child, were always a sore spot for Superman, and never more so than in that era of the inquisition. Newspapers glommed on to the tales. Eight-year-old Larry King of Columbus, Ohio, spread his homemade cape over his back and jumped from his second-floor fire escape, explaining from his hospital bed that "I thought the air would get under my towel and float me down like it does Superman." James Henderson, another eight-year-old second-story boy, took off in his Superman suit and landed with a sprained ankle. "The darned thing wouldn't work," the Des Moines youngster complained of his costume. Twelve-year-old Robert Van Gosig of New York wasn't so lucky: He slipped on a wet ledge while playing Superman on his tenement roof and plunged to his death.

After Jerry read articles like those, his comic book Superman warned readers that only he could perform such feats of derring-do without getting hurt. Superman costumes carried similar cautions. It was one thing for young fans to break their beds as they pretended to fly; it was quite another for them to break their necks. "We were very conscious of that," recalls Jay Emmett, who oversaw the licensing of Superman products. "We couldn't have kids buying costumes if they were going to jump out the window." George Reeves felt a special burden with kids who mimicked him. He gave up smoking and drinking in public. He pushed National Comics to stop selling costumes and capes. And, in a 1955 episode of *Adventures of Superman,* he warned listeners that "no one, but no one, can do the things Superman does. And that goes especially for flying!"

National's multi-front multimedia campaign worked. Making Superman more squeaky-clean on the printed page—and lightening up on the TV show's noir—eventually inoculated him against the attacks of critics like Wertham. The censorship campaign also backfired by turning Superman stories into the kind of forbidden fruit that made kids more determined to read on and tune in. Jack and Harry's most brilliant stroke was launching the new TV series in the middle of the assault on comic books, when other superheroes were running for cover. The publishing partners had always played better offense than defense. Their radio show, film serials, and animated movies had boosted rather than diminished the popularity of Superman comic books and comic strips, and TV did that in spades. Call it synergy, or just street smarts.

Another measure of success was the way Superman merchandising was taking off. It had always been done well, but in the early 1950s National capitalized on the popularity of its television series and "licensing income soared," says Emmett, who oversaw those sales. Building on his Superman success and his relationship with his uncle Jack Liebowitz, Emmett in 1960 launched a broader-based product-management operation called the Licensing Corporation of America, whose clients would eventually include Pat Boone, Batman, and the National Basketball Association.

TV also spread Superman's fame the rest of the way around the globe. Dubbed into Japanese, *Adventures of Superman* became that country's most popular TV show, with Emperor Hirohito writing George to say that Superman was his *ninkimono,* or fave. The show was playing in Paris, too, with simultaneous subtitles in French, Arabic, and Japanese. And all this was happening during the height of the comic book scare. Fredric Wertham had gone to war with the Man of Steel and, like so many Superman foes over the years, the venerable psychiatrist had been humbled.

THERE WAS ONE ADVERSARY SUPERMAN couldn't defeat: himself. Not that anyone imagined the Man of Tomorrow, the world's pre-eminent Pollyanna, trying to take his own life. The notion was so abhorrent that National Comics had banished any depiction of suicide—by Superman or anyone else—from its pages and airwaves. Yet on the morning of June 17, 1959, America woke to the headline TV SUPERMAN KILLS SELF. Parents tried to hide the paper from their kids. Kids were sure the reports had to be mistaken, since everyone knew bullets bounced off the Man of Steel. But the media spelled out the all too real and gruesome details: Friends had found George Reeves's naked body splayed across his bed, faceup in a pool of blood, with a bullet hole in his temple and a German Luger nestled between his feet.

To his admirers, George had everything to live for. *Adventures of Superman* had been reaching thirty-five million TV viewers a year, only half of whom were kids. After 104 episodes, there was practically no one in America who did not recognize George Reeves. He delighted moppets with a 1956 appearance on *Romper Room* and two days afterward he thrilled their parents and grandparents on Tony Bennett's variety show, the first time those with color TVs could see what he looked like in his radiant red-and-blue costume. Later that year he achieved the ultimate measure of celebrity: a guest slot on America's most-watched show, *I Love Lucy*. It was true that *Adventures of Superman* had stopped production in November of 1957, but re-runs were still airing and earning him as much as $1,000 a week, he had been approached about shooting twenty-six new shows, and, having already directed three episodes, he was bullish about directing more.

At the time of his death, George was due to be married in just three days. He was two weeks away from an Australian tour, in which he would play guitar in a band, then wrestle his sidekick Gene LeBell, a judo champion who dressed up as the evil Mr. Kryptonite. He had an offer to star in *Wagon Train*, a TV western that would go on to run for nearly ten years. "Nothing was bothering him," LeBell says of his friend, who was only forty-five. "He wasn't going to shoot himself."

Other observers offered a less rosy portrait, starting with George's offscreen appearances, which were part of his deal with National. They were the kind of thing Jerry Siegel had loved doing, but George never found them easy. In 1954 a young fan socked him in the eye "to see if he would flinch." Another pointed a loaded Colt .45 at him. The gun story became part of his legend and he played the hero, saying he had convinced the boy to put down the gun because, while Superman could fend off a bullet, a bystander could be hurt by the ricochet. His own variety shows, like the one planned for Australia, were financial disasters, and Noel Neill said he had been staying in his room more on these tours and drinking by himself. The low point was a stop in North Carolina where only three people showed up— a young boy and his parents. George's other investment schemes didn't fare well either, including one for a "Motel of the Stars" run by a con man who defrauded not just George, but Mickey Rooney, Burl Ives, and Debbie Reynolds.

At the time of his death, George hadn't had an acting job since *Adventures of Superman* went on hiatus nineteen months earlier. "Here I am wasting my life," he told Ben Welden, who played a thug on the Superman series. George had almost died twice in car accidents. The first was in March 1956, when a truck loaded with construction materials reportedly ran a red light and rammed into his sports car, sending him wheeling into another truck and leaving him in the hospital for a week. Three years later he took a curve too fast and skidded into an embankment, leaving him with a concussion and a five-inch gash on the forehead.

The last of his six Superman seasons was aimed more than ever at a young audience and had weak scripts as well as tired execution. He was looking and acting middle-aged now. Clark wore eyeglasses with actual lenses. Lingering pain from the first car crash prompted him to take pills and made it tougher for him and Superman to keep in shape. He strapped on a girdle these days before stepping in front of the camera. His hair was noticeably thinner, whiter, and in need of more frequent touch-ups with food coloring along with hair dye. Karate chops, which were easier to deliver and to fake, had replaced punches. George had always liked his olive, but now he liked it in the morning, too.

His love life was even more unsettled. It had begun promisingly and conventionally when, in 1940, he married a young actress named Ellanora Needles. They were separated first by his enlistment in the Army, then by separate careers and waning interest. The divorce was formalized in 1950, a year before he became Superman. The next year he started an affair with Toni Mannix, a former Ziegfeld Follies beauty who was eight years older than he was and fifteen years younger than her husband, Metro-Goldwyn-Mayer vice president and enforcer Eddie Mannix. She called George "the Boy." To him, she was "Mother" or "Ma," Eddie was "Pop," and the unorthodox relationship among the three churchgoing Catholics was "the Arrangement," which suited everyone perfectly. Eddie got to be with his exotic mistress and, given his weak heart, he had the security of knowing that Toni would have George to look after her. Toni got the man she loved, George, and an exhilarating lifestyle that brought her to the Superman set every day with a picnic basket brimming with gin, vermouth, olives, and hors d'oeuvres that made her a favorite with cast and crew. George got a house in Los Angeles's exclusive Benedict Canyon, an Italian sports car, a Minox camera, a sauna, and an open tab at his favorite restaurant, Scandia—all delivered by Toni and paid for by Eddie. It was a love triangle as tangled as Superman's with Clark and Lois.

The arrangement worked for everyone until George called it off early in 1958. One night at Toots Shor's Restaurant in New York he had met Leonore Lemmon, a barfly infamous for being the only woman ever tossed out of the Stork Club for fistfighting. George couldn't take his eyes off her ample breasts, jet-black hair, and white skin. When she turned up at his hotel room at two the next morning with wine and squab, they became inseparable. She moved to California and into his Benedict Canyon home, alienating his old friends and inviting new ones to what seemed like an around-the-clock party. "She makes me feel like a boy again," George told everyone. Toni called her "the whore" and allegedly had Eddie's yardman make harassing calls to George and Leonore. The two were due to be married three days after his death, or so Leonore said.

She rarely said the same thing twice and never seemed credible to George's friends, especially when it came to what happened the night he died. She told police that George had gone to bed about midnight, after which friends stopped by. George appeared in his robe and got into a squabble with one of the guests, then apologized and went back to bed. As he did, Leonore predicted that "he's probably gonna shoot himself." She could hear him open the dresser drawer and get out the gun. Minutes later, she said, a shot rattled the house. Those basic details remained relatively consistent in her retellings to investigators and friends until thirty years later, when she told a dramatically different version. George never came downstairs that night. She thought he might have planned to kill her, too. And given his difficulty finding work after being typecast as the Man of Steel, "the only thing that killed him is something very simple, very easy: Superman killed him."

The forensic details of the case were sketchy and spilled out haphazardly, fueling suspicion that the crime scene had been tampered with and casting doubt on the suicide declaration by the coroner and police. Why, researchers who have reviewed the evidence wonder, did the embalmer sew together George's head wounds before the coroner thoroughly analyzed them? How did the bullet casing end up under his body? Why were there no fingerprints on the gun or powder burns on his face? What about the extra bullet holes discovered in the floor under a rug in the bedroom? Why did it take forty-five minutes for anyone to call the police and why, in those anxious minutes, did Leonore phone high-powered Washington defense attorney Edward Bennett Williams? He told her to call the cops and keep her mouth shut, and later told friends that "only Lem can turn a suicide into a homicide."

The weeks after the shooting were a circus, with George's mother, Helen, as the ringleader. She came to town in a wheelchair, telling anyone who would listen that her son hadn't killed himself and hiring a prominent criminal attorney, a detective agency, and new pathologists to pore over the evidence. Toni visited the house with Jack Larson and—"to exorcise this evil"—used the heel of her shoe to nail tiny prayer cards over the bullet holes. Leonore went separately, with a friend who ripped the bloody sheets from George's bed and tossed them into the bathtub, then helped Leonore bundle up her things and leave L.A. for good. George's will bequeathed most of his fifty-thousand-dollar estate, including his home and car, to Toni and nothing to his fiancée, leading Leonore to insist there must have been a second will.

The chief coroner personally helped perform an autopsy a week after the death and confirmed it was suicide. George's funeral was held July 1; an open casket revealed his body dressed in a Clark Kent suit, with his head looking as if it had been hastily stitched back together. It would take another seven months for Helen to complete her probes and have her boy cremated. She tried to drown her grief in drink, which was the one thing she shared with Toni and Leonore. Helen died five years after George and her remains lie alongside his in a crypt at the Mountain View Cemetery and Mausoleum in Altadena, California. There are no gravestones, just her simple plaque honoring MY BELOVED SON "SUPERMAN."

Neither his burial nor the deaths of witnesses and investigators have quieted the storm. Was it murder, suicide, or accident? Arguments for all three have been made in fifty years of newspaper and magazine investigations, hours of TV exposés, and a trio of books, with more in the works. George's business manager died before he could complete his tell-all. So did Leonore. A 2006 movie called *Hollywoodland*, starring Ben Affleck and Adrien Brody, hedged its bets by imagining different death scenarios: Leonore shooting him accidentally, George killing himself, and Eddie Mannix hiring a hit man. Eddie had the contacts to do it but there is no evidence he did—and no motive, since he liked George enough to get him a cherished membership in the movie directors' guild and hoped he would get back together with Toni, who was driving Eddie crazy. Toni was mad enough at George to want him dead, and a young public relations man who was living at her mansion said he heard her confess to a priest that she was part of a murder conspiracy. But that didn't fit with her hope that George would come crawling back to her, or with the shrine she built after he died, where George's picture hung next to Jesus'. Leonore, with her mob friends and gutter diction, would have made a convincing bad gal if this had been a Superman TV treatment: Imagine George calling off their engagement, then Leonore shooting him on purpose or by mistake as they struggled over the gun. But even scriptwriters would have had a difficult time explaining how that happened with three witnesses in the house who vouched for Leonore.

George's young fans advanced their own theory after watching the rerun of *Adventures of Superman* that aired the day after he died. In "Disappearing Lois," Milton Frome played a thug who fired his pistol at Clark Kent at close range. Since Lois and Jimmy were present Clark was forced to play dead, hitting the deck with a thud. "That night," Frome recalled, "some neighborhood kids came by our house and told my son Michael, 'Hey, your father killed Superman.'"

No one will ever know for sure who or what killed the TV Superman, but good starting points are the typecasting that extinguished his film career and the three unhinged women in his life—Leonore, Toni, and Helen—each of whom wanted him as hers alone. He was aging and slowing, afflictions especially difficult for Superman to handle. On his last night he argued with Leonore and her houseguests, which boiled his blood. None of that would make a self-contained man like George do something he couldn't have imagined otherwise. But he had apparently talked about killing himself as far back as high school and as recently as a year or two before his death, according to one Reeves historian who has spent decades on the case. What might have pushed him to do it this time was the incendiary mixture of alcohol—the coroner said his blood level was .27 percent, three times today's legal limit in California and the equivalent of six martinis—and the painkillers he was taking for the migraines he had suffered since his car crash. His clothes were off because he slept in the buff, and the gun was within reach in the dresser. Whitney Ellsworth, who knew firsthand what dipsomania could do, labeled it temporary insanity. George's admirers then and now call it a tragedy.

There were silver linings even in that calamity. His fans adored him so much that many still remember where they were and what they were doing when they got the news of his death, the same way people do about John F. Kennedy's. Losing George meant being robbed of a touchstone of their youth. But decades of reruns—along with videotapes, DVDs, and an elegant and worshipful fanzine called *The Adventures Continue*—have let devotees visit with him again and have ensured that George, like President Kennedy, will remain forever young. The actor also seemed to say his own regretful goodbye on the last episode of the TV show. Waking from a dream in which he imagined he had superpowers, Jimmy said, "Golly, Mr. Kent—you'll never know how wonderful it is to be like Superman." After a considered pause, Clark answered: "No, Jimmy, I guess I never will."

As for Superman, the Reeves suicide could have disillusioned fans and tarnished the icon. Jack and Harry were worried enough that they contemplated bringing on another actor to play the part, or centering a series around Jimmy Olsen. Either move would have seemed panicky and neither was needed. While it would take thirty years for the superhero to make his way back to television in a fresh live-action series, he thrived in other media. The 1950s TV show, even more than his radio and film work, had taken Superman beyond the rarefied world of comic books and made him a centerpiece of popular culture. Television was now the medium that mattered in America, and no TV show mesmerized kids of all ages more than *Adventures of Superman,* which didn't surprise anyone who had watched the Man of Steel conquer comic books, radio, serials, and cartoons.

George's death also spawned a hypothesis called the Superman curse, which argued that misfortune befell anyone who was creatively involved with the Man of Steel. Jerry and Joe had been barred from their creation. Kirk Alyn couldn't land an acting job. Now George was gone. Any news, even the bleakest, added to the legend.

CHAPTER 7

Imagine This

FROM THE BEGINNING SUPERMAN FANS had longed for a story like this: "Mr. and Mrs. Clark (SUPERMAN) Kent!" Now here it was, in the new comic book devoted just to Lois Lane, with a cover sketch of her in an apron and pearls as her humdrum husband hurtles off in cape and tights to save the planet. "Hurry home, dear. Supper will be ready soon!" she chirps, thinking, "Would our neighbors be astounded if they knew my husband Clark is leaving our home through a secret tunnel, as . . . Superman!"

It started when Clark proposed and Lois said she couldn't, not if there was the faintest hope Superman might someday pop the same question. That did it. To her amazement, he doffed his spectacles, his business suit, and his covert identity. "Why did you wait so long?" she asked as they embraced. Superman: "I feared that if I married you, my enemies would seek to strike at me by harming you! But I've thought of a solution . . . as far as the world will know, you'll be marrying meek, mild Clark Kent! You alone will share the secret of my real identity!" And so it was, as they said their nuptial vows, then set up a snug household in the suburbs. Even her sister Lucy had to stay in the dark, telling Lois, "I'm glad you and Clark get along so well! Frankly, I thought you'd never get over your crush on Superman."

The tale, published in August 1960, was the first in a series of "imaginary stories" that helped define Superman during America's decade of discontent. This was a bid by National Comics to create fresh and arresting threads for writers who were running out of them. It also was an attempt to tap into the era's capsizing of conventions, even if the comic book outcome was more happily-ever-after than New Frontier. The very notion of tackling heretofore unthinkable topics and offering zany flourishes to timeworn plots was revolutionary, at least to the adolescent keepers of the Superman flame. When Jerry Siegel had proposed a working partnership between Lois and Superman in the K-Metal story in 1940, it was hushed up. Now those two were life partners, upending not just the love triangle and Clark and Superman's bachelorhood but the sacrosanct secret of Clark's alter ego. Romantics cheered, as did all the four-eyed boys who dreamed that a pretty girl would fall for the hero in them. Radical indeed, and vital to keeping Superman atop the sales charts. Yet the powers that be at National knew there were limits. Titillate readers, yes, but not to the point where it toppled the pillars of the Superman biography and canon, which comic book connoisseurs called the "continuity."

So they labeled this story and scores of others imaginary, as if the rest of the comics weren't. In the very first panel they made clear that they were looking into a future "several years hence, on a day that may or may not ever happen." The story ended on a comparably cautionary note, urging readers to "see future issues of this magazine for more stories about the imaginary marriage between Lois and Superman . . . that may come true . . . or may not!"

Other titles in the Superman family offered their own counterintuitive narratives. What would Superman have been like if his Kryptonian parents had come to Earth with him? How about if he, like Tarzan, had been raised in the jungle? Or if Ma and Pa Kent had adopted Bruce Wayne as well as Kal-El, making Superman and Batman brothers? We even met Superman's children, whether or not we knew their mother. There had been "imaginary" stories like these since the beginning, but the label was coined and the best of them were published during the Silver Age of comics, from 1956 to 1970. This was the most high-spirited, rules-be-damned Superman storytelling in decades and maybe ever. The World's Mightiest Citizen was letting his hair down.

There was one more unexpected twist to "Mr. and Mrs. Clark (SUPERMAN) Kent!": It was written by Jerry Siegel, or so he claimed, although another writer claimed the same thing. There were no bylines in the Superman comics once Jerry and Joe left, so no one can say for sure. But Jerry was back at Jack and Harry's publishing house, quietly working as a freelancer. It was the first in his series of bids to renew his ties to Superman. Imagining outlandish stories about the Man of Steel is what Jerry had been doing since he was a teenager, and now he needed the work and money more than ever. He brought to the task the insights of the battle-weary adult he was along with those of the lonesome boy who would forever define him. Now he had an opportunity to shape the future of a superhero he had brought to life, even if his legal settlement with National prevented him from whispering it to anyone.

EVERY ERA OF SUPERMAN had a defining medium. In the late 1930s and early 1940s it was comic books and comic strips that introduced the character and generated the buzz. Radio made a splash in the 1940s, with cartoons and serials building the wave. George Reeves and his TV adventures were the center of gravity from the beginning to the end of the 1950s, the decade of McCarthy and conformity. The 1960s were back to the future. The only action on TV was reruns of the Reeves series along with a new batch of cartoons that didn't start until 1966 and lasted just six minutes each. Superman had gone silent on the radio and was off the marquees. The big thing, again, was the comics.

Each medium likewise was defined by one or two creative personalities—from Jerry and Joe in the early comic books and strips, to Bob Maxwell and Bud Collyer on the radio, to Whit Ellsworth and George Reeves for most of the television boom. They were the handlers who tinkered with his biography, shifted his delivery mechanism, and made whatever other changes were needed to keep him alive and compelling. In the 1960s the towering figure was Mort Weisinger, one of the most inspired and influential of Superman's midwives, and hands down the most obnoxious.

This son of Russian-Czech immigrants was born on April 25,

1915—six months after Jerry and nine after Joe—and he matched them both in his passion for space-age fantasy. At sixteen he was being published in science fiction journals, and a year later he helped start the pioneering fan magazine *The Time Traveler*. By eighteen, he and his friend Julius Schwartz had launched Solar Sales Service, the first literary agency to specialize in fantasy and the first to sign up science fiction icons Ray Bradbury and H. P. Lovecraft. Weisinger's sensibilities were formed by the same forces that shaped other early comics leaders: roots in the rough-and-tumble Bronx, the worldview of a Jewish outsider, and teeth cut on the pulp universe of bug-eyed monsters. His parents, who had made a fortune in the shoe business and then lost it when their factory burned, pushed him to be a doctor. He pushed back. In 1941, Mort signed on as an editor with National and Superman—hired by Whit Ellsworth on Jerry Siegel's recommendation—and he stayed for three full decades. That was longer than Jerry, Joe, Whit, or even Harry Donenfeld lasted, and it was time enough for Mort to oversee the production of two thousand stories about Superman and his friends.

Weisinger framed TV and movie scripts and he had edited comics almost from the start, but his watershed came in 1957. That was when Ellsworth, who for years had been focusing on the broadcast world of Los Angeles, formally yielded to Weisinger the Superman realm in New York. Like any good potentate, Weisinger consolidated his authority and pressed ahead with his edicts. Mort's Rule No. 1: Know your readers. Superman's, he thought, were boys aged eight to twelve, a readership that turned over often enough that it was okay to recycle old storylines or reprint old stories. Rule No. 2: Don't let the kids get bored. Imaginary stories with epic sweep were just the beginning. He knew that everyone loves a party, so every six months he gave his youthful followers another reason to celebrate. It might be a new comic book (the two he liked most, even if his bosses didn't, were *Superman's Pal Jimmy Olsen* and *Superman's Girl Friend Lois Lane*), a new character (Supergirl, Superbaby, Krypto the Superdog), or a new explanation for an old conundrum (our yellow sun gave Superman his superpowers). The one enigma he couldn't explain away was why anyone bought Clark's disguise of a battered pair of horn-rimmed glasses. Mort called it the Cinderella Fallacy: "Everyone knows that at midnight all of Cinderella's finery changed back into rags. Yet has anyone ever asked why one of her slippers remained glass?"

Weisinger's last and golden rule was: Listen to your customers. That was why Jimmy got promoted from cub to full-fledged reporter. It also was why Lois got a bouffant hairdo like Jackie Kennedy's and, for her high-altitude flights with Superman, a spacesuit like Alan Shepard's. Not only did Mort publish adolescent fans' letters in all his Superman books, but he printed their home addresses so they could correspond with one another. It helped that he had been an avid science fiction fan as a kid and had never really grown up. He "glowed with an over-the-top enthusiasm for every meal, movie, or book he loved," recalled his daughter, Joyce Kaffel. "He was childlike in his exuberance in that everything he enjoyed was 'the best one' of its kind, even if the 'one' before it had been 'the best.'"

Before Mort came along, Superman's world was ad hoc and seat-of-the-pants, with Jerry and other writers adding elements as they went along without any planning or anyone worrying whether it all hung together. That worked fine when all the books centered around Superman and all the writing was done by a small stable. Now the pool of writers had grown and there were eight different comic books with hundreds of Superman stories a year to worry about. It would take a master choreographer like Weisinger to pull it together. He came up with story ideas and parceled them out to scripters, the way Ellsworth did for the TV shows. He divined a fairy-tale universe with its own laws of nature. Superman got a coherent past. He also got an extended family whose stories were scattered among the various books and collectively accounted for a quarter of National's output. "My greatest contribution to Superman," Mort explained after his retirement, "was to give him a 'mythology' which covered all bases. All this makes Superman credible."

Mort was good for Superman, but he wasn't popular. Everyone had a story about the editor's beastliness. He stole plot proposals from one writer and handed them to another, informing the first that it was a crappy idea and the second that it was Mort's. He took underpaid employees to lunch only when he had a two-for-one coupon, and his tie carried caked-on reminders of mashed potatoes, ketchup, and everything else that happened to be on his plate. He told one protégé, Jim Shooter, to be more like another, Cary Bates; told Bates to be more like Shooter; and told everyone that the people working for him were idiots. He had such trouble telling the truth that Julie Schwartz, his lifelong friend, joked that Mort's gravestone should read, "Here Lies Mort Weisinger—As Usual." Jack Adler, a colleague from the early days, recalled that "I had to bring something to him for approval and he wanted to know whether I was having an affair with someone. He said, 'If you tell me, I'll approve everything you bring to me.'"

Mort couldn't help himself. He was trying to make the important point that Superman, not the writers or artists, was the star. He was born with a heart made for storytelling and a tin ear for dealing with people. He wasn't well, as anyone who met him could see. Weighing three hundred pounds, he had developed a series of maladies: gout, inflamed ulcers, hypertension, insomnia, and what he said was a psychological hang-up that grew out of his being jealous of Superman. Blessedly, he hadn't lost the capacity to laugh at himself. Neal Adams, at the time a young artist, remembered asking Mort why he was so grumpy. "I'll tell you," the editor explained. "Try to imagine that you get up in the morning and you go into the bathroom to shave, and you look into the mirror, and you see *this* face."

Mort was a lot like his boss and benefactor, Jack Liebowitz, with whom he often commuted to work. Both knew the Man of Tomorrow was in a rut by the late 1950s, with storylines that seemed too yesterday and without the boost the franchise had gotten from George Reeves and *Adventures of Superman*. The newspaper strip was still going, but its nearly thirty-year run would end in 1966 as a growing number of outlets did not renew their contracts for Superman and other superheroes. Dr. Wertham and his watchdogs were making parents reluctant to shell out the money for comics, and television, now soaring in popularity, was competing for kids' time and interest. Superman needed a makeover and Mort delivered it. So what if he wasn't popular? Neither was Jack. The questions that mattered to bottom-line guys like them were *Would it work?* and *Would it last?*

It did work. In 1960, the first year in which sales data was made public, Superman was selling more comic books than any other title or character, and he stayed on top through much of the decade. The

Man of Steel was at the front of a charge that saw superheroes taking over from western and romance-themed comics. Some of that was a dividend from an easing of the comics scare and other, broader forces, but Weisinger's reinventions were key ingredients in Superman's comeback. "Mort kept it alive," says Carmine Infantino, a National Comics artist who would rise to editorial director, then publisher. "He was a damn good editor. Damn good."

You could see Mort's influence in the artwork. Curt Swan, who did his first Superman drawings in 1948 and his last thirty-nine years later, gave the hero a more refined look in the 1960s. Gone was Wayne Boring's muscular virility, replaced by a more dignified and human sensibility. Gorgeous had yielded to handsome. While story-lines leaped back and forth between science fiction and reality, Swan's artwork kept Superman grounded and credible. Swan also settled the question of how old the hero was: a clean-cut and youthful twenty-nine, which was how old he'd stay through the next two decades. Weisinger steered all these changes, as Swan and Boring have testi-fied. Swan said battling Mort gave him migraines. Boring said that, after nearly thirty years of drawing Superman, he couldn't believe his ears when Weisinger fired him in 1966, so he asked if he'd under-stood right. "Do you need a kick in the stomach to know when you're not wanted!?" the editor answered. His biggest nightmare, Boring added, was that "I'd die and go to hell and he'd be in charge!"

Weisinger's writers brought their own flourishes. Some stories, like "Mr. and Mrs. Clark (SUPERMAN) Kent!" used a liberated imagination to take readers places they never thought they would go. Characters also experienced extraordinary things—Clark ending up in a wheelchair, about to marry the magnificent Sally Selwyn—only to have them undone by amnesia. Other oft-used ploys: magic po-tions, instant aging and even faster rejuvenation, and short-lived su-perpowers for mortals such as Jimmy and Lois. Mort's favorite trick was making Superman temporarily lose his omnipotence, forcing him to fall back on his wits, à la Sherlock Holmes. Whimsical depar-tures like those would have been out of the question in the 1950s, when the comics were supposed to stay in sync with the TV show, which on its meager budget had trouble convincingly depicting sci-ence fiction. Now that the franchise was both flush and confined to print, the only limit was Mort's imagination, and his fanciful devices became so common in the Superman comics of the sixties that covers were often forced to assure fans that what they were about to read was *not* an imaginary story, a hoax, or a dream.

Reality was a more tender matter. Weisinger stories steered clear of the Vietnam War, the sexual revolution, the black power movement, and other issues that fired the 1960s. There was none of what Mort would have called "touchy-feely" either, much as readers might have liked to know how Clark felt about his split personality, or whether Superman and Lois engaged in the battles between the sexes that were a hallmark of the era. Mort wanted his comics to be a haven for young readers, and he knew his right-leaning politics wouldn't sit well with his leftist writers and many of his Superman fans. That didn't stop Otto Binder from sneaking pro-feminist and anti-homophobic messages into his fantastic Superman adventures. He also got away with insulting Weisinger to his face and surviving at National. "Called him every goddam name I could think of," said Binder, who claimed to have written the Mr. and Mrs. Kent story and to have planted with Jerry and Joe the original idea for a comic about an interplanetary orphan with special powers. After unleashing his invectives against his boss, Binder said, he "walked out, and went to see Julie [Schwartz], and Mort comes down the hall and says, 'Are you going to have lunch with me, Otto?' He didn't believe a word I'd said!"

Another writer Weisinger hired to breathe new life into Superman was the man who had breathed life into him to begin with. Mort called Jerry Siegel "the most competent of all the Superman writers. . . . What his successors did was just embroidery, including my own contributions. Siegel was the best emotional writer of them all." The feelings were not mutual. While he was glad to have a job, Jerry's correspondence from the early years made clear how he felt about Mort telling him how to write the character he had begotten. "What I find particularly distressing is the editorial attitude, as personified by Mort Weisinger, toward my SUPERMAN magazine scripts," Jerry wrote Jack Liebowitz in 1946. "Mort rejects 'em wholesale, and I find myself in the position of having an editor telling I, who created SUPERMAN, that I don't know how to write it. If this happened only occasionally, I'd shrug and figure every writer is entitled to some rejection slips, and forget it. But he rejects my stuff so consistently, with aggravating comments, that he puts me into a frame of mind where I find it almost impossible to write."

Whatever Jerry thought, it was Mort who now was Superman's boss as well as his mouthpiece. In Russia, Weisinger met Premier Nikita Khrushchev, who he said told him that "the Man of Steel cannot get through the Iron Curtain." In Washington, he sat down for a chat with President Kennedy's press secretary, Pierre Salinger. An MIT class sent Mort a letter from Albert Einstein, who asserted that nothing, not even Superman, could move faster than the speed of light. Mort consulted his "good friend" Isaac Asimov, the science fiction writer, who said that "Professor Einstein's statement is based on theory. Superman's speed is based on fact." Mort knew *everyone,* or pretended to, and he had no shame promoting himself and his comic book star despite his feigned modesty. "When people asked me what I did for a living, I would suppress the fact that I was editing *Superman*," Mort wrote. The truth, his psychologist son Hank said, is that "any time we went anywhere, it only took five minutes for him to let everybody know he was the editor of Superman."

Most helpful to National, Mort took on Dr. Fredric Wertham. In a radio debate, Wertham talked about how all of the two hundred inmates he had interviewed at reform school had read Superman, prompting Weisinger to ask, "Did you get them to confess that they also chew bubble gum, play baseball, eat hot dogs and go to the movies?" There was no joking in an "investigation" he did for *Better Homes and Gardens* in 1955 entitled "How They're Cleaning Up the Comic Books"—and no mention, as he outlined the "stern self-censorship" publishers were pursuing to purge comics of everything from sex to cannibalism and bad grammar, that Weisinger was not a disinterested investigator but a top editor at America's biggest comic book publisher.

In the end, Weisinger's 1960s remake of Superman was more earth-shifting than any changes the Man of Steel had undergone before, including when Jerry softened him up in the earliest years. Mort was a master plotter. His stories planted the hook with unexpected twists and threats—always by page six of a nine-page story—then reeled in young readers. His formula was to start with a thesis (Lois wants to marry Superman), follow with an antithesis (she is so obsessed she blackmails him into matrimony), and end with a synthesis (she backs out when she realizes an accident has changed her personality and takes a drug that cures her). That became a problem, though: His writers adhered to his rules so faithfully that a refreshing wackiness started looking predictable, and the writers started feeling creatively castrated. Even more limiting was Mort's focus on marketing gimmicks like ultra-powered villains and robotic universes when what kids craved was the hero's humanity and fallibility. Human foibles came naturally to a scarred and human creature like Batman, but not to the infallible Superman. They had come naturally to Jerry and Joe, but not to Mort.

That might not have been such a problem if Superman and National had had the playing field to themselves. Stan Lee and Marvel Comics were not going to give them any such gift. In 1962 Marvel introduced Spider-Man and all his teenage hang-ups. He joined the Hulk and Fantastic Four, and a year later came the ultimate outsiders, the mutant X-Men. Here was a new breed of superhero, insecure, vulnerable, and realistic—a dramatic and intentional challenge to the self-assured, all-powerful brand that was National's specialty. "I wanted to get characters," longtime Marvel boss Lee explains, "whose personal lives were as interesting as their superhero identity." What he really wanted, and found, was the anti-Superman. National now faced a dilemma that was partly of its own making, since it had hounded out of business heroes who were distant facsimiles of Superman and had stressed the Man of Steel's plots over his soul. Even the parent company's name, National Comics Publications, evoked a Wall Street stuffiness, one that fans on Main Street countered by referring to the publisher by its original title of Detective Comics or, simpler still, DC. Now upstart Marvel Comics was unveiling champions who really were different, posing a choice for every comics-reading adolescent who grew up in the 1960s and beyond: Superman or Spider-Man? DC or Marvel?

Spider-Man kids loved romance, Superman disciples were more classicists. It was the choice between the let-it-rip rapture of Little Richard and the self-contained genius of Duke Ellington. Marvel was in your face, the way Robert Maxwell and Phyllis Coates had been.

DC was softer-edged, like Whitney Ellsworth and Noel Neill. The competition between the two brands of superhero began slowly, but by the mid-sixties it had become fierce. Looking back, it has the feel of a friendly family squabble; at the time it was a cultural chasm, one built around beliefs so basic some still resonate a half century afterward.

Unused to that sort of challenge, DC second-guessed itself and its standard-bearer. The problem, however, wasn't Superman himself, who "done correctly was the greatest hero of all times. It was his writers who were out of touch, who were all about gimmicks and twists rather than honest emotion," says Jim Shooter, who was about to turn thirteen when he sold his first Superman story to Weisinger and who later became Marvel's top editor. "I was a kid and I knew how kids talked," Shooter explains. Mort realized he was in trouble as Spider-Man sales took off, but the realization came late. And the competition wasn't just Spider-Man: DC's own Sgt. Rock spoke in a way that Superman didn't to young people struggling with issues like the Vietnam War. Though Mort brought in young talent to help restore the youthful energy and relevance that Jerry and Joe had captured by instinct, it wasn't enough and it wasn't in time. The Superman family of comic books stayed the top sellers through the 1960s, but their sales were falling and their lead shrinking. Batman tumbled earlier and deeper, to the point where *Superman's Girl Friend Lois Lane* was outselling him and National contemplated killing off the Caped Crusader; he was saved by his campy TV show, which started in 1966. Marvel, meanwhile, was in the ascendant. The company not only had heroes in tune with the times, its ongoing storylines made young readers worry about missing a single issue the same way their grandmothers did about missing their TV soaps.

The declining sales and his increasingly grating style would put Mort Weisinger's job in jeopardy when new owners took over in 1968 and his patron Jack Liebowitz could no longer protect him. He admitted later he was losing touch with a new generation of kids and their notions about heroes and villains. He said he had tried for years to leave, repeatedly asking for raises big enough to ensure he'd be turned down—but he never was. Finally, as he reported afterward, he walked away in 1970. Carmine Infantino, the editorial director who had called Weisinger a "damn good editor," says it didn't happen quite that way: "Mort said, 'I'd like to stay.' And I said, 'No, Mort, I think it's time you moved on.'"

THE SUPERMAN UNIVERSE THAT Mort Weisinger left behind was more expansive than the world of any character in the comics, and perhaps in all of fiction. It began on a reimagined Krypton. In Jerry Siegel's first rendering, back in 1938, the planet lasted a single panel and had a simple, utilitarian purpose: to die so Superman could begin his life on Earth. Now that multiple comic book plots had to be contrived and more material was constantly needed, Otto Binder and other Weisinger writers had the chance to linger on Superman's planet of origin and make it into a jeweled paradise. The Gold Volcano spewed that precious metal instead of lava. Shrinkwater Lake reduced men to the size of ants. Pink leopardlike creatures had horns like unicorns' and, when they got angry, spit fire. Robots did all the hard work, the last war had ended thousands of years ago, and weather towers purified the air and stage-managed the seasons. It was a world that fulfilled science fiction's promise of a planet better than our own, anticipating the kind of intergalactic order that Gene Roddenberry would construct several years later for *Star Trek*. Krypton had gone from a mere launching pad to a wonderland that gave young readers goose bumps as they peered at the stars.

The most emotional of the Krypton tales was written in 1960 by Jerry Siegel, who got a three-part, twenty-six-page story called "Superman's Return to Krypton!" to fill in arcs in the plot he had rushed through more than twenty years before. A fully grown Superman found himself on Krypton before its destruction. He got to know his father and see the sacrifice his mother made by placing him in a rocket meant for her. He fell in love with the Kryptonian movie star Lyla Lerrol and imagined the life he might have lived on this faraway planet. He was getting the chance every child dreams of to see his parents when they were kids, especially boys like Kal-El and Jerry who had been robbed of their fathers, and Jerry was getting the opportunity every writer covets to spruce up an old story. Finally, Superman could purge himself of his survivor's guilt by seeing firsthand that there was nothing he could have done to rescue his planet or his mother and father. "It's impossible for me to save Lyla or my parents!" he told himself as he decided not to perish with them. "Earth needs me!"

The image of Kal-El as Krypton's solitary survivor was a central thesis of Jerry's early narratives. As heartrending as that was, it made for a lonely existence and made it difficult for Superman to learn about his past. Upon revisiting Superman's origins, Jerry discovered that his original thesis was wrong: Others had survived, too. Krypto, baby Superman's dog, had been blasted into space by Jor-El as a test before he dared launch his son. Miraculously, Krypto eventually drifted to Earth and into the arms of Kal-El, who could hardly resist this headstrong canine dressed in a crimson cape. Beppo the Super-Monkey and Titano the Super-Ape took similar paths to Earth. They would be joined by two other super-pets—Comet the Super-Horse and Streaky the Super-Cat—neither of whom came from Krypton but both of whom became members of the Legion of Super-Pets and delighted youthful audiences.

The fellow Kryptonian who gave Superman the greatest joy, and the most sleepless nights, was his cousin Kara Zor-El, known on Earth as Supergirl. While she wasn't launched as a character until 1959, we quickly got the full story. She and all of Argo City had been hurled into the cosmos when the rest of Krypton exploded. Later, when the orbiting Argo itself was threatened, Kara's father launched the child in a spaceship headed for Earth. Save for gender, her story mirrored her famous cousin's: She assumed a secret identity as the pigtailed Linda Lee, she had adoptive parents named Fred and Edna Danvers, she shunned her male admirers, and she had superpowers that she used to help humankind. The Maid of Steel, who would get her own comic book shortly after Mort Weisinger left National, gave Superman a blood relative and fellow outsider with whom he could let down his defenses. If youths of all stripes embraced Superboy, now girls had a heroine made in their own special image. And if H. G. Wells's *The War of the Worlds* had given aliens a bad name, Supergirl and Superman polished the image of the interplanetary interloper.

Argo wasn't the only city to outlast the cataclysm on Krypton. Its capital, Kandor, had been stolen by the space pirate Brainiac, who shrank it to microscopic size and saved it inside a glass bottle in his spacecraft. Superman eventually recovered the bottle and brought it to Earth. While he was able to shrink himself down to Kandorians' size so he could visit with them, he couldn't enlarge the city or its residents. Kandor, like all of Weisinger's inventions, opened up marketing and storytelling possibilities. It gave readers a dollhouse world where they could see sun lamps that mimicked Krypton's red sun, mental suggestion helmets that aided the mentally deficient, and jet-powered flying belts. Superman's enemies now had a way to get at him—via his defenseless fellow Kryptonians—and they never stopped trying. Kandor also made clear that even Superman couldn't get everything he wanted, since there was nothing he wanted more than to restore the Kandorians to their rightful size.

Superman kept Kandor and everything else that mattered most in his Fortress of Solitude, hidden on the side of a snowbank deep in the Arctic. It was a museum to his life as the Last Son of Krypton. There was a room in honor of Batman and Robin and another dedicated to Supergirl. He kept his atomic-powered robots there, and when he had a free minute he loved challenging them to a tug of war. There were rooms memorializing his birth parents from Krypton and his adopted ones on Earth. There was even a Doghouse of Solitude for the Dog of Steel, although it was situated in outer space rather than at the North Pole. The same way Superman's identity as Clark gave him a break from being Superman, his time at the Fortress let him get away from the pressures of being a hero and a reporter.

Brainiac, Kandor's kidnapper, looked human but was actually a computer. Two giveaways were his green skin and the lightbulbs in his head. Another was his tenth-level intelligence, which made him nearly twice as smart as a clever human. Each of Superman's recurring enemies claimed to be the most menacing and wicked, but none could back up the claim like this emotionless genius with infinite memory who had an unrivaled mastery of science and engineering and was programmed with a single-minded focus on wreaking havoc. He, or it, embodied everything that Space Age America worshipped and feared about technology. At the other end of the evil-genius spectrum was Lex Luthor, Superman's longtime archenemy, who was as smart as any human if not as smart as a computer—and made up for the gap with a kill-Superman obsession no artificial intelligence could match. While he first showed up in 1940, it was not until the 1960s that we learned the source of his hatred. Growing up together in Smallville, he and Superman had been friends, until an accident at Luthor's laboratory made him go bald, an accident he mistakenly blamed on the teenage superhero. Their clashes over the years were made more interesting because each craved what the other had—Lex wanted Superman's powers, Superman envied Lex's humanness.

Bizarro was Superman's twisted mirror image, built from lifeless matter and brought into the world by a scientist showing off his new duplicating ray. With a face the color of chalk and the texture of chiseled stone, the Thing of Steel got everything backward. He used dirt to wash himself instead of water, showed his respect for women by pulling their chairs out from under them, and took as his motto, "Anything Superman kin fix, us kin fix worser!" While he wore Superman's cape and colors, he looked more like Frankenstein. Bizarro, who first surfaced in 1958, offered a compelling device for Superman's writers: He made clear what Superman stood for—from impeccable hygiene to unmatched chivalry—but by doing so in reverse and tongue-in-cheek, he made the hero sound less preachy or self-righteous. Bizarro's monstrous imitation of Superman would have been straight-out funny if he hadn't had Superman's powers, which sometimes made him deadly and always made readers glad the real thing was around to save the day and end the story.

The enemy that had posed the greatest risk to Superman since it first surfaced on the airwaves in 1943 was kryptonite, which in the pre–Mort Weisinger days was a rare element and afterward cropped up all the time. Remnants of the planet Krypton at first were red, then gray, but writers finally settled on green for the metal that in small doses weakened Superman and with prolonged exposure would be fatal. Mort, however, decided that if a little kryptonite made for a good story more would be better, and he tapped the rainbow in coming up with new plots. Gold kryptonite robbed Superman of the powers that made him super. Blue was dangerous only to creatures from the Bizarro world, while the only life that white kryptonite could take was a plant's. Red-green was Brainiac's idea, and the combination was a double-edged sword: It gave Superman an eye he didn't need on the back of his head, but it provided him the extra heat vision he needed to lick the computer genius. Red-gold gave the hero temporary amnesia. Red kryptonite was Mort's favorite threat; it was able to split Superman in two or turn him into an ant. While its effects were unpredictable, as with anything Weisinger-related there were rules: Each scarlet-tinted piece had a unique impact, it worked on Superman just once, and its fallout lasted at most forty-eight hours.

Kara Zor-El, Krypto, and the other super spin-offs made clear how popular Superman was and how determined his handlers were to cash in on his legacy. They said the new additions were to keep Superman from feeling like he was on his own. Mort also used the evolving storyline to unite his universe, bringing old books like *Action* in line with the stories in new ones like *Superboy*. Mostly the changes were in response to the dip in sales of the Superman comics in the 1950s, and they paid off, at least at first. The Superman family led the rebirth of the costumed hero the same way it had the birth. National made no effort to disguise its devotion to the Man of Steel: In its annual report, the spot typically saved for a picture of the company president was instead used for a drawing of Superman, looking statuesque with his hands on his hips and his cape flowing behind him.

But Weisinger's innovations were taking a quiet toll on the story. Superman's world had become so complicated that readers needed a map or even an encyclopedia to keep track of everyone and everything. (There would eventually be encyclopedias, two in fact, but the first did not appear until 1978.) All the plot complications were beguiling to devoted readers, who loved the challenge of keeping current, but to more casual fans they could be exhausting. Still, Mort pushed ahead, soliciting ideas from neighborhood kids as well as readers and, at their urging, ordering up stories on Superman serving as a fireman (super-breath comes in handy), a postman (easy when you can fly), and even a millionaire (he gave it all away). Superman got a Social Security number (092-09-6616) and an honorary passport to the United Nations, which would have come in handy since he now was appearing in thirty countries. Before executing a new plot twist,

Mort would test it on his adolescent son, Hank, the same way "Jungle Sam" Katzman had on his; if Hank guessed the ending too fast, Mort would look for something more demanding.

It was easy to see the direction Mort was taking Superman's closest pals: He was dumbing them down and softening them up. Lois was more of a glamour gal now and less of a shrew or a barrier breaker. She had gone from being a dogged reporter to being fixated on proving that Clark was Superman and on landing Superman for herself. The very name of her comic book—*Superman's Girl Friend Lois Lane*—suggested the shift in tone, which happened just as the women's movement was firing up. No plotlines here about Lois taking birth control pills or burning her bras. Likewise, Jimmy was less interested in covering the news than making it. He had run-ins with aliens and sorcerers, and he had an ultrasonic watch that he used to signal Superman whenever he needed bailing out, which was usually. What he didn't do was experiment with marijuana, sex, or any of the other forbidden pleasures so tempting to teens of his generation. Even Superman himself was not quite the same. He was less of a firebrand, more of a smoothie. And while it was only in his imagination and comic strip dreams that he or Clark would marry Lois, he was affectionate enough to give little boys the shivers.

One thing neither Mort nor Jerry had trouble with was naming their characters. Both began with the premise that every name had to have two *L*s, ideally at the start. Jerry had signaled where he was headed with his spelling of Superman's Kryptonian name, Kal-L. The second-most important person in the Superman universe—Lois Lane—was the first to have the *L*s take their place up front. Lois's sister was Lucy Lane, while her parents were Ella and Samuel. Lana Lang, Superboy's neighbor and best friend, had a father named Lewis and siblings christened Larry, Alvin, and Ronald. Enemy number one originally had just one name, Luthor, but in 1960 editors decided to soften him up by adding a given name, Lex. His sister was Lena, his parents Lionel and Letitia, and Aunt Lena helped raise him. Over the years Superman, Superboy, or Clark fell in love with Lyla Lerrol, Sally Selwyn, Lyrica Lloyd, Lal Leta, Lahla, and Lori Lemaris, whose sister was Lenora. Superboy would team up with Lightning Lad and Lightning Lass against Lightning Lord.

Why the letter *L* and the alliterations? Jerry never said, nor did Mort. Not even Superman was talking. When Supergirl told him that she had chosen the name Linda Lee for her disguise, he commented how, "by sheer coincidence," she had picked the same initials as everyone else he held close. The truth was it was just for fun. The echo appealed not just to the ears of his writers and editors but to young readers, just as with fan favorites like Peter Parker, Bruce Banner, Archie Andrews, Mickey Mouse, and Bugs Bunny. Once Jerry got the style rolling, Mort turned it into a game for readers, scores of whom wrote in whenever they uncovered a new one or wondered why someone as close to Superman as Jimmy didn't have the two *L*s. Mort's answer: He did. Don't you remember the TV episode "The Talkative Dummy," which revealed Jimmy's full name as James Bartholomew Olsen?

SUPERMAN AS A song-and-dance man? It sounded like one of Mort Weisinger's imaginary stories. The Man of Tomorrow had triumphed in so many settings that a crew of theater people decided to give him a tryout in 1966. And this was not just any crew, it was Broadway's finest. Producer Harold Prince was on the way to making *Fiddler on the Roof* the first musical to run for more than three thousand performances. Music master Charles Strouse and his lyricist partner, Lee Adams, nearly swept the Tony Awards with *Bye Bye Birdie,* while scriptwriters Robert Benton and David Newman were a year away from their blockbuster movie *Bonnie and Clyde.* No one had ever tried before to build a musical around a comic character, but Superman was used to being first and no one had ever lost money gambling on him.

Jack and Harry gave their blessing in return for a modest share of the profits and—to protect the franchise—a promise that the play couldn't be called *Superman.* So the production was named *It's a Bird . . . It's a Plane . . . It's Superman.* Money wasn't a problem either: With Columbia Records on board, Hal Prince was able to raise half a million dollars. Strouse, Benton, and their partners had come up with a doozie of a story, in words and notes: Dr. Abner Sedgwick was convinced he had been cheated out of the Nobel Prize, not once but ten times, and he planned to make the world pay by eliminating its beloved Superman. When force didn't work, the mad scientist turned to psychology. In order to convince the people of Metropolis that Superman couldn't save them, he bombed City Hall while the hero was distracted, then persuaded Superman that he was a Man of Straw for doing nothing. "You're not stopping crime," Sedgwick insisted, "all you're doing is catching criminals after the fact." The logic was compelling. "Could that be true?" Superman asked. "Why must the strongest man in the world be the bluest man—tell me why?" Those were the kinds of questions Spider-Man might have asked himself, but not Superman, or at least not Mort Weisinger's Colossus of Krypton. Before the curtain fell, Benton and Newman's superhero recovered both his confidence and his powers in the nick of time.

The play blended the drama of the *Adventures of Superman* TV show with the burlesque of the comics for what looked like a winning touch of satire. Even the flying, which had stumped serial and TV producers, worked here by keeping it simple. A flying harness of light leather was strapped onto Superman's chest, upper arms, and back. A wire attached to a wooden clip and pulleys whisked him six feet above the stage. Making this work in front of an audience was a lot to ask, but theatergoers wanted more than anyone to believe. And the producers brought in the same technical staff that had made Mary Martin fly in *Peter Pan* and Tammy Grimes in *High Spirits.*

Hal Prince and his team knew enough about Superman to realize that everything turned not on stunts or even the story but on finding the right hero. So, like Bob Maxwell and Sam Katzman before them, they launched a far-reaching search. They didn't need a Broadway star to fit this bill; they would have plenty with Jack Cassidy, Linda Lavin, and the rest of the cast. The specs for Superman: He should stand six feet six inches and weigh 190 pounds. A seventeen-inch neck would be ideal, along with biceps of a minimum of eighteen and a half inches. Mid-thirties was the right age. Black hair was a must, along with blue eyes and legs that looked good in tights. And of course he had to know how to act, sing, and fly. Fifty-two actors showed up, including an Olympic pole vaulter and a bass-baritone from the New York City Opera. One fit the bill: Bob Holiday, a thirty-three-year-old singer and comedian on the supper club circuit. He had served overseas in the Army, spinning records for the Armed Services Network, and had been in a Broadway play once, singing the opening song. Most important, he weighed 190 pounds, stood six feet four, and had grown up as an only child in Brooklyn with Superman his favorite comic book friend. When he heard he had the part "a chill went through me. I said, '*Thank you. Thank you.*'"

To show his gratitude Holiday visited the gym every other day for up to two hours, curling hundred-pound weights and pressing 160 pounds. Breakfast consisted of powdered protein, milk, and wheat germ. Smoking was out, which wasn't easy for a two-pack-a-day guy, as was drinking in public. It all paid off when, after every performance, he would invite hundreds of kids backstage, letting them take their best shot at his midriff. It also helped when he fell from his harness, dropping six feet onto the stage. He bounced back up, turned to the audience as if it were rehearsed, and said, to a standing ovation, "That would have hurt any mortal man."

The first test of what an audience thought of *It's a Bird* was in February, in an out-of-town run in the historically loving city of Philadelphia. Not this time. "Is it low camp, high camp, medium camp? Is it a musical parody or a cartoon with music?" asked the Philadelphia *Bulletin*. The libretto, chimed in the *Philadelphia Daily News*, "has a form of humor but no great shining wit," while Strouse and Adams's songbook "only faintly recalls the animation these collaborators brought to *Bye Bye Birdie*." Disappointed but not done in, the creative team went back to work. The lead song was cut and a new showstopper written. Scenes were altered, costumes revised, and when there wasn't time to make the desired changes, outfits were simply turned inside out. Even the pricing at the Alvin Theatre was redone to give the New York opening its best shot. Prince offered the broadest range of rates on Broadway—two dollars at the bargain end, aimed at drawing a new and young audience, with the orchestra split into eight-, ten-, and twelve-dollar options, the last of which was $1.50 more than for any other musical and was meant to subsidize the cheap seats. It was equally novel to offer a third off the high-priced seats for early mail orders, and it worked: Advance sales topped those for *Fiddler* and Prince's Pulitzer Prize—winning *Fiorello!*

It's a Bird opened on Broadway in mid-March, with Mayor John V. Lindsay and much of the city's establishment on hand. Reviewers were there as well, and their verdicts were up-and-down. *Time* called it "amiable mediocrity . . . capable only of inspiring benign indifference." *The Washington Post* wrote that "on its appointed level of simple-minded casualness it works quite nicely." The New York papers were more generous, with the *Morning Telegraph* labeling it "a musical show loaded with entertainment" and the *World-Telegram and Sun* saying, "You leave the theater smiling, and the smile lasts all the way home." The biggest rave came from the highest-minded paper, *The New York Times,* whose critic Stanley Kauffmann pronounced the play "easily the best musical so far this season, but, because that is so damp a compliment, I add at once that it would be enjoyable in any season."

Prince was convinced he had a smash hit until he called the box office. "They said, 'My God, we haven't sold a single new seat.'" He, like nearly everyone involved with the production, felt like a kid again doing the show, and they all assumed the audience would grow to love it. The timing seemed perfect: Andy Warhol and Roy Lichtenstein were at the height of their popularity, and nobody better defined that pop art craze than the Man of Steel. But the wave had already crested and the crowds at the Alvin started shrinking two months in. Despite an unprecedented four matinees a week and a flurry of ads in the comic books, the curtain fell for the last time on July 17, after just three and a half months and 129 performances.

Everyone had a theory on what went wrong. "It should have had a little more muscle, and some teeth politically. We should have made it about the times," Prince says, looking back to the era when America was shipping young men en masse to fight in Southeast Asia and record numbers of draft dodgers were fleeing to Canada. To Strouse, the trouble was a combination of summer camp and "Capelash." Some kids were away swimming and boating when the show was playing, while others were watching a superhero for free on the new TV show *Batman,* which was such a hit it aired twice a week. To Benton, the difficulty was the very nature of his Superman story and whom it appealed to: "It was not a children's show and not an adult show. It sort of fell between the two."

Prince went on to produce and direct nearly sixty plays and win a record-setting twenty-one Tony Awards. Strouse wrote the music for twenty-two plays and six movies, including *Bonnie and Clyde*. Benton would make his name with films like *Kramer vs. Kramer* and *Twilight*. While *It's a Bird* was a mere footnote in their careers, for Holiday it was the highlight, just as playing Superman had been for Kirk Alyn and George Reeves. It had taken him onto the TV show *I've Got a Secret,* where he got to joke with Steve Allen and flirt with Miss America. He was a guest on Johnny Carson's *Tonight Show* and got to recast his Superman role in stage performances in St. Louis and Kansas City. And it had brought him to Broadway, which was a memory that kept him going as he became a home builder in the Pocono Mountains. "I don't think that the supposed 'Superman curse' hit me at all," he says. "It's still a kick to let people know that I was the Man of Steel. My doctor even hangs a picture of me in his office so that all his patients know he fixed Superman right up."

As for Superman himself, he escaped largely unscathed. The critics blamed not him but his handlers. The handlers learned valuable lessons, which they would apply repeatedly. The first was that when people had to pay to see Superman, the target audience should be adults who hopefully would bring along the kids. It also made sense, for a wildly popular character like the Man of Steel, to showcase him in mass media rather than a rarefied venue like a Broadway theater. Strouse and Prince say they wish they'd had a chance to put those lessons to the test. Benton and Newman did. A dozen years after *It's a Bird* closed, their names were listed in the writing credits for the first major superhero feature film: *Superman: The Movie*.

SUPERMAN WAS EVERYWHERE IN the 1960s. Audiences hooted when the director brought him onstage for the opera *Carmen* in Bologna, while three hundred thousand subscribers cheered when Superman comics finally appeared in West Germany. Forty-two countries, from Brazil to Lebanon, were translating every issue of the American comic book into their native tongues, which gave the Swedes a hero called Stålmannen, the Mexicans a caped cousin named Superniña, the Dutch an intrepid lady reporter whose byline read

Louise Laan, and the Arabic world an undercover male reporter named Nabil Fawzi who worked for the newspaper Al-Kawkab Al Yawmi. Andy Warhol hand-painted Superman into universal pop art fame. Superman and his family were the objects of parody in a comic called *Stupor-Man,* which also featured Stupor-Snake, Stupor-Rhino, Stupor-Grandpa, and Stupor-Old-Maid-Auntie. He was a star of Jules Feiffer's *The Great Comic Book Heroes,* which helped lift comic books to the status of high art even as its author prayed they would remain the lowest common denominator of America's fantasy life. "When *Superman* at last appeared," Feiffer reminisced in 1965, "he brought with him the deep satisfaction of all underground truths: our reaction was less 'How original!' than 'But, of course!' "

That was the reaction kids across America had when a new version of an animated Superman turned up on their TV screens in 1966, two months after Bob Holiday's Man of Steel took his final bows on Broadway. Youngsters who knew the hero from the comics thrilled at seeing him take on new shapes as well as new adventures. Those seeing him for the first time felt the glow of first love that their parents and grandparents had with Max and Dave Fleischer's cartoons a quarter century before. The show was aimed especially at young children but its title, *The New Adventures of Superman,* was chosen to appeal to older viewers who remembered popular programs of the same name on the radio in the 1940s and on TV in the 1950s. Much of what they heard and saw this time was brand-new: the first appearance in TV cartoons by Jimmy Olsen, Lex Luthor, and Mr. Mxyzptlk; the first time the cartoons came in six-minute features; and the first packaging of Superman shorts with ones starring Superboy and other DC stars, a twist that brought with it name changes to *The Superman/ Aquaman Hour of Adventure, The Batman/Superman Hour,* and finally back to reruns with the familiar if ironic title of *The New Adventures of Superman.*

The *New Adventures* borrowed more from the past than they changed. Filmation Studios, the producers, used the same low-budget rotoscoping technique the Fleischers had, tracing real-life characters frame by frame. Collyer was back as the voices of Clark and Superman, Joan Alexander reprised her radio role as Lois, Jackson Beck was again the narrator, and Jack Grimes returned in the role of Jimmy, which he had played during the last year of the radio show. Allen Ducovny, Bob Maxwell's partner on the radio show, was executive producer of these cartoons, which may explain why "Up, up, and away" was heard so often. The animated series conjured up one more specter from the past: the censors. This time they took the form of a grassroots group called Action for Children's Television, and their primary target was a worthy one: commercialism aimed at kids. The group, founded in 1968 outside Boston, hated being branded a censor, but that was the effect when it complained that there were too many punches thrown on the Superman cartoons. The result: The series was canceled in 1970, after its third full season.

Given the alarms being sounded by do-gooders, the last place one would have expected to find the Man of Steel was in the schoolhouse. But he had been there for twenty years, helping teach grammar to kids in thousands of classrooms. The number of unique words in a year of Superman comics was twice the vocabulary of the average fourth grader, studies found, and reading his adventures could help adolescents expand their language. Working with a high school teacher from Lynn, Massachusetts, National Comics in the early 1940s had prepared a Superman workbook with lessons on punctuation, grammar, and usage. Teachers across the country jumped aboard. As for the kids, "they loved it," reported *Magazine Digest.* "Children who had been bucking English grammar for years found themselves painlessly answering such questions as 'What punctuation mark ends Superman's speech?' and 'What kind of sentence does he use?' The sugar coating had been found for the pill."

Ron Massengill remembers the first compound word that he learned: Superman. "I couldn't read *bye-bye* but I could read *Superman.* There was the big *S* leading to the small *n.* I was sure I had seen that at the drug store or the grocery store," says Massengill, who was born the same year as the Superman comic book and has been a fan since he was a toddler. "Within four months I could read a Superman comic book all the way through. My mom had bought a dictionary, a huge dictionary that weighed like twenty pounds. She explained to me when I saw these groupings of letters in the comics that I could go through and find that grouping in the dictionary." Even more kids might have been using Superman in even more classrooms had it not been for Dr. Wertham, who convinced many parents and teachers in the 1940s and 1950s that it was dangerous to let comic books anywhere near their children.

By the 1960s, as the age of peaceniks and flower children gained steam, Wertham's influence had waned and Superman's had risen to the point that even the White House was laying out the red carpet. The Kennedy administration wanted the hero's help spreading the word about its campaign to close the "muscle gap." Mort Weisinger put two of his best writers on the story, which he called "Superman's Mission for President Kennedy." The Champion of Democracy flew across America pushing young runners to run harder, hurdlers to jump higher, and flabby journalists at the *Daily Planet* to do fifteen minutes a day of calisthenics. When *The New York Times* got wind of the preparations it scooped the comic book with an article headlined SUPERMAN MEETS KENNEDY ON VIGOR.

Weisinger's story was all set to run but was pulled back when the president was assassinated in November 1963. Shortly afterward, Weisinger got a call from President Lyndon Johnson saying, "We're waiting for the story. When's it coming out?" Mort explained his worry that running it might be in bad taste, at which point, as he recalled the tale, Johnson interrupted: "Horsefeathers. You can run it with a posthumous foreword, explaining that *I* ordered it!" Mort did.

It was not the first time President Kennedy had teamed up with Superman. That was in 1962, when Superman was ready to introduce his cousin Supergirl to the world and brought her to the White House to meet the president. High drama, indeed: The Camelot president on the same stage with the Lancelot of comic book heroes. More than a year later Superman took Kennedy into his confidence, sharing his dual identity as Clark Kent. "I'll guard your secret identity as I guard the secrets of our nation!" JFK promised, to which Superman replied, "If I can't trust the President of the United States, who can I trust?" The exchange took on a special poignance when the comic book, which was printed while the president was alive, showed up on newsstands just after he was gunned down in Dallas. There was one other time when the name Jack Kennedy had appeared in Superman's comic books. It was in the very first of the *Superman* series, in July 1939. A character named Kennedy was murdered and the newly

minted Man of Steel saved a wrongly accused man from being executed.

Inside Jack and Harry's business operations, there was a flurry of
activity that kept the cash registers ringing in the 1960s, though
Harry was less involved than ever. Ivy Leaguer Paul Sampliner, who
had supplied Harry with much-appreciated cash back during the Depression, remained the definition of the compliant partner, more interested in being a socialite and civic leader than a business executive.
Jack, as always, was looking for ways to boost profits and minimize
risks. As early as 1945 he had explored taking the company public,
and he would have done so if the stock market had been more bullish.
He tried again in 1961, but his broker said the stock exchange would
approve the arrangement only if Harry wasn't part of it. "His reputation," Jack wrote, "was not too good. His way of life was quite well
known in New York." Jack offered to make Harry, technically still his
boss, a millionaire if he resigned from the company. Harry took the
bait. Jack became president, with Sampliner still on the board. That
night, as Jack recalled, "I guess he [Harry] celebrated, he was drunk
and he fell on his head, was in a coma for weeks. He never knew that
we went public. Never knew." Doctors operated on Harry but there
was nothing they could do. He spent the last four years of his life with
round-the-clock nurses and no memory. He learned to recognize his
two children, his sister-in-law, and his mistress, but that was the ex-
tent of his engagement with the world. Harry died in February 1965,
when he was seventy-one and the comic book hero who made him
famous was twenty-six.

It was no way to go, and forty years later theories still percolate that
Harry's death might not have been an accident. That is what happens
when you live life as hard as he did and mix with people who make
accidents happen. Harry had spent his adult life in a marriage he
wanted out of and he had finally found a way. Gussie, his wife, had
just died and he was set to marry Sunny, his mistress. His fall put an
end to that. Peachy, his daughter, agrees with Jack that Harry's fall
was a drunken accident, but she adds, "We all said that momma came
down from heaven and kicked him."

Jack was no sentimentalist but he, too, celebrated the company's
listing on the stock exchange, not by getting drunk but by having a

chauffeur drive him to his old haunts across Manhattan. There was
the Lower East Side tenement where he had slept on the roof and
shared a bed with brothers Harry, Lenny, and Mac. He helped out all
three over the years with money and advice. (None did anything with
his largesse, or even said thanks.) Next stop was the Ladies' Garment
Workers' office, or at least the building where it used to be, and
where Jack used to be an idealist. On to Greenwich Village and New
York University, which taught him that he could be more than a
bookkeeper and gave him the skills and worldview of an accountant.
It was a *This Is Your Life*–type revisiting, shared not with a TV
audience—that was not Jack's style—but by himself and reconstructed
later for his two girls. His was an American success story—a Jewish
success story, of a boy from the Ukrainian ghetto making not good
but great. All accomplished, as he told older daughter, Linda, with
"no help from anybody."

After the nostalgic tour it was back to business. Jack's distribution
arm, Independent News, had always been his biggest moneymaker
and had helped National stay afloat in the 1950s when other comic
book companies were dying. Being a book distributor not only meant
that Jack trucked publishers' products from printer to wholesaler, it
made him their banker and gatekeeper. Major Wheeler-Nicholson
had seen what a vise that could be in the 1930s and now National's
biggest competitor, Marvel Comics, was learning the lesson. Independent had taken over as Marvel's distributor and Jack limited the
publisher to a dozen titles a month—a third of its peak output and
too few to unseat National as king of the comics. "We didn't want
the competition," Jack explained in his memoir. He handled *Playboy,*
too, which added thirty-five thousand dollars a month to his bottom
line, along with *Mad* magazine, whose sales he boosted from two
hundred thousand an issue to one million. By the 1960s, Independent
was America's largest distributor of magazines and paperbacks, and it
soon became a player in Europe, too. Jack's nephew Jay Emmett was
doing almost as well with his licensing business, cashing in on the
success not just of the over-the-top *Batman* TV show but of James
Bond's über-adventure movies. The numbers no longer were in the
hundreds of thousands of dollars, or even the millions. "These were

large accounts," Jack said of National's diversified holdings. "Tens of millions of dollars."

That money was pouring in to the newly christened National Periodical Publications, Inc., which included both the distribution and publishing operations. Revenues rose still higher in 1961 when National raised the price of its comics from a dime to twelve cents. But the bookkeeper in Jack couldn't keep his eyes off the expense side of the ledger. He knew from his days with the Ladies' Garment Workers how unions could boost employees' wages and benefits, and he wasn't about to let that happen in his shop. So when his workers had talked about a union in the 1950s, he had squashed the effort. When union talk resurfaced in the mid-1960s—talk of veteran freelancers getting health insurance, higher page rates, and partial ownership of the comics characters they created—Jack took a more subtle approach. He turned what became known as the Writers' Rebellion over to his lawyers to study. He said he'd go along with a union if Marvel's publisher would—knowing he wouldn't. Jack gave bonuses to artists who steered clear of the activists, knowing that artists were harder to replace than writers. "[Jack] turned to me at one point during the negotiations to say: 'You don't understand, I'm very sympathetic to the points you're making. When I was a young man, I was a Socialist, too!'" recalled writer Arnold Drake. "The problem was that Liebowitz had a youth of twenty minutes."

The rabble-rousers disappeared, slowly enough that it wasn't until years later that anyone realized how thorough the housecleaning had been. Few old hands were fired outright; rather, they were assigned to lesser comics, given fewer assignments, and supplanted by younger writers who had no idea they were scabs. Mort sided with Jack, as he always had, unaware that he, too, would one day be expendable. Not even Harry had been immune. It wasn't just National that was taking a hard line. Comic book publishers, as Drake said, had always run their businesses like brothels: "They were the madames, and the writers and artists were the girls."

To anyone who accused him of miserliness, Jack could tick off the names of all the employees and relatives he had helped buy a home or pay for a daughter's marriage. What better sign of his generosity could there be than lending yet another hand to the biggest ingrate he had ever hired? It happened in 1959, when Jerry Siegel once again was desperate. He had worked for other publishers, but these jobs never lasted long enough or ended the way he wanted. He and Joanne had been living in a one-bedroom apartment in Great Neck with their baby, Laura. The landlord had threatened eviction, the milk company and diaper service had cut off deliveries, and he couldn't make child-support payments for his and Bella's son, Michael. He went on a hunger strike. He wrote to the media. He touched up friends and neighbors for help. Finally, after years of her pleading on Jerry's behalf, one of Joanne's letters to National got a reply. With Jack's blessing, Harry's son, Irwin Donenfeld, brought Superman's creator back, as a freelancer, at what Jerry said was ten dollars a page, forty dollars less than when he'd left a dozen years before.

Jerry wrote with passion and precision, scripting stories about Superman, Superboy, Supergirl, Lois, Jimmy, and the Legion of Super-Heroes. He invented characters for Mort Weisinger's new universe, from Colossal Boy to Triplicate Girl, Chameleon Boy, Ultra Boy, Shrinking Violet, Sun Boy, and Bouncing Boy. He got along with Mort as well as he could and avoided Jack as much as possible. The arrangement lasted until 1966, when it was clear that Jerry and Joe were planning another lawsuit to try to reclaim the Superman copyright. It took three more years for the suit to be filed and the court didn't rule until 1973. The result was the same "no" as before, only this time Jerry didn't ask for his job back, and if he had Jack wouldn't have given it to him.

Joe never made it back to National as an artist, but he did as a delivery boy. "I was the oldest messenger boy in New York City," he recalled years later about the jobs he had had as a sales clerk, janitor, or gopher. "One day I had to deliver a message to an office located in the same building as the publisher of DC Comics. Someone from their office saw me in the hall, asked me what I was doing there, then told the publisher about it later. He called me that night—very upset—and asked me to come into his office so he could help me out a little. 'How does it look,' he said, 'for the artist/creator of Superman to be running around delivering messages—you're giving us a bad name!'" It looked worse to see Joe milling in front of the Alvin

Theatre the night *It's a Bird* opened, watching ticket holders head in to see his superhero onstage and wishing he had the money to join them. Another time police picked him up in Central Park as a vagrant. After he lost his 1947 lawsuit and his artist's income, he moved in with his invalid mother in Forest Hills, Queens. Later he and his brother shared an apartment in Queens, among broken venetian blinds, sofas with springs poking through, and boxes of yellowing Superman comics.

The best measure of Joe's state of mind, and his finances, was the work he had taken but never breathed a word about: drawings of bare-skinned or nearly naked women being whipped, spanked, and humiliated by men and by other women. Joe didn't sign the illustrations, but they were his. Comics historian Craig Yoe knew it right away when he found the booklets stuffed in an old box at a 1989 antique book sale, and Shuster experts have confirmed it. Most of the women looked like Lois Lane. Some men were dead ringers for Jimmy Olsen and Slam Bradley. The co-publisher was Joe's neighbor. One set of pamphlets, *Nights of Horror,* was said to have inspired the 1954 rampage by a group of teens known as the Brooklyn Thrill Killers. Dr. Fredric Wertham visited the gang leader in jail, carrying a copy of *Nights of Horror* but not knowing who had illustrated it. Neither, apparently, did the Supreme Court of New York when it ordered in 1955 the destruction of all copies of the inch-thick pamphlets, which it said were "pornography, unadulterated by plot, moral or writing style. . . . The many drawings that embellish these stories are obviously intended to arouse unnatural desire and vicious acts."

Why did Joe do it? "Neither he nor Jerry could get work for anything decent, so he had to tender that stuff to make a buck," says his friend and Batman illustrator Jerry Robinson. "I don't think that's the work he would like to be remembered by." Yoe, an author and former creative director for the Muppets, agrees but offers two additional theories: Depicting Superman characters in compromising poses might have been a way to strike back at Jack and Harry for firing him and Jerry. It also could have reflected Joe's fantasy life. "My guess," Yoe concludes, "is that it's probably some of all three of those things."

Jack almost surely never saw the pornographic drawings and he probably never saw Joe after the lawsuit. His preoccupation, starting as early as 1960, was with who would take over the empire when he retired. He was turning sixty and his only heirs were his daughters, whom he didn't want to see working in his business or any other. "I spent all my life accumulating some wealth," he said in his memoir, "but I have nobody to leave it with." So he hired Felix Rohatyn, a high-powered investment banker who would later help save New York City from bankruptcy, to start looking for a takeover partner. It took until 1967 to find one: Kinney National Services, which owned funeral homes, parking lots, rental cars, and an office-cleaning company. It seemed an unlikely match to everyone but Jack, who wrote that "I liked the people, they were hamisha people. Jewish, Jewish oriented. And they had a business that was prosperous." What he didn't say was that Kinney carried the same whiff of not-so-kosher underworld connections that Jack and Harry's businesses had. What mattered in the end was that Kinney paid National $60 million and National gave Kinney the toehold it wanted in the entertainment business. Two years later Kinney bought the Warner Bros. movie studio, and two years after that Kinney renamed itself Warner Communications, Inc.

Jack got a seat on the Kinney board of directors, then on Warner's board. Irwin Donenfeld, Harry's son, got a lot of money, but he lost his job. So did Mort Weisinger. Jay Emmett, Jack's nephew and the whiz kid behind the Licensing Corporation of America, made out best, at least to begin with. He became best friends with and right-hand man to Steve Ross, the ingenious dealmaker behind Kinney and Warner, although Ross later sacrificed his best friend to save himself from a federal racketeering indictment. Emmett said that Kinney's purchase of National was a great move for everyone, but that Ross—an "imaginative genius"—never appreciated that the most important assets he was getting were Superman and Batman: "He had no idea of the worth of those characters, none. They were just two comic characters to him."

CHAPTER 8

Believing a Man Can Fly

BARELY REACHING FIVE FOOT THREE, with a mop of blue-rinsed white hair, Alexander Salkind brought to mind a mole man more than a Superman. His taste ran to white bucks, silk ascots, and jeweled lorgnettes, the elegant spectacles favored by operagoers. His suits were strictly powder blue and Savile Row, with a Légion d'honneur rosette proudly pinned to the wide lapel. He held court amid the faded opulence of luxury hotels and refused to ride an elevator or an airplane. His exotic accent, a thick blend of old-school Romance languages, left no doubt that English was not his native tongue. Indeed, his background was Russian, his homeland Germany, his citizenship Mexican, his ethnicity Jewish, and his passport that of a cultural attaché to Costa Rica. He had bankers in every capital in Europe yet had never paid a bill on time. But this son of Greta Garbo's film producer knew how to make movies—his production credits ranged from Orson Welles's *The Trial* to the blockbuster *The Three Musketeers.* In the spring of 1974 he was looking for the next big thing.

"Why don't we do Superman?" his son and protégé, Ilya, asked expectantly over dinner at the Café de la Paix in Paris.

"What's Superman?" Alex asked back.

Not an auspicious beginning for the man who was about to define the Last Son of Krypton for a new generation in America and around

the globe. But what he lacked in appreciation of popular culture Alex
made up for with his instinct that a world disillusioned by Vietnam and
Watergate might need a superman. This was the intuition of the Holocaust survivor—an understanding that it wasn't the particular myth
that mattered but our aspiring to something bigger. His own life had
always been defined half by suspicions and anxieties, half by defying
norms and accomplishing the impossible. That fearlessness—what was
a tax problem or lawsuit to someone who had been hunted by the
Gestapo?—was precisely what was needed to revive Superman more
than twenty years after his last radio broadcast and fifteen after his TV
show and its star died, when he was again the limited province of adolescent readers of comic books.

"I told my father who Superman was—that he flies, that he's as
known as Jesus Christ, that we can't do it tiny—and why it has to be
a big movie," Ilya recalls. "He said, 'Sounds very interesting, this Superman. Flies. Powers. Stronger. Known. Ahhh, let me talk a bit with
my people.'"

His people were bankers and other moneymen from Switzerland,
the Netherlands, Germany, Britain, and Chicago. Some were repu-
table while others skated on the edge. It was the same combination
that had worked for Harry and Jack over the years. Enough of them
approved to give Alex and Ilya confidence. More than enough. Looking back, even his lawyer concedes that Alex sold or traded more than
100 percent of the production, in the style of a Ponzi schemer or of
Max Bialystock, Mel Brooks's double-dealing producer. He didn't go
to jail only because the film made enough money to pay everyone off
handsomely.

Step two was getting Warner Communications, Superman's new
owner, to hand over the keys. Warner Bros. executives were busy
with their own big films—*Alice Doesn't Live Here Anymore, Night
Moves, Dog Day Afternoon*—and had never imagined Superman as
much more than a comic book. A buoyant superhero seemed an especially poor fit at a moment when the nation was reeling from one
of the deepest recessions since the 1930s along with the resignation
and pardoning of its disgraced president, Richard Milhous Nixon. So
whatever they thought of the elfin Alex and his slightly taller son,
Warner agreed, turning over twenty-five years of moviemaking rights

to the Salkinds in return for $850,000 and the promise of millions
more in the unlikely event the producers cashed in. It was a golden
chance for Ilya and Alex and a lack of both vision and intestinal for-
titude by one of Hollywood's biggest dream factories. "It wasn't one
of the studios" that recognized what Superman could be, concedes
Terry Semel, Warner's former president. "I'd like to take credit for it,
but I think Alex Salkind saw it and he did it."

More than a thousand people would be involved in the production, including six writers and rewriters and three directors. Eleven
separate film units shot at three studios in eight countries on three
continents. More than a million feet of film were recorded, although
just twelve thousand were needed. It took the largest movie budget
ever to pull it all off, with more bounced or delayed paychecks than
anyone could count. A director, a writer, and the biggest stars all sued
the Salkinds afterward, and they all won settlements. Alex had to hi-
jack the film to squeeze the extra money he needed from Warner, and
his fear of flying—and of being arrested—kept him from the U.S.
premiere.

But what mattered to him, to Ilya, and to studio executives like
Semel was that it worked. Five years after that father-son dinner in
Paris, the Salkinds released *Superman: The Movie.* It was nominated
for three Oscars and took home a Hugo Award for best dramatic
presentation and a Grammy for best musical score. The box office
results were even more uplifting. It was the second-highest-grossing
movie of 1978, bested only by *Grease,* and the most profitable in
Warner Bros.' history. It was the first time a comic book hero had
starred in a serious movie and it launched Superman as a film franchise, with three sequels over the next decade. For the Man of Steel,
it meant a bold new adventure that would define him for Generation
Xers the same way George Reeves's *Adventures of Superman* had
branded him for baby boomers. And it was made possible by one of
the few people on the planet who had never heard of Superman.

BEFORE THE SALKINDS COULD MAKE a movie they needed a
script, and so, as they would with everything, they opened their
checkbooks and went hunting for a big name. Alfred Bester qualified,

having written *The Phantom* comics and award-winning novels like
The Demolished Man, and he was hired to produce a treatment. Ilya
loved what he wrote; Alex didn't. Bester might be a celebrity in the
world of science fiction, father Salkind said, but he wanted *big.* Bester
got a generous kill fee and Mario Puzo got a call.

Puzo's *Godfather* had recently been made into two movies that
earned him a pair of Academy Awards for best screenplay. An Oscar
was the kind of credential Alex could relate to, and Ilya signed Puzo
up for 5 percent of the film's gross sales. His Superman was a TV
anchorman at a station where Lois Lane was the weather girl and
there was no competition from the *Daily Planet,* which had folded.
Lex was there, too, or rather "Luthor Lux." When Superman went
looking for Lux he found a bald Kojak in a trench coat who, sucking
a lollipop, asked, "Hey! Superman! Who loves ya, baby?" Puzo
thought camp like that gave his movie pizzazz. Everyone who read it,
especially the National Periodical people, was sure it would undermine the film's credibility and Superman's. Puzo's opus, which
stretched to more than three hundred pages, read more like a novel
than a screenplay and would have cost a billion dollars to produce,
says Ilya. Yet both sides found silver linings when Puzo walked away
at the end of 1975: He eventually got his promised 5 percent, with
$300,000 of that up front and an on-screen credit for a largely useless
product, while the Salkinds got bragging rights to one of the world's
best-known writers, whose legend they used to refill their dwindling
coffers.

Next up were Robert Benton and David Newman, who had written the script for the Broadway production *It's a Bird,* along with
Newman's wife and writing partner, Leslie. Ilya offered the new team
a million dollars and simple instructions: "Fix it." They spent their
first three days tossing out big chunks of Puzo's work, then got their
own bead on the hero. "We decided that Superman is our King Arthur, he's our legend," says Leslie. What fascinated Benton was the
Clark Kent–Superman split: "Is he Clark Kent until that emergency
call happens, or is he Superman? Does he miss going full tilt or does
he get used to being this guy who sits in a coffee shop and has a
grilled cheese sandwich for lunch?" As for what the Salkinds wanted,

"They had no idea and couldn't have cared less," says Benton, although they made clear they wanted screenplays for a film *and* a sequel. Newman says Alex often asked about what was happening with "Mr. Superman and Mrs. Lois Lane," but "when we would start telling him he would fall asleep in about five minutes. I said to David, 'It's like telling bedtime stories.'" They did get paid—at the end of each day, in cash, with money from whatever country had the best currency exchange rate. They also got ongoing guidance from National's E. Nelson Bridwell, who was a living encyclopedia of everything that Superman had said, done, or imagined.

Heeding Bridwell's advice was less a matter of choice than of law, as spelled out in a fifty-four-page agreement between National and the Salkinds. It prescribed that the films "shall not be satirical or obscene." They had to be G-rated, or at worst PG, and had to be consistent with the way Superman spoke and acted in the comic books. National would get to vet the screenplay and be there during filming. Costumes for Superman and Superboy had to be preapproved, as did the actors who played them and Lois. Just to be sure, the publisher submitted its preferred lists for these parts. Superman and Clark, it suggested, might best be handled by any of twenty-four A-list actors, from Charlton Heston, known for his roles as Moses and Ben-Hur, to tough guy Charles Bronson. Lois's list had twenty-three actresses, from Natalie Wood, who had gotten rave reviews as Maria in *West Side Story,* to sexpot Raquel Welch.

Before they could worry about stars, the Salkinds needed a director. Tops on their list was *Chinatown* maestro Roman Polanski, who was still reeling from the murder of his pregnant wife, Sharon Tate, and would soon be accused of sexually abusing a thirteen-year-old girl. "Not exactly my kind of thing, Ilya," Polanski said of Superman. *Jaws* director Steven Spielberg approached him, Ilya says, but Alex worried that "the shark might go down, let's wait and see how this fish movie does." *Jaws* was a smash and now Spielberg was out of reach. From there they moved on to a who's who of top Hollywood skippers—from Francis Ford Coppola, who was busy with *Apocalypse Now,* to John Guillermin, whose hero of the moment was King Kong, to Sam Peckinpah, who pulled a gun on Ilya and said, "You gotta shut up, kid. What do you think you know about movies?" They finally settled on Guy Hamilton, who had made his name with *Goldfinger.* He looked like a gem until the production moved from Rome, where star Marlon Brando had a pending arrest warrant for sexual obscenity, to London, where Hamilton was a tax exile. Moving back to London, Hamilton decided, would cost him too much money.

Richard Donner was a perfect fit. He had grown up in the Bronx as a "comic book man" and his first true love was Lois Lane. He had just finished directing *The Omen* and was ready for new work. So he listened intently when he got a call on a Sunday morning from a man with what sounded like a Hungarian accent saying, "I am a world famous producer. I am making *Superman* and I want you to make it." Two hours later Alex Salkind's messenger was at Donner's door with a copy of the Puzo-Benton-Newman script. But the deeper he read, the more alarmed Donner became. "It was a parody on a parody. They were destroying Superman," he recalls. To see whether it could be salvaged, he invited over Tom Mankiewicz, a friend and the screenwriter for some of the James Bond movies. By the time Mankiewicz arrived, Donner had put on a Superman costume and convinced himself that if Mankiewicz agreed to rewrite the script, and Salkind agreed to hire both of them, he would do the movie. "I took the job to protect Superman," he says, "plus the fact that I was being paid a million dollars."

It actually was a million dollars as an advance against 7.5 percent of the film's gross, which made it even more attractive to Donner but still looked like a bargain to the Salkinds. They had already agreed to pay Brando more than any film star had ever received—11.3 percent of domestic gross and 5.6 percent of foreign, with a guarantee of at least $2.7 million—to play Jor-El, who was on-screen for thirteen and a half of the movie's 143 minutes. Two days later they signed up Gene Hackman for $2 million to play Lex Luthor. High-priced talent like that reassured anxious executives at Warner Communications and helped Alex woo his financiers. Still, with no final screenplay in hand, and without a frame of film, the Salkinds had just agreed to hand over a quarter of their profits, or 30 percent including earlier promises to Puzo. They were on the hook for another $10 million in salaries, agents' fees, and bills for gilded suites at hotels like the Plaza in New

York and the Beverly Hills in Beverly Hills. And they still had no clue who would be their Superman.

Saturdays were "Superman test day." By the time Donner and Mankiewicz came on board at the end of 1976, a lineup of first-rate stars had refused or been rejected for the part. Alex's first choice was Robert Redford, who said no. So did Paul Newman, although Ilya says Newman "vomited" when he heard later how much Brando was earning. Nearly two hundred other actors were considered, including Sylvester Stallone (too Italian), Arnold Schwarzenegger (too Aryan), Muhammad Ali (too black), James Caan (too greedy), Bruce Jenner (too little talent), and Clint Eastwood (too busy). Ilya's wife had her own favorite—her dentist in Beverly Hills—and he was flown in for a firsthand look (everyone agreed that he "looked terrific" and wasn't worth the risk). Gossip columnists were having a field day and Alex was having a conniption. It was reminiscent of the casting calls that eventually found Kirk Alyn and George Reeves, only worse, with shooting set to start in eight weeks. Ilya says he was all for using an unknown actor who wouldn't overshadow the role but Donner was intent on a big name; Donner says it was just the reverse. They agreed it was time to have a second look at the skinny Juilliard-trained actor whose photo the casting director, Lynn Stalmaster, kept putting back in the in-pile every time they'd toss it out.

Christopher Reeve was an unlikely choice. It wasn't just his honey brown hair, or that his 180 pounds did not come close to filling out his six-foot-four frame. He had asthma and he sweated so profusely that a crew member would have to blow-dry his armpits between takes. He was prep school and Ivy League, with a background in serious theater that made him more comfortable in England's Old Vic theater than in its Pinewood movie lot. He was picked, as he acknowledged, 90 percent because he looked "like the guy in the comic book . . . the other 10% is acting talent." He also was a brilliant choice. He brought to the part irony and comic timing that harked back to the best of screwball comedy. He had dramatic good looks and an instinct for melding humanism with heroism. "When he walked into a room you could see this wasn't a conventional leading man, there was so much depth he had almost an old movie star feeling," says Stalmaster. Alex loved the price: $250,000, or less than a tenth of what Brando would get. Donner asked Reeve to try on his horn-rimmed glasses. Squinting back at him was Clark Kent. Even his name fit: Christopher Reeve would be assuming the part made famous by George Reeves. "I didn't find him," Donner would say throughout the production. "God sent him to me."

Margot Kidder fell into her part. "She literally tripped into the door when she arrived for her test," says Donner, "and I looked at Lynn and said, 'That's Lois.'" Growing up in Canada's Northwest Territories, Kidder was banned from watching television, reading comic books, or doing anything else that would have put her in touch with Superman. She didn't have to be. To play Lois Lane she just had to be herself: "I'm manic and I'm overambitious and I'm often frantic and disorganized." When Donner told her she had the part that stars like Stockard Channing and Leslie Ann Warren wanted, she thought, "'Thank God, I really need the money!' Then I went out and to the best lingerie boutique on Beauchamp Place in London and bought six hundred bucks' worth of underwear!" She also went to charm school, courtesy of her director, learning how to wear high heels rather than cowboy boots and to sit in a skirt instead of blue jeans. In the end Kidder was what old fans had always imagined Lois Lane looked like, and what young ones would from 1978 on.

With the big roles filled and the big names signed, Donner and Mankiewicz could zero in on telling their story. Their key was recognizing that, to fans, Superman was not a fantasy character but an embodiment of real hopes and ideals. "It's as simple as that: truth, justice, and the American way. What other comic book hero could say that?" asks Donner. Over the years, Superman's handlers had labored over whether they should aim for kids or parents, longtime fans or new ones. Donner had a less complicated calculus: "I was making it for me. . . . This picture is the biggest Erector Set given to the biggest kid in the world." This was just what had driven Jerry Siegel to dream up the hero forty years before. To make sure his cast and crew understood his passion and never slipped into parody or pretension, Donner hung on his wall a plastic airborne Superman trailing a banner that read, VERISIMILITUDE.

The movie itself was equally straightforward and came in three acts: the science fiction birth and backstory on Krypton, Clark growing into his down-to-earth values and superhero persona on the wheat fields of Kansas, and nonstop adventures in Metropolis like rescuing Lois from a crashing helicopter and saving the president from a crashing Air Force One, which were what moviegoers had paid to see. Each segment had its own cast, with limited overlap. Each was filmed at its own location. Ground zero was Pinewood Studios, just west of London, where the crew assembled a crystalline version of Krypton along with the world's biggest soundstage. Alberta, Canada, doubled as Smallville, U.S.A. New York was the stand-in for Metropolis the way Metropolis had always been for New York. The settings and stories were truer to the spirit of the comic book Superman than anything filmed before. And it was more than Superman who benefited: Donner, Mankiewicz, and their collaborators were creating a prototype for the new genre of superhero epic, one that held old fans with an elegant rendering of nostalgic origins while it offered neophytes their first bite of the legend. It was a model that everyone from Batman to Spider-Man would follow. The Man of Tomorrow had again shown the way.

What wasn't straightforward was the flying. It never is, but moviegoers in the 1970s were not as forgiving as they had been in the low-tech 1940s and 1950s. Surely a world that had just unveiled videocassette recorders, neutron bombs, and a test-tube baby named Louise Brown could give us a convincing human airliner. Donner tried having his superhero skydive into the action. He hoisted him onto a three-hundred-foot crane behind a miniaturized Golden Gate Bridge. He experimented with flying harnesses and depressurized weightless chambers. Nothing worked. The solution came from an unlikely source: special effects wizard Zoran Perisic, who had read Superman comics growing up in Serbia and had been asked, "Who is Superman?" when U.S. authorities quizzed him for his naturalization papers. He was so convinced he could make Reeve fly that he offered to pay for the tests if his idea didn't work. He put zoom lenses on both the camera and the projector so that the projected image, as seen by the camera, never changed size. Superman, who was in front of that image, appeared to come closer or move farther away—and to be performing aerial maneuvers when the camera/projector rig rotated—when in fact he was standing still. Perisic called the technique "Zoptic." Donner called it a lifesaver. The producers didn't want anyone drawing attention to the invention for fear other filmmakers would use it before they did. The Academy of Motion Picture Arts and Sciences was impressed enough that it gave the film its Special Achievement Award for Visual Effects.

Gimmickry was just half the equation; the other half was Christopher Reeve. He wanted to do more than run and dive the way Kirk Alyn and George Reeves had done. As a licensed aviator, Christopher knew what it felt like to take wing. Even without an airplane or any movement, he banked the turns, rolled, and looped, all with the ease of a stunt pilot. Back on the ground, he studied his predecessors to see what else they did poorly or well. Like them, he performed many of his own capers. George offered critical lessons in how to play the role as if he believed it but none when it came to differentiating Superman from Clark Kent, something he had never managed to do. "How could a thick pair of glasses substitute for a believable characterization?" Christopher asked. "Lois Lane shouldn't have to be blind or dim-witted." His model for Clark was a young Cary Grant—shy, vulnerable, and charmingly klutzy—and his watchword was to underplay the character. By slumping his shoulders and compressing his spine, Christopher's Clark lost a full three inches from his Superman frame. His voice became more nasal and midwestern. He slicked back his hair, flipping the part from left to right and losing the spit curl. His demeanor now suggested a guy who not only couldn't get the girl, he couldn't even get a taxi.

Bulking up for the role was a different kind of challenge for Reeve. "We shoved food down Chris and got him lots of protein drinks, five to six cans a day," recalls Dave Prowse, a bodybuilder and gym owner in London who, having played Superman in a TV commercial, had hoped to land the movie role himself. When he didn't, he agreed to train the man who did. Working out five nights a week with free weights and a trampoline, Prowse and Reeve focused first on Reeve's pectoral muscles, thighs, and back, then on his arms, shoulders, calves, and abdominals. Teatime meant a plate of cakes, and mealtime came four times a day. In just six weeks Reeve put on more than thirty pounds, mostly muscle, adding two inches to his chest, two to his biceps, and enough overall that he could take the muscle padding out of his blue body stocking. Training him was easy at first, but when he had to leave for a week to be with another client, Prowse says, "Chris called me all the names under the sun. He said he was losing weight and strength. Donner called me over and said, 'He really thinks he is Superman.'"

And so he was. Superman himself changed with every artist who filled in his features, every writer who scripted his adventures, and even the marketers and accountants who managed his finances and grew his audience. Each could claim partial ownership. Actors like Christopher Reeve did more molding and framing than anyone and could claim more proprietorship. As each scene was shot it became clearer that he was giving the hero a different face as well as a unique personality. Christopher's Superman would be funnier and more human—if less powerful or intimidating—than any who had preceded him. He was more of a Big Blue Boy Scout now, in contrast to Kirk Alyn's Action Ace and George Reeves's Man of Steel. In the hands of this conservatory-trained actor, Supes was getting increasingly comfortable baring his soul.

As the filming slogged through its second year, the cast and crew were growing temperamental and the media were wondering whether it would ever be done. Ilya and Alex watched Donner spend their money all too freely. Donner says he was the first director ever who never got a budget, so he never knew whether his spending was under or over. Brando had shown up on the set with the flu and what he thought were humorous suggestions—that Jor-El the Kryptonian should look like a bagel, or perhaps a green suitcase—although he left calling the film "a fucking Valentine" to the superhero. Alex's wife, Berta Domínguez D., who called herself the Shakespeare of Mexico, attacked Mankiewicz with a steak knife when he made a joke about Alex's height. Alex apologized for Berta, saying Mexicans shouldn't drink, and he apologized for his perpetual lying, saying, "I can't help it." Jack O'Halloran, an ex-heavyweight boxer playing a Kryptonian supervillain, was so outraged when his paychecks took months to clear that he says he dragged producer Pierre Spengler across his desk, shouting, "This is bullshit. I signed a contract to work. I worked. Now pay me."

Thankfully, the relationship that mattered most off-screen as well as on, Lois and Clark's, was in good shape. The two actors behaved like brother and sister. Christopher was the uptight, ambitious sibling, Margot was loosey-goosey. She reassured him about being typecast as Superman. He pushed her to read the script, not a novel, while they dangled from cranes waiting for the next scene. She couldn't resist pinging his steel codpiece until he'd scream, "For God's sake, stop it!" Their chemistry was most apparent in the movie's most remembered scene, on Lois's balcony. Superman arrived saying, "Good evening, Miss Lane," then cuddled her in his arms for a flight over Metropolis's skyscrapers and bridges. Mankiewicz expanded the scene from two pages to seven and says that when he first heard Chris utter his greeting, "I remember putting my hands together and pleading that he would just keep going like that." He did. When Lois asked, "Who are you?" Superman answered sweetly: "A friend." Margot says they were indeed friends, which made it easy to act that way. What was difficult was summoning the sexual energy the scene demanded. "I had to pretend," she explains, "that Christopher was Harrison Ford." It worked. She asked the man with the X-ray eyes what color underwear she was wearing and, after awkward evasions, he told the truth: "Pink." But then, Reeve's Superman could make even a fib sound guileless, the way he did when he looked into Lois's eyes and promised, "I never lie."

The scene was more a Shakespearean drama—think *Romeo and Juliet*—than a comic book spoof, and Donner demanded an equally elevated tone for the music. "Superman was the perfect hero to be musicalized in quasi-operatic or balletic fashion," says John Williams, who composed the score and conducted the London Symphony's performance of it. There was a rousing "Superman March" for the opening and closing credits, a mysterious "Krypton crystal" motif to introduce the doomed planet, an all-American melody for Smallville, and a playful "March of the Villains" for Lex and his henchman, Otis. "My challenge and opportunity," Williams says, "was to capture musically Superman's optimism and invincibility and athletics and heroism. The perfect fifth and the perfect octave are heroic intervals that have a strength and a core power to suggest just those qualities of heroism and heroics."

While Donner and his team were working to assemble a movie

worthy of their hero, the Salkinds were building an audience that would want to watch. In 1975, before they had a final screenplay, they hired three planes to fly over the Cannes Film Festival every hour with a banner reading, SUPERMAN, SALKIND, PUZO. The next year five planes carried a slightly amended message: SUPERMAN, SALKIND, HAMILTON. By 1977 a blimp was carrying the message, along with a fleet of aircraft worthy of France's Armée de l'Air.

That was just the drumroll. The fully orchestrated rollout was plotted by Warner Bros., which was handling the film's distribution and was finally convinced it had real commercial potential. Super-secrecy was Warner's watchword, with paparazzi kept clear of the studio and street sets, even when the setting was the streets of New York. Pictures of Superman on cranes and wires could undermine the illusion of him flying on his own. There were none of the standard photo handouts, either. That would shatter the intrigue that was building over this new Superman and what he looked like in tights and cape. The secrecy campaign worked so well that someone broke into Pinewood Studios to try to filch shots. The first photographs of Christopher Reeve in uniform and in the air were published just where and when Warner wanted—in the two biggest newsweeklies, just before and after the film's release, with *Newsweek*'s shot consuming the full cover. As for paid advertising, the Warner team hatched a classic come-on that captured all that was new in the movie and happened to be true: "You'll believe a man can fly!"

But there was a last-minute glitch. Alex Salkind refused to deliver the completed film unless Warner executives agreed to kick in another $15 million. He said it would buy them additional distribution rights for "certain foreign territories." They said it was blackmail. Alex knew that 750 theaters were planning to screen the film, sight unseen, starting December 15, 1978. He also knew that his contract didn't require delivery until December 31. "There was an element of extortion in it," concedes Tom Pollock, Alex's lawyer, "but he was totally legally entitled." So Alex honored his contract, if not his word, and set a price that was $5 million more than Warner had paid for the distribution rights to all of North America and three-quarters of its international markets. The company knew it was over a barrel, and with just two weeks to spare, it agreed to pay.

Finally, five years after that dinner at a Paris café and just ten days before Christmas, the film was ready for viewing. President Jimmy Carter took his daughter, Amy, to see it at a premiere in Washington. Queen Elizabeth brought Prince Andrew to a royal unveiling in London. At the New York bash, Mario Puzo showed up in a blue Superman T-shirt and Norman Mailer wore a blue velvet tuxedo, but Marlon Brando stayed on vacation in Tahiti. A more confounding no-show was Alexander Salkind. He had been arrested by Interpol officers in Switzerland on charges of stealing $20 million from the German company that bankrolled his films and was released only after he displayed the diplomatic credentials he had secured years before courtesy of the president of Costa Rica. Rather than head to the *Superman* parties in the United States, where he feared another arrest, he overcame his phobia of flying by using heavy sedation and hired a jet to deliver him to the safe haven of Mexico. Had he come to the U.S. gala, Alex could have met Jerry Siegel. As the film ended, Jerry approached National's publisher in tears, saying, "It was exactly how I had imagined it."

Reviewers offered a mixed verdict on Alex's production. *Newsweek*'s Jack Kroll proclaimed it "a mass entertainment of high class and energy," while Roger Ebert called it "a wondrous combination of all the old-fashioned things we never really get tired of: adventure and romance, heroes and villains, earthshaking special effects, and— you know what else? Wit." Pauline Kael of *The New Yorker* seemed to be writing about an entirely different movie, saying it was "cheesy looking" and gave "the impression of having been made in a panic," by a director who "can't seem to get the timing right," with a score "that transcends self-parody." Vincent Canby of *The New York Times* began his review hopefully, writing that *Superman* offered "good, clean, simple-minded fun." Then he took his shot: "To enjoy this movie as much as one has a right to expect, one has either to be a Superman nut, the sort of trivia expert who has absorbed all there is to know about the planet Krypton, or to check one's wits at the door, which may be more than a lot of people are prepared to do for longer than two hours."

More people qualified than Canby might have expected. The film clocked in as the sixth highest grossing of all time, bringing in just over $300 million worldwide and appearing on screens as far away as Shanghai and Peking. With the average ticket in 1978 selling for $2.50, 120 million people watched Christopher Reeve fly across the screen—one hundred times more than were buying *Superman, Superboy,* and the rest of their family of comics that year. The movie won twenty-one awards, including best science fiction film of 1978 from the International Society of Science Fiction, Horror and Fantasy. It was an even bigger hit in pharmacies and department stores, where merchants couldn't stock enough thermoses, sneakers, lunch boxes, cereal bowls, cookie jars, and anything else with Christopher Reeve in blue tights. And it wasn't just little boys and their dads who were bewitched by the movie and its star. "I took my 7-year-old son to see the picture, not expecting very much," Penelope Hoover told readers of the *Los Angeles Times.* "When I emerged from the theater afterward, I felt like a 10-year-old kid who had just seen something wonderful. . . . It made me rediscover the little girl in myself and I'm happy to find her."

Hoover grasped what Warner Communications hadn't. Periodically we all need to recapture our youth and idealism, especially at a moment when America was mired in a malaise that President Jimmy Carter called a "crisis of confidence." Jerry Siegel and Joe Shuster understood that when they introduced their hero in the midst of the Depression and on the eve of a world war. The Salkinds understood it when they bought the rights to Superman and hired two grown-up kids—Donner and Mankiewicz—to make the movie. Superman, the world's biggest optimist, understood it better than anyone, which is why Hoover and her son so adored him.

One group that wasn't sure how to feel about the new film was scriptural literalists. They had plenty to mull over, starting with Marlon Brando as Jor-El. With a long-flowing white robe and a shock of silver hair, he looked as well as acted like God. "They can be a great people, Kal-El," he told his only son, explaining why the boy had been dispatched to Earth. "They wish to be. They only lack the light to show the way. For this reason above all—their capacity for good— I have sent them you. My only son." The Almighty couldn't have said it better. Similarly, Superman's adoptive parents, the Kents, were written into the script as "Christian folk whose morals are as basic as the soil they till." The movie was meant to have religious resonance, says screenwriter Mankiewicz, although the religion could as easily have been Muslim or Jewish as Christian. To many filmgoers, those references made *Superman* even more compelling, offering grist for editorials, Sunday school discussions, scholarly articles, and more than one book. To some, it was blasphemy. "I got major death threats," remembers Donner. "How dare I symbolize Brando as God and Christopher as Jesus? Studio security brought them to my attention. Some of them were just nuts, fanatics. There was talk of blood running in the streets."

Alex had his own problems. His film, he said, cost $55 million, making it the most expensive ever, although others insisted he was inflating the costs as a bragging right and to downplay his profits to his partners. Marlon Brando sued him for $50 million. Mario Puzo had Ilya served with his legal papers at the Washington premiere of the film. Richard Donner, Christopher Reeve, and Margot Kidder filed their own lawsuits with their own gripes about promises Alex had broken. But no one should have been surprised. Breaking promises had long been Alex's modus operandi. In one of his earlier films, *The Three Musketeers,* he had made history: He and Ilya paid their actors for one movie but came away with enough footage for a sequel as well. They got away with it that time, but the Screen Actors Guild insisted that all future contracts with them or any other producer have a provision—labeled a "Salkind Clause"—specifying how many films were being made. The lineup of *Superman* claimants realized too late that they should have included their own clauses to help them sort out which of Alex's movie production figures were real, which hotel and country he was currently calling home, and which of his "people" were real rather than fronts set up to inflate debts and disguise profits. Even Ilya ended up suing his dad, although that wouldn't come until later and it wouldn't get resolved to either's satisfaction.

Nearly all of what people alleged against Alex was true. He had few scruples and no shame. He always had one foot in his Citroën ready to leave town, and he would never say where he was calling from for fear the FBI or Interpol might be listening. He promised shares of *Superman* to everyone from Brando and Puzo to his German, French, and Swiss lenders. The part of his story that is seldom told is that "everyone got paid off from this movie every dollar they were entitled to," says Tom Pollock, the former MCA/Universal president who was Alex's lawyer when the lawsuits were percolating. "Dick Donner made millions and millions of dollars of profit, as did Marlon Brando, as did Mario Puzo. Warner Bros. made vastly more than anybody. I have no idea what Alex actually kept for himself. He walked away depleted and exhausted but not defeated. Through force of will and money, he put together the team that made a great movie, that generated and spawned other movies, and that created a huge business mostly for other people."

THE 1970S WERE A TIME for rebooting Superman's comic books along with his movies. Gone were Mort Weisinger's imaginary stories, along with Mort himself. Many of the Man of Steel's powers melted away, as did the robots that Mort had inserted in Superman's place to explain his absences when he was pretending to be Clark. The most surprising departure was kryptonite, which had been Superman's most effective adversary. The changes amounted to decluttering an encrusted story. The aim was about marketing as much as storytelling: Bringing Superman closer to Jerry and Joe's Golden Age creation would, his bosses hoped, win back older readers who missed the hero of their youth and educate younger ones on the brilliance of that more streamlined, less gimmicky vision.

Who better to oversee that restoration than an editor who had helped spawn the original, or claimed to have? The son of Romanian-Jewish immigrants, Julie Schwartz grew up in the Bronx—the place that had spawned more comics pioneers than any neighborhood in America. Julie and Mort attended the same high school, shared a passion for science fiction, and teamed up to publish a fan magazine, one of whose first subscribers was Jerry Siegel. Jerry liked what he read and launched his own publication, where he self-published "The Reign of the Super-Man." All of which led Julie to pose, only partly tongue-in-cheek, his Big Bang Theory: "If Mort and I had not created our fanzine, neither would have Jerry Siegel created his—and as a result may never have triggered his creation of the original Living Legend, Superman. No Siegel fanzine, no Siegel Superman!"

Julie had taken his first job in comic books in 1944, as an editor with one of the firms that would be absorbed into National. In the 1950s he was a central force in reviving the Flash and Green Lantern, kicking off a Silver Age of comics that lasted until 1970 and recaptured much of the energy and prosperity of its Golden Age beginnings. In the 1960s, while Mort was managing Superman, Julie was Batman's master. In the 1970s it was Julie's turn. He took over Superman not because he wanted to—he liked Superman but loved Batman—but because he knew the company's preeminent superhero was the comics world's definition of professional success. Now he was in the big time.

It was time for a change. Writers and artists had chafed under Mort's heavy hand. Circulation of the Superman family of comic books had been plummeting since 1966 and by 1970 its most popular title, *Superman,* was selling barely half what it had five years before. Archrival Marvel was moving up fast; within two years it would, for the first time, wear the mantle of industry leader. That got the attention of the Warner Communications executives who had taken over National and were asking whether they belonged in the comics business. Newly installed publisher Carmine Infantino was the man on the spot, and since his specialty was artwork, not writing, he turned to his friend Julie Schwartz, now in his mid-fifties, to come up with answers for Superman. Julie was the right choice, sharing Mort's deep grounding in comics yet with few of Mort's rough edges or insecurities. The Schwartz empire, however, was not as all-encompassing as Weisinger's, including *Superman* and *World's Finest* but not *Action* or the rest of the Superman-related titles that Mort had overseen.

Julie's impact was apparent from the first issues under his control in 1971. "Superman Breaks Loose" was the aptly named kickoff for a six-part series by lead writer Denny O'Neil in which a freak chain reaction converted all of the Earth's kryptonite into ordinary iron. Fans had complained that the deadly green metal was too omnipresent so, poof, it was gone, along with its gold, red, red-gold, and other rainbow of flavors. KRYPTONITE NEVERMORE! the cover promised. But kryptonite, O'Neil recognized, "was merely a symptom. The disease might have been called elephantiasis of the powers. Superman was just too mighty." Getting rid of kryptonite actually aggravated the illness by making Superman more invulnerable. The remedy, courtesy of Dr. O'Neil, was to have the explosion that rendered kryptonite harmless bring to life a demonic sandman who robbed Superman of critical powers. What was left was a streamlined hero, still super but now requiring both hands rather than the tip of a finger to hold up the world. The goal was to ratchet up the suspense by giving his enemies a better shot at taking him down. It also was to make the Kryptonian more human, more like the heroes that Stan Lee and Marvel were dreaming up.

Clark, too, was different under Julie, although in his case the change had more to do with modernizing than restoring. He moved from being a newspaperman on the *Daily Planet* to anchoring the news desk at the Galaxy Broadcasting System, which had bought the *Planet*. Young people, Julie explained, "got their news from the television, so therefore it was only natural that Clark Kent should take a job as a television reporter." Not so natural was that whenever Clark needed to change into Superman, the station took a commercial break. His reliable but crusty boss, Perry White, was supplanted by Galaxy president Morgan Edge, who was less steeped in journalism and less trustworthy. Clark's rumpled blue suits were out as well, with a new look snazzy enough to warrant an article in the real *Gentlemen's Quarterly*. More interesting to Marvel readers was Superman's internal struggle over which of his identities—the human reporter or the alien superhero—was the real him. The verdict: Both were indispensable.

Mort's successors took Superman places politically that he hadn't been since Jerry's early days. In "I Am Curious (Black)," which came out in 1970 just as Julie was about to take the reins, Lois was shunned by the black community she was trying to write about because "she's whitey." Superman helped darken her complexion for a day, which she spent exploring the world from an African American perspective. A taxi zoomed past her outstretched arm "as if I don't exist!" Other subway riders stared at her "as if I were a . . . a . . . freak?" In the end Lois asked Superman whether her temporarily black skin would stop him from loving her. His answer planted Superman squarely back in his 1930s role as Champion of the Oppressed: "You ask that of me . . . Superman? An alien from Krypton . . . another planet? A universal outsider?"

That wasn't the only story in which race was front and center, nor was racial justice the only hot-button issue on which Superman weighed in during the decade that brought us the legalization of abortion, the fall of Saigon, and mood rings. Something important was always at stake now for the hero and his friends. Lois helped recruit Dave Stevens as the *Daily Planet*'s first black columnist. Superman and Lois promoted Native American rights and she temporarily adopted an Indian baby. Pollution got him even more riled up. He sucked smog out of the air and expelled it into outer space a year after America celebrated its first Earth Day, and he worked to shut a dangerous chemical plant two years before toxins forced the evacuation of the Love Canal section of Niagara Falls, New York. Kal-El already had watched one home, Krypton, disintegrate when its inhabitants failed to acknowledge its impending environmental doom. He was determined to make sure the same thing didn't happen here on Earth.

Julie and his young writers collaborated in ways the scripters never had with Mort, and they answered, more convincingly than Mort's Cinderella Fallacy, the age-old question of why anyone believed Superman's lame masquerade as Clark Kent. Waking from a dream where his secret identity had been exposed, Superman put on his glasses and looked in the mirror, concluding, "That's the dumbest disguise I've ever seen!" By the end of "The Master Mesmerizer of Metropolis!" Superman and all of us had the answer. His power of "super-hypnotism" entranced anyone he met and "automatically projects my subconscious desire to be seen as a weaker and frailer man than I really am!" Not just that, but his glasses—made from the shattered glass of the Kryptonian rocket that sent him to Earth—had "some unknown property" that intensified the hypnotic effect. "Did you realize that the most successful practitioner of mass hypnosis in the world is Superman?" the editors asked as the story closed. "We didn't think so! After all—until today, Superman didn't even know it himself!"

The truth was that real fans didn't need a short-lived gimmick like that—or Christopher Reeve's shifting his hair part—to buy into Su-

Jerry Siegel (top) and Joe Shuster got things going for Superman in 1938, when their first story was published in *Action Comics* No. 1. The young collaborators from Cleveland had been working on that narrative for nearly four years, and their names eventually would become as conjoined and revered in the world of comics as those of Rodgers and Hammerstein in song and Tracy and Hepburn in cinema. *Photos courtesy of Laura Siegel Larson and Jean Shuster Peavy.*

Jerry Siegel's relationship with Jack Liebowitz would sour over the decades, but here they appeared to be the best of friends.

Bud Collyer was the voice of Superman for 2,008 radio shows, and across thirty years in various media. *Library of American Broadcasting, University of Maryland.*

Around the time Bud Collyer was bringing Superman alive on the radio, brothers Max and Dave Fleischer were taking him to movie theaters in the form of animated cartoons that many critics panned but most fans loved. They featured action and adventure, rescues and thrilling battles, such as the one above, in which Superman takes on mean-spirited robots, in a 1941 Paramount Pictures release called *The Mechanical Monsters*. The animators were Steve Muffati and George Germanetti. *Courtesy of Warner Bros. Entertainment Inc.*

Superman was a favorite of Allied troops during World War II, and they showed their gratitude by naming after him their jeeps, tanks, landing craft, and, pictured here, a B-17 Flying Fortress bomber. *Time & Life Pictures/Getty Images.*

While he was a favorite of parents and even grandparents, Superman's success in the early years resulted from his capturing the imagination of youths like this boy, seen reading a comic book in New York in 1946. Another favorite reading spot: under the bedcovers, at night, where a flashlight illuminated the pages. *Time & Life Pictures/Getty Images.*

The 1950s TV series *Adventures of Superman* welcomed back old fans of the comics and radio productions and introduced new ones to the Man of Steel narrative. For millions of children who grew up glued to that show, and for others who have watched it in reruns, when they envision Superman they see George Reeves, who is shown here nabbing two thugs. *ABC via Getty Images.*

It was the ultimate measure of celebrity in 1956: a guest slot on America's most-watched TV show, *I Love Lucy*. It is tough to tell here who was having more fun: George Reeves as he flexed his biceps, or Lucille Ball as she felt his super-strong muscle. *Getty Images.*

The pace on the *Adventures of Superman* set was frenetic, given the measly budgets and tight deadlines, but off the set George Reeves could relax with Noel Neill, who played Lois Lane alongside him for five seasons and earlier had starred next to Kirk Alyn in such film serials as *Atom Man vs. Superman. Colorized photo courtesy of Larry Thomas Ward.*

Jack Larson, who was just twenty-three when he signed up to play Jimmy Olsen, connected so completely with viewers that he took the character from a supporting role to a star. Larson and Neill, shown here in 1956, have sustained their friendship through the decades. *Colorized photo courtesy of Larry Thomas Ward.*

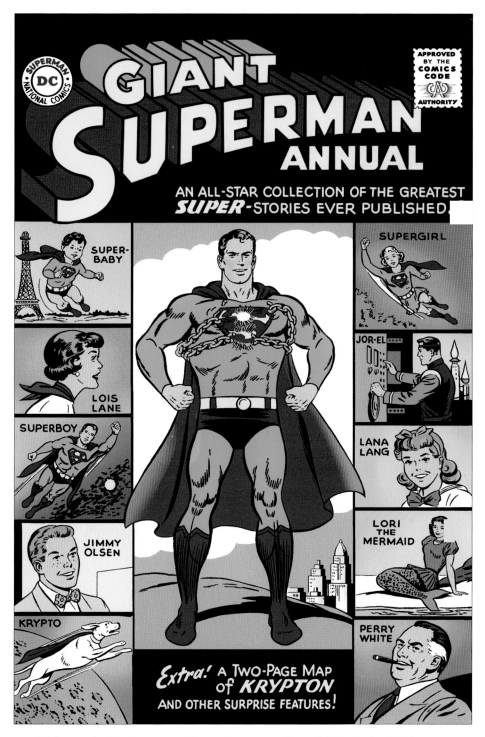

This comic book cover—from *Superman Annual* No. 1 in 1960—was drawn by Curt Swan and colored by Stan Kaye. Swan, who did his first Superman drawings in 1948 and his last thirty-nine years later, gave the hero a more dignified and human sensibility. *"Superman Annual"* No. 1 © 1960 DC Comics. Used with Permission.

Two of Superman's most insidious, relentless, and hairless enemies—the evil genius Lex Luthor and the computerized space pirate Brainiac—join forces in this comic book from 1964. *"Superman" #167 © 1964 DC Comics. Used with Permission.*

Superman spends much of his life fending off Lois Lane's bids to ensnare him, even as she is doing the same with Clark Kent. In this comic from 1966, the Man of Steel offers a novel line of reasoning: He can't marry any-one dumb enough not to see through his lame disguise. *"Superman's Girl Friend, Lois Lane"* #63 © 1966 DC Comics. Used with Permission.

Superman became a regular at the Macy's Thanksgiving Day Parade in New York as early as 1940, when the biggest balloon was an eighty-foot-high replica of the Man of Tomorrow. This shot is from the 1966 parade. *New York Daily News via Getty Images.*

To sleep-deprived parents in the 1970s, a cartoon like *Super Friends* was a twofer: Kids were mesmerized by the animation, orchestrated by Hanna-Barbera, and the collaboration between Superman and such heroic friends as Aquaman, Wonder Woman, Robin, and Batman; Mom and Dad, meanwhile, delighted in the extra hours they got in bed. *ABC via Getty Images.*

Many fans of the 1978 movie *Superman,* the first in a series starring Christopher Reeve, wondered what the sequel would have been like if Richard Donner had been kept on as director. They found out twenty-five years later, when, thanks to their lobbying, Warner Bros. released on DVD a re-edit called *Superman II: The Richard Donner Cut.* Donner is shown here with producer Michael Thau (right) and a cutout of Reeve. *Getty Images.*

The Superman TV show launched in 1993 was called *Lois & Clark: The New Adventures of Superman*. As the title suggested, the show was more interested in the relationship between the two journalists than in the adventures of the superhero, and at least as interested in Lois as in Clark. Teri Hatcher played Lois while Dean Cain doubled as Clark and Superman. *ABC via Getty Images.*

Smallville debuted on the WB network just a month after the 9/11 terrorist attacks. The long-running series let young viewers see why their grandparents and parents were so smitten with Superman, and it gave them a version of the superhero who was theirs alone. Tom Welling (left) played a youthful Clark Kent, and Michael Rosenbaum (below) portrayed what may have been the most riveting Lex Luthor ever. *Warner Bros./Getty Images.*

After nearly seventy-five years in which scores of artists have offered up their unique visions of Superman, it isn't easy to stand out. But Alex Ross's mournful rendering—from the 1999 collection *Peace on Earth*—does. *From* Superman: Peace on Earth © *1998 DC Comics. Used with Permission.*

In the early 1990s DC Comics decided to kill off Superman, and while it was for real, it wasn't forever. Readers lined up on the street and around the block outside comic stores to buy *Superman* No. 75, the death issue, which tallied the biggest one-day sale ever for a comic book, with more than six million copies printed. *"Superman" #75 © 1993 DC Comics. Used with Permission.*

perman's disguise as Clark Kent. They loved all that he stood for, from his idealism to his unflinching heroism. Too many of their flesh-and-blood heroes were gone now. Assassins got Jack Kennedy, then Martin Luther King and Jack's brother Bobby. Drugs took Elvis and Marilyn. Baseball great and humanitarian Roberto Clemente died in a plane crash, his body lost at sea. A breakup spelled the end of the Beatles. They were all gone, but Superman endured, seemingly forever, and all those who looked to him as an archetype were grateful. If all he wanted back was for them to play along while he switched in and out of his cape and tights, his fans were ready.

For his part, Julie Schwartz added personal touches that he hoped would make his hero even more appealing and abiding. Julie drew on his Jewish heritage in stories pitting Superman against the galactic golem, Lex Luthor's evil incarnation of the mythic character of clay that watched over Jews. The editor dropped into his comics notes steering readers to old stories or explaining arcane terms, sometimes signing them with an impersonal "editor" and sometimes as "Julie." He tipped his hat, or rather Clark's, to his predecessor: The Kent apartment was furnished with a sculpted bust that looked like Weisinger and when Clark came home he tossed his hat on the statue, saying, "Evening Morty." Julie also tipped his hat to his writers and artists, including their bylines along with his on every story. And, with help from writers like the legendary Jack Kirby, the family of Superman books showed a flourish for the science fiction Julie had been raised on—giving readers a handheld computer decades before it came into use, and delving into genetic research and cloning before they were part of our vocabulary.

Many fans applauded the changes Julie brought as a return to first principles. Others mourned the dulling-down of Weisinger-era tomfoolery. In any case, most of the plot shifts didn't last long and some never made it into *Action* and other DC titles beyond Julie's control. By 1973 Superman was back with the world on his fingertip and Denny O'Neil was back to Batman. Kryptonite returned as Superman's Achilles' heel in 1977. By the end of 1978, to realign Clark Kent with Christopher Reeve's wildly popular incarnation, Julie's comic book journalist again had print flowing through his veins and a job at the *Daily Planet*. Like reboots of Superman that came before and would follow, Julie Schwartz's arrived with fanfare and fizzled without notice.

That is less a commentary on Julie and Mort than an observation on how Superman shaped his own reality. The same way parents, through a blend of nature and nurture, influence their child's values, politics, and looks, so Superman's handlers animated who he was and what he did. But at some point a child grabs hold of his fate, and so, too, did the superhero. His writers, artists, and editors thought they were in control when it was Superman's personality and legend—what he stood for and what his fans demanded—that set their boundaries. If the DC creative team moved him too close to Clark and away from Superman, or made him more (or less) powerful than he needed to be, he quietly tugged them back toward Jerry and Joe's original vision. Sometimes it took decades, as with Mort's imaginary world; "Kryptonite Nevermore" and Julie's other tinkering unraveled more quickly. Alvin Schwartz was one of the few who saw that it was the fictional hero who was pulling the strings. "Superman directed his own destinies," says Schwartz, who ghostwrote Superman comic strips in the 1940s and 1950s. "All of us were merely his pawns."

By the mid-1970s, even Superman's magic had stopped working. His troubles had less to do with him, his editors, or his writers and more to do with the wider business of comics. Marvel had pulled ahead of National, but both were slumping. Readers continued to age, sales at newsstands were still in free fall, and while specialty comic book stores were catching on, it was not enough to make up the difference. Movies, meanwhile, were making a comeback with special effects blockbusters like *Star Wars;* TV was attracting young viewers with shows like *All in the Family* and *Saturday Night Live;* and video games like Atari's *Pong* were making a claim on the time and money of bell-bottomed preteens. Even *The New York Times* wondered whether America's most popular superhero, once a symbol of vitality, had fallen victim to that dreaded affliction: the irrelevancy of middle age. "The famous blue long-john union suit, now faded to the color of old jeans, sags loosely where steely abdominals once stopped speeding locomotives dead on the tracks," humor columnist Russell Baker wrote. "The double chin is nearly a triple. On the back of the skull the hair is sparse, and a bit too blue to be persuasive."

Superman may never have looked like that, but it was a generous take on the cigar-chomping sixty-year-old men who ran National. New blood was needed to spice up the company and refill its coffers, and it arrived in 1976 in the person of Jenette Kahn. At twenty-eight, National's new publisher was the youngest senior executive at Warner Communications and in the world of comics. This daughter of a rabbi also was everything that Jack and Harry hadn't been: college-educated, with a degree from Harvard; an art history major who believed comic books were a form of art; and a neophyte to the industry, although she had grown up reading Superman by flashlight under the bedcovers. Most unsettling, she was a woman in a field where there were almost none. One male colleague later confided that when he heard about her hiring he headed to the men's room and threw up.

But Kahn knew publishing, having launched three successful kids' magazines, and she was willing to try anything to raise her heroes' profiles. When Bill Sarnoff, the head of Warner Publishing, was interviewing her for the job, he actually proposed terminating publication of any new comic books and focusing on licensing and other media, which was where the firm made its money. "Whether he really would have done that I can't say," she says looking back, "but I said that if we were to do that, the characters would have a radioactive half life and all the other revenue would dry up." She sensed she had limited time to make her case, so she started pushing from the day she arrived. One symbolic move was to change the company's name from National Periodical Publications, a colorless title that hid what the company did from would-be censors, to what young readers had always called it: DC Comics. Superman novels were not new, but there were more of them now, including *Superman: Last Son of Krypton*. Kahn's company also was anxious to get more free publicity, as it did when Henry Kissinger showed up on the cover of *Newsweek* wearing a red cape, blue tights, and the moniker SUPER K, and when a former DC intern began teaching the first accredited college course on comic books. His class was approved only after Michael Uslan convinced the Indiana University dean that Superman and Moses shared an origin story and a teachable moment. Carmine Infantino made history just before he left as publisher with a special-issue comic book teaming Superman with Marvel's Spider-Man; Jenette Kahn did him one better with a book in which Superman partnered with Muhammad Ali to defend the Earth against an alien attack.

She recognized that with so many new forms of entertainment to distract the young, Superman never again would be a million-seller, and that even steep price hikes—comic books began the decade selling for fifteen cents and ended at forty—couldn't make up for the revenue lost with declining circulation. So Jenette and her business-savvy sidekick, Paul Levitz, started viewing comics as creative engines rather than cash cows, able to spin off profitable enterprises in other media. It was a process that Jack Liebowitz had started when comic books themselves were big moneymakers; now those efforts were re-doubled.

Superman animated cartoons had come and gone since the Fleischers pioneered them in the 1940s, but by the late 1970s the Colossus of Krypton and Froot Loops were once again a Saturday morning ritual across America. The animator this time was Hanna-Barbera and the lineup of characters came from the *Justice League of America* comic book. Teamwork was the theme, with Superman collaborating with such heroic friends as Batman, Robin, Wonder Woman, and Aquaman. A not-so-subtle subplot, given the target audience of four- to eight-year-olds, was that violence was verboten the way it had been during the scare of the 1940s and 1950s. The show took on various names, all but one of which included the words *Super Friends,* and each made friends of sleep-deprived parents, who delighted in the extra hours they got in bed while their kids were mesmerized by Superman.

But the Hanna-Barbera cartoons were more than a distraction. If reach and duration are the measure of a medium's influence, *Super Friends* gave Superman his biggest stage yet with the small fry. The series ran, with occasional interruptions, from 1973 to 1986. At its height it attracted several million children, most of whom were getting their first look at Superman and many of whom would form a lifelong bond. The show became a paradigm for Kahn's new DC, and it was Superman's most successful venture into animation. *Super Friends* "drew a humungous audience compared to the comics," Levitz says. "It introduced more kids to our hero than Reeves or Reeve."

Luis Augusto was one of those kids. The forty-year-old architect says the *Super Friends* cartoons were "totally real to me, then, and Superman was more real than all of them. He could fly! He could bend steel with his bare hands! Nobody could bully him (unless he was pretending to be weak)! Oh, how I dreamed of all these [things]." For Augusto as for so many children, the cartoons were a gateway to other Superman experiences—feasting on Superman comic books, entertaining himself with Superman toys, and cherishing the way Christopher Reeve brought his hero alive in the movies. Superman became a part of Augusto's life, no matter that Metropolis was thousands of miles away from his home in Salvador, Brazil. Superman was "not just some action hero," says Augusto, who today writes and draws his own comic strips, "but a model. A goal to achieve in my life."

Back in the United States, Big Blue had returned to the newspapers with a strip that was launched in 1978 as *The World's Greatest Superheroes* and the next year was renamed *The World's Greatest Superheroes Presents Superman*. Movies offered even more potential for the synergy that Kahn and Levitz were so keen on. Comics lovers had been gathering for ever-bigger conventions since the mid-1960s, and DC capitalized on these gatherings to get fans geared up for Christopher Reeve's Superman film long before it hit the theaters. Not long after its release in late 1978 they published the first comic book miniseries, *World of Krypton*, along with a behind-the-scenes book on the movie and a Superman dictionary for kids. The film and its stars also hitched themselves to the Special Olympics, which was good for the charity and for the company's bottom line. Movie-related marketing had become standard fare by then, but it had never been seen on this scale. Two hundred licenses were awarded for more than twelve hundred products, from soap packaged like a telephone booth to velour sweatshirts that sold at Bloomingdale's. Companies paid even more to see their names or merchandise on the screen. It was no accident that we could easily read the name of Lois's Timex watch when she romanced Superman on her balcony, and in the sequel Philip Morris paid forty thousand dollars to get its Marlboro delivery truck into the fight scene with Kryptonian bad guys.

Kahn and Levitz weren't just focused on the present. They were building for a future when comic books would again pay their own way without offshoots like licensing. The turnaround didn't come as soon as they expected—the "DC explosion" of new titles quickly and embarrassingly became the "DC implosion" when many old and new books couldn't pay for themselves—but comics did eventually regain some of their profitability. Advertising helped. Comic books had drawn ads from the beginning, but they took up fewer than two of the sixty-four pages in *Action* No. 1. Advertising copy quickly grew to 10 percent of the publications and stayed that way through most of the Golden Age. By the 1970s, DC was running up to sixteen pages of ads in books that were down to thirty-six pages, which would prove to be the high-water mark for advertising space in comics, although still not at the 50 percent level of most magazines. The nature of the ads was shifting, too, reflecting comic books' changing readership and society's changing priorities. Gadgets were replaced by beauty aids and muscle manuals. "Sex education" products came and went quickly, thanks to the Comics Code. Breakfast cereals were a perennial advertiser, along with Oreo, Reese's, and other sweets. Pitches for correspondence courses suggested that high school dropouts were a key part of the fan base, just as pitches for older comics made clear how many collectors there were.

The DC brain trust also realized that it paid to treat the creative talent better. When Kahn arrived in 1976, she began giving artists and writers 20 percent of licensing fees for characters they dreamed up, and in 1981, when she became president as well as publisher, she began paying them 5 percent of revenues on comic books that sold more than one hundred thousand copies, a milestone that Superman hit regularly. Freelancers were now getting medical insurance and yearlong contracts, the very benefits that had made Jack Liebowitz blanch. Giving creators a financial stake measurably improved their work. Suddenly a job at DC was a better deal than one at Marvel or at other competitors, which helped lure away the best talent, at least until the competition started matching the benefits.

DC Comics, which thanks to Jerry Siegel and Joe Shuster had been a poster child for the old feudal system, now seemed the model of enlightenment.

EVEN JERRY AND JOE would benefit from the new ownership, not that it was easy.

Jerry had spent the first half of the 1970s hoping to win his lawsuit against National and settling into his new life. He was in dire enough straits that he took work first as a writer and then as a proofreader at DC's archrival, Marvel, then he moved his family to California, where there was a healing sun for him and Joanne and inexpensive colleges for their daughter, Laura. To pay for the move, he had to sell off some of his treasured collection of comic books. To make a living, he took a seven-thousand-dollar-a-year job as a clerk-typist with the state of California, while Joanne sold Chevrolets at a car lot in Santa Monica. Jerry earned extra income by writing stories about Mickey Mouse, Goofy, and Donald Duck for Walt Disney's Italian line of comic books. He had fallen so far that he sometimes thought about killing himself, as George Reeves had. A living wage and the California weather helped overcome his depression, but now he worried about his weakening heart and how, if he needed an operation, he would pay for it.

No one found out about any of that until later because Jerry had gone underground, declining to talk to the press and steering clear of most old friends and colleagues. He emerged from the shadows in the fall of 1975, just as Mario Puzo was turning in his movie script and Superman was back on center stage. The creator of Superman knew how to grab the spotlight when he wanted to, and now he did. "Jerry Siegel, the co-originator of SUPERMAN, put a curse on the SU-PERMAN movie!" read the press release he tapped out on his manual typewriter and distributed to all the major media. "I hope it super-bombs. I hope loyal SUPERMAN fans stay away from it in droves. I hope the whole world, becoming aware of the stench that surrounds SUPERMAN, will avoid the movie like a plague." For anyone unfamiliar with the stench, Jerry filled them in with a single-sheet summary and a nine-page exposition. National Periodical Publications and Jack Liebowitz especially had "killed my days, murdered my nights, choked my happiness, strangled my career. I consider National's executives economic murderers, money-mad monsters."

It was Jerry at his melodramatic best, showing the same passion and single-mindedness he had tapped to compose and sell his first Superman story forty years before. What led him to cook up Superman? He was inspired by President Roosevelt's fireside chats, by the Nazis' slaughter of fellow Jews, and by a depression that left him and millions of others jobless, which gave him "the great urge to help . . . help the despairing masses." What would he do if he had the strength of his superhero? "Rip apart the massive buildings in which these greedy people count the immense profits from the misery they have inflicted on Joe and me and our families." What did he want now? A cut of the profits.

Jerry had always been torn as well as tortured, as demonstrated in years of letters to Jack. The angry young man who felt wronged quietly did battle with the lonely one aching to be embraced. His memoir would reflect the latter; his press release bared his mad-as-hell side. No matter that Jack was just a board member now while others ran the company, or that Jerry had promised in his legal settlement never to rehash these issues. It was not just he who was hurting now but his wife and child, and he was out for blood.

The press saw this for the great story it was. A *Washington Star* reporter visited Joe Shuster in 1975 in the dingy apartment in Queens where he was "slowly going blind, still hoping his Superman would come to his rescue." The next month a *New York Times* reporter talked to Jerry. "For years," he said, "I've been waiting for Superman to crash in and do something about it all." Their stories played even better on TV, as the *Today* show, the *Tomorrow* show, and Howard Cosell appreciated. Orchestrating the publicity was Neal Adams, whose fiery art had brought new life to the Green Lantern, Batman, and Superman. Adams chaperoned the aging creators around New York, persuading the media to pay for their hotel rooms and cartoonist Irwin Hasen to draw his wide-eyed war orphan *Dondi* with a huge tear on his face and the words, "Is it a plane? Is it a bird? No, it's a pity." Adams remembers that "Joe was like an angel sent from heaven, I never heard him utter an angry word. Jerry was very bitter." Adams drew on both and, with help from *Batman* artist Jerry Robinson and the Cartoonists Society, he made the case with Warner Communications. "What was my leverage?" Adams asks. "Humanity. Pity. Common sense. I mean, truth, justice and the American way."

Warner's point man in the publicity struggle was Jay Emmett, Superman's longtime marketing whiz and now a man in the middle. On one side, his uncle Jack Liebowitz was adamant that Jerry and Joe had voluntarily signed away their rights and didn't deserve anything more. On the other, morality dictated that Warner, flush with cash from its Superman franchise, help the creators of that golden goose. Business logic bridged the difference. "We were about to put out a movie worth tens of millions and I said, 'Let's not worry about chicken feed,'" recalls Emmett. So after back-and-forth over particulars, Emmett and his company agreed—two days before Christmas—to give Jerry and Joe $20,000 a year for life, an amount that was intended to be fixed but that rose substantially over the years. Their medical expenses, which were enormous, were covered, along with a one-time bonus of $17,500 for each of them. Their bylines were back on the comic books and nearly everywhere else Superman appeared, including a prominent opening credit in *Superman: The Movie* and its sequels. In return, the creators agreed, again, not to sue for more.

"Joe and I are very happy to be associated with our 'Superman' creation again," Jerry wrote in his memoir, with his joyful tears at the movie premiere making clear he meant it. Joe was happier still. The money let him move to California, where he could be in the sun, in an apartment of his own, back near Jerry and Joanne. It also let him get married for the first time, in December 1976, to Judith Ray Calpini, who seemed to have everything he had been looking for. The attractive blonde was three years younger than he was and five inches taller. Their marriage license listed her as a nurse, while a press photo called her a former showgirl and current writer and artist. It was her fourth marriage, her third having ended nine months before, and it happened almost exactly a year after his settlement with Warner Communications. It lasted eleven months and nineteen days, although their official divorce wasn't granted for another three and a half years. The divorce proceedings listed Judith as a housewife and spelled out what possessions Joe had left: three suits, a topcoat, a color TV, a lounge chair, an eight-year-old Mazda, a few thousand dollars' worth of comic art, no job, and declining health.

Being abandoned was nothing new for Joe Shuster and he didn't let it spoil the fun he was having being reunited with Superman. The settlement with Warner "has meant a tremendous change in our lives," he told *The New York Times*. "We've received marvelous recognition for the Superman movie and our names also appear in the comics. A whole new generation knows us."

CHAPTER 9

Back to the Future

HIS MISSION WAS TO SCRAPE off the barnacles. Take us back to Jerry Siegel and Joe Shuster's primal vision, John Byrne's bosses at DC told him in 1986, but make him a Man of Today. Rewrite Superman's forty-eight-year history, from day one, preserving everything essential and killing all that was timeworn. Don't worry about consistency or the rabid fanboys. Borrow anything you like from the Fleischer brothers' cartoons, Mort Weisinger's imaginary stories, and the Reeves and Reeve Supermen and Clarks. The choices are yours. Just make us remember why we first fell for him.

The moment demanded it. DC Comics had just marked its fiftieth anniversary by blowing up its wider universe, setting the stage for streamlined versions of the heroes who lived on. Who better to point the way than DC's leading man, who was about to celebrate his own golden jubilee? Jenette Kahn had promised bold change and, after a decade of tinkering, it was time to deliver. The new comics-only shops were begging for headliners. Could anyone be more compelling to their baby-boomer patrons than a harder-edged Man of Steel custom-built for the grimmer, edgier Dark Age of comics that kicked off in the mid-1980s?

That didn't mean it would be easy. Recasting the sacred Superman legend was as perilous as trying to jazz up the Bible or formulate a New Coke. It would take somebody with ingenuity, finesse, and a super-sized ego. Byrne had all of those, along with a proven record revitalizing Marvel's cornerstone team of superheroes, the Fantastic Four. No matter that he was born in the British Isles and raised in Canada. Hadn't the Salkinds shown that outsiders could not only be spot-on about an American hero but could even take him to new heights? Byrne said he was scared, but the truth was he was itching to get at it.

Byrne delivered a Clark with flesh and spirit. No more mild-mannered wimp. The new Mr. Kent was a newspaper columnist modeled after the gritty Jimmy Breslin, with stylish round glasses, hair brushed straight back, and the tough-guy demeanor of George Reeves. "More aggressive," explained Byrne. "Not so squeaky clean." Superman changed in reverse, losing his time-traveling powers, freeze breath, and annoying tendency to make any job look easy. He sweated, cursed, and used the toilet. "You can't do interesting stories with a god," Byrne pronounced. "He used to be a *super*man; now he's a super*man*." The Champion of the Oppressed's politics were moving rightward in an era when Ronald Reagan occupied the White House, Rambo always drew first blood, and "shop till you drop" was the national motto. "If Reagan has done nothing else," Byrne said, "he's gotten us to wave the flag again. Superman practically wears the flag. I'll be shamelessly exploiting that." Byrne's most radical role reversal happened in Superman's head: After half a century of Superman disguising himself as a human—which made him stand out from Batman, Spider-Man, and other humans masked as heroes—now the earthbound Clark would be the real thing and the alien from Krypton the alter ego.

Superman's supporting cast underwent its own retooling. The new Lois was a woman to contend with. Her hair had gone from basic black to in-your-face russet. She could shoot an Uzi and had learned from the Green Berets how to kick a terrorist where he would feel it. When she wasn't winning a Pulitzer Prize for the *Daily Planet* or signing a lucrative book deal she was fending off advances from Lex Luthor. No time for curling up with Superman or unmasking Clark Kent. Krypton, meanwhile, was more antiseptic and Superman once again was its sole survivor. No more Superdog, Super-Monkey, or Supergirl. Superboy was gone, too, with Clark not emerging as a superhero until he arrived in Metropolis as an adult, which was the way Jerry had written it. The good news for Superman was that his adoptive parents, the Kents, lived on in this romantic retelling and could revel in the man that Clark had become. The bad news was that Lex was even more deadly as a power-grabbing billionaire than he had been as a power-grabbing scientist. Kryptonite was back, but only in the form of a single chunk that had stuck to Superman's spacecraft, and only in green.

This was not the first time Superman had needed a remake. That had come in the early 1940s, with Jerry and Joe doing the work. Mort was the architect of change in the 1960s and Julie Schwartz oversaw 1971's powering down and tossing out of kryptonite. Those revisions were the equivalent of a haircut and nail trim. Byrne performed open-heart surgery, cleaning out arteries that had hardened over the decades and recasting the hero and his universe. The makeover was unveiled in a six-part miniseries called *The Man of Steel*, released in the summer and fall of 1986. DC then sent Superman on a three-month vacation, suspending his comic book adventures for the first time since 1938. When they resumed in January, the company signaled the milestone and its marketing savvy by launching a new version of the *Superman* title and starting it off with No. 1. Byrne wrote and drew that and *Action Comics,* and a year later he was writing the old *Superman* book, too, which had been renamed *Adventures of Superman.*

There are several ways of judging an overhaul like Byrne's, starting with whether anyone notices. Everyone seemed to, beginning with America's most influential newspaper. *The New York Times* published four stories—one just before the six-part miniseries, one just after, a third after Superman's hiatus from the regular comic books, and even an editorial, which said to DC Comics, "We write as friends. We like your plan to modernize Superman." *The Washington Post, Los Angeles Times, Time,* and a lineup of other publications added stories of their own. The last time the comics industry had gotten that kind of coverage was in the 1950s, when it was under siege by Dr. Fredric Wertham and the PTA.

Another measure of change is whether it lasts. Most of Mort's adjustments in the 1960s disappeared when he did in 1970. Julie's remake in 1971 was gone in a year, as was his Superman writer. Byrne's backstory became Superman's defining one for the next eighteen years. It would form the basis for two television series, two TV cartoon shows, and a BBC radio play, and was translated into Chinese. All that meant cash in the DC tills. So did the million copies the first issue of *Man of Steel* sold, which was the kind of circulation Superman hadn't seen in thirty years. Sales came down to earth once the regular comic books were back on the racks, but at a level above where they were before the remake.

The reaction from longtime readers was harsher and quicker. This was the early days of email, and complaints flooded Byrne's computer. How dare you? they asked, although dare wasn't their four-letter word of choice, and most told rather than asked. "Excoriated" is how Byrne describes the reaction. Thanks to the advance publicity, "anal retentive fanboys" let him have it "even before the work saw print." Paul E. Akers was slightly kinder in his guest column in *The Washington Post,* arguing that, thanks to Byrne, "the comic book hero, once virtually a deputy of the deity, has fallen to the source of secular superhumanism. Thus confused, comics today try to do almost everything but the one thing they can and should do: tell a simple, imaginative story." Critics drowned out supporters like Russell Hexter, a high school senior from Armonk, New York, who started out skeptical about the need for a reboot but told *The New York Times* he was delighted to find a Superman who was "more believable and more weak, more like you and me." Over time sentiment has shifted toward the Hexter view, with fans upset by later changes wishing that Byrne would come back, but in 1986 and '87 it was difficult to hear anything but the anger.

Byrne took it to heart. He was equally upset with DC for killing his ideas to keep Superman's Kryptonian mother alive long enough for her to give birth on Earth to Superbaby, bring back a still-learning-the-ropes Superboy, and make other changes he was promised he would be free to undertake. "Double-crossed" is the word he uses, although DC executives say they gave him more money and freedom than anyone had had since Jerry Siegel. And like Jerry, Byrne remained scarred by the wall he had run into. "My time with Superman should have been a dream come true, but it was closer to a nightmare," he says twenty-five years later. "Virtually everything I contributed to the character has been expunged—deliberately—so, in the end, I qualify as little more than a footnote."

BYRNE WALKED AWAY FROM SUPERMAN in 1988, just as the comic book industry was turning around financially. There are two ways to earn money in publishing, as in most enterprises: sell more of what you make, or earn more on each item you sell. DC did both.

Expanding the readership seemed like a lost cause by the 1980s, a decade defined by break dancing, Cabbage Patch dolls, and an *Official Preppy Handbook*. A comics industry that had sold nearly a billion books a year in the 1940s was down to 175 million. *Superman*'s numbers had been plummeting since 1965, when it reached 823,829 copies per issue. Sales fell to 446,678 in 1970, 296,000 in 1975, 178,946 in 1980, and a paltry 98,767 in 1985. That same year the comic strip, which by then ran in just fifteen newspapers, called it quits for a second time.

Then something happened. In 1987, sales nearly doubled from the year before—from 98,443 to 161,859. Behind-the-scenes initiatives by Kahn and her colleagues finally started to pay off, all at once. Christopher Reeve's movies had introduced Superman to tens of millions of new fans, made millions of aging fans feel young again, and motivated subsets of both to have a look at the hero's comic books. John Byrne's radical remake, and the press attention it was generating, added to the buzz and stirred up collectors. The new look and the newly numbered *Superman* book made many think the Byrne titles would become classics. They stocked up, keeping the books in their closets wrapped in protective plastic, unread, waiting until the right moment to sell. Not even DC was sure how much each of those factors contributed, and the trends became impossible to monitor after 1987 because the publisher stopped making its circulation figures public. But everyone agreed that, finally, the Superman news was good.

That wasn't enough by itself. Whether the bump lasted a year or several, it was temporary, and sales figures would never rebound to anywhere near their 1950s peak or even the level of the 1970s. The comics business had undergone what *Time* called an adultification. Older buyers were replacing younger ones, a trend that had begun when Americans replaced their radios with TVs, and kids found CDs, PCs, MTV, and other faster-paced ways to sate their thirst for fantasy. Hard-core fans were the norm now, with fewer casual ones and comics no longer the mass medium they had been for half a century. A survey by Marvel Comics found that its average reader was twenty, which meant he or she was born just after the postwar boom in babies and funnies. On average readers were spending ten dollars a week on comic books, which was beyond the allowance of the average kid. And that ten dollars didn't go very far, since a comic that cost fifteen cents in the 1960s and fifty cents in 1980 was generally a dollar by the end of 1990, with *Superman* and *Batman* holding out a bit longer at seventy-five cents.

To DC, predictability was as important as total sales. Historically, comics publishers printed two or more books for every one they sold. Candy stores, five-and-dimes, groceries, and other retailers could return any that were unsold for a full refund, which gave them little incentive to be realistic when ordering and left publishers with garbage bins loaded with untouched comic books. Direct sales changed all that. Kids who had grown up loving comics and still did started opening stores that sold nothing else. Beginning in the 1970s, they made a bargain with publishers: Knowing their customers in a way that general newsstands couldn't, they could predict how many copies they would sell and were willing to give up the right to return unsold ones. In return, publishers gave them lower prices. It worked well enough for both sides that by 1986, when the Byrne reboot was being unveiled, there were four thousand specialty comic shops nationwide accounting for half of all sales. And DC once again was making money from its comics.

OVER THE YEARS SUPERMAN became entangled in a web of inconsistencies. In the 1940s he fought alongside a super-fast hero named Flash who under his scarlet costume was a college student, Jay Garrick, and who lived in the same world we do. In the 1950s he fought beside a Flash named Barry Allen, a police scientist who lived in a parallel Earth where Jay was a comic book character and Barry's inspiration. Superman and Batman were honorary members of the Justice Society of America, a first-of-its-kind team of superheroes formed in 1940, and in 1960 they were founding members of the Justice League of America, which had never heard of the Justice Society. More confounding was how Superman had spent his youth. Did he slowly discover his powers and keep them hidden until he arrived in Metropolis and took on the identity of Superman, as Jerry told us from the first? Or did he start out as an adolescent hero named Superboy until he became a man, as Jerry and others started telling us later? And why, as he carried on decade after decade, didn't Superman ever look a day older than thirty?

Contradictions are a given for comic books, which are fantasies and, in the case of a long-running character like Superman, have been written and drawn by hundreds of different people, each of whom added his own flourish. One way to deal with the incongruities was to have fun, then tell readers it was an imaginary story or a dream. Another was simply to ignore them, the way Superman's handlers did when Pa Kent turned up as John, Jonathan, and Eben, and the Man of Steel went from outrunning a speeding train to flying faster than a wave of light. That worked fine when readers were eight or nine and stayed with the comics only into their teens. It became a problem as Superman's audience shrank, aged, and became at least as versed in everything that had come before as his writers and editors.

So, in time-honored science fiction form, those writers and editors concocted new laws of nature and systems of logic. The Superman adventures from the Golden Age of comic books, from 1938 through the early 1950s, were said to have occurred in a dimension called Earth-2. The Silver Age Superboy and Superman lived in an alternate reality called Earth-1. The parallel dimension concept had been around in science fiction for decades, but DC first introduced it to comic books in 1961, in a story where the Barry Allen Flash met the earlier Jay Garrick version. The two universes occupied the same physical realm but never intersected because they spun at different speeds of vibration. They were given counterintuitive names—Earth-2 for the older reality and Earth-1 for the newer one—in 1963. The changes were made under Julie Schwartz's leadership and they filled in the black holes that had troubled faithful readers since Superboy showed up in 1945. The Justice Society was on Earth-2, where Superman returned to the original spelling of his Kryptonian name, Kal-L, and his adoptive parents were John and Mary Kent. The Justice League was on Earth-1, as were the hero called Superboy and Jonathan and Martha Kent. When the Earth-1 Superman was in his prime, Kal-L started showing his age, which wasn't surprising since he was almost twenty-five years older, and he went into semiretirement. Most supporting characters were tough to tell apart, but not Supergirl, who was Power Girl on Earth-2, where she took over for her cousin when he called it quits.

Over time it got even more muddled. If two Earths were good, why not an Earth-3, Earth-4, Earth-5, Earth-6, Earth-K, and Earth-Prime? Superman was part of several of the new worlds, and each came with its own special heroes and villains. Characters crossed between universes and comics titles at dizzying speed. Superman fans now had to buy other heroes' books to follow his exploits, and vice versa, which was part of the motivation for DC. New readers were left with their heads spinning and many gave up. Even some veterans had trouble keeping track and pined for the simplicity of one Earth and Jerry and Joe's singular Superman.

That is the beauty of comic books: When things get out of control, editors can blow up one reality and create a more reader-friendly one, which is what they did in 1985 for DC's fiftieth anniversary. It came in twelve parts, required years of careful research, and was something that author Marv Wolfman had been aching to try since he was a kid reading comics on his stoop in Brooklyn. They called it *Crisis on Infinite Earths,* but it could as easily have been named *Let's Start Over.* In a battle between the ever-powerful Monitor and Anti-Monitor, planets were annihilated, heroes died, and archenemies joined forces to save their skins and their worlds. The five worlds that weren't destroyed were condensed into one and no one remembered that there had ever been more. Gone were Luthor 1, Barry Allen's Flash, and Supergirl, among millions. There was but one Superman now, one Lois, one Lex, and one set of stories to keep track of. It was the most cataclysmic event in the history of the Multiverse, rebooting DC's entire line in one swoop, and it set a template both for future comic-cleansings and for impending changes in Superman.

After the *Crisis* stories and before John Byrne's restart, DC published one of its most moving Superman stories ever, a two-parter called "Whatever Happened to the Man of Tomorrow?" It was Julie Schwartz's goodbye after more than forty years at DC and fifteen years overseeing Superman. It also was the perfect segue into the superhero's new era and new bosses. Julie's first choice to write it was Jerry Siegel, whom he called a "genius," but legal hurdles nixed that idea and he ended up with a more contemporary comic book celebrity, Alan Moore. The story opened by explaining that Superman had died ten years before and a *Daily Planet* reporter was interviewing Lois (Lane) Elliot to find out what his last days had been like. His bitterest enemies had teamed up against him, she said, and his friends came to his defense. He broke his no-kill rule by slaying Mr. Mxyzptlk. Jimmy Olsen and Lana Lang died, too, and a disheartened Superman had disappeared into the Arctic cold, where he presumably froze to death.

But wait. On the last page, we could see that Lois's husband, Jordan, was in fact Superman and that their son, Jonathan, had inherited his powers. It was the Superman franchise's trademark wink, the kind that George Reeves had perfected in the 1950s and that Julie carried on decades later. It effectively said, "Hold on, readers. Just between us, there's more to the story." No need to spell it out—simply show baby Jonathan playing with a pile of coal, and, just by rubbing it, turning one chunk into a sparkling diamond. In the last panel Jordan looked out at his readers, suggestively closed one eye, and said, "What do *you* think?" As for the answer to the title's question—Whatever happened to the Man of Tomorrow?—the upshot, as Julie ordained and Moore wrote, was that he, his wife, and his baby were destined "to live happily ever after."

He was actually destined to live the way John Byrne wanted him to, which was more like a human and less like an alien. That approach was why Marvel's heroes were outselling DC's, and that was the kind of Superman that Christopher Reeve had been in the movies. His Kryptonian past, the way Byrne wrote and drew it, was more otherworldly than ever. He came to life not through bodily conception but in a gestation chamber, to parents who looked less human than when Joe Shuster sketched them, and he was rocketed into space not as a cuddly baby but as an unborn child sealed in a futuristic birthing matrix. The idealized Krypton of earlier origin tales was replaced by what Jor-El called "a cold and heartless society, stripped of all human feeling, all human passion and life." No wonder Clark was quick to affirm his Midwestern surroundings and the down-to-earth side of his split personality.

Other Byrne changes were answers to critics who said the superhero had degenerated into a stodgy old man. It was true: Not just Superman but all those around him were showing their age, making him look less like a Man of Tomorrow than Yesterday's Hero. Al Capone had been the right role model for villains in the 1930s, Adolf Hitler in the 1940s, and the Dr. Strangelove–like mad scientist in the 1960s. But in the 1980s the bad guys were corporate raiders who wore Ralph Lauren suits and ID badges to the stock exchange. Enter the new Lex Luthor, Metropolis's wealthiest and slimiest citizen, fashioned in the image of The Donald (Trump), Ivan Boesky, or perhaps Marvel's Kingpin. The new Lois was even more a creature of her times. No more distressed damsel or columnist to the lovelorn—the model now was the sassy Margot Kidder, who had set the standard on-screen by telling Superman, "I've seen how the other half lives. My sister, for instance. Three kids, two cats, and one mortgage. I would go bananas in a week." Byrne's Lois pumped iron and showed thighs and breasts in a way that reflected a far less prudish Comics Code and America. And sex wasn't only for heterosexuals anymore. Policewoman Maggie Sawyer tried a closeted life and marriage but over time became more open to herself and to readers about her attraction to women.

Evolution was inevitable for a character who had lasted as long as Superman. Stasis would have doomed him. New writers and artists picked from a sprawling buffet of ideas and approaches, reflecting what mattered to them and their generation, the same way authors had with folktales like Little Red Riding Hood and with sacred texts like the Torah and the New Testament. "It's a collective work," says Paul Levitz, the former DC publisher who helped steer the 1980s reboot. "It's a long conversation. People come into the room and leave the room and the story keeps getting told. The goal in any process like that is always to preserve the essence of the character."

That is where Byrne got into trouble. He rebuilt the mythology not just around the edges but at its core, changing what not just fans but fellow mythmakers thought should be immutable. "The notion that Clark is the disguise and Superman is the real man was accepted through the 1940s, '50s, '60s, and even the '70s," says Mark Waid, who came to DC just after Byrne did and would get to do his own remake a generation later. "One thing that struck me as off-note with John Byrne's big revamp was the reversal of those roles, with Superman just another disguise. It struck me as taking away one thing that made him unique and it gave short shrift to his alien heritage." What stuck in the craw of Elliot Maggin, another longtime Superman writer, was the idea that Superman had to become less powerful to be more accessible. "You don't define the most powerful character in the world by his limitations. The whole point is that if you have all the power in the world, what do you do with it? How he answered that question is what makes him such an important American character." The most piercing critique came from Len Wein, who, like Byrne, wrote for both Marvel and DC. Byrne's Krypton, Wein says, was so sterile that it "deserved to blow up." And the new Superman "wasn't Superman. He had no heart."

Byrne, many fans agreed, had gone too far. He forgot that the key to Superman is that he is like us even though he isn't us. He isn't human but is a shining example for everyone who is. Sometimes it takes an alien to show us what is special about ourselves, or what could be if we really tried. The Last Kryptonian's greatest powers are his mind and his heart, which are why baby boomers embrace him as much as the greatest generation did.

The Byrne remake and the controversy it spawned came just in time for Superman's fiftieth birthday jubilee, which was perfect timing for DC. Rather than the anniversary conversation being about how calcified he was, it was about what made him a classic. The Smithsonian showed how central it thought Superman was to the American psyche with a yearlong celebration called "Superman: Many Lives, Many Worlds." George Reeves was there alongside

Christopher Reeve, in the continuous clips the museum aired from
TV, movies, and cartoons. There was a battery-operated Superman
wristwatch, a box of Pep cereal with Superman on the back, and, as
recognizable as Judy Garland's ruby slippers, Jimmy Olsen's bow tie.
Time thought the occasion important enough to justify a cover feature. CBS ran a special assembled by *Saturday Night Live* creator Lorne
Michaels, whose ex-wife was Joe Shuster's niece Rosie. Playwright
David Mamet paid tribute, too, writing, "I admire anyone who can
make his living in his underwear." And DC ran back-to-back-to-back
birthday parties at New York's historic Puck Building, with Mayor
Ed Koch toasting the ageless superhero, "May you live to 120!"

The tribute Superman himself might have enjoyed most was a
book of essays called *Superman at Fifty! The Persistence of a Legend!* It
explored serious questions such as why Lois was so attracted to Superman ("Because he represents freedom. Freedom from a conventional life. Freedom from the roles women are expected to play.
Freedom, in flying, from the gravity that pulls on humans") and fun
ones such as is there anything Superman can't do. (A Man of Steel
can't get a tattoo, a tan, a vaccination, or a vasectomy.) As to why he
persisted for a full half century, the editors concluded it was his "el-
emental power—a simple grandeur of conception—that sticks in the
soul and finds its way to the corner of one's smile."

ALEX AND ILYA SALKIND celebrated their success with *Superman:
The Movie* by doing it again. And again. Then they sold the rights to
make a fourth to someone else. Sequels were their specialty—and
how they turned red ink black. But by the third, the plot lines were
testing the faith of even Superman's fiercest defenders and budgets
were plummeting along with box office receipts.

The first of the new movies, *Superman II,* was the most successful
creatively and financially. Relieved of the need to retell the origin
story, which the 1978 film had done, this 1980 release could get right
into the action, although setting the opening on Krypton served as a
reminder of Superman's alien beginnings. The new movie also didn't
have to start from scratch with writers and rewriters. Nearly all the
story was there in the Puzo-Benton-Newmans-Mankiewicz script,

with David and Leslie Newman returning to do touch-ups and write a new ending since the original had been filched for the first movie. Part of the second film had been shot alongside the first, although precisely how much would be hotly contested.

Like its precursor, *Superman II* was partly a love story. Lois and Clark were dispatched by the *Daily Planet* to Niagara Falls, where he stuck his hand into a fireplace to rescue her hairbrush—and she realized that he didn't get burned. To her, that proved he was Superman. After half a century of denying it, he inexplicably fessed up. Then he took Lois to his Fortress of Solitude and shared with her the story of his Kryptonian roots. But being with a human like her carried a cost: He must give up his special powers. He did, spending the night of his life with her and intending to spend more. He also experienced what it was like not just to fake physical weakness but to actually be a weakling, as he got throttled by a burly trucker in a seedy diner. Tasting his own blood for the first time, he said to Lois, "Maybe we ought to hire a bodyguard from now on." Lois: "I don't want a bodyguard. I want the man I fell in love with." Clark: "I know that, Lois. And I wish he were here." Humor *and* romance. What more could a movie-goer want?

What kids wanted was a Superman adventure story, not a yucky love tale. They didn't have to wait long. Three criminals who had been sentenced by Jor-El and his fellow elders to the Hades-like Phantom Zone escaped and came to Earth to exact revenge on Jor-El's son and his adopted planet. They were vicious and single-minded, in stark contrast to the stumblebum villains of the first movie. After subduing the president of the United States they went looking for Superman, who, upon hearing of the havoc they were wreaking, managed to restore his powers. Lex Luthor joined with the murderous trio and they kidnapped Lois. What followed was the most heart-stirring on-screen battle ever for Superman, waged in the streets and into the skies of Metropolis. Weapons were anything they could find—buses, manhole lids, humans ducking for cover—and the action was worthy of Jerry and Joe's early comics. Afraid there would soon be no city left, Superman eventually lured his adversaries to his Arctic fortress. Knowing he couldn't beat three Kryptonians, each with strength comparable to his, he feigned defeat, then stripped them of their powers by exposing them to the same crystalline red light that had weakened him. He had won the battle but was about to lose his love—the toll for getting back his superpowers was forfeiting his dream of human romance. The next day Clark kissed Lois, which he knew would eliminate her memory of his being the Man of Steel, and Superman promised the president that he would never again falter in his primary mission to safeguard humanity.

Director Richard Donner had started filming this story while he was working on the first movie, but he never got to finish it. "My feeling at the time was that if the first picture had been a failure, the Salkinds would have demanded that I come back for the second" just to torture him, Donner recalls thirty years later. "Since it was a success, they figured they could make the second one without me. One day I got a telegram from them saying my services no longer were needed and that my dear close friend Richard Lester would take over. To this day I have never heard from them." Ilya Salkind has a different version: "Dick Donner said, 'I will do the second movie on my terms and without [Pierre] Spengler,'" who was the producer and money manager. "Spengler was my friend since childhood and my father and I were very loyal guys. We said no, and it really boiled down to that."

Much of the cast sided with Donner, including Christopher Reeve, who at the time said, "The mind boggles at the prospect of doing it with someone else, because Dick was so marvelous to work with." A doubling of Reeve's salary to five hundred thousand dollars and a promise that it would be doubled again for a third movie helped unboggle him, as did knowing that enough of the work had been completed to ensure that shooting the sequel would take a fraction of the time he had spent on the first film. Margot Kidder, true to her Lois Lane persona, was less diplomatic and more loyal. She lashed out at the Salkinds, explaining to *People* magazine that "if I think someone is an amoral asshole I say so." It earned her the admiration of Donner's many fans—and assured that Lois would have fewer than five minutes of screen time in the third movie.

Lester, who had directed two films with the Beatles, had been brought on near the end of the first Superman movie, supposedly to act as an intermediary between Donner and his producers but in fact, he acknowledged later, "to make [Donner] quit and walk out of it and they wouldn't have to pay him any more." Lester was paid twice for shepherding the second movie, first by the Salkinds and again by an anxious Warner Bros., assuring him the highest salary ever for a director. He earned it. First there was the need to substitute Lara for Jor-El in scenes that were supposed to feature the latter. The Salkinds, Lester explained, "decided not to pay Marlon Brando to be in 2, so they had to get rid of all his footage." Gene Hackman already had shot with Donner everything he needed to, and wherever adjustments had to be made, his double stood in for him. As for Kidder, she was in "uncontrollable despair" over problems with her real-world husband and daughter but had to gear up for the scene where Superman would kiss her and make her forget the life they had planned together. "It was the only time that I've ever been quite so manipulative," Lester said. "We shot that scene, and she was so out of it and so emotionally distraught that it was really a lovely performance."

Flying and other special effects continued to be a challenge, especially for the actors. Sarah Douglas, who played the sexy villainess Ursa, started each day by having her long hair tucked into a short-cropped wig. Her freckles needed coating in white makeup—"supervillains don't have freckles"—while her eyebrows were pasted up with glue to make her look haughty and false nails were baked on so they wouldn't keep falling off. The worst part of the job was hanging in the air during flying scenes, held up with just two wires on rings. Her runny nose was repeatedly wiped by a man holding a forty-foot pole with a tissue on the end. All the flying and fighting hurt so much that by the end a nurse had to be on the set to tend to the twenty-year-old Douglas. "I have injuries to that shoulder blade to this day," she says, while fellow villain Jack O'Halloran ruptured a disc and needed an operation. Douglas also earned fans who continue to follow her and her leather-clad, lizardlike Ursa, including "a terrific gay following. Guys say, 'I was struggling with my sexuality and I looked to you.'"

With Brando gone, religion played less of a role in Superman II, although one of its most memorable lines was whispered by an elderly woman as Superman was rescuing a young boy about to topple into Niagara Falls. "What a nice man," she says out of the blue but not out of the script. "Of course he's Jewish." The sets and background, meanwhile, were even more elaborate and expensive for the sequel than for the original. The Fortress of Solitude was completely rebuilt. New York was re-created in miniature in the London studio, with scores of tiny cars with working headlights. Niagara Falls was there, too, along with a look-alike Times Square that would be torn apart by Superman and the trio of villains and showed how quickly costs could mount. Simulating that slice of Manhattan at the British studio required 5,500 tons of sand, cement, and tar; 500,000 feet of scaffolding; 250,000 feet of lumber; 6,000 cubic yards of concrete; and 10,000 square feet of glass. Total cost for the re-creation: $10 million. Total cost for the film: $53 million, which was a record at the time.

To ensure that everyone made back their money, Warner Bros. flipped on its head the conventional marketing strategy used for the first film. Instead of pumping up publicity, the studio did everything it could to avoid attention, at least at first. That was because it had reversed the usual schedule for release, opening the film overseas rather than in America, as was the tradition for blockbuster movies. The goal was to hit every country that mattered during its peak moviegoing season—Christmas in France, South Africa, Spain, Australia, and Italy, and Easter in West Germany and England—and still be ready for a premiere in the United States and Japan during the summer, when kids were out of school and ready for fun. For that to work, Warner's marketing mavens said, it was critical that word not leak back to America about what was happening abroad. They weren't afraid that the film would bomb so much as that it would seem stale once it reached the United States, a concern that had never bothered moviegoers overseas. So while the publicity budget was double what it had been for the first film, and the 1,397 theaters scheduled to air it nearly tripled the first film's bookings, all the ads in newspapers and on radio and TV were held until just three weeks before its June 1981 opening. The all-expenses-paid junket to Niagara Falls for reporters also was last-minute. It was the kind of gamble that Alex Salkind relished but that was anathema to Hollywood studios.

It paid off better than even Alex could have conceived. Its opening day was the highest ever for an opener and for a Friday, at nearly $4.5

million. The next day it smashed the all-time one-day record with $5.6 million, besting *Star Wars* by more than $2 million. Its $24 million first week was a record, too, $4 million higher than *The Empire Strikes Back*. For the year, *Superman II* earned $108 million—enough to place third among all releases in 1981, trailing only *Raiders of the Lost Ark* and *On Golden Pond* and topping such favorites as *Arthur, Body Heat,* and James Bond's *For Your Eyes Only.* That jackpot, plus more than $100 million in overseas ticket sales, dug the Salkinds out of their hole from the first film. Still, says Ilya, having spent $120 million to produce the two movies, they "barely broke even."

Critics were split over how good the second movie was and how it compared with the first. "It is that rarity of rarities, a sequel that readily surpasses the original," wrote Richard Schickel of *Time.* "Suffice it to say *Superman II* is a movie no kid need be ashamed to take his parents to." Janet Maslin of *The New York Times* was equally effusive: "'Superman II' is a marvelous toy. It's funny, it's full of tricks and it manages to be royally entertaining, which is really all it aims for." But *The Wall Street Journal's* Joy Gould Boyum called it "as loud and distracting as a carnival" and *The Washington Post's* Gary Arnold wrote, "What seems to have been lost is the straightforward heroic exuberance of the original film." Most damning of all was Gay S. Gasser, whose *Los Angeles Times* commentary said, "This Superman is prone to the ugliest of human faults—petulance, envy, vengefulness. He reneges on his commitment to Lois; he throws a temper tantrum when his 'identity' is revealed; he spews out clichés in moments when sincerity would seem vital. What can Lois possibly see in him?"

While fans turned out in numbers unusual for a sequel, loyalists of Richard Donner, whose *Superman: The Movie* was becoming a classic almost on the scale of the George Reeves *Adventures of Superman,* were steaming about his having been dumped from *Superman II.* They resented the fact that Donner wasn't listed as director of the second film, given all the work he had done on it. They argued over whether what was left was 25 percent his or 75, and whether the cuts had been made for artistic reasons or so Lester and the Salkinds could claim the work as theirs. The Donner faithful weren't really satisfied until twenty-five years later, when, thanks to their lobbying, Warner Bros. released on DVD a re-edit called *Superman II: The Richard Don-*

ner Cut. While the storyline was largely the same, half the footage had been shot by Donner decades before but never used, including fifteen minutes of Marlon Brando as Jor-El. Donner, not Lester, was credited as the director. Finally Donner fans had the film they longed for and answers to the what-ifs. Ilya took perpetual ribbing when the old Donner crew got together in Los Angeles to watch the new version, but years later he got the last word, saying, "It was mainly because I agreed with Warner's" that the Donner cut came out. "I called Dick after that and I said, 'I love you, man.' And I do."

The Salkinds had made their own special cut of the first Superman movie in 1981. It was aimed at television, and money—not art—was the motive. They added forty-five minutes of footage, knowing that each extra minute meant more money from the ABC network. Gone was a nude baby Kal-El, along with any profanity. The 182-minute film, shown over two nights during the sweeps ratings period in 1982, finished tops in that month's Nielsen survey.

The Salkinds, Lester, Reeve, and the Newmans were back for a third movie in 1983, which, in the spirit of the first sequel, was titled simply Superman III. Luckily for him, Donner was long gone, and Margot Kidder was only there long enough for a cameo hello and goodbye. The romance this time was between Superman and Lana Lang, his childhood friend, played by Annette O'Toole in her first appearance in the Superman mythology that she would help redefine a generation later. The villain was an industrialist played by Robert Vaughn, TV's Man from U.N.C.L.E. The real star was Richard Pryor, as an unemployed ne'er-do-well who discovered that his skills with a computer were just what Vaughn needed to dominate the world economy. Pryor had caught the Salkinds' attention when he mentioned on Johnny Carson's Tonight Show that he would love to be in a Superman film, but he ended up distracting the writers and director as they looked for a way to play to the comedian's strengths while staying true to the Superman story. It was futile. The one thing that did work was a literal junkyard brawl between a dark version of the Man of Steel, who'd been corrupted by kryptonite, and his still good-guy alter ego Clark Kent. "The whole good versus evil Superman is something we'd always wanted to fool around with," says Leslie Newman. "Superman is a love triangle with two people in it,

BACK TO THE FUTURE

it's got multiple personalities built in, and we wanted to take it one step further."

Superman III as a whole indulged in the sort of camp that Donner had consciously avoided in the first movie and Lester only occasionally dabbled in during the second. Its most generous review came from *The New York Times,* which called it "enjoyable enough." *The Washington Post* branded it "a high-flying disappointment" and Reeve conceded that it "became more a Richard Pryor comedy vehicle than a proper Superman film." The frankest appraisal came from Pryor. "The movie was a piece of shit," he wrote in his memoir. Why did he do it? "The producers offered me $4 million, more than any black actor had ever been paid. 'For a piece of shit,' I'd told my agent when I finally read the script, 'it smells great.'"

Pryor wasn't the only one the filmmakers were throwing money at. Reeve got more than $1 million this time, along with script approval. Warner added $1 million to what the Salkinds were paying Lester. The film grossed barely half what *Superman II* did, although the hero still had enough star power to finish eighth at the box office for 1983, ahead of classics like *The Big Chill* and *Silkwood.* The Salkinds, however, knew that sequels are all about cashing in on old sets, old scripts, and old techniques, which become cheaper each time around. So despite declining ticket sales, Ilya says this was the film where he and his father went from breaking even to "making money," although he won't say how much.

This film stood out in another way: It was the first where Alex found a way around his travel phobias and legal struggles to be at the premiere, which included a reception at Ronald Reagan's White House complete with a picnic, a Beach Boys concert, and a picture with the president. Reagan, like Jack Kennedy before him, was the upbeat kind of leader Superman could relate to, in contrast to the more glum Jimmy Carter and Gerald Ford. But Reagan knew he had no fan in Christopher Reeve, who had publicly branded him a cold-hearted leader who only cared about the rich, so the movie actor turned ruler of the Free World worked his charms on Reeve at the picnic dinner. "I'm just optimist enough to think he might have changed his mind," Reagan wrote in his memoir.

Superman IV could have been Reeve's answer to Reagan. In it, the

Man of Steel tried to do what Reeve felt the president ought to be doing but wasn't: work to rid the world of nuclear weapons. The villain this time was Nuclear Man, a radioactive clone reminiscent of the 1940s Atom Man, although Nuclear Man had neither the flair nor the compelling Nazi backstory of his predecessor. The good news for the Salkinds was that they had no part in the 1987 film, having sold their rights to Cannon Films for $5 million. The bad news for Reeve was that he starred in the film and set its theme, which was to wake the world up to the hazards of the escalating U.S.-Soviet atomic arms race. "I thought the character could be used effectively in the real world once again," Christopher wrote later. "Big mistake." He could have saved himself the embarrassment by looking back at how Superman's handlers had dealt with World War II, when they saw that even a superhero couldn't clean up some human messes. Worse still for Reeve, he and the producers were hit with a $45 million lawsuit from two writers who said he stole their idea for the film; he won the legal battle, but at the price of steep legal fees and a tarnished reputation.

Reviewers already had delivered their verdict on *Superman IV.* "One of the cheesiest movies ever made," slammed *The Washington Post. The New York Times* called the flying sequences "chintzy," the special effects "perfunctory," and the cinematography "so sloppy that Superman's turquoise suit is sometimes green." Critics' reactions to Superman had dimmed with each new film, according to Rotten Tomatoes, the website that compiles and weighs the critiques. Ninety-four percent of reviews for *Superman: The Movie* were upbeat, a stunning record. The favorable score for *Superman II* was a still impressive 88 percent. The third film plummeted to 24 percent positive, and *Superman IV* scored an anemic 10 percent. That movie, which had its world premiere in Cleveland, made just shy of $16 million at the box office. That was less than a third of the disappointing result for *Superman III* and a signal to Warner and the world that the Reeve Superman saga had run its course.

The Salkinds might have run out of steam for productions about Superman, but not about his youthful offshoots. In 1984, after *Superman III* and before *IV,* they released *Supergirl,* a movie that followed the *Superman* model by casting an unknown actress, Helen Slater, in the title role and saving the high-priced stars—in this case Faye Dun-

away and Peter O'Toole—for the parts of the villain and the Kryptonian elder. Reeve was slated for a cameo but wisely decided against it.
The plot saw Supergirl battling Dunaway's evil witch, with a love
story buried between the battles much as it was in movies featuring
her superhero cousin. The numbers told the real story: Only 8 percent of critics liked *Supergirl,* an even lower score than for *Superman
IV.* The film cost $35 million to make and took in just $14 million at
the box office, but Ilya says that the finances were structured in a way
that for him and his father, "*Supergirl* was huge."

With Superboy, the Salkinds opted for the small screen. The
half-hour TV series featuring the Boy of Steel ran for one hundred
episodes over four seasons, starting in 1988. The timing was para-
doxical, since John Byrne had recently killed Superboy in the comic
books. Yet many of the show's best scripts were written by Cary
Bates, Denny O'Neil, Mike Carlin, and other DC comic book writers who knew the character best. The TV Superboy was a college
man, attending the Siegel School of Journalism at Shuster University.
He also was pointedly not Christopher Reeve, especially in the first
season, when John Haymes Newton played the part. "I just wanted
Superboy to be a little introverted and insecure, not bumbling,"
Newton says looking back. "But I didn't make enough of a distinction [between Superman and Clark]. . . . I went overboard not to do
what Chris Reeve did." Newton may have been trying not to think
of Reeve, but Stacy Haiduk, the actress who played Lana Lang,
couldn't think of anyone else. "He was and always will be the only
Superman," she says.

What was on Stan Berkowitz's mind when he wrote scripts for
Superboy was how many bosses he was answerable to and the contra-
dictory notes they were sending him. The media conglomerate Viacom was the series' distributor, the Salkinds were the producers, and
DC Comics was the keeper of the flame. "DC people were the Jesu-
its, saying Superboy can't do this and can't do that," recalls Berkowitz. "The single biggest one was killing. He couldn't kill anyone,
anywhere, at any time. Otherwise everyone would be afraid of him,
even the good people." While *Superboy* had an audience a hundred
times bigger than any comic book, with "the *Superboy* show on your
résumé you are just dirt," the scriptwriter says. "It pretty much de-

stroyed my live-action TV career. They think all you're capable of writing for is children." For producer Julia Pistor it had the opposite effect, especially in England, where she grew up and where "Superman was ubiquitous." *Superboy* "was the most fun I've ever had in anything I've ever done," she says, "and it did wonders for my career." The show died after its fourth season less because of anything Berkowitz, Pistor, or any of the actors did than because Viacom had the hundred episodes it needed for syndication and amortization and because Superman's owners wanted to reclaim the rights to the character they had turned over to the Salkinds two decades before.

Alex and Ilya, meanwhile, were having a falling-out over money matters involving a movie they were making about another iconic figure, Christopher Columbus. Getting sued for breaching a contract and committing fraud was nothing new for Alex, but this time the plaintiffs were his son and daughter-in-law. She was Jane Chaplin, Charlie's daughter, and she had loaned Alex nearly $7 million to make *Columbus*. When the film bombed, Alex said he had no money to pay her back. "This is a very delicate situation for me because he is my father and I am an only child. I can't even talk to my mother," Ilya said at the time. Alex felt equally aggrieved: "This is all very surprising, very upsetting to see my son come after his father." Looking back, Ilya says he deeply regrets the split and never seeing Alex again before he died in 1997. Their breach also prevented Ilya from moving ahead with plans for a *Superman V* film, not to mention his dreams of a sixth, seventh, and even an eighth. Alex, he says, "immediately sold the rights for Superman back to Warner's so I couldn't get them."

The Salkinds weren't the only ones whose lives were rocked by the Superman movies. Christopher Reeve grew up over the course of the four films, not always in ways he had wanted. He started out as a twenty-four-year-old actor in serious theater whose role model was Laurence Olivier, not Cary Grant or George Reeves. When the chance arose to play Superman, his mother recalls, he saw it as a "big breakthrough" that could launch his career, but he didn't see himself staying for long in the unfamiliar world of popular culture.

By the time *Superman IV* came out, Christopher was a thirty-four-year-old millionaire and pop culture icon. Fans' first Superman is the one they hold on to forever, and for millions of young Americans Reeve was it. Typecasting wasn't a problem for him: He had a personality strong enough to resist that, says Gae Exton, his partner at the time and the mother of his first child. "People would say, 'Superman?' and he'd say with a smile, 'No, Christopher.'" The problem, those who knew him best say, is that those ten years had robbed him of energy and at least some of his idealism. He had to count on the makeup department now to keep his hairline youthful and he did painful sit-ups to rein in a bulging gut. He worried that he was offering a negative example to kids, some of whom tried to fly like him and ended up injured or worse, as an earlier generation of kids had when imitating George Reeves's TV Superman. "By the time of *Superman III* and *IV,* Christopher didn't see it anymore as his pathway to success and recognition," says his brother, Ben. "It was much more a job and something he did to make money." Christopher himself called *Superman III* "mostly a misconception," and as far as the next one, "the less said about *Superman IV* the better." His father, a professor of literature, says that Christopher "asked me not to see 3 and 4. What I saw happening to his career he later agreed with, but at the time he couldn't help himself." He was in a series of films after *Superman,* including serious ones such as *The Remains of the Day,* but never as the leading man and never with as much notice as when he was playing the Man of Tomorrow.

One of the few people to play Superman who wasn't transformed by it was Aaron Smolinski, who at age three had the part of baby Clark in *Superman: The Movie.* "When I was cold, Richard Donner would wrap me in a blanket and let me talk on his walkie-talkie," Smolinski recalls. When he first met Christopher Reeve, which wasn't until *Superman III,* "I thought, what a big man. My hand disappeared in his hand. . . . It wasn't until I was four or five that it really dawned on me who Superman was and what I had actually played." Is there a curse? "Let's be honest," Smolinksi says. "Having a 'Superman curse' isn't the worst thing to happen. For me, it was and is an incredible experience that I wouldn't trade for anything."

Joanne Siegel had a different take on the curse and a different kind of trade in mind for her husband and his old partner. The three were doing better since they had moved to California, and Warner Communications had hiked Joe's and Jerry's pensions to sixty thousand dollars a year. But even with that, "the quality of our lives is so demoralizing," Joanne wrote to Warner CEO Steve Ross early in 1988. The mailboxes at her and Jerry's apartment building had been broken into, water seepage was rotting the walls, termites were eating their kitchen floor, and they had to haul their soiled laundry to a public Laundromat where "people's dogs and screaming children run up and down the aisles" and "weird looking street people wander in and out." As for Joe, "his rent, like ours has been raised regularly," and if his building were converted to condos he could be evicted.

What did Joanne have in mind? She had worked it out down to the penny and the publicity. "What I'm suggesting is a spectacular gift," she wrote Ross, "presented by you, at a special media event, a gift in the area of 5 million dollars for each, in the form of tax free, gift checks. One million to represent each ten years of Superman's success. In addition, lifetime incomes of $200,000 plus royalties to equal that of top writers and artists working at DC." What if he refused? Joanne didn't threaten the Warner boss, she just reminded him that, in the wake of the triumphant Superman movies and the fiftieth anniversary hoopla, "US, Canadian and Europian [sic] media of every kind, has been and currently are trying to get interviews from the three of us." If those journalists were made aware of Jerry's and Joe's plight, Joanne added, it would be "obvious to the media that DC's reform and ethical standards are a sham." In the end the creators didn't get checks for $5 million, but they did get another boost in their annual payouts, to $80,000 a year, with a one-time bonus for each of $15,000 and an agreement that thereafter the annuities would rise with the consumer price index. Ross, the ultimate gamesman, knew when he had met his match.

CHAPTER 10

Till Death Do Us Part

IT STARTED AS A JOKE. Every year Superman's writers and illustrators would hole up in a conference room, sometimes high above Manhattan and other times as far away as Florida, to plot story lines for the next twelve months. Mike Carlin, the editor in charge, taped to the wall a giant chart divided into four columns, one for each monthly book of the interconnected Superman comics. Then the fifteen creators would shout out ideas. "Team Brainiac up with Bizarro," one might say. "What about Lex running for president, and winning?" After a while Jerry Ordway would pipe up with a suggestion he had offered so often that it was a tradition: "Everyone dies—the end!" Ha ha ha.

No one was laughing this time. The team at the 1991 summit wasn't quite desperate, but close to it. The cartoonists had counted on Clark and Lois getting hitched, a story arc that had started six years before with the John Byrne reboot. Lois had fallen out of her infatuation with Superman and into love with Clark. He proposed, she accepted, and the road was paved to their wedding and a year of ready-made storylines. Now that was out. Warner Bros. was developing a television series called *Lois & Clark* and suddenly the DC honchos were insisting that the marriage wait for TV to catch up, which could take years. The comic book creators would need something new, and fast. So while few took seriously Ordway's tension-breaking refrain, Carlin jotted it down and Ordway, who had been writing and inking Superman for six years, added a refinement. Let's not kill everybody—"Why don't we just kill *him*."

It wouldn't be the first time. Just five years after he came to life, Superman was snuffed out by a second-rate crook, or so it seemed until we learned that it was a ruse to get the thug to confess. The Last Son of Krypton became terminally ill in 1950 in "The Last Days of Superman," which turned out not to be, after all. And so it went, as he appeared to expire in 1957, 1958, 1961, 1962, 1963, 1966, 1968, 1984, and twice in 1987—with each story proving to be his inventive artifice or his writer's imagination. But what if it wasn't? What if Superman really faced off against a villain who was his equal and he couldn't fight or reason his way out? What if he really did die? That would be more riveting even than his getting married, and comic book fans might regret having taken the aging hero for granted. At the very least, it would take the pressure off Carlin and his Super-Team to find a replacement for the wedding stories.

"I'll cop to the fact that I tossed it out there," Ordway says looking back, "but I didn't know how it would work." Writer and artist Dan Jurgens walked into the meeting with two ideas on his scratch pad: "death of Superman" and "bestial foe." Carlin kept the conversation going. "Okay, wise guys," he said, "*if* we kill him, then what happens?" Next he scribbled on his story board "doomsday for Superman." Others chimed in, trying to imagine a villain omnipotent enough to do in Superman and how a world without him would look. By the time they left the room they had a rough outline for a series of stories. Superman would duke it out with an all-new evil predator who was tearing apart Metropolis. What to call him or it? The answer was there on Carlin's chart: Doomsday. Superman would die as he slew Doomsday. Metropolis would give its savior a royal send-off. Then, after months lying in the grave, he would be brought back to life through an unspecified combination of Kryptonian technology and human faith in resurrection. Good ideas, although all would need amending and none seemed especially radical for a hero who had died and been reborn a dozen times.

Little did they know. Martha Thomases, DC's publicity person, sensed something was brewing over Labor Day weekend in 1992, when editors from TV's *Entertainment Tonight* tracked her down at the country club in Youngstown, Ohio, where she was celebrating her dad's birthday. What was this about Superman cashing it in? They had read all about it in a front-page story in *Newsday* titled "The Death of Superman" and now they wanted the full scoop. Cleveland's *Plain Dealer* provided context in its headline: SUPERMAN TO DIE SAVING METROPOLIS. *The New York Times* added a touch of whimsy: LOOK! IT'S A BIRD! IT'S A PLANE! IT'S CURTAINS FOR THE MAN OF STEEL. The frenzy had begun, with nearly every paper and station nationwide and many worldwide picking up the story and late-night TV hosts having a feast. It was a distraction for a country mired in a recession and an endless presidential campaign. Having its longest-lived icon die said something about America, even if nobody could agree what. The stories made clear one more thing: Journalists, along with most of their readers and viewers, didn't understand that heroes regularly perished in the comics and almost never stayed dead.

Carlin, who was the only person on Team Superman authorized to talk, played it coy. "Never say we wouldn't kill Superman," he told reporters. "Never say we wouldn't bring him back." The truth was that DC was reeling at all the publicity. The higher-ups at Warner Bros. were caught by surprise when they saw a CNN report on the superhero's impending death. First they were mad as hell. "How dare you kill him without consulting me?" Warner CEO Bob Daly demanded of DC president Jenette Kahn. Then they were embarrassed when a Superman ad for long-running Duracell batteries ("He runs like he's on Duracell") ran in *People* just before a story about their unflappable mascot meeting his maker. Finally they asked the same question as the people picketing their headquarters: Why would DC liquidate its most cherished character? "Of *course* he would survive— we weren't stupid!" Carlin would explain later. "None of us wanted to write ourselves out of a job. Or worse, be labeled the people who really did end the Neverending Battle."

The corporate bosses stopped complaining when they saw the consumer response. Readers lined up on the street and around the block outside comics stores. *Superman 75*, the death issue, tallied the biggest one-day sale ever for a comic book, with more than six million copies printed. A special collector's edition, at $2.50, came in a sealed black polybag and included an obituary from the *Daily Planet* as well as a black mourning armband. The spin-offs seemed endless, from a wildly successful graphic novel, novel, and young adult book to a beat-'em-up videogame and a tribute ballad from the Crash Test Dummies. T-shirts were flying off the racks, especially the one with blood oozing from a red-and-yellow *S* shield. It worked so well that DC tried the same thing with Batman, conjuring up a backbreaking assault that temporarily took him out of action. It was the kind of moneymaking lollapalooza worthy of Harry, Jack, and the Salkinds.

For Kahn, this was why she had come to DC sixteen years before. "Our mission was to torture our readers," she explains, "and the best way to torture them is to torture our characters." For Carlin, it was a godsend. He was living out a childhood dream by overseeing Superman but was at a loss as to how to revitalize a character whose comics had resumed their free fall not long after the Byrne retooling. Now he had it. "Okay, world," he told himself, "you want to embrace the antiheroes of the time . . . and you think Superman is old-school and corny. . . . Well, how about we take him away?" It was perfect. "To save him," Superman's guardian concluded, "we had to kill him."

KILLING HIM TURNED OUT to be the easiest and most predictable chapter of "The Death of Superman" saga, although it took ten weeks to play out. Superman had confronted a long lineup of evildoers over fifty-four years—from the Ultra-Humanite and Toyman to Lex the mad scientist and Lex the ruthless capitalist—any one of whom would have relished a shot at the ultimate retribution. No prankster or bad guy in a lab coat was man enough for this job. It had to be someone whose very name suggested he was more heinous, more powerful than any evildoer the world had known. His life story would come later, but at first he was a cipher, by design. His unexplained recklessness and unquenchable rage made him ominous in the style of the mindless action comics of the day. All we knew for sure was that he had broken through his burial chamber and cast off most of his chains, that his face and body were masked by a green rubber suit, and that he was a single-minded killing machine.

His first victim was a yellow bird that he crushed in his fist, sending feathers flying. Next came big rigs and other vehicles that happened to be passing on the highway. "HAH . . . HA HA HAAA," he bellowed, one hand still chained behind his back. The Justice League heroes got word of his rampage and vowed to stop him. Bad idea. The Blue Beetle and Bloodwynd were mere cannon fodder, but the glory-seeking Booster Gold at least put a name to the unrelenting creature when he wondered if it "is biological . . . or some kind of doomsday machine!"

Then Superman stepped in. It wasn't a fair fight from the start. Doomsday was not distracted by the voices of his victims the way the Man of Steel was. "Superman—you're the only one—help us!" a boy cried as he, his mother, and his baby brother were ensnared. And so their hero did, giving a human dimension to his crusade and making his adversary seem even more maniacal. The stakes quickly became apparent, with Superman promising, "I'll stop Doomsday . . . if it's the last thing I do!" And so the slugfest proceeded toward Metropolis, with Doomsday turning uglier still as he shed his green covering to reveal stringy white hair and a body rippling with muscles and pocked with bony spurs. Superman's family and friends offered support and concern. "That's our son, Jonathan!" Martha Kent cried to her husband. "He's being beaten to a pulp—and those TV reporters are treating it like entertainment!" In the tenth and last installment of the series, *Superman* 75, Superman embraced Lois, telling her, "Just remember . . . no matter what happens . . . I'll always love you. Always."

That issue was a rarity in comic books, less for its storyline than its storytelling technique. Preceding chapters had scaled back their panels from four per page to three to two, building to the climax. In this last book, each of the first twenty-two pages was a single breathtaking panel documenting another stage of the bone-crushing, beat-to-a-pulp showdown. Fists were clenched, blows were landed, and fists were clenched again, like those of boxers; elbow blows to the body ended with arms interlocked, like wrestlers'. By the end hero and villain had shredded their costumes and battered their bodies. Forget about DC's no-killing rule: This Armageddon was kill or be killed. As the narrator recounted, "In the years to come a few witnesses will tell of the power of these final punches . . . that they could literally feel the shockwaves." The last two drawings were spread across four foldout pages showing an anguished Lois cradling a dying Superman. "You stopped him!" she said. "You saved us all! Now relax." The narrator had the last words: "But it's too late. For this is the day—that a Superman died."

It was that comic book with the tombstone cover that journalists and fans had been anticipating, and that collectors thought would someday pay for their kids' college education. And it might have, if millions of others hadn't been thinking the same way. *Superman* 75 went on sale in mid-November 1992, two weeks after Bill Clinton was elected president and two months before its cover date. "Copies in New York sold out the first day as customers ranging from Wall Street business people to Greenwich Village artists swamped stores," *The Wall Street Journal* reported. Much of the world mourned Superman's passing, including humor columnist Dave Barry, who urged him to "go on the *Larry King Show* and announce that he would come back to life if people in all 50 states wanted him to." A few fans were angry enough to call or mail in death threats to DC, one of which looked as if it had been written in blood. But *New York Times* culture critic Frank Rich said: good riddance. "Superman," he wrote, "was a goner long before Doomsday arrived, as was the heroic ideal ('very phallic, glossy, gleamingly hard-edged, hyper-masculine' in the words of the writer Camille Paglia) he symbolized in American culture."

DC writers knew better, and they already had their next series of tales plotted out. It came in an eight-part package called "Funeral for a Friend," with two stories appearing in each of the four Superman titles, followed by an epilogue. Everybody had a chance to weigh in on the lost hero. Lex Luthor II was distraught—not at Superman's demise, but at someone else getting to claim his scalp; not in public, where he was playing the concerned citizen by planning the funeral; and not for real, since Lex II was really Lex masquerading as a non-existent son. Jimmy Olsen felt guilty for having snapped the last photo of a dying Superman. Lois wondered how she could go on. The Kents had to watch the funeral on TV because the world didn't know that its loss of a champion meant their loss of a son. Bill and Hillary Clinton were there, though, along with more heads of state than had ever been in one place at one time. At least as impressive was the turnout of the DC superheroes, led by Batman and Wonder Woman, all wearing black armbands with the S logo.

Even more than Superman's death, this funeral was the real story. It was a chance for mankind to reflect on what Superman meant to it, and for DC to remind readers why they should buy his comic books. Nobody captured the memories and meaning more movingly than Bibbo Bibbowski, Superman's tough-talking friend and snitch from Suicide Slum. Standing in his darkened bar, the Ace O'Clubs, Bibbo communed with his divinity: "God? 's me . . . Bibbo . . . Been awhile since we talked. I know my pal Superman is with ya now . . . So I guess he don't really need my prayers. . . . But the rest 'o us sure do . . . Take good care o' Superman . . . Okay, God? I miss 'im . . . I 'spect just about ever'body misses 'im. God? I gotta ask ya . . . why? Why should Superman die . . . when a washed-up 'ol roughneck like me goes on livin'? It ain't right, God . . . . . . It just ain't right."

In the comics, even stories about last rites and eulogies had to have action. An enigma was even better. Superman's body was stolen from his grave by the head of the Cadmus Project, a super-secret, government-backed experiment in genetic engineering. The corpse was eventually recovered, with Cadmus's vision of cloning Superman presumably having failed. Also falling short was the bid by Supergirl and other heroes to check the spike in crime rates that greeted Superman's death. Jonathan Kent took his adopted son's loss harder than anyone. He suffered a heart attack and, on the verge of death, had a vivid dream in which he rescued Clark from the afterlife. The series ended with a cliffhanger worthy of the 1950s serials, with Superman's remains again disappearing from his grave. The clear message was: Stay tuned.

All the Superman comic books took the next three months off, time that let readers absorb the loss, gave the press a chance to speculate on what would come next, and allowed DC writers and artists to hold an emergency summit to figure that out. "If this many people are caring about Superman's death—we REALLY need to amp up his return!!!" Carlin told himself as he and his crew headed back to a conference room, this time at a hotel north of Manhattan, in Tarrytown. The meeting was held behind a veil of secrecy in the dead of winter, 1992, and the writers of the four Superman books had four very different ideas on who should replace him while he was deceased and on how to bring him back to life. "It was making me nervous that we'd have to pick one of the 4," Carlin recalls, "and have 3 writers participating in a big story that THEY had less invested in." Then Louise Simonson, one of the quartet, shouted out a solution: "What the hell . . . Why not do all 4?" It fit the bill as brilliantly as Ordway's "kill him" idea had, and turned into a twenty-two-part series called "Reign of the Supermen." The first book in the resurrection sequence hit the stores on April 15, 1993—four days after Easter. Carlin says that timing was just luck, but its appearance on tax day wasn't. "Now," he explained, "only taxes are certain for Superman."

Back in the world of Metropolis, it was just days after Jonathan Kent had dreamed about Superman's soul following him back to the world of the living. Suddenly, four Superman look-alikes were sighted across the city. The Cyborg Superman was one-quarter human, three-quarters machine, and with his wiring and skeleton showing he was 100 percent creepy. Claiming to be the real thing, he announced, "I'm back." The Metropolis Kid was a teenage clone of Superman, constructed by the Cadmus Project using genetic material from Superman's stolen corpse. He loved sunglasses and women and hated being called Superboy. The Last Son of Krypton was a solar-powered alien who had some of Superman's memories but none of his warmth or aversion to killing. Steel, the last new arrival, was an ironworker who used his expertise in weapons design to fashion a suit of armor, mighty sledgehammer, and S shield. Superman had once come to his rescue and told him to "live a life worth saving." He was. He had tried to assist Superman in fending off Doomsday and now he was helping safeguard Metropolis. He had no superpowers, made no claim to be Superman, and was African American, which was still an oddity in the world of comics.

Each would-be hero battled demons and laid out his worldview in a separate comic book—Cyborg in *Superman,* the Metropolis Kid in *Adventures of Superman,* the Last Son in *Action Comics,* and Steel in *Superman: The Man of Steel.* The first issue of each came with a poster of that hero. Readers got to decide for themselves over more than five months which, if any, seemed a worthy successor to the dead superhero, or whether one of the four might actually be that hero in disguise. In the end, succeed though they did in picking up parts of Superman's mantle, the more his replacements tried to take the place of Superman the clearer it became why he had reigned for so long. None had the real hero's blend of empathy and strength, brains and a story so compelling that readers prayed it never would end. The series' name, "Reign of the Supermen," turned out to be more ironic than literal, calling to mind the miscreant a teenage Jerry Siegel gave us in "The Reign of the Super-Man."

The final stories exposed as evil imposters the two Supermen who had made the strongest claim on being the real one. The Cyborg had hatched a plot to conquer the Earth, with help from Superman's old enemy Mongul. The Last Son of Krypton turned out to be the Eradicator, an ancient Kryptonian originally created as a weapon and re-created by Superman's robots after he died. The Eradicator drew his energy from Superman's stolen body, but his wreckful intentions slowly mellowed, and in the end he joined with the Metropolis Kid, Supergirl, and the Green Lantern in standing up to the Cyborg. As the battle unfolded, the real Superman returned to life just in time, via the birthing matrix that had empowered the Eradicator. While the explanations for how that happened came from science fiction, the very fact of his rebirth affirmed writers' and readers' faith in humanity and, for many, divinity. The Christ-like nature of his journey could not have been clearer—from a noble death to the discovery of his empty tomb, the resurrection itself, and his making clear that he was back to redeem mankind.

The narratives dreamed up at the two DC conference summits were paying off in ways that were easy to tally. While they couldn't hope to reach the stratospheric levels of *Superman* 75, the "Reign" issues sold more than a million copies a week month after month, which was better than Superman had done since the 1940s and better than he has done since. "That became our most successful year in the history of DC," remembers Kahn, "and probably in the history of comics." It was a gold mine not just for the company but for its writers and artists, all of whom were earning royalties that, thanks to publishing sales and licensing spin-offs, were bigger than anyone could have imagined. It also was a reminder that both storytelling and marketing were essential to Superman's success, just as they had been when Jerry Siegel teamed up with Jack Liebowitz.

The nearly yearlong death chronicle left a lingering imprint on Superman, too. His hair had grown to shoulder length during his time away and it stayed that way through most of the 1990s. He had more powers now, including being able to survive in space, which was a partial about-face from his depowering by John Byrne. Another reversal was the return of Superboy, who again got his own comic book and a place in the wider DC universe. Steel did, too, although his didn't last as long, and the Eradicator and Cyborg would eventually be back. How would Jerry Siegel have felt about his successors erasing his hero, even temporarily? Mike Carlin worried about that, so he asked and Jerry gave him a splendid answer. "He said, 'I love what you guys are doing,'" Carlin recalled, "and it didn't matter what anyone else thought."

EVEN AS SUPERMAN WAS being resurrected in the comic books, he was back on TV in 1993 in a series bigger than any he had done since George Reeves went off the air. It was called *Lois & Clark: The New Adventures of Superman.* As the title suggested, the show was more interested in the relationship between the two journalists than in the adventures of the superhero, and at least as interested in Lois as in Clark. Money also played a role in that formulation: Down-to-earth entanglements were cheaper to film than flying sequences and other superheroic special effects.

Teri Hatcher portrayed a Lois who was a lot like the one from Superman's earliest days and the one Margot Kidder played in the movies: feisty and ambitious, sexy, and, at first at least, disdainful of her *Daily Planet* colleague Clark Kent. Hatcher was a known quantity from the soon-to-be-number-one TV show in America, *Seinfeld,* or at least her breasts were: Jerry Seinfeld ended his relationship with Hatcher's character after being told her buxom build was the product of implants, then he lamented the decision after he learned they were real. It was just the sort of legend that *Lois & Clark* creator Deborah Joy LeVine relished. "I didn't want her to be this sweet woman, I wanted to make her more of a businesswoman who was getting that story no matter what," recalls LeVine. ABC "thought she was too bossy, too bitchy, not nice enough. I used to get notes from the network saying she's unlikable, which of course was not true. I used to say, 'Guys, don't you get it? Clark puts on a cape and it doesn't really matter what she says to him.'"

Dean Cain's Clark was less the one Jerry Siegel imagined and more John Byrne's remake. Gone was the good-natured bumbler. In his place was a confident, funny hunk in the person of the six-foot, 190-pound Cain, a former football star at Princeton whose dating résumé included actress Brooke Shields and *Baywatch* siren Pamela Anderson. Another Byrne carryover: Clark was the dominant personality, Superman his alter ego. Breaking with tradition was easier if, like LeVine, you hadn't grown up with it. In her childhood home, Shakespeare passed for popular culture and comics were verboten. "Just doing a show about a heroic guy who helps people was not that interesting to me," she says. "I was much more interested in what his problems were emotionally, how he falls in love with Lois, who is pretty horrible to him. I told ABC I didn't want to do Superman but I would love to do a show that was a love story between this alien and this Earth woman he knows he probably never will be able to have a real relationship with. I wanted to do it as a romantic comedy."

LeVine had other ideas on how to rewrite the myth. She wanted James Earl Jones to play Perry White, and she says he was "very interested," but "the fact that he was black was anathema to a lot of people" at the network and studio. They rejected her choice for Jimmy, too. "I didn't want him to be so wide-eyed and naïve. I wanted him to be more of a player." As for Perry, the most noticeable change she could manage was having him mumble "Great shades of Elvis" instead of "Great Caesar's ghost." Rather than upending the lore the way she had hoped, LeVine had to settle for tinkering around the edges.

Timing, however, was in her favor. America needed a break and a hero in the fall of 1993. It was still reeling from the Branch Davidian fiasco in Waco, Texas, which left dead close to eighty men, women, and children. A Somali warlord slaughtered twenty-three United Nations peacekeepers, a car bomb at the World Trade Center killed six and injured a thousand, and two Los Angeles police officers were convicted of violating the civil rights of Rodney King, whose vicious beating had been videotaped by a bystander. TV, as always, brought us the gruesome images, then offered viewers who stayed tuned a great escape. The fantasy diet for 1993 included *Murphy Brown, Roseanne, Grace Under Fire,* and, the most romantic and escapist of all, *Lois & Clark.*

That first season fell short on some expectations but exceeded others. Its time slot, 8 P.M. on Sundays, saw more American households with their TVs on than any other time during the week or weekend, and more of those sets were tuned to *Lois & Clark* than to Steven Spielberg's ballyhooed science fiction series *seaQuest DSV.* The problem was that far fewer were watching the new Superman series than the old standby *Murder She Wrote.* Yet it was advertising money that mattered most to the networks, and advertisers were more interested in high-spending eighteen- to thirty-four-year-olds who were watching *Lois & Clark* than in *Murder She Wrote*'s over-fifty audience. The bottom line: By the end of the second season, ABC was charging advertisers $132,000 for a thirty-second spot on *Lois* while CBS was getting just $116,000 for ads on the more popular *Murder.*

That was no accident. Warner Bros. and the network purposefully wooed those young, profitable viewers. Erotic innuendo was one key. They tried to craft a Katharine Hepburn and Spencer Tracy–style on-screen electricity, updated for a more modern, less restrained, and less clothed era. Publicity placards showed Cain and Hatcher embracing in their undershirts. AOL promoted pin-up posters of Hatcher that set a record for Internet downloads, making her as much a part of the fantasy life of young men in the 1990s as Noel Neill had been for GIs in the 1940s. Cain was equally appealing to their female counterparts, earning his own reputation as the thinking woman's sex toy. And fans tapped into the exploding World Wide Web to let producers know what they liked, what they hated, and what dialogue and plots they had scripted in case the show's writers were interested. The marketing teams were smart enough not to write off older viewers even as they were trolling for young ones: Phyllis Coates and Jack Larson were back for cameos, to the delight of parents and grandparents who had watched them alongside George Reeves in *Adventures of Superman.*

LeVine got to see Coates, but she was no longer around by the time Larson guest-starred. The final episode of season one was the writer-producer's last, and the full-blown romance she had imagined wouldn't take hold until she was gone. By the end of the first season Lois still was infatuated with Superman but had almost married the ultra-rich, super-evil Lex Luthor. Their wedding was interrupted when Superman burst in, exposing the cunning groom's true persona and watching as Lex seemingly jumped to his death. By the start of season two a male producer was in charge and the show was more action-oriented. The ratings went down, Clark and Lois started dating, and, in the final episode of the year, Clark proposed marriage.

The TV show finally was catching up to the comic books, where Clark and Lois had gotten engaged five years before and where Mike Carlin and his team had been biding their time since 1991. Their wait was not over. At the start of season three, Lois signaled to Clark that she knew his secret identity when—true to her profession as a reporter—she answered his proposal with a question: "Who's asking, Clark or Superman?" Then she turned him down. By the seventh episode she had changed her mind and proposed to him, although that was not the last word either. The wedding was postponed twice—first when television scriptwriters were told to wait for them to get hitched first in the comic books, then to make it even more romantic by delaying it until Valentine's Day. But in a story arc that was part science fiction and part cartoon, Clark ended up marrying a frog-eating clone of Lois while his real fiancée was kidnapped by Lex, who had miraculously survived his fall and been pardoned for his crimes by a cloned president of the United States.

Loyal Superman fans would have known that getting their hero wed wouldn't be any easier than getting him killed. Clark had married Lois for the first time in the *Superman* comic strip, in a walk down the aisle that started in September 1949 and didn't finish until February 1950. It took another two years for Clark to summon the courage to tell her that he was Superman, and as he did, he awoke to realize that their courtship and nuptials had been a dream. In 1955 the wedding story was in the comic books and it was Lois who was dreaming. They tried and failed again in 1959, and sixteen times in the 1960s. Their record in the 1970s and 1980s was better: six swings, five misses. The one wedding that took, in 1978's fortieth anniversary

issue of *Action Comics,* seemed as if it, too, was going to fizzle, since
Clark was under a spell that caused him to forget his heroic side and
Lois only discovered it during their seaside honeymoon. She got the
spell lifted and offered Superman a way out of his vows, but, shock-
ingly, he and his handlers didn't take the bait. Lois and Clark/Super-
man actually tied the knot a second time, Krypton style. The only
catch was that this was the Earth-2 Superman at a time when most
of the comic books were following the adventures of the Earth-1 version.

It was in December 1996 that Clark and Lois got married for real,
with no equivocations or caveats. It happened in the same week on
TV and in the comic books, with Superman part of the bargain. It
was for better as well as worse, since the union of an intrepid reporter
and a mettlesome superhero was sure to carry double doses of good
and evil.

In the comics, the union occurred in a ninety-six-page *Superman*
issue called "The Wedding Album." DC gave a role to everyone
who wanted one and had contributed to the nearly sixty years it took
the wedding trio to make it to the altar, which added up to an
unheard-of thirty-five writers, pencillers, inkers, letterers, and color-
ists. The plot was simple, although the scripters had been thinking
about it at least since that summit in 1991. Clark and Lois had split up
a year before but Lois thought better of it, returning home from her
assignment as a foreign correspondent and agreeing to marry a
ponytailed Clark, who had temporarily lost his superpowers as part of
an attack on the Earth by a sun-eating demon. Time was made for the
bridal shower, gown and tuxedo fittings, and apartment hunting, but
not much attention was paid to Superman, making clear this was
Clark's affair. The entire Superman family was at the ceremony.
Jimmy was best man and his on-again, off-again girlfriend, Lucy,
Lois's kid sister, was maid of honor. The wedding was held at the
Metropolis Chapel of United Faiths, a big tent of a church, and the
service was conducted by a cleric who looked a lot like Jerry Siegel.
In the pews was the creative talent who had drawn and written Superman's chronicles. The story ended the only way a love triangle
could: with Clark kissing Lois and, superimposed on that image at
twice the size, Superman kissing her, too.

The TV wedding was staged in season four's third episode, appropriately named "Swear to God, This Time We're Not Kidding." As always when it came to Superman and his bride, the wedding almost didn't come off. The problem this time wasn't at the studio but in the script, where a scary-looking female prison escapee dubbed the Wedding Destroyer was willing to do anything to undermine Lois and Clark's bliss. They managed to stop her and got married on a mountaintop, but the wedding itself was short enough on particulars that real fans had to refer to the comic book version for the full story—and its aftermath spelled the series' demise.

Call it the *Moonlighting* Effect. That popular 1980s TV show lost viewers once sexual tension gave way to sex. With *Lois & Clark,* interest had started to fade even before domesticity set in, perhaps because of the false starts and stops with the wedding. By the time the nuptials actually happened, only 7.5 million viewers were watching, as opposed to the 12 million who had tuned in the previous season to see Clark marry Lois's clone. With competition stiffening from the rival networks, ABC dropped the show at the end of that season even though it meant having to pay Warner Bros. more than $40 million to cancel the last season of its contract. "Maybe we shouldn't have had them get married," said Robert Singer, the show's executive producer. "But people seemed to be clamoring for that. I guess we bent under the pressure." Jenette Kahn, who had dreamed up the series at her offices at DC Comics and sold Warner on it, says that at the time "marriage was the natural progression. Retrospectively, marrying them off took away some of the excitement of the relationship."

Hatcher, who played Lois, credits the show with making her believe "I was that special," and she went on to a series of movie and TV roles before settling in with the wildly popular *Desperate Housewives.* Cain had less success after *Lois & Clark,* but he said he wasn't disappointed to see the show canceled even though he was earning a reported thirty to sixty thousand dollars an episode, or more than fifty times what George Reeves had. He didn't relish the regimen of living on steamed chicken and vegetables and counting every beer he drank, which is what it took to keep a form that could be shoehorned into his blue-and-red spandex uniform. "There comes a time when you get tired of it," he confessed, adding, "I've been in that costume far, far longer than anyone in history." It was true, as least in one sense. With his show running an hour compared to Reeves's half-hour, Cain had nearly doubled the airtime of his longest-lasting predecessor. Was he afraid of being typecast after Superman? "That's the dumbest thing in the world," he said. "Everybody who's ever been President of the United States—except for four guys—are all dead. So you shouldn't be President of the United States because you might die?"

SUPERMAN WAS ALWAYS a multimedia character, but in the old days that meant one or two formats at a time and those could be tracked with a pencil and ledger, the way Jack Liebowitz did. Now media came in countless segmented forms, and Superman's new boss as of 1990 was the world's largest media conglomerate, Time Warner, Inc. At first, executives at the parent company saw DC as a distant and not especially interesting cousin. What did comic books mean to buttoned-down titans who spent their days fretting about media behemoths like *Time* magazine and Warner Bros. studios? But the "Death of Superman" bonanza and the success of *Lois & Clark* had them rethinking the relationship and looking for ways that comic book characters like Superman could contribute across the Time Warner family.

The potential was there to see at Six Flags Magic Mountain, the amusement park near Los Angeles that had the world's tallest and fastest ride, called "Superman: The Escape." Where he was escaping from was unclear, but kids with queasy stomachs had to be thinking getaway when, in just seven seconds, the roller coaster accelerated from zero to one hundred miles per hour—going backward. It also rose 415 feet, which was thrilling heading up and terrifying coming down. Why name it after Superman? Perhaps because anything that powerful conjured up images of the world's fastest, most powerful hero. Or because Time Warner owned Six Flags.

Superman was appearing at Carnegie Hall, too, where the Baltimore Symphony Orchestra performed the five-part *Metropolis Symphony,* with Krypton, Lex, and even Mr. Mxyzptlk getting movements named for them. Superman was also back in the theater, although not on Broadway. In 1992 the Goodspeed Opera House in Connecticut restaged the 1966 musical *It's a Bird . . . It's a Plane . . . It's Superman,* and a year later the show appeared at Theater Three in Port Jefferson, New York. The Man of Steel even had his own Nintendo video game, *Superman 64,* although video kids gave it a thumbs-down and *The New York Times* called it a poor fit: "In Virtual Metropolis, Superman is out of his element. He lacks the reflexive grace of characters born and bred in the video game universe so he seems befuddled and trapped. . . . Suddenly, you realize that Superman from behind looks just like Al Gore with a cape. After that, it's hard to take him seriously."

It was easier to take him seriously in the cartoon show that inspired the video game. This was produced by Warner Bros. and broadcast on Time Warner's WB Television Network, beginning its run in 1996, just before Lois and Clark got married on competing ABC stations. There wasn't much overlap in viewership, with the cartoons targeting the Saturday-morning Froot Loops audience of preadolescents while *Lois & Clark* aimed at their older siblings and parents. At first called just *Superman,* then *Superman: The Animated Series,* these cartoons may have been the character's best ever. They used animation techniques that the Fleischer brothers couldn't have imagined, borrowed half their story line from Jerry Siegel and the rest from John Byrne, and picked up an Emmy nomination. The series lasted through the end of the century, with the last episode being broadcast in February 2000.

When he wasn't starring in his own TV program Superman was guest starring in someone else's. Hawkeye Pierce referred to him at least a dozen times in the 1970s and 1980s on *M*A*S*H,* and the prankish Army surgeon spent an entire episode dressed as the Man of Steel. In the 1990s, *Seinfeld* went *M*A*S*H* several episodes better. In a 1994 show called "The Visa," George observed that Jerry's "whole life revolves around Superman and cereal." The next season, in "The Marine Biologist," Jerry told Elaine that "when Superman saves someone no one asks if he's trying to hit on her." Elaine: "Well, you're not Superman." Jerry: "Well, you're not Lois Lane." Seinfeld's obsession with Superman, the ultimate man of action, was ironic given that Jerry's show was, by design, "about nothing" and that his career and life were all talk, almost no action. That was precisely Superman's appeal: It would have been difficult for the comedian to dream up a better straight man for contrast. So strong was the bond that in 1998 Jerry teamed up with an animated Superman for an American Express TV commercial in which Superman tried to help Lois when she forgot her wallet at the market, but his uniform had no pockets to carry money in and Jerry had to rescue her with his AmEx card. The ad made Superman as regular a guy as Seinfeld, and it made enough money for him, Time Warner, and American Express that they would do it again six years later in a pair of four-minute web-based commercials directed by film maven Barry Levinson.

Superman's handlers would not let him shill just any product. Jeeps were in; liquor was not. Also in were causes to which DC thought that Superman could be of service. That was the case in 1996 when it collaborated with the Defense Department and UNICEF in publishing a special comic book in which Superman swept down and saved two boys about to step on a landmine. The safety lessons were written in Serbo-Croatian, printed in both the Cyrillic characters used by Serbs and the Roman ones used by Muslims and Croats, and half a million copies of the comic were shipped to Bosnia and Herzegovina. More of the same lessons, in Spanish, would be shipped to war zones in Central America. Why Superman? "He is a citizen of the world," explained Jenette Kahn.

Canada knew that, but Canadians liked to think of Superman as one of their own, since Joe Shuster was born in Toronto, so in 1995 Canada Post issued a Superman stamp in honor of Joe. The U.S. Postal Service followed suit three years later, making clear that whatever else he was, the Big Blue Boy Scout was as all-American as baseball and jazz. The fifteen-stamp set of which Superman's was a part honored icons of the 1930s, from Franklin and Eleanor Roosevelt to Jesse Owens. But rather than choose FDR's hometown of Hyde Park, New York, in which to unveil the series, or Owens's birthplace of Oakville, Alabama, it picked Superman's home, Cleveland, Ohio. It was the Man of Steel's picture and life story that headlined the Postal Service's press release, and he was front and center on the special-edition comics sent to three hundred thousand classrooms nationwide. The first book in that series became DC's largest-circulation title ever, reaching more than 10 million people and helping teach Americans of all ages a little bit about their history.

Comic book collectors had less noble intentions. There had been hobbyists since the beginning, most of whom loved the Superman stories and art and who traded issues with one another. The trend was fueled in the 1970s and 1980s with the opening of specialty stores and publication of limited-edition books. By the early 1990s, the land-scape looked decidedly different. Collectors now could cash in and even achieve a certain status by showing or selling a special issue or artifact. Many illustrators were selling their original art while Chris-tie's and Sotheby's were staging "comic art" auctions, with bidders wearing business suits and thinking of vintage *Superman* books as commodities not unlike pork belly futures. No wonder. A copy of *Action Comics* No. 1 fetched $54,625 at a Sotheby's sale in 1994, which was more than the auction catalog price and more than what a copy of the first *Batman* brought in (a surprise only to Batman boosters who had argued for years that Bats had left Supes in the wings).

DC and other companies targeted this new market by manufactur-ing comics aimed at the new breed of collectors with their get-rich-quick fantasies. Some books had gimmicks like glow-in-the-dark covers; others, like the Superman death special, came hermetically sealed in plastic. The latter paid off in two ways: It cost twice as much as the normal comic book, and anyone who actually wanted to read it had to buy a second copy, since the first would stay in mint condition only if the seal remained unbroken. But ultimately it was a comic book's scar-city that gave it value, which made the mass-marketed collector's edi-tion a contradiction in terms and ensured that the Death of Superman books would, in the end, be worth no more than the cover price. By the end of the 1990s the collector's market was stronger than ever, but only for truly rare comics starring time-tested heroes.

Even as auction houses were soliciting bids for old Superman clas-sics, a stable of DC writers was trying to create new ones. *Kingdom Come* showed how good the new crew could be. It was a comic book series published in 1996, and two years later a different author turned it into a no-pictures book. In both, Batman's archnemesis, the Joker, attacked the *Daily Planet,* killing everyone but Lois. Then he finished her off, too. A superhero called Magog killed the Joker, yet was acquitted by a jury that believed he had done the world a service. The only one who objected was Superman, who even after losing Lois maintained his credo that murder couldn't be justified. He was so disillusioned at the jury's verdict and Magog's new celebrity that—in this story, at least—he retired for a decade, coming back only when the world seemed about to self-destruct. After a long battle pitting one set of superheroes against another, and eventually against the United Nations, Superman finally picked up the pieces of his old existence, then, in a confirmation of his faith in the future, conceived a child with Wonder Woman. The Man of Steel imagined his baby as "a battler for truth . . . justice . . . and a new American way. I can hardly wait to see it for myself."

The plot was complicated, action-packed, and beside the point. The real aim of the series and book were for Mark Waid and Elliot Maggin, two of Superman's most loyal and skilled disciples, to reaffirm first principles. Superheroes weren't gods, the writers told us, but with their strengths came responsibilities they couldn't walk away from the way Superman had. Rules mattered, too, including ones that seemed quaint, such as murder being wrong even when the murderer meant well and the victim deserved to die. Never forgetting anything was Superman's greatest burden, especially while he was mourning Lois, and his ability to inspire hope in others was more powerful than his X-ray vision. Waid underlined the spirituality of his tale by making his narrator a minister. Maggin called the mantra about truth and justice Superman's "personal Torah." Both writers treated the superhero as if he were real. "You absolutely have to, otherwise you're just writing a cartoon," explains Waid. While he and his bosses originally conceived of *Kingdom Come* as a story about the broader DC universe, they soon realized that "Superman is such a strong character that any story with Superman in it becomes a Superman story. He is a first among equals. If he retires, if he gives up, if he surrenders, nobody else wants to get out of bed. A world without Superman would be a world in which everybody else who's followed in his footsteps would just throw up their hands and go, 'Why go on?'"

Another landmark from the era was Jeph Loeb's 1998 *Superman for All Seasons*. Each of its four issues was a season of Superman's life, and each was told from the perspective of a new narrator. Jonathan Kent spoke of a father's love for and legacy to his son. Lois Lane described the coming to life of her superhero. Lex Luthor explained the genesis of a vengeful rival. Lana Lang talked about Superman becoming comfortable with his two sides, the human and the heroic. Like Maggin and Waid, Loeb was a devotee and wanted to get back to fundamentals. For him, though, the heart of the character was the Kansas-bred Clark Kent, who "made a choice to put on a costume and realized he had a greater destiny." Loeb thought that having him marry Lois was a mistake, that it made her and Superman more predictable and less interesting. He also wanted to make clear how Superman differed from other characters he had worked on, including Batman and Spider-Man. "Spider-Man tells us that even heroes are human and can be hurt, and that *you* can be a superhero. Batman tells us this is a dark, terrible thing and you don't want to do it. He says, 'I'm here to scare the hell out of you,'" explains Loeb. "Superman is here to say, 'This is as good as we can be. I'm not going to preach to you. I'm not going to tell you this. I'm just going to show you through my actions that, as in the line from the Superman movie, "There are good people." ' "

This was what every DC partisan had dreamed of since the 1960s, when the world split into DC versus Marvel people, Superman versus Spider-Man. Here, thanks to writers like Waid, Maggin, and Loeb, was a Superman who was not just in touch with his motivations, as Spider-Man was, but with his and our aspirations. Spider-Man had been telling us what he thought and felt in a way that seemed self-indulgent and even narcissistic. Now Superman was showing us in a way that made us want to listen and follow. "I don't want to relate to a superhero," twenty-three-year-old Chris Clow, a political science major at Western Washington University, says in explaining why he prefers Superman to Spider-Man. "Superman continues to inspire me not because I can relate to him, but because I aspire to act as he does. He, and by extension the storytellers that have given him life, have taught me how to live well. Not financially, but socially. Spiritually. Morally. And I am better for it."

In his regular line of comic books, meanwhile, Superman was changing with the times, as he had every decade since his birth. His costume underwent tinkering, as did his haircut and his powers, which now included making himself invisible and teleporting across dimensions. His Reagan-era boosterism and bellicosity were tempered to fit the Clinton era of lowered U.S. rhetoric and America as the single superpower. There also were new characters, many of whom came from the childhood worlds or adult fantasies of their writers. Bibbo Bibbowski, Superman's pal from Suicide Slum, was the reincarnation of Jo Jo Kaminski, a hard-as-nails softie whom Jerry Ordway had adored growing up in Milwaukee. Elliot Maggin managed to insert into his stories names of girls he was dating.

Such stories were more likely than ever to play out over months and even years, which let writers develop intricate plots and subplots that they weaved in and out of *Superman, Adventures of Superman,* and *Action.* For readers, this meant purchasing every title and issue if they wanted to keep up, which was more than okay with DC. Such ongoing narratives had been around since the 1930s, but they became more frequent in the 1960s, were ramped up again in the 1970s and 1980s, and by 1991 DC had added a numbered triangle to the covers of each primary Superman series to let fans know the order in which they should be read.

More remarkable and counterintuitive was the injection of race into Superman stories and into the staff at DC, which for twenty years had struggled with its reputation as the home of heroes who were both white and white-bread. Now the "Reign of the Supermen" story arc had parachuted a black man, John Henry Irons, into the middle of the most popular comics narrative ever. He was the least egocentric of the four replacement heroes and the easiest to warm to. When the real Superman came back, Irons—known as the Man of Steel, or by Superman as simply Steel—got a comic book of his own. That led to appearances on two cartoon shows, a role on a BBC radio series, and a feature film in which Irons was played by the biggest Superman fan of all, Shaquille O'Neal.

Was the comic book Steel a credible African American character and role model? Louise Simonson thought so when she and artist Jon Bogdanove dreamed him up, seeing him as embodying Superman's spirit if not his powers. She didn't want to make him a racial stereotype or a generic good guy, which would have been the kiss of death in an escapist medium like the comics. "Steel was a character who had made a mistake in inventing weapons, doing what he thought was a good thing until they fell into the wrong hands, and he felt guilty about it," Simonson says. It seemed to work for more than three years—until plans for the *Steel* movie picked up steam and her bosses at DC started paying more attention. "I was told I was fired because I had sent Steel into space and he should be an earthbound character," Simonson says. "I think I was fired because if there was any publicity related to the movie they didn't want a middle-aged white woman being the face of Steel." Christopher Priest, who took over, is African American, but he says he "wrote John Henry a lot whiter than Louise wrote him. I made him droll." It didn't matter, Priest adds, because few at DC still seemed to be paying attention, and not many readers were, either. As for making Superman more appealing to black readers, Priest says that would have been difficult sixty years into the legend. Superman, he explains, "represents white culture in an intensely megalomaniacal way. To many blacks, he is not Superman so much as he is SuperWhiteMan. There's no sign on the comics shop window that reads WHITE POWER, but the sensibility is implied."

Not to everyone. Growing up in the 1950s, Harvard professor Henry Louis Gates, Jr., "used to watch *Superman* on television every Monday night, sitting in a galvanized tub in the kitchen while my mother did the laundry." To Gates, the African American literary critic, filmmaker, and scholar, "Superman was America's big brother, getting us out of every scrape. Watching him was as soothing as the warm, soapy water in our tin tub." Celebrity weatherman Al Roker was even more dazzled growing up in Queens, reading about Superman in the comics and watching him on TV: "There was something about this guy, the fact that he's theoretically invulnerable, that he can't be killed, that he's a stranger from another planet." His hero's being white didn't enter into it, says Roker, who is black. "He was, after all, an alien, which was as different as being African American or Jewish." No one was or is more of a fan than Shaquille O'Neal, the fifteen-time NBA All-Star with size 23 shoes, who had more than five hundred framed Superman comic book covers hanging in his home in Orlando, Superman logos engraved in the headlights of his silver Mercedes, and a Superman *S* tattooed on his left bicep. When he dies, the sports star wants to be entombed in a mausoleum "with Superman logos everywhere." While he relishes being a role model to kids, especially black ones, Shaq has looked to Superman as his own role model since he was seven. He is drawn to the Man of Steel mainly because he is a force for good, but he also identifies with his hero's split personality, which made O'Neal even more anxious to star in the film *Steel*. "Shaquille is corporate, nice-looking, soft-spoken, wears suits, and is very cordial to people, whereas Shaq is the dominant athlete," he explained. "It's kind of like Clark Kent and Superman. During the day, I am Shaquille, and at night I am Shaq."

Another sign of the changing times for Superman was when, in a three-part series in 1998, he traveled back in time to take on the horrors of the Holocaust. It was the kind of story Jerry and Joe probably wished they had done from the start in 1938, although the world knew much less then about what was happening in Germany, and editors would have been reluctant for Superman to step in, just as they were for him to get involved in a war he couldn't stop. While there was a minor flare-up over why the word *Jew* wasn't used in the 1998 stories, there was no question who the victims were and how much Superman and his writers wanted to help. Before he was transported back to the present, Superman did manage to break up a Nazi rally in America and free some of those trapped in the Warsaw Ghetto. "I'm not a golem and I'm no angel . . . but it's time Superman got busy," Clark told a community elder and two young boys who were stand-ins for Jerry and Joe. Jon Bogdanove, who drew and co-wrote the series and was so taken with Superman that he named his son Kal-El, said, "I wanted to do a story that didn't just look in the style of Jerry and Joe, but could have been a story that they would have done."

All the comic books and books, TV shows and licensed products, added up to a mixed balance sheet for DC. An optimist would have reveled in the records that the death stories set and the revenues flowing in to Time Warner from licensing and subsidiary products. Realists worried that comic books—the core business built by Jack

Liebowitz and Harry Donenfeld—would never again be the money-makers that they had been. In 1991, DC accounted for slightly more than 28 percent of the nation's comic book sales, with Marvel topping 46 percent. In August 1992, DC for the first time fell to an embarrassing albeit temporary third place, with 17 percent of the market compared to Marvel's 39 percent and 18 percent for the short-lived upstart Malibu Comics. Specialty comic book stores, which in the late 1980s were the industry's savior, were in trouble, in part because they got stuck with so many nonreturnable copies of special series like the ones on Superman's death and Batman's crippling. By the late nineties, two-thirds of the stores operating earlier in the decade had shuttered their doors and direct-distribution sales had plunged from $900 million to $300 million. Even market leader Marvel was slashing production, laying off staff, and, in 1996, filing for bankruptcy protection. Superman's death and resurrection yielded spikes in sales, but the abiding death story was what was happening to comics in an age of video games and high-tech toys.

The silver lining for Superman, if not DC, was that he remained king of whatever hill was left. A Gallup poll taken around the time of the death stories showed that just 25 percent of respondents saw him as passé, compared to 60 percent who wanted him brought back to life. The nationwide survey, which included people age eighteen and older, showed Superman to be more popular than all the other superheroes combined—with 44 percent picking him as their favorite, 8 percent liking Batman, and just 5 percent choosing Spider-Man. Thirty-nine percent knew Superman came from Krypton and 66 percent said Lois Lane was his girlfriend. By comparison, just 13 percent of Americans knew that Delaware was the first state and only 34 percent recognized John Adams as the second president, according to another Gallup survey done a year earlier. "The public," the pollster concluded, "evidently knows more about Superman than it does about American history."

It wasn't just that people recognized the hero's name. He was their main man. He made them soar and moved them to imagine the best in themselves. Bill Necessary of Tyler, Texas, fell in love with Superman when he saw Christopher Reeve's first movie. Today, the forty-seven-year-old cleric is known at his Catholic church as "Superdeacon" because "of my great love for the character and for the fact that I always wear an *S* t-shirt under my clergy shirt. . . . I have around 80 different versions of the *S*." Donald Wurzelbacher, a religious studies teacher in Cincinnati, is fifty and the father of four— a son named Kirk Allan, after Kirk (Superman) Alyn; a daughter named Kara, after Kara (Supergirl) Zor-El; another daughter whose middle name is Therese, after Teri (Lois Lane) Hatcher; and his oldest daughter, who was born on Christopher Reeve's birthday. The last is a matter of chance, but the first three are matters of love, as is the basement in Wurzelbacher's new home, which is dedicated to Superman memorabilia from as far back as the 1940s.

Ken Cholette, a corrections officer in Massachusetts, grew up in the 1960s watching reruns of the George Reeves *Adventures of Superman*. When he got married in 2008, his wife surprised him with a wedding cake topped by a statue of Superman carrying Lois Lane, which she had had shipped from Japan, and the couple walked down the aisle to John Williams's theme song from *Superman: The Movie*. His first Father's Day gift was getting the Superman *S* painted on a stone in their front yard. Best of all, Cholette says, "she bought me a belated wedding gift: The Superman tattoo that I now wear proudly on my right forearm."

What makes grown men feel such connection to and even ownership of a fantasy character from their long-past childhoods? "It's the belief that with all the things that are wrong in the world there is still one thing that can't be corrupted," explains Cholette. "Superman is something that stands for everything that is good and decent." Wurzelbacher finds it sad "that many young people today seem to want a DARK hero." Superman, he adds, not only isn't dark but has shown other superheroes the light. "There would not be other superheroes if it weren't for Superman." Necessary's love is simpler and closer to home: "When I was a freshman in high school, *Superman: The Movie* came out. I was in the balcony of the Tyler Theater on opening night, Dec. 15, 1978. I think that was when Superman became my favorite hero. I could so relate to Clark Kent. I wore glasses, I stuttered and was clumsy. I was even the manager of my high school football team, just as young Clark was in the film. That film sealed in my heart that, like Clark, I could always do good for others. I may not have his powers, but I could have his heart!"

WITH SUPERMAN ENTERING HIS seventh decade in the 1990s, it isn't surprising that many of those who were with him early on were getting old and some were dying. For those who believed that a curse of Superman brought misfortune to his friends and handlers, there was more evidence.

Joe Shuster was the first to go, with his heart giving out in the summer of 1992, just as DC writers were plotting Superman's death. Joe had been living in a one-bedroom apartment in West Los Angeles, surrounded by the clutter of his life and Superman's. There was sheet music from the Broadway musical, enlarged photocopies of his earliest Superman sketches, and clippings from *Reader's Digest* that he needed a magnifying glass to read. Just signing his name had become a chore; his right hand trembled and his left was unable to grasp a pencil. His great escape was classical music, which he listened to on his collection of turntables, tape decks, and CD players, the sound pulsating through any or all of his dozens of stereo speakers. Jerry lived nearby and they got together for dinner regularly until Jerry had his heart bypass surgery.

Just what things were like for Joe near the end became clear in a letter his sister, Jean, wrote to Time Warner three weeks after his death. "I was shocked to learn that Joe did not only not have much money in the bank but that he had almost $20,000 in credit card debts and unpaid bills," she wrote. He had three bank accounts, one with $23,773, the others with $167 and $11. He had no life insurance. What he did have was tax returns documenting that Time Warner had, as Steve Ross promised, increased his pension to $80,000 a year. Where did it all go? His closets were stuffed with sports jackets and other clothing. Stereo components were stacked floor to ceiling in every room. Joe, Jean said, apparently had become "a compulsive buyer triggered by years of deprivation." He showered everyone in his orbit with gifts, including his "ladyfriend" and her son. He also made out a $1,200 check every month to Joanne Siegel. "She had been taking 20 percent of his income as an agent's commission," Jean wrote, "for getting pay raises for Siegel and Shuster." Jean asked that Time Warner help her out and it did, agreeing to give her $25,000 a year for the rest of her life. It also arranged Joe's memorial services, as it would for Jerry.

In 1995, the bad news involved the actor millions still thought of as Superman, Christopher Reeve. Eight years after his final Superman film, he was competing in an equestrian event. His horse inexplicably stopped as they approached a three-foot jump and he was thrown, landing on his head and snapping his spine clear through. "This is called a hangman's injury," he would explain in his memoir. "It was as if I'd been hanged, cut down, and then sent to a hospital. I was heard to say, 'I can't breathe,' and that was it." He lost all movement from the neck down. The world was shocked. How could something like this happen? How could it happen to Superman? The children of baby boomers were asking the same questions the boomers themselves had asked thirty-six years before, when George Reeves shot himself.

The difference was that Christopher Reeve not only would survive, he would offer a different and in ways more compelling model of the hero after his accident. His odds of having any function at all were daunting after doctors used wires to essentially reconnect his head to his body. In despair, he thought about suicide. But his wife, Dana, helped him believe in himself and his potential to recover. He exercised beyond exhaustion. He used electric shocks to stir his moribund nerves. He was rewarded with a wild success: He moved an index finger. His doctors were startled; other patients were inspired. Continuing the backbreaking work of rehabilitation, he regained sensation above his neck, around his shoulders, and down his left leg and arm. From a wheelchair, he directed an HBO film that was nominated for five Emmys. He played the lead in a remake of Alfred Hitchcock's *Rear Window*. He wrote an autobiography that spent eleven weeks on the *New York Times* bestseller list. He lobbied for federal funding of stem cell research and he became the leading advocate for people with spinal cord injuries. "'What is a hero?'" he wrote. "I remember how easily I'd talk about it, the glib response I repeated so many times. My answer was that a hero is someone who

commits a courageous act without considering the consequences. . . .
Now my definition is completely different. I think a hero is an ordinary individual who finds the strength to persevere and endure in
spite of overwhelming obstacles."

Reeve was not the only one from the Superman movies who was
suffering. In 1990, Margot Kidder had a serious car crash that left her
in a wheelchair for about two years. That was just the beginning for
the actress whose Lois Lane had seemed almost as invincible as Superman. After several surgeries and unsuccessful appeals to her insurance
carrier, she declared bankruptcy. She had been married and divorced
three times. In 1996 she was back in the hospital, this time a psychiatric one, after being found in the backyard of a suburban Los Angeles home, bedraggled and disoriented, claiming she had been stalked
and attacked. "She was frightened for her life," a police spokesman
said. "We do not feel there has been a crime at this time." The explanation was bipolar disorder. Since then she has reengaged in the world
and in politics, and she has introduced her grandson to Superman.
"It's the first movie that little boys really get," she says. "For little
kids, mostly boys, it's their introduction to morality and I think that's
a pretty powerful thing."

Reeve and Kidder both confirmed and refuted the chestnut about
the Superman curse. Yes, unimaginably bad things happened to them,
but what did that have to do with Superman? Yes, they had been
typecast, but to themselves as well as to the public, any future role
seemed like a footnote. It was their assignments with the Man of Tomorrow that stuck in their minds and America's. They believed in his
story and became part of it. For Reeve, Kidder, and most of the artists
associated with Superman, he was more of a blessing than a curse.

It was true even for Jerry Siegel. His heart had been giving him
trouble for years and it gave way in January 1996, after a short illness.
His last years were relatively comfortable. He had moved to Marina
del Rey, a seaside enclave of Los Angeles, into a waterfront apartment
much nicer than the one Joanne had complained about. He was collecting the same pension Joe was from Time Warner along with re-
imbursements for steep medical bills, and occasionally he got the
acknowledgment he craved from Superman's latest midwives. It had
happened during a visit to the *Lois & Clark* set, when Joanne was

introduced to Teri Hatcher, the 1990s model for Lois. It happened again when the Siegels were guests of honor at a dinner of the DC creative team during the Death of Superman run. "The fact that he was so gracious to us at all was amazing, given the past history with legal issues over Superman," says Jerry Ordway, whose shout-out had launched the death project. "None of us would have had jobs without that amazing literary creation." Paul Levitz, DC's second-in-command, was equally touched: "There was an intergenerational blessing going on."

Jerry also made his peace with the new bosses at DC and some of the old ones. "Mort Weisinger had visited him and he and Jerry went out to lunch together, hung out a bit, and became buddies," says Mark Evanier, a comic book writer and historian who visited Jerry six weeks before he died. "Jerry also talked about how much he owed to Paul Levitz of DC, that Paul was responsible for him and Joe getting whatever they had, and I thought to myself, 'Wow, when I first met Jerry if you mentioned anybody at DC Comics to him he'd put a curse on them and he'd turn orange.' It was so pleasing to me to see that he was getting some closure."

Alex Salkind was the next of Superman's intimates to go, in 1997, when he was seventy-five. Since he was ever the enigma, it is fitting that his spokeswoman refused to tell the press what killed him, although he had been hospitalized outside Paris for a stomach ailment. He spent the last years of his life the way he had earlier ones: living in hotels or on his boat, with his wife or mistress, still a fixture in Cannes and still trying to put together movie deals. Two years after Salkind's death, the first on-screen Superman, Kirk Alyn, died at the age of eighty-eight. While he had often said that playing the superhero made it difficult for him to find other movie parts, the truth was that he relished the celebrity the role brought him and, until the last, he would talk to anyone and everyone about his glory days flying over Metropolis.

Jack Liebowitz outlived them all and was proud of it. He survived his loquacious partner Harry Donenfeld by thirty-five years, and his silent partner Paul Sampliner by twenty-five. He mourned the deaths of Bob Maxwell and Mort Weisinger, both of whom went in the 1970s, both at the relatively young age of sixty-three. He never got over the breach with Jerry Siegel and would get livid when anyone mentioned his name. Jack wasn't actively involved with DC when it was shepherding the Christopher Reeve movies and the new TV shows, but he kept a seat on the board with Warner Communications, then with Time Warner, until 1991, and he went into the office every day. For a man whose comic book business and Superman character had helped define twentieth-century America, it was fitting that Jack Liebowitz came into the world in 1900 and left it in 2000, at the age of one hundred.

CHAPTER 11

Tights and Fights

SMALLVILLE WAS *LOIS & CLARK* in the throes of puberty and raging hormones. The new TV show also was just what the Time Warner doctors ordered to introduce Superman to America's millennial generation, which didn't know George Reeves from Christopher Reeve and in fact barely knew the Man of Steel himself. *Smallville* had two aims: Let young viewers see why their grandparents and parents were so smitten with Superman, and give them a version of the superhero who was theirs alone.

The show zeroed in on Clark Kent's high school years in the town of Smallville, Kansas, while he was discovering his powers and before he assumed the identity of Superman. It was the Superboy story that Jerry Siegel had imagined nearly sixty years before, but with the focus now on his heart, not his muscles. There would be "no tights, no flights," the producers announced from the first, meaning their reluctant hero wouldn't don the Superman costume, wouldn't fly, and wouldn't stick to the rest of the credo built up over sixty years if that got in the way of exploring his fears and longings. What they wanted was to look deep enough inside this ordinary kid to see how he handled his extraordinary possibilities. Could he have sex? Would the world let him alone if it knew what he could do? What did life have in store for an alien who wanted so badly to be normal? These were the very questions every tortured teen was asking then about his—or her—own life.

To make the point that this was not your grandfather's Superman, *Smallville*'s pilot episode offered a twist on the standard creation story. Clark's arrival on Earth brought with it a shower of green meteors that struck and transformed the idyllic Smallville, whose previous claim to fame was as Creamed Corn Capital of the World. The damage became clear in everyone close to Clark—from the girl he loved, Lana Lang, whose parents were squashed by the falling kryptonite, to his friend Lex Luthor, who lost his hair and his innocence. A succession of others turned up with strange and evil powers in a story arc that became known as the Freak of the Week. The comic book Superman may have blamed himself for being Krypton's sole survivor, but his TV stand-in was faced with a more proximate and disabling font of guilt: a body count that grew with each new episode. This revised backstory was half Norman Rockwell, half Stephen King. It also was 100 percent suited to kids weaned on the horrors of 9/11 and craving a hero to help them cope. The new show, debuting a month after the 2001 terrorist attacks, didn't allow young Clark an easy coming of age, but it did explain why a fully grown Superman felt so driven to save the world.

Knowing how the story would turn out made it more fun to imagine how it began. But being familiar with all the details of the grown-up champion wasn't a prerequisite for enjoying *Smallville*. "We made no assumptions that anybody knew anything about Superman," explains Al Gough, one of the show's creators. "When we tested it with teenagers, the boys had to tell the girls that they were watching Superman. The girls were completely engaged in the show but they had no idea that Clark was Superman." For old fans, Gough and his colleagues gave Superman something every hero needs to be believable: a past. For new ones, they offered teenage love, duels of good versus evil, and a gateway to the myth.

Religion was infused in *Smallville* as it had been in other Superman renditions, only more so, as befit an age when public figures felt obliged to pledge allegiance to a deity along with a flag. Divinity was front and center in the first show of the first season. Football players took Clark on what they intended to be a simple hazing ritual, tying him to a scarecrow stake in a cornfield, unaware that kryptonite had made him so weak he couldn't escape. There stood a hero descended from the heavens, stripped nearly naked, on what looked like a crucifix. The image was so powerful it was splashed on billboards and in magazines as well as at the start of each episode in the early seasons. And that wasn't the only insinuation of faith. Clark was filmed next to the statue of an angel, its wings seeming to sprout from his shoulders. He was bathed in halos of light. There were allusions to the Holy Grail, the wise men, and the Romans. "We were very conscious of the religious tones. We also knew it was dangerous, there's a line you don't cross," recalls Ken Horton, a writer and producer. "The most extreme use of religious symbols was in the pilot with the scarecrow. After that we were far more subtle."

Tom Welling had a lot in common with earlier on-screen Supermen. He didn't read comic books or know much about Superman. He was an unknown, having worked in construction, modeled for Tommy Hilfiger and Calvin Klein, and played minor parts on TV. And he was a hunk, standing nearly six foot three with an oh-my-gosh innocence reminiscent of the young Christopher Reeve. That was an asset, since fans were being asked to believe that the twenty-four-year-old Welling was a student at Smallville High. Eighteen-year-old Kristin Kreuk was a closer match as Clark's classmate Lana Lang. This wasn't the feisty Lana we had met in the movies and comics but a subtle beauty made brittle by the loss of her parents in the meteor storm. She and Clark were two sides of the classic love triangle: He longed for her while she befriended him and dated a football star. But a triangle takes three, and without Superman in the picture the producers had to invent a new character. Chloe Sullivan, editor of the school paper, pined for Clark even as she investigated the strange doings in town and their possible connection to her wished-for boyfriend.

No one planned for Michael Rosenbaum to steal the show, but they didn't rein him in when he portrayed the most riveting Lex Luthor ever. His bald pate made him alluring, in a Yul Brynner sort of way, leading fans to brand him "Sexy Lexy" and the media to crown him the "hairless heartthrob." When he went out in public it was with a toque on his head and, when he was feeling playful, with a fake mustache plastered to his lip. The same way Welling's Clark couldn't help but rise to heroism, Rosenbaum's Lex didn't try to be evil but knew that a descent into darkness was his destiny. Rosenbaum had "just the right mix of creepy entitlement and helpless longing" to make him "the most ambiguous character on any prime-time series," Tom Carson wrote in *Esquire*. "You don't even know if he's lovelorn young Clark's rival for the affections of Lana Lang . . . or her rival for his." That last element—whether Lex's longing gazes at Clark meant he was gay—was fodder for fans and pundits. "I love it," Rosenbaum said. "In fact, if there's a line where I look at Clark and I say, 'If you need me, I'm there,' we laugh our asses off. It takes us ten takes to get it out. Let the audience think what they want to think."

Pete Ross was Clark's best male friend in the comic books and in *Smallville*. He was mad about Chloe, which added another romantic spin to the plot. And he was played by an African American actor, Sam Jones III, in a casting choice that would have been too controversial for *Lois & Clark* but that *Smallville* fans liked so much that they set up an online site lobbying for him to get more airtime. He did and was let in on Clark's secret identity, which hadn't been part of the plan. Jones left the show after three seasons, but he was back for a guest appearance in season seven and might have returned again if real-world DEA agents hadn't arrested him in 2009 on drug trafficking charges.

The first season's Freak of the Week aura was toned down by season two, with true crimes, natural disasters, and other stories mixed in with the monster ones. The world apparently had enough real-life monsters to satisfy even the kids. Clark stayed in high school through the first four years, but after that he grew up and the show ventured into more familiar Superman settings like the *Daily Planet*. He explored his origins on Krypton and heard from Jor-El, even if he didn't see him. He battled familiar villains (with new aliases) like Brainiac, General Zod, Doomsday, and a "really hot foreign exchange student" named Mikhail Mxyzptlk. Most of all, he slowly learned to live with each one of his expanding powers, from seeing through tall buildings to being able to leap over them. Lex left seven seasons in, by which time his friendship with Clark had soured, although he came back for a final face-off in season ten. By then the no-tights-and-flights rule had been lifted and Clark was out of high school, living in Metropolis, and ready to take on the full-time role he had been training for.

The new era opened opportunities for new characters. Newspapers across the country had strong-willed women editors, so it was no surprise that Chloe Sullivan was not just popular on *Smallville* but was written into the mainstream Superman comic books. Lex's father, the diabolical industrialist Lionel Luthor, was made for TV and a poster child for extreme parenting. Perry White was back, this time as a television hack and a drunk. Settings were different, too. Rural Smallville was a bulwark against the industrialization and urbanization pushed by the likes of Lionel Luthor. Violence and sex were okay now in ways that would have been inconceivable in the finger-wagging era of Dr. Fredric Wertham. Computer graphics finally made what little flying there was seem believable and a world removed from Kirk Alyn's cartoons, George Reeves's wires and springboard, and Christopher Reeve's trick photography.

For all the changes in plots and cast, and his own self-doubts, Clark/Superman was the hero he had always been. He still had an instinctive sense of what was right and acted on it. His love interests were as tangled as ever. He remained the handsomest, mightiest, most captivating super-being on TV and in the universe. No wonder a new generation of kids was smitten.

Behind the scenes of *Smallville* the watchword remained product synergy, but the cooperation was now broader and deeper. Merchandise ranged from two soundtrack albums to T-shirts, hats, posters, and a monthly magazine. "Save Me," the show's theme song, soared on the *Billboard* charts, and, in a strange twist on product placement, in one scene a CD of *Smallville*'s songs was being sold. There were two series of *Smallville*-inspired young adult novels with eighteen titles. The normal pattern whereby a comic book generated spin-offs was turned on its head, with the TV show launching the bimonthly *Smallville: The Comic* and inspiring cartoonists to redraw Superman to look more like his televised counterpart. There also were webisodes and a tie-in with Verizon that let registered users watch plot updates. True fans could make their own digital comics in a deal worked out between the network and a chewing-gum company.

The most lucrative of the synergies was playing out at the newly created AOL Time Warner, showing the troubled conglomerate what a merger could mean when its moving parts got in sync. The WB network broadcast the show not just across America but around the world, from San Salvador and Berlin to refugee camps in Nairobi. DC Comics safeguarded the legend, which was easier with Superman comic book writer Jeph Loeb also writing and producing for *Smallville*. Warner Bros.' TV studio oversaw the project, and its film division watched for any overlap with the new Superman movie. Expertise was shared. Money was saved. And sometimes limits were set, like keeping Lois Lane off the show until season four, because DC and Warner wanted to save her for what they hoped would be a new film focused on Superman's early years.

Christopher Reeve was a metaphor for that sharing of Superman across divisions and generations. He watched *Smallville* and loved it, so much so that he agreed to be a guest star. He played Dr. Virgil Swann, a wheelchair-bound scientist who revealed to Clark that Kal-El was his real name, Krypton was his first home, and he had a mission to fulfill on Earth. The aging star who had defined Superman for baby boomers was, in effect, passing the torch to the young one who would define the hero for generation next. The nostalgia was ramped up a notch when Reeve's Lois, Margot Kidder, came back to play Swann's emissary. The producers also brought in Annette O'Toole, who had played Lana in the 1983 Superman movie and now was Clark's adoptive mother, Martha. Making cameo appearances in new roles were *Lois & Clark*'s Lois and Clark, along with the Salkind-era actors who played Jimmy Olsen, General Zod, and Supergirl. "We were winking to the mythology," says Gough, and it wasn't just in casting. Smallville's high school newspaper borrowed its name from Jerry Siegel's high school paper, the *Torch*. Lana wore a kryptonite stone in a necklace, a reminder of her parents and Superman's. In one episode, when Clark dropped a copy of a book by Nietzsche, Lana asked whether he was a "man or superman?" Clark: "I haven't figured it out yet."

But he did figure it out in new ways that drew rave reviews. "'Smallville' is one of the few new shows this season to have attained breakout status," wrote Hal Hinson of *The New York Times*. "'Smallville' peddles its own brand of classic all-American corn, which, when served with a pinch of teenage angst, a hint of paranormality and a fresh take on one of the most durable icons in pop culture history, makes an immensely satisfying meal." *Esquire*'s Carson was even more swept away, writing, "Seeing the Superman myth in terms of innocence lost gives the material a poignancy it's never had before." *Entertainment Weekly* added that "finally, Clark Kent has an adolescence that actually makes sense," and *Smallville* "is luring in those who don't know kryptonite from crapola."

It happened at just the right moment. For the WB, the new show cushioned the blow of losing *Buffy the Vampire Slayer,* a hit that had jumped to a competing network. For the nation, *Smallville*'s launch in the wake of 9/11 gave America a hero it could believe in when it needed one, the same way Jerry and Joe had more than sixty years earlier.

Smallville drew the biggest-ever audience for a debut on the WB network, 8.4 million viewers, and by its second season it was the WB's most popular program. The show set viewership records for the age groups that AOL Time Warner executives craved: eighteen-to thirty-four year olds. It attracted young men to a network that had catered to teenage girls. Fathers watched with their daughters, the former loving Superman and the latter thinking Clark was hot. While its audience slowly declined over the years, even at the end it was drawing several million viewers, not bad for a cable network.

This wasn't the first Superman TV show to explore the hero's early life. *Superboy* did that, although he was in college rather than high school, and he wasn't afraid to don his uniform or take flight. The link to *Lois & Clark* was even clearer, with the title snubbing Superman and the program showing more interest in Clark than in his heroic alter ego. But *Smallville* was more interesting, maybe because it focused on a more troubled period of Clark's (or anyone's) life: adolescence. It was a story about family, too. Martha and Jonathan were not mere props here but down-to-Earth parents with rock-solid values, anxious to help their son. Lionel Luthor made the same point in reverse, raising Lex to be a chip off his bad-guy block. The upshot was that while *Superboy* and *Lois & Clark* died after four seasons, *Smallville* lived for ten years, making it not just the longest-lasting of the Superman shows but the most enduring of any TV series based on a comic book hero.

RECASTING SUPERMAN FOR A RETURN to the big screen was harder. Warner Bros. had bought back the movie rights from Alex Salkind in 1993 after he had a falling out with his son, Ilya, and the studio trumpeted its acquisition almost as brashly as Alex had his. It should have known better. For starters, it didn't have in hand a Superman story worth telling. Its earliest version began with the hero dying just after immaculately impregnating Lois with a child so super that he grew to adulthood within weeks. It took even less time for Warner to realize it needed a more plausible narrative. Subsequent scripts traded in Superman's blue-and-red costume for an all-black one, sat him down with a psychologist, built him a robot named L-Ron (patterned after Scientology's L. Ron Hubbard), gave him a third persona, pitted him against Brainiac and Batman, resuscitated not just his birth parents but his home planet, and wrote in references to 9/11 then wrote them out for fear the country wasn't ready. Ten writers came and went over eleven years, along with countless producers, directors, and stars ready to don the cape and tights, at a cost to the studio of tens of millions of dollars and a stack of embarrassing news clippings. Even a title for the movie proved elusive, with the options including *Superman Reborn, Superman: Flyboy, Batman vs. Superman, Superman V,* and the unintentionally ironic *Superman Lives.*

Finally, in the summer of 2004, Warner Bros. hired Bryan Singer to produce and direct his idea for a story he called *Superman Returns.* The title showed that he understood what fans were thinking seventeen years after the Man of Steel's last appearance on the big screen: Give us back our hero. It also made clear that Singer wasn't planning to rewrite the character but wanted to resurrect the Superman millions of Americans had fallen for in the comics and, more to the point, in the two films directed by Richard Donner. Singer had proven his superhero bona fides by bringing to the screen two successful movies about Marvel Comics' X-Men. He had vetted his Superman ideas with his friend Donner before presenting them to Warner, which was desperate to make good on the promises it had made when it reclaimed the movie rights a decade earlier. Just how delighted it was to have Singer on board became clear when the studio gave him a budget of $210 million for the new film, which might have been a record. Just how novel what he was attempting was wouldn't become clear until later, when a movie historian called *Superman Returns* the first feature film ever to be part of a franchise without being a remake, a prequel, or a sequel. What it was, Wayne Lewellen added, is "a modern blending of the core elements that have endured for nearly 70 years."

Singer's film, released in June 2006, couldn't answer why it had taken nearly twenty years for Superman to return, but it did explain what the hero had been doing for the last five. He was off looking for what astronomers said were the remains of Krypton. While he didn't find any survivors, he did find his earthly world transformed by the time he got back. Lois had had a son, gotten engaged, and won a Pulitzer Prize for her story "Why the World Doesn't Need Superman." Lex had married an old widow whose fortune would finance his latest plot to dominate the world. Stopping his old enemy was as instinctual as flying for Superman, but it was certainly hard getting used to seeing Lois in another man's arms. Harder still for the Man of Steel: not knowing whether her son, Jason, was his son, too.

The first clue came when the boy seemed to be weakened by the kryptonite Lex had stolen from the Metropolis Museum. The evidence became conclusive when Jason saved himself and his mother by using a piano to crush Luthor's thug. In the end, Lois whispered a secret into Superman's ear when she and Jason visited him in the hospital, unsure if he would come out of a kryptonite-induced coma. When Superman woke up, he visited a sleeping Jason and recited to him the parting words he had heard from his father, Jor-El, in the first Salkind film: "You will be different. You will sometimes feel like an outcast. But you will not be alone. You will never be alone." Lois, meanwhile, wrote a corrective to her award-winning story, calling it "Why the World Needs a Superman."

The dialogue wasn't the only part of *Superman Returns* intended as an homage to Alex and Ilya's first two movies. Its star was, too. Bryan

Singer was looking for an unknown, just as Richard Donner had been when he chose Christopher Reeve, and both directors picked actors who needed to add ballast and brawn to convince anyone they were strongmen. Brandon Routh, like Reeve, had acted in a soap opera, and both were twenty-six when they assumed the mantles of Clark and Superman. Routh, who had an angular jaw and six-foot-three-inch frame, had been told all his life he looked like Reeve, especially when he wore his blue-tinted contact lenses. When, as a young boy, he saw Reeve's first film, he got so excited that "I gave myself a migraine. I was puking through half of the movie." Years later, when Routh was picked to succeed Reeve, Christopher's widow, Dana, told him she was struck by the resemblance. She said he was a fitting successor to her husband, who had died just months before. "I can't tell you what that was like to get her blessing," Routh said. "It's frightening trying to fill Christopher Reeve's shoes." Dana herself died of cancer in March 2006, seventeen months after Christopher and three months before the opening of the movie, which was dedicated to both of them.

Singer took another cue from the earlier movies by signing up big names to play Lex Luthor and Jor-El. Kevin Spacey, whom Singer had gotten to know when Spacey delivered an Oscar-winning performance for the director ten years before in *The Usual Suspects,* gave his audience a villain who knew how to use humor as disarmingly as Gene Hackman had and was even better at anger. As for Jor-El, Singer couldn't have topped Marlon Brando and he didn't try. Rather, he and Warner Bros. negotiated with the estate of Brando, who died in 2004, for the rights to use not just the footage that had already appeared in the first movie but other scenes unearthed from a warehouse in Kansas.

The Superman legend didn't begin with the Salkind movies and Singer didn't stop with them in trying to reel back old fans. He cast eighty-five-year-old Noel Neill, the original live-action Lois Lane, as Lex's dying wife, Gertrude Vanderworth. Jack Larson, whose Jimmy Olsen played alongside Neill's Lois on TV, was back for his own movie cameo as Bo the bartender, wearing his distinctive bow tie and looking younger than his seventy-eight years. While both were delighted to be part of the ongoing legend, "Our George," as Neill explained, "will always be Superman to us."

One way to measure the change in Superman over the decades was to watch him fly. As determined as George Reeves was, and as much as Christopher Reeve lived up to the hype of making us believe a man could fly, Brandon Routh set a new standard. In scenes where animation was used, a cyber scan of the actor duplicated him down to the hair on his ears and the tastebuds on his tongue. For shots of the real Routh airborne, a new digital camera brought intimacy and editing ease, while computers painted out the wires and cranes as they had for Tom Welling in *Smallville* but couldn't when Reeve was doing his tour of the city with Margot Kidder. Even Routh's skin-tight supersuits were space-age. At a cost of hundreds of thousands of dollars, the sixty tricolored costumes were fitted not with clothespins or caster molds, but using an electronic mapping device so precise that the actor wasn't allowed to add or shed even an ounce until the film was out.

Michael Dougherty, who with his co-writer managed to craft the movie-ready script that had eluded a lineup of other writers, says the experience was both universal and highly personal. "Writing a story like this is almost biblical, when you hear how the Bible was passed down orally from year to year. The Superman character has been passed from one person to the next and one generation to the next," he says. "My grandmother still loves more than anything the black and white George Reeves show, the Superman that she grew up with. For Bryan and I and Dan it was the Donner films, and today's teenagers gravitate towards *Smallville,* which I can appreciate simply because I love the character. There's a Superman for every generation." Staying true to that history was just half the process for Dougherty. The other half was pure fun: "It's indescribable—what it's like to stand on the Fortress of Solitude set. To walk into a room and there's Superman standing there. To hang out at the *Daily Planet*. It's really emotional. It's a blast."

That's not the way things started out for John Ottman, who composed the score. "I was practically getting death threats from fans of the Donner version," says Ottman, who had edited and composed for Singer in *The Usual Suspects*. "They worried I wouldn't do the right thing with the music and asked why John Williams wasn't writing the scores the way he had for Donner. I started getting crippled, worrying what fans were thinking. Finally I said to myself that I have to ignore all that and weave in my own sensibilities and style, and of course nod to the Williams theme, which I'd always intended to. The fan reaction was that if they could have sent me flowers, they would have. They all were very happy."

Bryan Singer was under the most intense microscope. It wasn't just that he wasn't Donner, but he was openly gay, and film critics wondered whether his hero would be, too. It was a fair question; the mutant X-Men in Singer's movies concealed their powers, were shunned as outsiders, and had characters in their orbit who were openly lesbian or gay. "Superheroes—let's face it—are totally hot," arts editor Alonso Duralde argued in a cover story titled "How Gay Is Superman?" in *The Advocate,* a gay-oriented magazine. "Not for nothing does gay director Bryan Singer have an eye for how to make the Superman suit most flattering to Brandon Routh." It wasn't the kind of publicity Warner Bros. had hoped for, and Singer felt compelled to publicly assure fans that *Superman Returns* was the "most heterosexual movie I've ever made." Any remaining doubts were washed away when Singer made clear that Superman had fathered Lois's child and still was in love with her, no matter that she had a fiancé.

Sex wasn't the only hot button for the producer-director. America-first bloggers were livid about a superhero who they said had been made too global in his outlook and thereby not all-American enough. The flash point came when Perry White told his reporters to find out whether Superman, after being away for five years, still stood for "truth, justice . . . all that stuff." "Warner Brothers, the studio distributing the movie, doesn't want to tee off any foreign viewers with pro-U.S. sentiments," railed Bill O'Reilly. "It's bad enough Superman was raised in the Midwest; we can't be having the hero actually standing for the American way, now can we? Some jihadist in Pakistan might throw popcorn at the screen." It was left to Erik Lundegaard, who wrote about movies for the liberal MSNBC.com, to come to the defense of Singer and Superman. "There's no reason to be upset," he wrote in a *New York Times* commentary. "Superman is right back where he began: fighting a never-ending battle for truth and justice. That should be enough to occupy any man. Even a Superman."

Singer had to coordinate not just with editors at DC Comics, who were determined to keep Superman true to his roots, but with the producers of *Smallville,* who wanted exclusive rights to Superman's adolescence. He had to cope with mishaps—from his producer being mugged, to his editor puncturing a lung when he fell through a window, to a cameraman fracturing his skull in a tumble down a flight of stairs—that added to the legend of a curse. And he had to do everything in record-setting time. It took just two years from his deciding to make the movie, without a script in hand, to its premiere in movie theaters—a process so demanding that "at one point I just stopped shooting," Singer says. "I was physically exhausted and mentally destroyed. I needed to take three weeks off."

Even with those constraints, Singer told the story he wanted to. Like the Death of Superman comic book series a decade earlier, *Superman Returns* answered the question of whether the hero still mattered. He did, more than ever. The movie revisited the Christ story by looking at whether society still wanted and needed a savior. The answer was yes. Like the previous Superman films, this one was about secrets, but the secret that mattered here wasn't Superman's alter ego but his past intimacy with Lois and the son they had conceived. The only ones who knew were Lois, Superman, and the sixty million people who watched their movie. Millions more saw it in 3-D, and it was the first live-action film Hollywood had produced in the IMAX format.

"They're very important, these comic book movies, because they're our modern myths," said Singer. "What Superman represents is idealism in a physical form." The film also had a personal resonance for its director, who, like Superman, was an only child, an orphan, and an outsider. "*Superman Returns,*" he says, looking back, "suddenly opened that whole history to me."

Critics understandably compared Singer's film to the Donner and Reeve renditions, which had turned into icons over time. "Earlier versions of Superman stressed the hero's humanity: his attachment to his Earth parents, his country-boy clumsiness around Lois," wrote Richard Corliss of *Time.* "The Singer version emphasizes his divinity. He is not a super man; he is a god (named Kal-El) sent by his heavenly father (Jor-El) to protect Earth. That is a mission that takes more than muscles; it requires sacrifice, perhaps of his own life. So he is no simple comic book hunk. He is Earth's savior: Jesus Christ Superman." But was it a good movie? Corliss asked himself. "You bet," he answered. "Made with precision and vigor, the film never forgets to entertain. . . . The best Hollywood movies always knew how to sneak a beguiling subtext into a crowd-pleasing story. *Superman Returns* is in that grand tradition. That's why it's beyond Super. It's superb." Richard Donner agrees, saying the Singer film "stayed very much within the honest traditions. When that little child shoots the piano [across the room] I thought, 'Oh my God.' Bryan did a super job, a really sensational job."

Others felt the film didn't measure up. Routh "offers not so much his personal interpretation of Superman as his best impersonation of Christopher Reeve playing Superman. This feels constrained, to say the least," Anthony Lane wrote in *The New Yorker*. "Singer's casting errs toward the drippy and the dull, and your heart tends to sink, between the rampant set pieces, as the movie pauses listlessly for thought." Mike D'Angelo of *Las Vegas Weekly* was harsher still, writing, "Fidelity is one thing; slavish imitation another." And *The New York Times*' Manohla Dargis called *Superman Returns* "leaden." Rotten Tomatoes gave it a composite critics' rating of 76 percent—a record that would make any director proud unless they were comparing themselves to Donner, who scored 94 percent for his 1978 film and 88 percent for *Superman II: The Richard Donner Cut*.

Results at the box office also were mixed. The film took in $200 million in domestic sales and another $191 million overseas, which sounded like a lot but wasn't stacked up against production costs and what Marvel Comics had raked in for its blockbuster movies. The original Spider-Man grossed $822 million in 2002, and its sequel two years later hit $784 million. The third X-Men movie, out a month before *Superman Returns,* brought in $459 million. Superman was even losing out to his DC brother Batman, whose masterwork back in 1989 had taken in $411 million—or $668 million in 2006 dollars—while his *Dark Knight* in 2008 would gross just over $1 billion. *Superman Returns* "was a very successful movie, but I think it should have done $500 million worldwide," said Warner Bros. president Alan Horn. "We should have had perhaps a little more action to satisfy the young male crowd."

The box office may have been how Horn measured his studio's success, but parent company Time Warner took a broader view. *Superman Returns* cashed in on a big-time deal with Burger King under which the hamburger chain displayed Superman toys, Superman banners, and Superman fast-food wrappings at 8,500 of its restaurants. Pepsi rolled out more than a billion cans of super-strength Superman soda. Frito-Lay encouraged its customers to test their super hearing at displays that amplified the sound of them munching Lay's and Cheetos snacks. Mattel sold inflatable muscle suits, Cap'n Crunch cereal came with red S-shaped shields that turned milk blue, an Orlando game maker released a *Superman Returns* video game, and Brandon Routh sported a white mustache in "got milk" ads. A&E aired a Superman documentary just before the film came out, narrated by Kevin Spacey, and the National Geographic Channel countered with a *Science of Superman* special. In total Warner Bros. collected more than $80 million from *Superman Returns* licensing deals in America, and substantially more overseas.

Superman had once again demonstrated why he belonged as a summertime Hollywood blockbuster, even if his handlers had not made the same case for themselves. Singer had been hired with the hope of launching a new film franchise for America's signature superhero, just as Routh was intended to replace Christopher Reeve as the defining Superman for his generation. Even the ending of *Superman Returns*—with the hero passing the mantle to his son and letting Lois know he was back to stay—was tailor-made for a sequel. But a new film called *The Man of Steel,* intended to air during the summer of 2009, died on the vine. While Warner Bros. is making another Superman movie, neither Singer nor Routh is involved.

JERRY SIEGEL AND JOE SHUSTER's story read like a movie script from the beginning, and the drama didn't end with their deaths.

To Jerry's widow, Joanne, it was a tragedy, and after decades of Jerry being the victim, she and her daughter, Laura, now assumed that role. Joanne may have been the model for Lois Lane's looks, but it was Laura who lived Lois's life as an award-winning radio newscaster and talk show host, TV reporter and anchor, and news and documentary producer. Now Laura had multiple sclerosis and couldn't work, and Joanne was getting old. They notified DC, Warner Bros., and Time Warner in 1997 that they planned to reclaim the copyright Jerry had signed away in 1938. So much for the promise not to sue that he made back in 1948 and reaffirmed in 1975. Since then federal laws had made it easier to redress perceived wrongs from the past, and the Siegels had had two more decades to stew over how shabbily they had been treated. It was Jerry's dying wish that they set things right, his daughter said. What she and her mother wanted was the nest egg they felt they deserved. So their attorneys and DC's sat down to talk.

They talked and talked some more. Finally, in the fall of 2001, it looked as if the lawyers had agreed on a deal. On October 16, DC set out the general terms of a plan to pay Joanne and Laura nearly $1 million a year each for the rest of their lives. Three days later, their lawyers signed on. Sensing how near they were to a resolution, DC had already given the Siegels a nonrefundable advance of $250,000, and four months later the company sent them a full-blown agreement. That is when things imploded, although why remains a matter of heated dispute.

"We were stabbed in the back with a shocking contract" that included "new, outrageous demands," Joanne wrote to Time Warner boss Richard Parsons. "The document is a heartless attempt to rewrite the history of Superman's creation and to strip Laura and me of the dignity and respect that we deserve. . . . My disabled daughter still has not received the medical coverage she and her children were promised several years ago," she added, her anger building as the three-page letter proceeded. "Just like the Gestapo, your company wants to strip us naked of our legal rights. Is that moral?" In spite of the letter, negotiations continued for another four months, at which point the Siegels fired their old attorney, hired a new one, and sued Time Warner, Warner Bros., and DC.

While there were changes between DC's preliminary and final proposals, the switch that mattered more was the Siegels' new legal counsel. The Hollywood studios whom he had skewered regarded Malibu's Marc Toberoff as a Svengali who manipulated vulnerable clients. Admirers, like the heirs of Winifred Knight Mewborn, whose short story became the TV classic *Lassie,* called him a Robin Hood for restoring rights they had given up for next to nothing half a century before. Everyone agreed that the low-budget filmmaker turned high-stakes litigator had mastered an arcane area of copyright law and exploited it to benefit his clients and himself. In the Superman case, DC argued that Toberoff deceptively lured in the Siegels as clients, falsely promising them $15 million in immediate payouts and the chance to make their own Superman movie. His real motive, the company said in a legal filing against Toberoff, was to secure for himself the right to 45 percent of any payout the Siegels would get and the role of kingmaker in future Superman films. Toberoff called DC's allegations a desperate "smear campaign" and part of Warner Bros.' "last-ditch effort" to hang onto its rights to Superman, a property he believes is worth a billion dollars.

Whoever was right, the result was that the Siegels and Jerry's old employers were back in court. Scores of witnesses were deposed and thousands of pages of yellowing documents were unearthed that traced Superman's development from Jerry and Joe's earliest rendering to the latest TV incarnation in *Smallville,* which Toberoff claimed was a Superboy knockoff and thus belonged to Jerry's heirs. For historians, the legal battle yielded a trove of material—from Jerry and Joe's original $130 contract to stacks of correspondence between the young creators and their editors and publishers. It also produced Jerry's unpublished memoir.

The documents revealed a Jerry Siegel whose personality was at least as split as his superhero's. One side of him was a creative and bereft boy looking to escape his real life by inventing one in fantasy. Less appealing was the angry young man who never recovered from the real and imagined wounds inflicted by the entrepreneurs to whom he had entrusted his sacred Superman. There were two Joannes as well. One was the nurturing beauty who had Jerry and Joe fawning over her. She coaxed the hard-hearted Jack Liebowitz into rehiring her husband after he had repeatedly burned bridges with the publisher, and looked after her man and girl when Jerry was an emotional wreck and there was barely cash enough to keep Laura in milk and diapers. Joanne's other side was that of a lioness protecting her cubs. She was the mouthpiece for Jerry and Joe, writing letters to DC

Comics demanding settlements, cost-of-living raises, and other benefits the aging creators lacked the gumption to ask for. If strong language was needed to get a CEO's attention, she'd brand his company
as the Gestapo. When an old classmate of Jerry's was written up as the
model for Lois Lane, implying that Joanne might not have been,
Joanne had her lawyer send a cease-and-desist letter. No matter that
the claims weren't the classmate's, but old ones by Joe and Jerry, and
that by the time Joanne was posing for Joe, Lois already was part of
the story. Superman over time became Joanne's, too, to the point
where she told people she planned to write her own memoir on the
whole sordid history.

The legal proceedings dragged on long enough that seven different
federal judges pored through the evidence. Their preliminary
rulings—in 2008, 2009, and 2011—gave the Siegels much but not all
of what they wanted. They had the right to sue despite the agreements they had signed with DC Comics. They also had a right to the
Superman story in *Action* 1 but not the cover, the Superman story in
Action 4, parts of *Superman* 1, and the first two weeks of *Superman*
newspaper strips, which Harry and Jack had authorized Jerry and Joe
to produce on their own. That gave Jerry's heirs ownership of Superman's blue leotards, red cape, and boots, as well as his early powers to
leap tall buildings, repel bullets, and run faster than an express train.
Time Warner owned the flying superhero, the *Daily Planet*, Jimmy
and Perry, the Kents, X-ray vision, and kryptonite, along with the
overseas rights to everything. In practice the rulings meant that, for
the full-fledged Superman to appear on-screen or anywhere else, Jerry's heirs and Jack and Harry's would have to pool their bifurcated
holdings and share the profits. Just how that should happen and how
much the Siegels already were owed, the court said, would have to be
settled in a trial.

While all that was playing out in public, behind the scenes checks
continued to arrive each month from DC to Joanne. By the end of
2010 the payments had exceeded $3.8 million, including coverage of
Joanne and Jerry's medical bills, which had peaked at $89,000 the
year he died. When a Superman TV show or film did especially well,
there was a bonus of between $10,000 and $50,000. The agreement
signed in 1975 had called for cutting off benefits to Joanne fifteen

years earlier, but DC said it would keep them coming in spite of Jerry's death and Joanne's bid to reclaim the ownership of Superman. In 2001, the company said it would continue paying so long as Joanne was working toward a settlement of the copyright dispute; settlement talks broke off in 2002, but again DC kept sending the checks. Annual payouts that had started at $20,000 were up to $126,000 at the end.

Even as Warner Bros. lawyers have been arguing with Toberoff and hoping for a settlement, they are steeling themselves for October 2013, when Joe Shuster's nephew, Warren Peary, will try to restore his uncle's Superman copyright and make the same claim the Siegels have. After Joe died in 1992, DC agreed to clean up his $20,000 in debts and pay his sister, Jean, $25,000 a year for the rest of her life, which so far has yielded her more than $500,000. In return she promised not to sue. But Jean's son, Warren, never gave his word, and he hired Toberoff to sue DC for what he thinks the Shuster heirs will be entitled to under an amended federal copyright law. This time the lawyer and his client would split the rights 50–50, giving Toberoff a total stake of 47.5 percent in the Siegel-Shuster holdings, compared to 27.5 percent for the Siegels and 25 percent for the Shusters.

Is that excessive? Toberoff is entitled to that much, some legal authorities say, since his firm isn't charging a fee and is absorbing the huge costs of the multiyear lawsuit. Others say any contingency share over one-third is excessive and that Toberoff should have persuaded his aging and ill clients to take the tens of millions DC has offered even though he believes they deserve and can get more. "The whole purpose of these termination provisions [in federal law] is to give authors and their heirs a second bite at the apple, to enable them to finally profit from the market value of their creations," says Toberoff. What about the fear—voiced not just by DC and Warner Bros. but by fans—that the lawsuit could impair and even end the Superman franchise itself by clouding the question of who owns the hero? "The notion that this could be the death of Superman is nonsense and studio counter-spin," Toberoff says. "It's clear that this is simply a financial matter. The Siegels are ready and willing to relicense their recaptured copyrights to Warner Bros. at a price that properly reflects the market value."

Toberoff also tried to strike a deal with Jerry's son, Michael Siegel, saying he had an investor who was interested in buying out Michael's interest in the Superman copyright, which would have been 25 percent of any settlement agreed to by Joanne and Laura. But Michael died suddenly in 2006 from complications of knee surgery—without having approved Toberoff's proposal, which was a fraction of what he would have received under DC's settlement offer, and without a will to pass on his share of a future payout. Michael had never gotten the annual payments that Joanne did and he would never see a penny from his father's role in creating Superman, which was par for Michael's course. Jerry was in the Army for much of his only son's early life. After he and Bella got divorced, when Michael was four, Jerry seldom visited, and he stopped paying child support when he hit hard economic times. Michael became a plumber, like Bella's father, and lived with Bella in Cleveland until she died, just four years before he did. Near the end each took care of the other and both felt abandoned by Jerry.

It was a strange way for a son who never got over the loss of his father to treat his own son, but Jerry was wrapped up in his own troubles and his new family. Jerry told everyone who asked how proud he was of Laura, his own Lois Lane and Supergirl, but seldom mentioned Michael. Michael kept a low profile and seldom talked about Superman or his father, who was a cherished native son in Cleveland and would eventually have his birthplace restored, with a plaque dubbing his street Jerry Siegel Lane and the cross street Lois Lane. What little Michael did say about Jerry, to friends and others, showed how torn he was. He didn't want to be angry but couldn't help it. He was crushed every time Jerry was supposed to pick him up at Howard Johnson's for a custody visit but didn't show up. He wished his dad had been around to see what an athlete he was, which was something Jerry had wanted to be but couldn't. It hurt, again, when Michael turned up as an afterthought in Jerry's will. "Even in death," the aggrieved son wrote, his famous father "continues to shun me! Why?" Michael likely died without knowing the high hopes Jerry had had at the beginning for his firstborn, high enough that he named him after his own hallowed dad.

Like Michael, Joanne died without seeing a dime of settlement money. With her passing in February 2011 at the age of ninety-three, the checks from DC were cut off as agreed back in 1975, which presumably gives Laura more incentive to settle her lawsuit. Warner, meanwhile, has two extra motivations to meet its June 2013 target for a new Superman movie: The judge in the Siegel case has made it clear that any delay could be interpreted as holding back on potential earnings for the heirs, and in the fall of 2013 Warren Peary will be asking to reclaim Joe Shuster's copyright. Other comic book creators have been following the suit in hopes it helps them, while other publishers and studios hope it doesn't threaten their ownership rights. Superman fans, too, are keeping a close watch—praying that if the two sides can't settle, the judge shows the wisdom of Solomon by ensuring that the bid by the heirs of Superman's creators to reclaim him does not kill him.

OFFSCREEN, THE FIRST DECADE of the new millennium looked like the worst of times for Superman. Readership continued to sag for comic books generally, and specifically for Superman titles. The bestselling of those, *Superman,* had fallen from 720,000 copies a month in 1966, to 98,000 in 1986, to just 62,000 in 2006. Circulation was down again early in 2011, to 42,000, with optimists hoping for a rebound and realists noting that *Action* and other Superman titles were faring even worse. The remaining audience was dedicated to the point of fanaticism, a trend that was self-reinforcing. No longer did casual readers pick up a comic at the drugstore or grocery, both because the books increasingly required an insider's knowledge to follow the action and because they simply weren't being sold anymore at markets, pharmacies, or even the few newsstands that were left. Cost was another constraint: Superman comics that sold for 10 cents in 1938 were $2.99 to $3.99 by 2011, an increase that was about twice the rate of inflation. The core fan now was a worldly-wise twenty-six-year-old who was shelling out a thousand dollars a year for new comics. And it was a he; females made up barely 10 percent of the readers. Comic books had gone from being a cultural emblem to a countercultural refuge.

Superman's fortunes had soared with those of the comic book, but he didn't crumple when the comic book did. That was partly because, after seventy years, he was as recognizable an American trademark as Mickey Mouse or the Playboy bunny and more resilient than either of them. He had his own Graceland in Metropolis, Illinois, which celebrated its native son with summertime festivities that drew thirty thousand people and were as much grassroots love-fests as the ones that Memphis organized for Elvis. When VH1 compiled its list of the two hundred greatest pop culture icons of all times, Superman ranked second—behind Oprah Winfrey and just ahead of Elvis Presley and Lucille Ball. The superhero was back onstage in Dallas, a featured attraction in Warner Bros.' bustling store in Shanghai, a prominent player in movies as eclectic as *Kill Bill* and *Hollywoodland*, the focus of college courses on everything from sociology and immigration to gender studies, and a centerpiece of exhibitions at Jewish museums in Berlin, Paris, and Amsterdam. In the Philippines, a thirty-five-year-old man had extensive cosmetic surgery to make himself look more like Superman. Collectors still traded his oldest stories; a copy of *Action* No. 1 sold for $1 million in February 2010, a record for any comic, and another copy smashed that mark two years later with a sales price of $2.2 million. Even the cheapest of his old trinkets, if they were in good enough condition, could fetch fat prices: $150 for a 1943 Superman-Tim birthday postcard, $750 for a 1945 Pep cereal box with the picture of a Superman button, $3,500 for a 1948 Superman felt beanie, and $20,000 for a brass ring that could be had in 1941 for two bottle caps and ten cents.

Music is a touchstone in any culture, and Superman's omnipresence in the American songbook underlined the chord he had struck. The Crash Test Dummies despaired that "the world will never see another man like him." Donovan boasted that "Superman or Green Lantern ain't got a-nothin' on me." The Kinks wished they "could fly like Superman," while Hank Williams, Jr., said his "friends all call me Superman." Herbie Mann professed his love and ours for the hero. Bluesmen sang about him as wistfully as country boys, rockers, balladeers, and big bands. Rappers, too, although they were less sentimental. "You could be my boyfriend, you surely can, just let me quit my boyfriend called Superman," the Sugarhill Gang recited in "Rapper's Delight," the first hip-hop single to crack the Top 40 Hits.

"I said he's a fairy I do suppose, flying through the air in pantyhose, he may be very sexy or even cute, but he looks like a sucker in a blue and red suit."

While his place in American lore was rock-solid, what sustained Superman as a Man of Tomorrow rather than a dusty icon was the same alchemy that had brought him alive three-quarters of a century earlier: the resonance and relevance of his story. That magic was dramatically displayed in *Superman: Red Son,* a miniseries published by DC in 2003 that challenged not just the premise of the Man of Steel as a symbol of the red, white, and blue, but the outcome of the recently concluded Cold War. What if his rocket ship had taken a slightly different trajectory and, rather than landing in a Kansas cornfield, it had come down on a collective farm in Joseph Stalin's Ukraine? What, writer Mark Millar wondered, would it mean if instead of the bold *S* on his chest Superman sported a hammer and sickle? The tale was part Mort Weisinger, part George Orwell. Superman managed to virtually eliminate poverty and ignorance behind the Iron Curtain, along with any vestiges of resistance to the Communist Party, which now presided over a global empire with six billion supplicants. America, not Russia, was economically and politically imploding in the brave new order. Its last hope lay with its most brilliant scientist and new president, Lex Luthor. It was a new way of seeing not just Superman and his supporting cast but our world and ourselves.

Millar wasn't the only one reimagining Superman's roots. Mark Waid got to replot Superman's interplanetary beginnings and terrestrial circumstances in *Superman: Birthright.* "Who am I and why am I here?" the hero asked himself. And, in terms more suited to science fiction fans, "Am I an Earthman or a Kryptonian?" His answer, laid out in twelve comic books published in 2003 and 2004, was that embracing his alien heritage wasn't just a possibility, it was his destiny. Along the way Waid gave us a Superman who was less defensive of the status quo and more like the rebel that Jerry Siegel had envisioned. It was a vision compelling enough that it would supplant John Byrne's reboot and become the defining mythos, at least until the next big reboot seven years later.

Superman and Batman teamed up anew in a comic book called

Superman/Batman that premiered in 2003 and explored their mutual empathy and antipathy. They still were DC's most glittering stars, and their differences still offered an illuminating lens on what made each special. Superman played Dudley Do-Right to Batman's Dirty Harry. Metropolis was Central Park and 59th Street at ten on a sunshiny morning on the first day of spring; Gotham was the Lower East Side in the middle of a rainy night in November. Now the two worlds and two heroes, who had forged their friendship on the radio in the 1940s, were united in a single book whose kickoff issue was ominously entitled "Public Enemies."

Crackerjack stories like those generally debuted in the comics, but many were collected into graphic novels and novelizations. Some were written by Superman pundits like Jeph Loeb, Mark Waid, and Cary Bates, who were aching for a chance to remind us why their hero mattered. Others came from newer hands like J. Michael Straczynski, who dispatched Superman on a year-long trek across the country to reconnect with the American way, and David S. Goyer, who took Superman in a different direction by having him renounce his American citizenship. Even Stan Lee, Marvel's longtime boss and DC's old-time nemesis, kicked in with a comic book called *Just Imagine: Stan Lee's Superman*. With no facts to rely on, Superman stories had always been about imagination. They also had been about the Metropolis Marvel giving a mouthpiece to the dreams of his starry-eyed writers and to the star-gazer in all of us. "Hold fast to dreams," Harlem Renaissance poet Langston Hughes had admonished, "For if dreams die / Life is a broken-winged bird / That cannot fly."

In the summer of 2011, DC made a bold gambit to expand its narrowing audience of comic book readers by recasting and simplifying not just Superman but its full lineup of superheroes. In the *Superman* series, the Man of Steel and his alter ego once again were bachelors, Lois was back on the dating scene, and the touchstone red briefs and blue tights were replaced by high-tech ceremonial armor. *Action Comics*, meanwhile, was relaunched with a new number 1 and a Superman who was younger, sported jeans and a T-shirt along with his red cape and S logo, and was still finding his way in his new world. It was the most daring makeover in years, one aimed at teenagers and adults rather than the adolescents of old, and early returns were bull-ish: Sales of the reconstituted comics were the highest in twenty years, with both print and digital versions doing brilliantly.

DC is counting on its newest stories to be a gateway not just for new readers but for Hollywood. Warner Bros. has never needed a research and development department when it came to its super-heroes; DC Comics has been the best idea mill in the business. Read-ing a comic is like watching a film frame-by-frame, letting studio executives see how audiences respond to characters and scripts before they commit millions of dollars. It is no accident that one comic book special after another has ended up on the big screen. *Doomsday* was a 2007 animated adaptation of the 1990s "Death of Superman" story. It also was the first in a series of cartoon movies based on DC heroes that included *Superman/Batman: Public Enemies, Superman/Bat-man Apocalypse,* and *All-Star Superman.* What Warner Bros. hopes will be its biggest Superman movie ever is due out in June 2013, with Hollywood heavyweights in charge. Director Zack Snyder's credits include *Watchmen,* a superhero drama modeled after the comic book of the same name, and *300,* based on Frank Miller's graphic novel about the Battle of Thermopylae. Creative consultant Christopher Nolan and his wife, Emma Thomas, who is producing the new Su-perman film, are responsible for rebooting the Batman film franchise and overseeing the science fiction thriller *Inception.* Picking up the red cape and blue tights (or will it be jeans and a T-shirt?) of Christo-pher Reeve and Brandon Routh will be British actor Henry Cavill, a relatively unknown hunk who played the first Duke of Suffolk on the Showtime series *The Tudors.* As is the tradition in Superman films, more conventional stars will fill in around Cavill, with Russell Crowe playing Superman's Kryptonian father and Kevin Costner his Earth-bound dad.

And it was no accident that in 2009 DC got its first chief executive whose background was in movies, not publishing, and that DC Com-ics was subsumed under DC Entertainment, which also has movie-making, online, and digital publishing arms. The move came just nine days after the Walt Disney Company announced its purchase of Marvel Comics, with all the promise that held for making Spider-Man and other Marvel characters even bigger screen stars. Diane Nelson, the new DC president, had shepherded Harry Potter from the printed page to movie screens, toy stores, home videos, and theme parks. Now, she told DC's writers and artists, she was determined to do the same for Superman and the rest of DC's heroes. Her announcement made many old-time comic book fans shudder, but it would have been music to the ears of Jack Liebowitz. The technology may have changed from radio waves to the World Wide Web, and kids are more likely to be reading Superman under the covers using an e-reader with a backlit screen than a flashlight and printed page. But the formula for success is the same one that Jack pioneered a half century earlier: Hire the best writers, artists, and actors; stay true to what made Superman resonate with audiences from day one with *Action No. 1*; and get his story before as many eyeballs as possible to keep the cash register ringing. Ka-ching.

WILL THE TWENTIETH CENTURY's longest-lasting hero endure deep into the new century and millennium? That is what fans and pundits are asking as Superman approaches the ripe age of seventy-five, just as they did at his first birthday and his tenth, and at his silver and golden jubilees. He has belied every prediction of his demise and defied the life expectancy for cultural icons and literary properties. We saw what happened when his handlers tried to kill him off: America would not have it. Kids want to be like him, and parents like that because they did, too. Many still do. He has proven tougher and more embedded in our DNA than even Jerry Siegel and Joe Shuster dared dream.

Whether he lives on depends in part on those telling his story—in the comic books, on TV, in the movies, and online—and whether they continue cultivating the richness of his character and illuminating his role in a world that never stands still. All signs suggest they will. It depends, too, on the steadfastness of his owners. If he thrived in the hands of a couple of Jewish kids from the ghetto, he should flourish when backed by the muscle of one of the world's biggest media conglomerates, which would be mad to let its billion-dollar franchise languish. In the end, however, it comes down to us, and whether we remain as besotted by Superman as our parents and grandparents were.

Why wouldn't we be? Heroes like Doc Savage, Ty Cobb, and even Teddy Roosevelt can become dated, reduced to interesting reflections of their era but not ours. Others, like Sherlock Holmes, Babe Ruth, and Franklin Roosevelt, still resonate, tapping into something primal. Superman defines that archetype. Part of it is the irresistible allure of taking flight. Part of it is the seduction of the love triangle and his secret identity. Part of it is just being ten years old again. The more that flesh-and-blood role models let us down, the more we turn to fictional ones who stay true. With them, and especially with Superman, it is about the possibility—of getting the girl, saving the world (or at least Lois and Jimmy), and having it our way. Our longest-lasting hero will endure as long as we need a champion, which should be until the end of time.

Acknowledgments

WE KNEW HIS FACE WOULD tell us whether he liked the book idea or hated it, probably in the first fifteen seconds. So my agent, Jill Kneerim, and I decided to make our pitch in person to editor Will Murphy, without even hinting at the topic. We took the train from Boston to New York and marched over to Random House's offices. "Will, I want to tell the story of the longest-lasting American hero of the last century," I announced bluntly. "Who do you think it is?" A shadow of skepticism appeared, but Will played along. He made half a dozen guesses—politicians, sports stars, literary luminaries—all of them wrong. Then Jill carefully positioned on his desk a picture of Christopher Reeve's Superman in the classic red-and-blue uniform.

A smile spread across Will's face well before my fifteen seconds were up. Then he started asking the same exacting questions Jill had. What new could there possibly be to say about the planet's best-known superhero? What credentials did I have to tell his story? Why did the world, which already had two hundred books about the comics and their leading man, need two hundred and one?

Their refusal to accept anything on faith is part of what I like about Jill and Will. The other part is their willingness to listen, then to get as fired up as I do. There are endless books on Superman, I explained, but most are sociological surveys or picture books, or deal exclusively with the comics, TV shows, or some other limited aspect of his expansive, multimedia career. None is a full-fledged account that approaches him as if he were human, which he is to tens of millions of fans who have followed his loves and deaths, reinventions, resurrections, and redemptions. The fact that he is ethereal lets us fill in our image of Superman from our own imaginations. Our longest-lasting champion, I said, offers a singular lens into our deep-rooted fears and our enduring hopes.

They were sold. Jill, who knows as little about Superman as she did about my last subject, Satchel Paige, helped me flesh out my ideas, pored over my manuscript, and held my hand. Will didn't know much about baseball when he did a crackerjack job editing and advocating for *Satchel*, but he is crazy about comics and has helped make my story worthy of his passion.

The Superman idea came from the same place so many good things do for me, my wife, Lisa, and she was the first to go at my manuscript with a red pencil and sharp intellect. I enlisted two kinds of readers. First were the experts, and I had the best: Paul Levitz, the longtime boss and guiding light at DC Comics; Superman writer Mark Waid, who doesn't just know more than anyone about the superhero but cares more; and Michael Hayde, whose own book demonstrates his nuanced understanding of Superman on the radio and TV. My other readers were old friends: Tom Maguire, whose blend of humor and serious-mindedness gives counterculturalism a good name, and Lou Ureneck, a seasoned newspaper editor and journalism professor who writes inspired memoirs. Even as she was finishing her own book, Sally Jacobs found the time to help me find the words I needed. Claudia Kalb did the same even as she was making a career change.

Two last words on readers: Evan Camfield. Production editors don't come any better. He caught errors of fact and context, fine-tuned prose, and made what often is an exasperating process a pleasure. Two more Random House people to whom I am grateful: designer Chris Zucker, whose creative flair is here for you to see, and publicist David Moench, who is passionate about Superman and selling books.

Every city I visited and every issue I probed turned up questions and gaps. I filled them in with help from hundreds of authors, experts, and friends, all of whom I list in the bibliography and am grateful to. Those I went back to more than I had the right are Cary Bates, Rick Bowers, Nicky Wheeler-Nicholson Brown, Mike Carlin, Richard Donner, Jay Emmett, Danny Fingeroth, Gary Grossman, David Hyde, Jenette Kahn, Jack Larson, Brian McKernan, John Jackson Miller, Will Murray, Denny O'Neil, Jerry Ordway, Tom Pollock, Louise Simonson, Michael Uslan, and, last and most especially, John Wells.

I hired a stream of student researchers, in Boston, Cleveland, Washington, and Los Angeles, to help with library searches, courthouse and schoolhouse searches, and other inquiries. The ones who stayed the longest were Nick Catoni, Michael Goldsmith, Tim Lewis, Chris McElwain, Maryrose Mesa, Elliot Schwartz, and Josh Willis. The ever-deft Katie Donelan was my in-house, go-to person at Random House. I also had two in-home experts on comics and kids, Alec and Marina. Jim Cahill kept my computers running and me online. Thanks, finally, to my parents, Dot and Mauray, for letting Superman into your house and my heart, which was no small thing in the 1950s.

A couple of notes on style: I quote people I interviewed in the present tense, and use the past tense with those whose words came from earlier writings and recordings. My endnotes generally are abridged listings of sources, with the full references in the bibliography.

Appendix

SUPERMAN (KAL-EL): CURRICULUM VITAE

- **Permanent:** 344 Clinton Street, Apt. 3-B, Metropolis, USA
- **Getaway:** Fortress of Solitude, North Pole

Personal
- **Parents:** Lara Lor-Van and Jor-El (birth); Martha and Jonathan
  Kent (adoptive); Jerry Siegel and Joe Shuster (creative); Jack
  Liebowitz and Harry Donenfeld (mercantile)
- **Hometowns:** Kryptonopolis (Krypton); Smallville, Kansas (USA,
  Earth)
- **Planetary homes:** Earth-2 (as Kal-L, 1938 on); Earth-1 (as Kal-El,
  mid-1950s on)
- **Girlfriends/wives:** Lana Lang, Lois Lane, Lori Lemaris, Wonder
  Woman, Lyla Lerrol, Sally Selwyn, Maxima
- **Best friends:** Pete Ross, Jimmy Olsen, Perry White, Inspector
  Henderson, Chloe Sullivan, Batman, Krypto
- **Nemeses:** Ultra-Humanite, Lex Luthor, Mr. Mxyzptlk, Brainiac,
  General Zod, Myrtle Beech (aka the Wedding Destroyer)
- **Aliases:** Clark Kent, Man of Steel, Last Son of Krypton, Big
  Blue, Supes
- **Age:** Over 29
- **Social Security No.:** 092-09-6616

Education

- Smallville High School (yearbook: "highest grades—boy most likely to become famous")
- Metropolis University (journalism major; cheerleader football team; fraternity pledge; Bachelor of Arts with honors)

Work Experience

- *Daily Star* and *Daily Planet* (Metropolis): Police reporter, war correspondent, advice-to-the-lovelorn editor, Bombay correspondent, editor-in-chief
- WGBS-TV (Galaxy Broadcasting): Reporter and news anchor
- *Newstime* magazine: Publisher

Publications

- *The Golden Throne*
- *The Janus Contract*
- *Under a Yellow Sun*
- *The Confessions of Superman*
- *I Superman*
- *The Krypton Chronicles*

Special Skills

- Flight (like a bird)
- X-ray vision (can see through buildings)
- Super-strength (can squeeze coal into diamonds)
- Immune to aging (no hair loss, graying, wrinkles, or paunch)
- Super-hearing (can hear an ant's footfall)
- Super-breath (can blow out a celestial star)
- Photographic memory (can digest a 300-page book in seconds)

Vulnerabilities

- Kryptonite (green, red, gold, black, red-green, red-gold)
- Virus X
- Magic
- Unbending moral code

Other Media Training
- Comic books (1938–present)
- Comic strips (1939–1966)
- Radio (1940–1951)
- Cartoons (1941–present)
- Novels (1942–present)
- Movie serials (1948–1950)
- Television (1952–2011)
- Feature films (1978–present)

Professional organizations
- Justice Society of America
- Justice League of America
- Atlas Club
- Strong Man Club
- Round Table Club
- Metropolis Press Club
- Club of Heroes
- Legion of Super-Heroes

Languages
- Kryptonese, English, Atlantean, Interlac, Romance languages, Russian

Honors
- Honorary citizen of all United Nations member countries
- Ambassador for Physical Fitness under President John F. Kennedy

References
- Perry White, *Daily Planet*
- Morgan Edge, Galaxy Broadcasting
- Colin Thornton, *Newstime*
- Batman, Gotham City
- Supergirl (Linda Lee, Kara Zor-El)
- Diane Nelson, president, DC Comics

Notes

PREFACE

x **LETTER WRITER:** A. L. Luther, "Vigilantes Not Needed," Cleveland *Plain Dealer*.

xii **"HOW DID YOU":** Author interview with Aaron Smolinski.

xii **"THE GODFATHER":** Email to author from Donald Wurzelbacher.

1. GIVING BIRTH

3 **HIS TROUBLE BEGAN:** Siegel, *Creation of a Superhero,* unpublished memoir, Chapter 1: pages 2–4. This memoir was likely written in stages over the years, with two earlier versions being titled *The Story Behind Superman #1* and *The Life and Times of Jerry Siegel*. While none of the three were published or made public, Jerry did register *Creation of a Superhero* with the Copyright Office of the United States in 1978, when he was living in Los Angeles. The application was made in his name, along with those of his wife, Joanne, and daughter, Laura. He wrote his autobiography, he said in the preface, because so many people had asked him to "straighten out some misconceptions" about Superman's creation and "tell the full story."

4 **ON VALENTINE'S DAY:** Siegel, *Creation of a Superhero,* 1: 6–7.

4 **RECESS, TOO:** Siegel, *Creation of a Superhero,* 1: 7, 18–19.

4 **WITH THE REAL:** Siegel, *Creation of a Superhero,* 1: 9–10.

5 **POINTING TO:** Author interview with Jerry Fine.

5 **HE EVEN TRIED:** Siegel, *Creation of a Superhero,* 1: 19.

6 **IT HAPPENED:** Coroner's report (June 3, 1932), police report (June 3,

1932), and death record (June 4, 1932) on Michel Siegel. The Siegel family, and even the coroner, have raised suspicions that violence was involved in Michel's death, but there was no evidence of that. While the theft probably induced his heart attack, his death was ruled to be the result of natural causes.

6 **"BLISS"**: Siegel, *Creation of a Superhero,* 1: 2.

7 **"LET ME DIE"**: *Tanakh: Holy Scriptures,* 407.

8 **SHELLEY REFLECTED**: Moskowitz, *Emperors of the Infinite,* 33.

8 **"WHAT IS THE APE"**: Nietzsche, *Thus Spoke Zarathustra,* 12.

10 **HIS PROTAGONIST**: Burroughs, *A Princess of Mars.*

10 **HUGO DANNER**: Wylie, *Gladiator.*

11 **KNOWN TO THE:** Dent, *Man of Bronze.*

11 **HAVE AS A MODEL**: Murray, "The Pulp Connection," *Comic Book Marketplace.*

11 **AMERICA WAS READIER**: Author interview with and emails from Will Murray.

12 **EARNED HIM A VISIT**: Siegel, *Creation of a Superhero,* 1: 13.

12 **"MASTER OF DEDUCTION"**: *Glenville Torch,* "Master Sleuth."

12 **PEN NAME**: Jerry's other pseudonyms included Joe Carter, Jerry Ess, Herbert S. Fine, Cleve Jerome, Bernard J. Kenton, Hugh Langley, and Leger (Bails, "Who's Who of American Comic Books").

14 **GREW UP POOR**: Kobler, "Up, Up and Awa-a-y!" *Saturday Evening Post.*

15 **JOE SHUSTER HAD**: Mietkiewicz, "Great Krypton!" *Toronto Star.* Comic scholars argue over whether Joe Shuster adorned his Canadian roots and their role in shaping the Superman story.

15 **"HE WAS IN"**: Author interview with Jerry Fine.

16 **"RHEUMY AND SOFT-FOCUSED"**: Author interview with Rosie Shuster.

16 **THEIR FIRST BIG**: Herbert S. Fine, "The Reign of the Super-Man," *Science Fiction: The Advance Guard of Future Civilization* No. 3.

16 **"I SEE, NOW"**: "The Reign of the Super-Man."

17 **"WAS A GIANT"**: Siegel, *Creation of a Superhero,* 1: 20.

17 **"WITH THE FURY"**: Siegel, *Creation of a Superhero,* 3: 4.

17 **HAL FOSTER**: Siegel, *Creation of a Superhero,* 3: 6–10.

18 **AND HE DIDN'T:** There apparently are no surviving copies of that or other early versions of the Superman story.

18 **"WHEN I TOLD"**: Siegel, *Creation of a Superhero,* 3: 7.

18 **BEEN DISLOYAL**: Others say they, too, were approached by Jerry. Reuben Schrank remembered Jerry asking him to collaborate when both were at Glenville High. While his college plans prevented that, Schrank told his daughter decades later, he did introduce Jerry to an artist he said was "a better cartoonist than I am." That artist was Joe Shuster, and Schrank was one of several friends who believed he was Jerry and Joe's matchmaker (material provided by the Schrank family).

18 **THEY EXCHANGED:** Letter from Jerry Siegel to Russell Keaton, July 12, 1934.

19 **KEATON TOLD HIM:** Siegel, *Creation of a Superhero,* 3: 18.

19 **SAYS THE ILLUSTRATOR:** Author interview with Denis Kitchen.

19 **HIS MOST CONSIDERED:** Siegel, *Creation of a Superhero,* 3: 18–20. One detail that Jerry could not recall, or at least didn't include in his memoir, was the date of this restless night of writing. Judging from dates he did specify, it did not happen on a hot summer night as he would later dramatically recount, but at the end of 1934 or the early months of 1935, which in Cleveland probably were chilly and wintery.

19 **"THIS WENT ON":** Siegel, *Creation of a Superhero,* 1: 18.

20 **"I CONCEIVED":** Bishoff and Light, " 'Superman' Grew out of Our Personal Feelings About Life," *Alter Ego* No. 56, 6.

20 **JERRY BEGGED:** Siegel, *Creation of a Superhero,* 1: 20.

20 **LOIS WAS HARDER:** " 'Superman' Grew," *Alter Ego* No. 56, 8.

21 **JERRY REMEMBERED:** Siegel, *Creation of a Superhero,* 1: 21. Jerry's son, Michael, among others, suspected that Joanne made up the modeling story, and that Jerry and Joe played along. Drafts of the earliest comic, with Lois included, already had been drawn by the time the modeling session supposedly happened in 1935, skeptics point out, and Joanne would have been just eighteen then—or twelve, according to the white lie she told about her age on her certificate of marriage to Jerry. And why would she have bothered lying to Jerry about her age if he knew her as early as 1935? But Joanne, Jerry, and Joe insisted until their dying days that the story was true. And it might have been: Joanne could have been hired to help Joe better visualize a character that he already had sketched out and Jerry had written about.

21 **"I HAVE A FEELING":** Siegel, *Creation of a Superhero,* 1: 23

22 **WHEELER-NICHOLSON'S BIOGRAPHY:** Author interviews with and emails from Nicky Wheeler-Nicholson Brown; Brown, "He Was Going to Go for the Big Idea," *Alter Ego* No. 88, 39–51; and Brown, "Major Malcolm Wheeler-Nicholson, Cartoon Character or Real Life Hero," *International Journal of Comic Art* 10, No. 2, 242–53.

22 **UNLIKE ITS PROGENITORS:** Historians point to a long line of "firsts" in the evolution of the modern American comic book, starting with a collection of newspaper strips published in 1897. Over time they shrank to look more like magazines and less like tabloids, soft covers replaced hard and color pages supplanted black-and-white, newsstands began offering the publications for general sale and publishers stopped relying on special orders from companies like Procter & Gamble, and comic books attracted devoted readers who may or may not also have read newspaper comic strips. Benton, *Superhero Comics of the Golden Age,* 14–20.

23 **"DOCTOR OCCULT":** For their "Doctor Occult" stories, Jerry and Joe used the pen names Leger and Reuths, which Jerry said were anagrams of their real names.

23 **THE BELL SYNDICATE:** Siegel, *Creation of a Superhero,* 4: 5.

24 **WHEELER-NICHOLSON WROTE:** Letter from Malcolm Wheeler-Nicholson to Jerry Siegel, October 4, 1935.

24 **THIS POSTSCRIPT:** Letter from Wheeler-Nicholson to Siegel, May 13, 1936.

24 **BUT THE BOYS:** Jerry explained in his memoir that he and Joe didn't get the 15 percent of profits or 50 percent of chain store sales for the first comics they sold to Wheeler-Nicholson. "Joe and I were not sold on Wheeler-Nicholson," he added, "and hoped to place 'Superman' with what we hoped would be a more responsible organization" (Siegel, *Creation of a Superhero,* 4: 7–8).

24 **THAT IS WHAT:** Douglas Wheeler-Nicholson, "His Goal Was the Graphic Novel," *Alter Ego* No. 88, 29.

24 **PULSATING STREETS:** Jones, *Men of Tomorrow,* 8.

25 **"HE COULD SELL":** Author interview with Jack Adams.

25 **HERBIE SIEGEL:** Younger workers at DC would speculate over the years on just what Herbie did. Was he Harry's bodyguard or friend, gofer or babysitter? The truth is that he was all those things. As for Harry's misdeeds, he testified in April 1939 that he was never convicted of a crime but "I pleaded guilty in General Sessions for publishing magazines and paid a fine." *Detective Comics Against Bruns Publications.*

25 **JACK LIEBOWITZ WAS:** *Jack S. Liebowitz,* 1993, 1–23. This unpublished memoir consisted of his transcribed responses to a series of questions posed by his daughter, Linda Stillman. One effect of having to share a bed when he was growing, Jack said, was that "when I married I refused to have [a] double bed. I wanted my own bed."

26 **JACK WORKED OUT:** Liebowitz memoir, 25–26, 40.

27 **PAUL SAMPLINER:** He apparently owned 25 percent of Harry Donenfeld's publishing operation and 75 percent of the distribution company, with Harry owning the remainder of both.

27 **WALLET EMPTY:** Comics historian Michael Uslan says that in 1973, he saw evidence in the DC archives that the Major received a payment of $19,703, in addition to having his debts canceled (*Superman: The Action Comics Archives,* Vol. 3, 6). Neither the Major's family nor DC can find evidence of a payout, although the company acknowledges that many of its files have been lost over the years.

27 **ABSOLUTELY, ACCORDING:** Liebowitz memoir, 47.

27 **HARRY HAD ORCHESTRATED:** Malcolm Wheeler-Nicholson, agreements with Donny Press, Inc., World Color Printing Co., and Photochrome, Inc. Nicky Wheeler-Nicholson Brown, the Major's granddaughter, is assembling evidence that she says will raise further questions about the bankruptcy's legitimacy (author interview with Brown).

27 **"SHE HATED THEM":** Amash, "His Goal Was," *Alter Ego* No. 88, 33.

28 **UNITED FEATURE SYNDICATE:** Siegel, *Creation of a Superhero,* 4: 12.

28 **LEDGER SYNDICATE:** Siegel, *Creation of a Superhero,* 4: 13.

28 **AS JACK WROTE:** Liebowitz memoir, 48.

28 **CHARLIE AND JACK:** *Detective Comics Against Bruns,* 131–36.

29 **IT WAS THE QUESTION:** Siegel, *Creation of a Superhero,* 4: 21.

29 **A SWINDLE:** In fairness to Harry and Jack, most investments for them and other publishers didn't pay off and theirs was fair within the dealings of the times. Were Jerry and Joe as naïve as the natives who were handed trinkets by the Dutch West India Company? Not entirely, since they spoke the language and were aware of what they were doing. But they were naïve, and desperate to make a sale and a living. So while Harry and Jack had lawyers covering their backs and knew they could drive as hard a bargain as they chose, Jerry and Joe had barely any clout or clue.

29 **WERE BUYING NOT:** Letter from Donenfeld to Siegel and Shuster, September 22, 1938. There is disagreement among relatives and others familiar with the case as to whether Jerry and Joe sought legal advice before signing that famous contract. Some say the boys did, at the suggestion of Jerry's mother, and the lawyer said to sign. Others say they got no counsel. In his memoir Jerry writes, with uncharacteristic understatement, "The legal release, which Joe and I signed, caused us much grief later" (Siegel, *Creation of a Superhero,* 4: 25).

In a comic book world where everything was written concisely, that legal release included one of the longest sentences ever: "In consideration of $130 agreed to be paid me by you, I hereby sell and transfer such work and strip, all goodwill attached thereto and exclusive right to the use of the characters and story, continuity and title of strip contained therein, to you and your assigns to have and hold forever and to be your exclusive property and I agree not to employee said characters or said story in any other strips or sell any like strip or story containing the same characters by their names contained therein or under any other names at any time hereafter to any other person, firm or corporation, or permit the use thereof by said other parties without obtaining your written consent therefor" (release form signed by Siegel and Shuster, March 1, 1938).

30 **ARTWORK WAS DESTROYED:** While there has been some confusion over what happened to that artwork, Jack Adler says, "Absolutely, it was destroyed." Adler worked for the engraver of *Action* No. 1 and later for National Allied Magazines, where it was his job to destroy original art like that. Author interview with Jack Adler.

30 **JOSEPH STALIN:** Stalin was born Iosif Vissarionovich Dzhugashvili. He adopted the name Stalin, a takeoff on the Russian *stal,* which means "steel." He liked the notion that he was a Man of Steel, but the more fitting reference is to the iron fist with which he ruled.

31 **"PLEASE CLARK!":** Siegel, *Action Comics* No. 1.

32 **SUPERMAN BUILT ON:** Siegel, *Creation of a Superhero,* 1: 15 and 5: 7.

32 **DOC SAVAGE LENT:** Author interview with and emails from Murray; and Murray, "The Pulp Connection."

32 **CASE FOR A CONNECTION:** Murray, "Gladiator of Iron, Man of Steel," *Alter Ego* No. 37, 3–18.

33 **"DID YOU EVER":** Wylie, *Gladiator,* 46.

33 **"USED DIALOGUE":** Letter from Philip Wylie to J. Randolph Cox, January 28, 1970.

33 **"OUR CONCEPT":** "'Superman' Grew," *Alter Ego* No. 56, 7.

2. A HERO FOR HIS TIMES

35 **THERE WERE TWO:** *Detective Comics Against Bruns,* 43–46; and author interviews with Adams and Paul Levitz.

36 **ALL THE NUMBERS:** *Detective Comics Against Bruns,* 52. Conventional wisdom says that National Comics printed 200,000 copies of *Action* No. 1, but Jack Liebowitz testified that it was 202,000.

36 **RAN A TEST:** *Detective Comics Against Bruns,* 37–38.

36 **DRIVE DEMAND:** Liebowitz memoir, 48.

37 **CONTINUED TO CLIMB:** Uslan figures from DC Archives.

37 **LIBRARIES GOT:** Seldes, "Preliminary Report on Superman," *Esquire;* and Sheridan, *Classic Comics,* 234–35. Enoch Pratt Free Library in Baltimore was the first to use Superman to attract kids in 1940, and the technique spread.

37 **ALL-STAR PITCHER:** Cramer, *The Hero's Life,* 109.

38 **FIRST CHARACTER:** *Detective Dan* appeared in 1933, but as a one-shot deal with the character thereafter appearing as the star of the *Dan Dunn* comic strip.

38 **FIRST PRESS RUN:** Uslan figures from DC Archives.

38 **THERE WERE A DOZEN:** Benton, *Superhero Comics of the Golden Age,* 23.

38 **"WE LIKED IT":** Liebowitz memoir, 48.

39 **FRED ALLEN'S RADIO:** Transcript by author of Allen's radio show on October 9, 1940; and "Up in the Sky! Look!" *Alter Ego* No. 26, 29–33. When "Superman" pretended to lift Donenfeld into the air, the publisher pleaded, "I've got a weak stomach and any minute I'm going to lose it. Please take me down!"

39 **HARRY WOULD WEAR:** Jones, *Men of Tomorrow,* 159.

40 *ACTION* 1 **REFERRED:** Siegel, *Action Comics* No. 1.

40 *SUPERMAN* **NEWSPAPER COMIC:** "The Superman is Born," *Superman: The Dailies,* 13.

40 **ON DAY FIVE:** "Krypton Doomed!" *Superman: The Dailies,* 15.

40 **FIVE INSTALLMENTS:** "Speeding Towards Earth," *Superman: The Dailies,* 17.

40 **FIRST *SUPERMAN* COMIC:** Siegel, *Superman* No. 1.

40 **IN *ACTION* 1:** Siegel, *Action Comics* No. 1.

40 **"AN INSTANT AFTER":** "Speeding Towards Earth," 17.

41 **IN *SUPERMAN* NO. 1:** Siegel, *Superman* No. 1.

42 **FIRST *SUPERMAN* BOOK:** Historians have assumed that Joe, Jerry,

and their editors merely stuck back pages cut from *Action* 1 to fill out *Superman* 1. But in his memoir, Jerry said that "the additional pages were specifically created for use in Superman Magazine no. 1." Siegel, *Creation of a Superhero,* 6: 3.

42 **"ARE YOU SURE"**: Siegel, *Action Comics* No. 1.

42 **NO TAKE-OFF:** His first flying actually was in the Fleischer cartoons, which first aired in 1941.

43 **"MILLION-DOLLAR MARATHON"**: Siegel, *Action Comics* No. 65.

43 **"TO FLY"**: Siegel, *Creation of a Superhero,* 1: 2.

43 **WASN'T THE FIRST:** Pinpointing who *was* the first isn't so simple, historian John Wells says, since the first widely distributed comic book in which the Sub-Mariner took flight, in October 1939, also featured a flying Human Torch. As for Superman, "the transition from leaping to flying was a gradual, organic process with some subsequent backsliding and emphasizing of the leaping along with other stories where Superman HAD to be flying. To my mind, though, Superman was flying (or at least doing a great imitation) by the end of 1939. That's important because 1940 saw an explosion of flying heroes, including (in rough chronological order) Hawkman, the Spectre, Black Condor, Bulletman, Doctor Fate, and Green Lantern. Captain Marvel was definitively flying by the latter half of 1940, too." Email to author from John Wells.

43 **FOLLOWING THOSE TWISTS:** Helping me follow the twists and turns were Fleisher, *The Great Superman Book;* Greenberger and Pasko, *The Essential Superman Encyclopedia;* and Wells emails.

44 **"WHICH IS THE"**: Siegel, "Superman Joins the Circus," *Action Comics* No. 7.

44 **EXCLAMATION POINT!:** That punctuation was at least partly a function of the metal plates used to print the comics back then. "Someone in the printing process could accidentally clean out a period, thinking it was a speck of dust, because it was so small," explains Levitz, the former DC publisher. Because exclamation points were bigger they were more likely to survive, which meant that early writers were more likely to use them. "Today, with offset printing," adds Levitz, "that worry is totally irrelevant and there is very little reliance on the exclamation point in comics. It is used more than in the average literature but mostly for melodrama."

44 **"HIS FIGURE ERECTS"**: Siegel, "Superman in the Slums," *Action Comics* No. 8.

44 **"THE BOYS DON'T"**: Siegel, "Superman in the Slums."

44 **WORD LIKE "SARDONIC"**: Siegel, "The Million-Dollar Marathon," 172.

45 **"TOUGH IS PUTTING"**: Siegel, "Superman, Champion of the Oppressed," *Action Comics* No. 1.

45 **"THE MOTHER'S RIGHT!"**: Siegel, "Superman in the Slums," 42, 52, 54.

46 **"IN THE EYES"**: Siegel, *Creation of a Superhero,* 7: 1.

47 **SURPASSED IN POPULARITY:** Slater Brown, "The Coming of Superman," *New Republic.*

48 **"I WROTE, WROTE"**: Siegel, *Creation of a Superhero,* 7: 2.

48 **HE STILL DID:** Kobler, "Up, Up and Awa-a-y!"

49 **AS TIME WENT:** The instructions were laid out in a letter from Liebowitz to Siegel on January 23, 1940, and in letters from Whitney Ellsworth to Siegel on January 22, 1940, November 4, 1940, and February 19, 1941. The "Murray" in Ellsworth's 1941 letter almost surely is Murray Boltinoff, although he wasn't believed to have started working at National for another two years.

50 **"HOW FOOLISH YOU"**: Waid, "K-Metal: The 'Lost' Superman Tale," 13.

50 **NO ONE KNOWS:** Thomas Andrae argues that it was "editorial quibbles" and the story's length that killed it (*Creators of the Superheroes,* 54–55). Will Murray says it is more likely that the profound changes the story proposed were too much, too fast, for a superhero as successful as Superman ("The Kryptonite Crisis," *Alter Ego* No. 37).

50 **THERE WAS MORE:** Again, there was a series of letters from Liebowitz to Siegel—on September 28, 1938, January 23, 1940, and January 29, 1940.

52 **IT WAS ENOUGH:** Kobler, "Up, Up and Awa-a-y!"

53 **"HE LOVED *SHIKSAS*"**: Andrae and Gordon, *Funnyman,* 79.

53 **"AFTERWARDS I SAID"**: Author interview with Jerry Robinson.

53 **DATING BATMAN AND SUPERMAN:** There is an old joke that Superman is the guy girls want to marry, but Batman is the one they want to date.

53 ***WASHINGTON POST:*** "Superman Rescues His Creator," *Washington Post.*

54 **NO SURPRISE THERE:** *Detective Comics Against Bruns,* 79–105; and Andelman, *Will Eisner: A Spirited Life,* 43–45.

55 **"A MONGOLOID"**: "'Superman' Grew," *Alter Ego* No. 56, 11.

55 **RETIRE THE CAPTAIN:** Twenty years after the settlement, DC Comics licensed the rights to Captain Marvel, and in 1973 DC brought him back to life in a comic book called *Shazam!*

55 **OTTO BINDER:** Emails to author from science fiction writer Richard Lupoff, who was a friend of Binder's.

55 **"IT IS PERFECTLY CLEAR"**: *Jerome Siegel and Joseph Shuster Against National Comics,* June 5, 1947, 17.

55 **TOLD A JUDGE:** Kane told Will Murray that if it hadn't been for Siegel and Shuster, "I wouldn't have created Batman nor would there be a comic book industry" ("Mark of the Bat," *Comic Scene Yearbook* No. 1).

56 **HOW RICH:** Kobler, "Up, Up and Awa-a-y!"

56 **WHAT IS CLEAR:** Jones, *Men of Tomorrow,* 159–64.

56 **"HE WAS MANY"**: Author interview with Sonia "Peachy" Donenfeld.

57 **JACK REGULARLY REMINDED:** Liebowitz memoir, 47.

57 **COMBINED CIRCULATION:** "Superman's Dilemma," *Time.* The three comic books he starred in back then were *Action, Superman,* and *World's Finest,* which was launched in 1941 and featured Batman along with (and sometimes teaming up with) Superman.

57 **ROSE AND THE GIRLS:** Author interview with Joan Levy.

58 **CARTOON STORY:** Siegel, "How Superman Would End the War," *Look.*

59 **"TO RAP THE":** Uslan, *America at War,* 27.

59 **"AS THE MIGHTIEST":** "Superman's Dilemma," *Time.*

59 **"YOU'RE PHYSICALLY":** Untitled comic strips, February 16–19, 1942, *Superman in the Forties.*

60 **THE U.S. MILITARY:** "All's Well in Britain Now—Admiralty Enlists Superman," *Washington Post;* and Kobler, "Up, Up and Awa-a-y!"

60 **AFTER D DAY:** Weisinger, "Here Comes Superman!" accessed at superman-through-the-ages.nu.

61 **AT U.S. MILITARY BASES:** "Comic Culture," *Time;* Robinson, *Zap! Pow! Bam!* 21; "Superman's Dilemma," *Time;* and "Superman Stymied," *Time.*

61 **"THE FBI CAME":** Overstreet, *The Comic Book Price Guide* No. 13 (1983), A-65. Superman editor Mort Weisinger went a step further, as always, saying, "I'd discovered the bomb two years before it was first exploded" (Peterson, "Superman Goes Mod," *Indianapolis Star Magazine*).

61 **A 1945 DOCUMENT FROM:** "Superman and the Atom Bomb," *Harper's;* and "Superman vs. Atom Man—the Prequel—and the Sequel!" *Alter Ego* No. 98, 13.

62 **ALVIN SCHWARTZ:** Author interview with Alvin Schwartz; and Schwartz, "The Real Secret of Superman's Identity," *Annual of the Modern Language Association.*

62 **IN A 1944 LETTER:** Letter from Siegel to Liebowitz, January 1, 1944.

63 **IT WAS CALLED:** "Introducing 'SUPER GI,'" *Midpacifican.*

63 **GEORGE LOWTHER:** He already had experience writing Superman stories on the radio, and would go on to an eclectic and impressive career in print and writing, producing, directing, and even acting on television and radio.

63 **MONTHLY SALES:** De Haven, *Our Hero,* 76; "Escapist Paydirt," *Newsweek;* Rossen, *Superman vs. Hollywood,* x; and "Superman Scores," *Business Week.*

64 **"YOU DID NOT":** Letter from Liebowitz to Siegel, February 3, 1947.

64 **POPULARITY FADE:** The only three comic book superheroes to survive in the same form and without interruption from the pre–World War II Golden Age until today are Superman, Batman, and Wonder Woman, although Wonder Woman experienced a brief hiatus in 1986. Aquaman and Green Arrow also still are around, but have come and gone as stars of their own series (Wells emails).

3. A MATTER OF FAITH

65 **KAL IS SIMILAR:** The Hebrew word for voice is *kole* and for vessel is *kol*. *Kal* itself means "light," as in weight.

66 **KANSAS FARMERS:** Just where the Kents lived wasn't made clear for decades. An early Superman radio show placed them in southeastern Iowa. In the 1950s and 1960s, Metropolis was set on the East Coast, with the Kents seemingly not far away. By the 1970s it had been pinpointed as Maryland. But promotional material for *Superman: The Movie* talked about Clark having been raised on the plains of Kansas, no matter that the film itself didn't say that, or that the Kansas scenes were shot in Canada. One influential moviegoer, John Byrne, liked the idea of Clark being from Kansas, and it stuck when Byrne led his reboot of the franchise in 1986. Today it is generally accepted that Clark and his adoptive parents lived in the town of Smallville and that Smallville is in Kansas. Or at least the original Earth-2 Smallville was. On Earth-1, it was back in Maryland (Wells emails; and *The Essential Superman Encyclopedia*).

66 **A 1940 ARTICLE:** "Jerry Siegel Attacks!" *Das Schwarze Korps.*

67 **THE JEWISH 100:** That is one in a series of books that explore Superman's Jewish roots. Others include *Disguised as Clark Kent, From Krakow to Krypton, Jews and American Comics,* and *Up, Up, and Oy Vey!*

67 **JULES FEIFFER:** Feiffer, *Backing into Forward,* 73.

69 **FATHER JOHN CUSH:** Emails to author from John Cush.

69 **"THE WORD BECAME":** Cornell, "Superman/Jesus Similarities Examined," *Los Angeles Times.*

69 **"SUPERMAN, I'VE":** Friedrich, Austin, and Simpson, "Up, Up and Awaaay!!!" *Time.*

69 **SUPERMAN KNEW:** Schwartz, *An Unlikely Prophet,* 204–5.

70 **HE COULD CRAWL:** Author interview with and email from Michael Green.

70 **IT ALSO IS:** Author interview with Geoff Johns.

70 **"SUPERMAN IS NOT":** Author interview with Mark Waid.

70 **THE GOVERNOR WOULDN'T:** Siegel, "Superman Goes to Prison," *Action Comics* No. 10.

70 **"YEARS AGO":** Waid and Ross, *Kingdom Come,* 194–95.

71 **"I'VE NEVER HAD":** Ramos recently got married—to a "huge Supergirl fan." The pastor who married them "made mention during the ceremony how Superman made me the man I am," he says, and "we even had the Superman theme song played at the end of the ceremony (right after they pronounced us husband and wife)" (emails to author from Emilio Ramos, Jr.).

71 **"UP UNTIL I":** Author interview with Peter Lupus.

71 **"I HAD WHAT":** Author interview with and emails from Tom Maguire.

73 **"LET ME GET":** Andrae and Gordon, *Funnyman,* 17.

73 **BY ONE COUNT:** Andrae and Gordon, *Funnyman,* 5.

74 **"I WRITE ABOUT":** Andelman, *Will Eisner: A Spirited Life,* 346.
74 **BOTH CHANGES WERE:** "I Didn't Want to Know," *Alter Ego* No. 56, 36.
74 **BOYHOOD PAIN:** Andelman, *Will Eisner: A Spirited Life,* 113.
74 **THEIR NAMES:** Fingeroth, *Disguised as Clark Kent,* 99–100.
75 **"I NEVER CONSCIOUSLY":** Author interview with Stan Lee.
76 **FEWER NAME CHANGES:** Julius Shuster and his family were listed in the 1930 U.S. Census as Schuster, which Rosie Shuster says almost certainly was a mistake by the census taker. "People," she adds, "just want to put that 'c' in there. My epitaph will be—'no "c" in Shuster'" (email to author from Rosie Shuster).
76 **CLEVELAND BACK THEN:** Vincent, *Memoirs of a Life in Community Service;* and Rubinstein, *Merging Traditions.*
77 *HOW TO BE FUNNY:* The Library of Congress lists Siegel as the sole author, although his address is given as the Siegel-Shuster School of Humor. The book came out in 1938, just after the first Superman story was published in *Action Comics.*
78 **WASN'T ENTIRELY TRUE:** Emails from Dwight Decker to author, and Decker, "The Reich Strikes Back," *Alter Ego* No. 79.
79 **MORE THAN ANYONE:** There were other Jewish superheroes over time, although none with nearly the reach of Superman. Gardner Fox's Sandman, for instance, was half Jewish, but that incarnation of the character, who came to life a year after Superman, faded during the 1940s.
79 **"DONENFELD," HIS:** Author interview with Peachy Donenfeld.

4. THE SPEED OF SOUND

82 **HE HIRED:** Josette Frank, head of the Child Study Association of America, was Maxwell's primary expert. The strategy was outlined in a May 20, 1946, letter from Mrs. Hugh Grant Straus to the editor of *PM* magazine (Child Study Association Files, University of Minnesota).
82 **"CLAN OF THE FIERY":** Author's transcript of the radio broadcasts.
83 **MAXWELL USED:** Hayde, *Flights of Fantasy,* 78.
83 **BUMP IN THE RATINGS:** Whiteside, "Up, Up and Awa-a-y!," *New Republic.*
83 **"TOLERANCE IS RAMPANT":** "It's Superflight," *Newsweek.*
84 **THE ANGLE THAT:** Whiteside, "Up, Up and Awa-a-y!"
84 **KENNEDY PICKED UP:** Kennedy, *The Klan Unmasked,* 91–94.
84 **IT WAS A:** Hayde, *Flights of Fantasy,* 77–78; and Patton, "Investigation of Stephen J. Dubner & Steven D. Levitt Article," *Florida Times-Union.* Dubner and Levitt, in their bestseller *Freakonomics,* lionized Kennedy, calling him "courageous and resolute and unflappable." After they learned that Kennedy likely had embellished, the *Freakonomics* authors questioned his credibility in a *New York Times Magazine* story entitled "Hoodwinked?" The truth is that Kennedy wasn't the hero he was painted, nor the villain. He did help expose the Klan and he did enlarge his role—which Dubner and Levitt could have determined by asking researchers familiar with Ken-

nedy's work or comparing tapes of "Clan of the Fiery Cross" with Kennedy's claims about the Superman broadcasts. Bids to determine what fact-checking the *Freakonomics* duo performed were unsuccessful: Levitt referred questions to Dubner, who said he would try to answer, then didn't. Kennedy was more forthcoming. He said he sent the Klan passwords to Superman producer Maxwell, who apparently didn't use them, but that syndicated columnist Drew Pearson did. Kennedy, who died in August 2011, was mentioned in at least one Pearson column (May 6, 1947) that talked about leaked Klan passwords.

84 **THE VETERANS:** Hayde, *Flights of Fantasy,* 78–79.

85 **"SLAP A JAP":** In an undated comic strip called "Superman Scores Again," Jerry and Joe showed U.S. troops destroying a Japanese invasion fleet. But they reminded readers that "most Japanese-Americans are loyal citizens. Many are in combat units of our armed forces, and others are working in war factories. According to government statements, not one act of sabotage was perpetrated in Hawaii or [the] territorial U.S. by a Japanese-American."

85 **"WE HAD BEEN":** Whiteside, "Up, Up and Awa-a-y!" Not everyone was clapping. Dorothy Lewis of the National Association of Broadcasters wrote that "while Superman often tries to crusade in civic affairs, he does so at the expense of the dignity of the community. This leads to confusion and lack of faith" (November 13, 1947, letter from Lewis to Josette Frank, Child Study Association Files).

And while Maxwell led the chorus for more shows on civil rights, he was less broad-minded when it came to portraying America's wartime enemies to his juvenile listeners. "I am, at the moment, teaching this vast audience to hate. If not to hate individuals, to hate that for which they stand," he wrote in an April 12, 1943, letter to George Zachary at the Office of War Information. "A german is a Nazi and a Jap is the little yellow man who 'knifed us in the back at Pearl Harbor.'" Zachary was taken aback, and consulted his colleagues for their reactions to Maxwell's letter. They observed, Zachary wrote, that "the notion that it is necessary to hate our enemies is crude and childish and unreal. It is the invention of frustrated civilians who don't know anything about war" (April 3, 1943, letter from Zachary to Allen Ducovny, Maxwell's partner at Superman, Inc. Both letters are in the Child Study Association Files).

86 **COLLYER DREW:** Hayde, *Flights of Fantasy,* 33; and Tollin, *Smithsonian Historical Performances: Superman on Radio,* 12–13.

87 **EVEN THOUGH THEY:** "It's Superflight," *Newsweek.*

87 **PORTRAYING SUPERMAN:** Tollin, *Superman on Radio,* 14.

87 **"THE PRODUCERS":** Jane Hitchcock's eulogy for her mother, Joan Alexander.

89 **THE LAST FOUR:** Superman's motto of "Truth, Justice and the American Way" debuted on August 31, 1942, when his live radio serial debuted on the Mutual Broadcasting System. Prior to that, he fought for "Truth and Justice." Olga Druce—a writer, actress, and child psychologist—took

credit for the famous phrase. There was only a one-word difference between the Mutual Broadcasting prelude and the one that would later be used on the George Reeves television show. On radio, the narrator says, "strange visitor from another world," while the TV narrator says, "strange visitor from another planet" (email to author from Michael Hayde).

90 **"KIDS CAN DETECT"**: Tollin, *Superman on Radio*, 17.

90 **"A RAILROAD TRAIN"**: Interview with Edward Langley by Brian McKernan, July 9, 1985.

91 **SUDDENLY FEEL**: Tollin, *Smithsonian Historical Performances: Superman vs. Atom Man*, 7.

91 **"SUCCEED WHERE"**: Freeman, *The Superman Radio Scripts*, 1–43, 199, 203.

92 **"UP IN MY ARMS"**: Author's transcript of "Clan of the Fiery Cross."

93 **REASSURE PARENTS**: Hayde, *Flights of Fantasy*, 63.

93 **THERE WERE ACTUALLY**: Hayde, *Flights of Fantasy*, 115–16.

94 **THEY THOUGHT BUILDING**: Fleischer, *Out of the Inkwell*, 105.

94 **THE BROTHERS WERE**: Dooley and Engle, *Superman at Fifty!* 64–65; Daniels, *DC Comics: Sixty Years*, 68–69; Rossen, *Superman vs. Hollywood*, 7–9; and Cabarga, *The Fleischer Story*, 174–77.

95 **"THE MOVIE CARTOON"**: "The New Pictures," *Time*.

95 **"THE FLEISCHERS SHOW"**: Maslin, "Film: Animation Art of the Fleischers," *New York Times*.

95 **"THESE FILMS"**: Maltin, *Of Mice and Magic*, 122.

95 **"SOME 20,000,000"**: "The New Pictures," *Time*.

96 **REACTIONS LIKE**: Hayde, *Flights of Fantasy*, 47, 58.

96 **ONE BIT OF**: Younis, "Superman and the Phone Booth," www.supermanhomepage.com.

97 **SHORTS IN FRANCE**: France blew hot and cold when it came to Superman's comic books. Some were published under alternative names and ascribed to French authors during the Nazi occupation. But the postwar French government banned them, either because they were seditious capitalist influences or, as some reports suggest, because it was too much of a stretch to say he could fly. In any case, they were back by the 1960s (Wells emails; and Bart, "Advertising," *New York Times*).

98 **"IF THEY GUESS"**: "Jungle Sam," *Time*.

98 **"I SAID, 'WAIT'"**: Brennan, "Kirk Alyn: Man of Steel," *Washington Post*.

98 **FIRST ACTOR**: Technically, the very first was Ray Middleton, an actor hired to portray Superman at the 1940 World's Fair in New York.

98 **"I VISUALIZED"**: Tollin, *Smithsonian Historical Performances: Superman with Batman & Robin on Radio*, 22.

99 **KATZMAN ANNOUNCED**: Alyn, *A Job for Superman*, 6.

99 **"I WAS SAVED"**: Alyn, *A Job for Superman*, 18.

99 **PRODUCERS ALSO**: Grossman, *Superman: Serial to Cereal*, 43–44.

100 **PARTS OF THE**: Schoell, *Comic Book Heroes*, 23–25.

100 **TWO YEARS**: Schoell, *Comic Book Heroes*, 25–28.

101 **HE LOVED IT:** Grossman, *Superman: Serial to Cereal,* 23, 30.

103 **BILL FINGER'S TALE:** "The Origin of Superman," *Superman* No. 53.

103 **IT TOOK ANOTHER:** Finger, "Superman Returns to Krypton," *Superman* No. 61.

104 **COMICS TO GIVE:** Siegel, "The Archer," *Superman* No. 13.

105 **WHO WAS THE INSPIRATION:** Joanne Siegel, "The True Inspiration for Lois Lane," supermanhomepage.com; Sherwood, "Superman Still Makes Millions," *Washington Star;* and author interview with Lois Amster.

106 **WILSON HIRSCHFELD:** Emails to author from Dan Hirschfeld, Wilson's son, and materials supplied by Dan.

107 **"NO MAN ON EARTH":** "The Origin of Superman," 55.

107 **ALTHOUGH JOR-EL BECAME:** The *el* became *El* in the comic book letters columns of the 1960s (Wells emails).

107 **"IT WAS NOT":** Lowther, *The Adventures of Superman,* 24–28.

108 **BETTER FIX ON:** Waugh, *The Comics,* 334–49.

109 **"I THOUGHT":** "The Archer."

109 **"WHAT SORT":** Siegel, "Europe at War," *Action Comics* No. 23.

110 **"LET'S TEST":** Cameron, "The Mxyztplk-Susie Alliance," *Superman* No. 40.

110 **"A CHANGE OF":** Siegel, *Creation of a Superhero,* 5: 3.

5. SUPERMAN, INC.

112 **"BE A WHOO":** National Comics Publications, *Superman-Tim,* 1949.

113 **THE NEW NAME:** The comic book publisher's name changed often enough that it was difficult to keep track. It started in 1935 as National Allied Magazines, became National Comics Publications in 1946, and switched to National Periodical Publications in 1961. National Periodical Publications merged with Kinney in 1967 to become Kinney National Services, and Kinney National was renamed Warner Communications in 1971, although National Periodical Publications continued to be used to describe the publishing operations. There were other iterations in between, including the holding company called Superman, Inc. Only one title was there from the very first, with Major Malcolm Wheeler-Nicholson, and has survived: Detective Comics. It was there on the banner of America's longest continuously published comic book, was sometimes used to refer to the company as a whole, and was the only name most readers recognized. In 1976 the company let its fans have the final word by adopting an abbreviated version—DC Comics—as its official title (www.dccomicsartists.com; and author interview with Levitz).

114 **"LOOKS EXACTLY":** Murray, "The Kryptonite Crisis."

116 **"LED TO HER":** Author interview with Jerry Fine.

116 **"BELLA WENT":** Letter from Siegel to Liebowitz, November 11, 1946.

116 **"I NEVER":** Andrae and Gordon, *Funnyman,* 53.

117 **"PRACTICALLY NONE":** *Siegel and Shuster Against National Comics Publications,* 1947, 204.

117 **"IN LINE":** Letter from Siegel to Shuster, September 18, 1946.

117 **THEY DESPAIRED OF:** Jones, *Men of Tomorrow,* 215–16, 228; author interview with Peachy Donenfeld; and "Company Formed," *Middletown Times Herald.*

119 **IN THE TEN YEARS:** *Joanne Siegel and Laura Siegel Larson v. Warner Bros. Entertainment Inc.,* 2004.

119 **SIGNED AN AGREEMENT:** *Siegel and Shuster Against National Comics Publications,* Final Judgment, May 21, 1948, 6.

119 **BOB KANE PROVED:** There has been endless speculation whether Kane got a better deal than Siegel and Shuster, and if so, why. Some say his deal was comparable but looked more lucrative because he didn't have to split it in two the way Jerry and Joe did. Others say Kane's father helped him negotiate better terms, in part by tapping the father's friendship with Liebowitz, and that Kane used Siegel and Shuster's lawsuit to get Liebowitz to settle amicably and lucratively with him.

120 *LI'L ABNER:* Capp, *The World of Li'l Abner,* 120–26.

120 **BELLA SUED:** *Bella Siegel vs. Jerome Siegel,* Petition for Divorce, July 14, 1948.

121 **CARTOONISTS SOCIETY:** Siegel family lore says that Marlon Brando judged the costumes (Weber, "Joanne Siegel, the Model for Lois Lane, Dies at 93," *New York Times*).

121 **"JERRY AND I":** Andrae, "Of Supermen and Kids with Dreams," *Nemo* No. 2.

121 **THE MARRIAGE COULDN'T:** Winchell, "'Superman' Artist Weds a Model," *Syracuse Herald-Journal;* Jolan Kovacs and Jerome Siegel's applications for marriage license, October 13, 1948, and November 3, 1948; and Jolan's birth certificate. One possible explanation for the dual marriage licenses was that court fees were not paid in Jerry and Bella's divorce settlement until October 29. Could that mean Jerry was still married to Bella when he married Joanne in October 1948? No, say Ohio matrimonial lawyers, explaining that paying the fees is a technicality and should not have held up his divorce or his remarriage.

122 **AFTER HIGH SCHOOL:** Handwritten letter from Joanne to unknown recipient, May 25, 1992.

123 **"THE URCHIN IN":** Ellison, "It Ain't Toontown," *Playboy.*

123 **THAT CELEBRITY LET:** Kobler, "Up, Up and Awa-a-y!"

124 **SUPERMAN, INC., STARTED:** Matetsky, *The Adventures of Superman Collecting.*

125 **"LET SUPERMAN BE":** Daniels, *The Golden Age,* 48; and Daniels, *DC Comics: Sixty Years,* 74.

125 **IT WORKED:** Matetsky, *The Adventures of Superman Collecting,* 17.

126 **"SUPERMAN TURNED":** Matetsky, *The Adventures of Superman Collecting,* 138.

126 **"FOR THE WHOLE UNIVERSE":** Email to author from Vincent Maulandi.

6. THE DEADLY TRUTH

127 **ON A COOL:** "Boy Kills Self Showing Chum Gun Roulette," *Washington Post*. While his mother said he read about Russian roulette in a comic book, police said they were told he had learned about the dangerous revolver gamble in a movie.

127 **TWO MONTHS:** "'Comics' Blamed in Death," *New York Times*.

127 **THE COMMON:** Wertham, *Seduction of the Innocent,* 34, 97, 118.

128 **"UNLESS WE":** North, "A National Disgrace," *Chicago Daily News*.

128 **"WHAT'S WRONG":** Doyle, "What's Wrong with the 'Comics'?" *Catholic World*.

128 **"THE SUPERMAN FORMULA":** Legman, *Love & Death,* 39–40. Similar warnings were coming from Moscow. "The word superman, as is known, comes from the ideological inspirer of the German Fascists, Nietzsche," charged Korny Chukovsky, a leading writer of children's books. "Mass fascisization of the children fully corresponds to the perspectives of the present bosses of America" ("Russian Says Comic Books 'Fascisize' U.S. Children," *New York Times*).

128 **"COMIC-BOOK READING":** Crist, "Horror in the Nursery," *Collier's*.

129 **YEARS LATER:** Nyberg, *Seal of Approval,* 1–21.

130 **"WE ARE":** Crist, "Horror in the Nursery."

130 **"BELIEVING THAT":** "600 Pupils Hold Burial Rites," *Washington Post*.

131 **A GALLUP POLL:** Hajdu, *The Ten-Cent Plague,* 294.

131 **IT WAS EASY:** Hajdu, *The Ten-Cent Plague*, 190.

131 **"YOU FIND":** Crist, "Horror in the Nursery."

131 **HE WAS ONE OF FOUR:** Hajdu, *The Ten-Cent Plague,* 149, 264.

132 **MAXWELL AND HIS DIRECTOR:** Grossman, *Superman: Serial to Cereal,* 80.

132 **NEVER SERIOUSLY:** Whitney Ellsworth heard Alyn's claim that he was offered the TV role, but said, "It just is not true" (transcript of Grossman interview with Ellsworth). And Noel Neill says, "I found out later that [Alyn] was very, very depressed by not being asked to do Superman on the television show" (author interview with Neill).

132 **MAXWELL'S CO-PRODUCER:** Grossman, *Superman: Serial to Cereal,* 80, 316. Studio releases told a more dramatic story about casting George: "Maxwell was on a vacation when he saw a man taking a sun bath on Southern California's Muscle Beach. In his sunglasses the man surprisingly resembled Clark Kent." Glut and Harmon, *The Great Television Heroes,* 26.

134 **"TAKE THE MONEY":** Grossman, *Superman: Serial to Cereal,* 82.

134 **"WELL, BABE":** Author interview with Phyllis Coates; and Weaver, *Science Fiction Stars and Horror Heroes,* 22.

134 **"I'D NEVER":** Author interview with Coates.

134 **"WEAR A SUIT":** Warren, "Superman's Girl Friday," *TV People*.

134 **"I MET BOB":** Weaver, *Producers and Writers,* 20.

135 **"MY GOD"**: Grossman, *Superman: Serial to Cereal,* 128.

135 **"WE WENT"**: Weaver, *Producers and Writers,* 21–22.

136 **OTHER MONEY-SAVING:** Glut and Harmon, *The Great Television Heroes,* 28–29.

137 **ON BUDGET:** There were varying recollections of what that budget was. Co-producer Robert Luber said it was $18,500 per episode. Outside producer David Wolper recalled it being $20,000. Jack Liebowitz said the ad agency paid $17,000, Maxwell said he could do it for $14,000, and it ended up costing $28,000. (Grossman, *Superman: Serial to Cereal,* 316; Wolper, *Producer,* 18; and Liebowitz memoir, 52.)

137 **"THAT'S ENOUGH"**: Hayde, *Flights of Fantasy,* 155.

137 **"GEORGE CAME"**: Grossman, *Superman: Serial to Cereal,* 127.

137 **"HE DECKED"**: Weaver, *Producers and Writers,* 24; and Bifulco, *Superman on Television,* 3.

137 **"WHAT IS A MAN"**: Noel Neill in *Biography* TV show, February 9, 2000.

137 **THERE WAS A SILK:** Hayde, *Flights of Fantasy,* 144.

138 **"THIS DROVE"**: Weaver, *Producers and Writers,* 25–26.

138 **"THIS," HE:** Author interview with Jack Larson.

139 **TRADEMARK BOW TIE:** Smithsonian officials say the tie is in their collection and that while it isn't currently on display, it may be soon.

139 **SHOW'S SPONSOR:** Whitney Ellsworth reportedly said that Kellogg's wanted Shayne fired and that Ellsworth insisted the actor be retained (Will Murray, "The Driving Force That Really Made DC Great," *Alter Ego* No. 98, 17). But Ellsworth told Gary Grossman that "never did either Kellogg or their agency make any suggestion that we not use Shayne or anybody else, in spite of all the talk about the blacklists and everything else" (Grossman interview with Ellsworth).

140 **"MONITORED PROGRAMS"**: Hayde, *Flights of Fantasy,* 180.

141 **"TELEVISION HAS"**: Wertham, *Seduction,* 381.

141 **WAS AFRAID OF:** William H. Young and Nancy K. Young, *The 1950s,* 42. In those earliest years of television, sponsors routinely engaged in the kind of content control that Kellogg's did with Superman.

141 **"THAT FAVORITE"**: Hayde, *Flights of Fantasy,* 165.

142 **"HEY JIMMY"**: Author interview with Larson.

142 **"I HAD TO"**: Warren, "Superman's Girl Friday," *TV People.*

142 **"SO HE WAS"**: Liebowitz memoir, 52.

143 **WHITNEY ELLSWORTH:** He wrote under several pen names, including Fred Whitby and, when he collaborated with Robert Maxwell, Richard Fielding.

143 **HE DID:** Ellsworth letters to Siegel on February 21, 1940, November 4, 1940, and February 19, 1941.

144 **"WE NEVER"**: Grossman interview with Ellsworth.

144 **"MAXWELL'S FIRST"**: Grossman interview with Ellsworth.

144 **A RECENT COMIC:** "The Menace from the Stars" was published in *World's Finest Comics* No. 68, which hit the newsstands just as "Panic in

the Sky" was hitting the airwaves. While it is impossible to say for sure which came first, it's likely that "Panic" was inspired by "Menace." Comic books then were written as long as six months in advance of the cover date, whereas Jackson Gillis, who wrote "Panic," said he often gave an idea to his producer at lunch, then sat down and wrote the screenplay almost immediately and not long before its airing. But Gillis also said that the rip-off process was a two-way street, with comic book writers both borrowing from and offering up ideas to the TV screenwriters (Hagen, "From Lassie to Superman: Jackson Gillis," *Comics Interview*).

145 **"PURE FANTASY":** Author interview with Jackson Gillis.
145 **LISTENED CLOSELY:** www.tv.com/shows/adventures-of-superman/panic-in-the-sky-90378; and Bifulco, *Superman on Television,* 75.
145 **"I HAD TO":** Grossman, *Superman: Serial to Cereal,* 128.
146 **"I LOVED":** Author interview with Larson.
146 **SHE ALSO WORRIED:** Author interview with Coates.
146 **"I'VE HAD":** Weaver, *Producers and Writers,* 24–25.
146 **"COMIC BOOKS IN":** Author interview with Neill.
147 **NEILL FOUND IT:** Author interview with Neill; and Ward, *Truth, Justice, & the American Way,* 82.
147 **DIDN'T LIKE ONE:** Ward, *Truth, Justice,* 73; *The Adventures Continue* No. 2, 66; and Weaver, *Producers and Writers,* 27.
147 **"JACK, I GOT":** Grossman interview with Ellsworth.
148 **THAT SAME KID-FRIENDLY:** Hajdu, *The Ten-Cent Plague,* 326, 329, 800.
148 **"MERCENARY MINORITY":** Weisinger, "How They're Cleaning Up the Comic Books," *Better Homes and Gardens.*
149 **"THE SAME TYPE":** "Are Comics Fascist?" *Time.*
149 **"EXPRESSIONS HAVING":** Memo from Ellsworth, "Editorial Policy for Superman-DC Publications."
149 **NEWSPAPERS GLOMMED:** "Superman Emulation Puts Boy in Hospital," *Washington Post;* "Miscellany," *Time;* "'Death-Defying' Leap Kills Boy," *Los Angeles Times.*
150 **"WE WERE VERY":** Author interview with Jay Emmett.
150 **"NO ONE":** Grossman, *Superman: Serial to Cereal,* 84.
150 **NATIONAL CAPITALIZED:** Author interview with Emmett.
150 **EMPEROR HIROHITO:** Grossman interview with Ellsworth; and "Reeves, Superman of TV, Kills Himself," *Los Angeles Times.*
151 **$1,000 A WEEK:** Grossman interview with Ellsworth.
152 **"NOTHING WAS BOTHERING":** Author interview with Gene LeBell.
152 **"TO SEE IF":** Ames, "Superman George Reeves and Producers Disagree," *Los Angeles Times.*
152 **HIS OWN VARIETY:** Ward, *Truth, Justice,* 100–101.
152 **"MOTEL OF THE STARS":** Hayde, *Flights of Fantasy,* 277.
152 **"HERE I AM":** Grossman, *Superman: Serial to Cereal,* 275–76.
152 **GEORGE HAD ALMOST:** Hayde, *Flights of Fantasy,* 260.

152 **THREE YEARS LATER:** "TV Superman Hero Injured in Auto Crash," *Los Angeles Times.*

152 **HE WAS LOOKING:** Hayde, *Flights of Fantasy,* 283.

154 **"HE'S PROBABLY":** Transcript of Lee Saylor interview with Leonore Lemmon.

154 **FORENSIC DETAILS:** Author interviews with Craig Harvey, chief coroner investigator, Los Angeles County, and Dr. Eugene Mark, pathologist, Massachusetts General Hospital.

154 **RESEARCHERS WHO:** Author interviews with Jim Beaver, Chuck Harter, Hayde, and Jan Alan Henderson

154 **"ONLY LEM":** Thomas, *The Man to See,* 145.

154 **TONI VISITED:** Author interview with Larson.

155 **PUBLIC RELATIONS MAN:** Edward Lozzi says Toni kept George's clothes in a bedroom in her mansion that became a shrine to him. "Her deathbed confession was totally the opposite of what she had been telling me," Lozzi says. "She was blaming it all on Leonore Lemmon." Author interview with Lozzi.

156 **GEORGE'S YOUNG:** Grossman, *Superman: Serial to Cereal,* 102; and Hayde, *Flights of Fantasy,* 272.

156 **NO ONE WILL:** Author interviews with Beaver, Harter, Harvey, Hayde, Henderson, and Eugene Mark.

7. IMAGINE THIS

158 **STORY LIKE THIS:** "Mr. and Mrs. Clark (SUPERMAN) Kent!" *Superman's Girl Friend Lois Lane.*

160 **ACTION ON TV:** The airwaves were dominated then by Westerns like *Bonanza* and *Wagon Train* and personality-driven comedies like Red Skelton's and Andy Griffith's.

161 **"EVERYONE KNOWS":** Weisinger, "I Flew with Superman," *Parade.*

162 **HE "GLOWED":** Joyce Kaffel, "Digging up Superman," *Alter Ego* No. 98.

162 **EIGHT DIFFERENT:** The eight were *Action Comics, Superman, World's Finest, Superman's Pal Jimmy Olsen, Superman's Girl Friend Lois Lane, Adventure Comics, Justice League of America,* and *Superboy.*

162 **"MY GREATEST":** Will Murray, "Superman's Editor Mort Weisinger," *The Krypton Companion,* 12.

163 **"HERE LIES":** Jones, *Men of Tomorrow,* 131.

163 **"I HAD TO":** Author interview with Adler. Jim Shooter says Weisinger called him a "fucking retard who couldn't spell." But his family was poor, Shooter adds, and the work Weisinger gave him "saved our house and kept us alive. That was the two sides of Mort" (author interview with Shooter). Others say that various DC staffers were so frustrated with Weisinger that they tried to toss him out the window, although with steel mesh surrounding the frame he wouldn't have gone very far.

163 **"I'LL TELL":** Michael Eury, "Neal Adams Interview," *The Krypton Companion,* 101.

164 **"MORT KEPT IT"**: Author interview with Carmine Infantino.

164 **CURT SWAN**: Zeno, *Curt Swan: A Life in Comics*, 173, 734–75.

164 **"DO YOU NEED"**: Pachter, "A Rare Interview with Superman's God-father," *Amazing Heroes* No. 41, 33. After he was fired from DC, Boring worked on several newspaper strips, then took a part-time job as a security guard.

165 **STEERED CLEAR:** There were exceptions, like the imaginary story in 1963—"The Amazing Story of Superman-Red and Superman-Blue"—in which the hero got Khrushchev to dump all his missiles into the sea and Fidel Castro to free all his political prisoners. And in 1969, Mort sent Clark Kent, Lois Lane, and Superman to Vietnam in a story entitled "The Soldier of Steel!" It was written by DC's war comics whiz, Robert Kanigher, and illustrated by longtime war artist Joe Kubert.

165 **"CALLED HIM"**: Schelly, *Words of Wonder,* 39, 142; and Lupoff email.

165 **"THE MOST COMPETENT"**: Murray, "Superman's Editor Mort Weisinger," 13.

165 **"WHAT I FIND"**: Letter from Siegel to Liebowitz, July 13, 1946.

166 **WEISINGER MET**: Murray, "Superman's Editor Mort Weisinger," 14.

166 **"WHEN PEOPLE"**: Lillian, "Mort Weisinger: The Man Who Wouldn't Be Superman," *Amazing World of DC Comics.*

166 **"ANY TIME WE"**: Murray, "Superman's Editor Mort Weisinger," 17.

166 **"DID YOU GET"**: Weisinger, "I Flew with Superman."

166 **AN "INVESTIGATION"**: Weisinger, "How They're Cleaning Up the Comic Books," *Better Homes and Gardens.*

167 **"I WANTED"**: Author interview with Lee.

168 **"DONE CORRECTLY"**: Author interview with Shooter.

168 **BATMAN TUMBLED:** Evanier, Beerbohm, and Schwartz, "There's a Lot of Myth Out There!" *Alter Ego* No. 26, 23; and author interview with Infantino.

168 **FINALLY, AS HE REPORTED:** In another version, Mort said he had the economic security to quit DC after Columbia Pictures paid him $250,000 for his novel *The Contest.* How did he feel about leaving Super-man after all that time? "I guess my baby has grown up," Mort said, "and doesn't need daddy any more" (Peterson, "Superman Goes Mod").

168 **CARMINE INFANTINO:** Author interview with Infantino. Julie Schwartz's version is that "every year or so Mort would tell our boss Jack Liebowitz that he wanted to retire, and Jack (he always wanted us to call him Jack) would talk him out of it. Then one day in 1970, (surprise! surprise!) he accepted the resignation since he himself was leaving DC" (Schwartz and Thomsen, *Man of Two Worlds,* 131).

169 **THE MOST EMOTIONAL:** Siegel, "Superman's Return to Krypton!" *Superman* No. 141.

171 **TENTH-LEVEL:** Lex Luthor would amp up Brainiac's intellect from level ten to twelve.

172 **"ANYTHING SUPERMAN"**: Siegel, "The Bizarro Invasion of Earth!" *Superman* No. 169.

172 **THE ENEMY:** Waid, "Red Kryptonite," *Amazing Heroes* No. 41, 44–45.

173 **IN ITS ANNUAL:** Bart, "Advertising: Superman Faces New Hurdles," *New York Times.*

173 **SOCIAL SECURITY:** That number was issued to a real person, Giobatta Baiocchi, who was born in 1887 and whose relatives say they don't know of any connection he might have had to Superman.

173 **BEFORE EXECUTING:** Eddy Zeno, "A Fond Remembrance of Mort Weisinger by His Son," *The Krypton Companion,* 17.

174 **COMIC STRIP DREAMS:** Those dreams lasted from 1949 to 1952, with Clark waking just as he was about to tell Lois he was Superman. The story was dreamed up by Whitney Ellsworth, who started to write it, but then got distracted, and Alvin Schwartz claims he wrote nearly all of it.

176 **"YOU'RE NOT":** Newman and Benton, *It's a Bird . . . It's a Plane . . . It's Superman: The New Musical Comedy.*

177 **"A CHILL":** Holiday and Harter, *Superman on Broadway,* 18.

177 **THE FIRST TEST:** Schier, "'Superman' Needs a Quick Course in Muscle Building," Philadelphia *Bulletin;* and Murdock, "'Superman' Lands in Town," *Philadelphia Daily News.*

178 *IT'S A BIRD* **OPENED:** "Paper Cutups," *Time;* Coe, "Not Peter Pan, It's 'Superman,'" *Washington Post;* Nadel, "'Superman,' Airy, Merry," *New York World-Telegram and Sun;* and Kauffmann, "'It's a Bird . . . It's a Plane . . .'" *New York Times.*

178 **"THEY SAID, 'MY'":** Author interview with Hal Prince.

178 **EVERYONE HAD:** Author interviews with Prince, Charles Strouse, and Robert Benton.

179 **"I DON'T THINK":** Author interview with Bob Holiday.

179 **SUPERMAN WAS:** Shabecoff, "Look! Up in the Air!" *New York Times;* and Weisinger, "Superman and His Friends Around the World," *Superman's Pal Jimmy Olsen* No. 113.

180 *STUPOR-MAN:* Not to be confused with *Mad* magazine's Superduperman.

180 **"WHEN *SUPERMAN*":** Feiffer, *The Great Comic Book Heroes,* 17.

181 **"THEY LOVED IT":** Thomas, "Superman Teaches School," *Magazine Digest.*

181 **"I COULDN'T READ":** Author interview with Ron Massengill.

182 **TWO OF HIS BEST:** The two writers were Bill Finger and E. Nelson Bridwell. "Superman's Mission for President Kennedy," *Superman* No. 170.

182 **WHEN *THE NEW*:** "Superman Meets Kennedy on Vigor," *New York Times.*

182 **"WE'RE WAITING":** Weisinger, "I Flew with Superman."

182 **IT WAS NOT:** *The Essential Superman Encyclopedia,* 151–52.

183 **COMPLIANT PARTNER:** Sampliner served on the boards of the Anti-Defamation League, the New York City Anti-Crime Commission, and the New York State Commission Against Discrimination. He stayed on as an owner of DC Comics until 1967, and in 1969 he was named

chairman of the board of Independent, the distribution company (Kleefeld, "Paul Sampliner," kleefeldoncomics.blogspot.com).

183 **AS EARLY AS:** Liebowitz memoir, 55–56.

183 **HE NEVER KNEW:** Others, including Jack Adams, say the accident happened after the company went public.

183 **"WE ALL SAID":** Author interview with Peachy Donenfeld.

183 **HAVING A CHAUFFEUR:** Liebowitz memoir, 56, 62.

184 **"WE DIDN'T WANT":** Liebowitz memoir, 51.

185 **"TURNED TO ME":** Barr, "The Madame and the Girls," *Words & Pictures* No. 5, 5.

185 **"THEY WERE THE":** Barr, "The Madame and the Girls," 10.

186 **WAS DESPERATE:** Knutzen, "Man of Steel Splinters an American Dream," *Los Angeles Times.*

186 **"I WAS THE OLDEST":** Knutzen, "Man of Steel Splinters an American Dream."

186 **IT LOOKED WORSE:** Author interview with Neal Adams.

187 **THE BEST MEASURE:** Yoe, *Secret Identity: The Fetish Identity of Superman's Co-Creator Joe Shuster.*

187 **"PORNOGRAPHY, UNADULTERATED":** *City of New York v. Kingsley Books,* Supreme Court of New York.

187 **WHY DID JOE:** Author interviews with Robinson and Craig Yoe.

188 **"I SPENT ALL":** Liebowitz memoir, 57. He could, of course, have brought his daughters into the business, but that was unthinkable to an old-school father like him.

188 **SO HE HIRED:** Liebowitz memoir, 57.

188 **STEVE ROSS:** Bruck, *Master of the Game,* 129–33.

188 **EMMETT SAID:** Author interview with Emmett.

8. BELIEVING A MAN CAN FLY

189 **"WHY DON'T WE":** Author interview with Ilya Salkind.

190 **HIS LAWYER:** Author interview with Tom Pollock.

190 **OWN BIG FILMS:** Curiously, Warner Bros. was willing to make a movie about *Doc Savage: The Man of Bronze,* but not about Superman, the caped hero who had borrowed from Doc, then left him in the dust.

191 **"IT WASN'T":** Author interview with Terry Semel.

191 **MORE THAN A:** Petrou, *The Making of Superman the Movie,* 21.

191 **BOUNCED OR DELAYED:** The Salkinds' producer and money man, Pierre Spengler, concedes, "there were times of extreme cash flow difficulties." But he adds that "everybody got paid in full" (emails to author from Spengler).

192 **GROSS SALES:** That is money received by the distributor(s) of the film, in this case mainly Warner Bros. It includes about half of box office receipts along with the distributor's share of proceeds from television, VHS/DVD, and other offshoots.

192 **EVERYONE WHO READ:** Author interviews with Salkind, Tom Mankiewicz, Richard Donner, and Infantino. Infantino says the Puzo

script was "the worst thing you ever saw in your life." Transcripts of meetings with Puzo show Infantino and others trying to tone down the script's sexuality and beef up its fealty to Superman and his forty-year history.

192 **NEXT UP:** Author interviews with Leslie Newman and Robert Benton.

193 **AGREEMENT BETWEEN NATIONAL:** Agreement with Alex and Ilya Salkind, November 6, 1974.

193 **NEEDED A DIRECTOR:** Author interview with Ilya Salkind.

194 **PENDING ARREST:** The warrant had to do with Brando's role in the film *Last Tango in Paris*. His interest in Superman was piqued by an old girlfriend.

194 **IT ACTUALLY:** Author interviews with and emails from Spengler and Pollock.

195 **A LINEUP:** Petrou, *The Making of Superman the Movie*, 36–37.

195 **PREP SCHOOL:** Christopher said that his poet-professor father, upon hearing his son was playing Superman, assumed he meant George Bernard Shaw's *Man and Superman*. Frank Reeve, the father, says that is "a great line" apparently dreamed up by Christopher and his buddy, comedian Robin Williams. "Later," Frank adds, "it became a line said so often he [Christopher] came to believe it." Frank says he watched all his son's movies except those Christopher asked him not to. "I found *Superman 1* delightful and enthusiastically said so." (Emails from Frank Reeve to author.)

195 **"LIKE THE GUY":** Dangaard, "Reeve Flies to the Rescue of 'Superman,'" *Los Angeles Times*.

196 **"SHE LITERALLY":** Author interview with Donner.

196 **"I'M MANIC":** Petrou, *The Making of Superman the Movie*, 48.

196 **"IT'S AS SIMPLE":** Author interview with Donner. Christopher Reeve, in his 1978 film, was the first Superman to explain for himself that he was fighting for "truth, justice and the American way," to which Lois, with characteristic sarcasm, replies, "You'll wind up fighting almost every elected official in this country."

196 **"THIS PICTURE IS":** Anderson, "It's a Bird! It's a Plane! It's a Movie!" *New York Times*.

197 **THE SOLUTION CAME:** Author interviews with Zoran Perisic and Donner.

198 **HIS OWN CAPERS:** Spengler says Reeve would have liked to do *all* of his own stunts but "I had to stop him at times for security and/or insurance reasons" (Spengler email).

198 **"HOW COULD A":** Reeve, *Still Me*, 192.

198 **"WE SHOVED":** Author interview with Dave Prowse.

199 **WAS SO OUTRAGED:** Rossen, *Superman vs. Hollywood*, 90.

200 **BEING TYPECAST:** Sean Connery, who played James Bond in seven films, told Reeve not to worry. If the first film isn't good, he said, there won't be more. If you do a low-budget film next, it might hit big by the time *Superman* airs. And if the producers or studio give you trouble, "get a good lawyer and sue the bastards" (Davis, "Marketing the Man of Steel!" *Maclean's*).

200 **"FOR GOD'S SAKE":** Transcript, *Studio 360,* "American Icons" series.

200 **MANKIEWICZ EXPANDED:** Author interview with Mankiewicz.

200 **"I HAD TO PRETEND":** Author interview with Margot Kidder.

200 **"SUPERMAN WAS THE":** Author interview with John Williams.

201 **LAST-MINUTE GLITCH:** Author interviews with Donner, Semel, and Ilya Salkind; author interview with and emails from Pollock; and Blue and Delugach, "'Superman': Rare Look at Film Finances," *Los Angeles Times.* Semel says that Warner Bros. sent a plane to Europe and managed to get a copy of the negative from Technicolor, the film storage people. "We called Alex in London to say, 'Oh, by the way, the negative is here, in Burbank, we're printing—we started printing last night—maybe we'll see you at the premiere, maybe we won't,'" recalls Semel. Tom Pollock has a different take on what happened more than thirty years ago: "Technicolor denied it, and in any case, had they [Warner Bros.] used it, it would have opened them up to lawsuits, as well as Technicolor. The letters of credit were contingent on DELIVERY by FilmExport, not by theft by Warners."

202 **CONFOUNDING NO-SHOW:** "'Superman': Rare Look at Film Finances."

202 **"IT WAS EXACTLY":** Author interview with Jenette Kahn.

202 **REVIEWERS OFFERED:** Kroll, "Superman to the Rescue," *Newsweek;* Ebert, "Superman," *Chicago Sun-Times;* Kael, "The Current Cinema," *New Yorker;* and Canby, "Screen: It's a Bird, It's a Plane, It's a Movie," *New York Times.*

203 **AND PEKING:** The *Peking Evening News* said that Superman is not really a savior but "a narcotic which the capitalist class gives itself to cast off its serious crises." There were no problems anywhere else in China and all this happened in 1985, when China finally was catching up with old movies from America (Mann, "'Superman' Shanghaied in Peking Screen Test," *Los Angeles Times*).

203 **"I TOOK MY":** Hoover, "What Women See in Man of Steel," *Los Angeles Times.*

204 **THE MOVIE WAS MEANT:** Author interview with Mankiewicz.

204 **"I GOT MAJOR":** Author interview with Donner.

204 **$55 MILLION:** Spengler says that "the aggregate cost of the first two movies was $109 million. The split would be approximately 75 for the first and 34 for the second" (Spengler email).

204 **FILED THEIR OWN LAWSUITS:** Tom Pollock says it wasn't just Alex who was targeted in the lawsuits, but "everybody under the sun. Alex, Ilya, Pierre [Spengler], all of Alex's companies, Credit Lyonnais Bank, Warner Brothers, etc etc etc." (email from Pollock).

204 **PRODUCTION FIGURES:** That matters because the percentage payouts to Puzo, Donner, and the others specified that they were a share of the profits left after Alex recovered his production costs. No postproduction profits, no payouts.

205 **"EVERYONE GOT PAID":** Author interview with Pollock. He says

that Warner made more than $100 million, with Spengler adding that it was "considerably more." Credit Lyonnais, one of Alex's banks, "made the next most," says Pollock, and DC Comics got 5 percent of the gross. Spengler adds in an email that DC got "7.5% domestic or 5% worldwide, which ever is greater."

205 **BIG BANG THEORY:** Schwartz and Thomsen, *Man of Two Worlds,* 15. If Julie had asked Jerry for his response to Big Bang, the Superman creator likely would have pointed out that he already had a magazine by and for fans, *Cosmic Stories,* which predated not only Mort and Julie's fanzine but Jerry's own *Science Fiction.*

206 **"WAS MERELY":** O'Neil, *Superman: Kryptonite Nevermore,* 189.

207 **YOUNG PEOPLE:** Schwartz and Thomsen, *Man of Two Worlds,* 134.

207 **"I AM CURIOUS":** Kanigher, "I Am Curious (Black)!" *Superman's Girl Friend Lois Lane* No. 106.

208 **"THAT'S THE":** Pasko, "The Master Mesmerizer of Metropolis!" *Superman* No. 330.

210 **"SUPERMAN DIRECTED":** Author interview with Alvin Schwartz.

210 **"THE FAMOUS BLUE":** Baker, "Sad Feet in the Sky," *New York Times.*

211 **HE ACTUALLY PROPOSED:** Author interview with Kahn.

212 **MUHAMMAD ALI:** It was bad karma: By the time the book came out, Ali had been dethroned as boxing champ by Leon Spinks.

212 **PRICE HIKES:** The price rise was even steeper if you start in 1969, when a DC comic book sold for twelve cents, and go until 1981, when it was fifty cents. The number of pages fluctuated, often rising as the price did.

213 **"DREW A HUMUNGOUS":** Email to author from Levitz.

213 **"TOTALLY REAL":** Email to author from Luis Augusto.

213 **MOVIE-RELATED:** Harmetz, "The Marketing of Superman and His Paraphernalia," *New York Times;* Levin, "'Protect Children Act' Aims to Ban Cigarette Deals," *Los Angeles Times;* Scivally, *Superman on Film, Television, Radio and Broadway,* 95; and author interview with Kidder.

214 **ADVERTISING HELPED:** Gabilliet, *Of Comics and Men,* 134–37.

215 **AS A WRITER:** Much of his writing for Marvel was under the pseudonym Joe Carter.

215 **"JERRY SIEGEL":** Siegel, "Superman's Originator Puts 'Curse' on Superman Movie," archives.tcj.com.

216 **THE PRESS:** Sherwood, "Superman Still Makes Millions, but Not His Creators," *Washington Star;* Breasted, "Superman's Creators, Nearly Destitute, Invoke His Spirit," *New York Times;* and Vidal, "Mild-Mannered Cartoonists Go to Aid of Superman's Creators," *New York Times.*

216 **ORCHESTRATING THE PUBLICITY:** Author interviews with Neal Adams and Irwin Hasen.

217 **"WE WERE ABOUT":** Author interview with Emmett.

217 **ROSE SUBSTANTIALLY:** In 1979, Jerry and Joe each got a check for $15,000 in recognition of the success of *Superman: The Movie.* The next year their annual payments jumped to $30,000. In 1981, after the release of

Superman II, the pensions rose again, to $60,000, and they each got one-time bonuses of $50,000 that year and $25,000 the next. After Joanne Siegel made her first formal request for additional money in 1988, the annual payouts were increased to $80,000, with a cost-of-living inflator.

217 **"JOE AND I":** Siegel, *Creation of a Superhero,* 7: 5.

217 **DECEMBER 1976:** Most references to their marriage say it was in 1975, but public records make clear it was December 24, 1976, in Del Mar, California. Wedding pictures show each with a flower pinned to their breast, him wearing a suit and slightly raised shoes, her in a full-length gown standing before their three-tiered wedding cake. Joe was sixty-two then, Judith fifty-nine. Their handwritten notes invited guests to a reception at the Atlantis Restaurant in Mission Bay, an oceanfront oasis at the mouth of the San Diego River.

217 **THE ATTRACTIVE:** Certificate of Registry of Marriage, Joseph Michael Shuster and Judith Ray Calpini; and Request and Declaration for Final Judgment of Dissolution of Marriage, *Joseph Michael Shuster vs. Judith Ray Calpini.*

218 **"HAS MEANT A":** "Follow-up on the News," *New York Times.*

9. BACK TO THE FUTURE

220 **"MORE AGGRESSIVE":** Parrott, "For Clark Kent, Wimpery Is Out," *Los Angeles Times.*

220 **"YOU CAN'T DO":** Melvin, "Cartoonists Explain Superman's New Image to His Fans," *New York Times.*

220 **"HE USED TO":** Akers, "Bring Back the REAL Superman," *Washington Post.*

220 **"IF REAGAN HAS":** Kempley, "Superman: The Ramboization of the Comics' Man of Stale," *Washington Post.*

220 **SUPERMAN'S HEAD:** Psychologists and psychiatrists have suggested that Superman is the classic schizoid personality, although even they have trouble deciding whether Clark or Superman is the primary identity.

221 **RENAMED *ADVENTURES*:** *Adventures of Superman* picked up the numbering from the old *Superman* comic book, and a new *Superman* was launched with a new number one. *Superman* and *Adventures of Superman* were published concurrently from 1986 through the spring of 2006, when *Adventures* was killed and *Superman* reclaimed its numbering.

221 **"WE WRITE AS":** "Dear DC Comics," *New York Times.*

222 **"EXCORIATED":** Email to author from John Byrne.

222 **"THE COMIC BOOK HERO":** "Bring Back the REAL Superman."

222 **"MORE BELIEVABLE":** "Cartoonists Explain Superman's New Image to His Fans."

222 **"DOUBLE-CROSSED":** Byrne email.

223 ***SUPERMAN'S* NUMBERS:** Miller, "Superman Sales," blog.comichron .com.

223 **THE PUBLISHER STOPPED:** DC stopped making public its circula-

tion figures when it stopped mailing its comic books second class, a discount privilege that carried with it the reporting requirement.

224 **ADULTIFICATION:** Friedrich, Austin, and Simpson, "Up, Up and Awaaay!!!" *Time.*

224 **A SURVEY:** Eichenwald, "Grown-ups Gather at the Comic Book Stand," *New York Times.*

224 **FULL REFUND:** The black market for comics listed as destroyed was so effective that, in 1974, it was estimated that as few as a quarter of all printed comic books were actually placed for sale at retailers. Many if not most of the rest presumably were sold illicitly, then listed as destroyed so wholesalers and distributors could profit a second time by claiming a credit from publishers (*Of Comics and Men,* 141).

225 **COUNTERINTUITIVE NAMES:** Julie Schwartz later acknowledged having made a "horrible mistake" by naming the older planet Earth-2 and the younger one Earth-1. "If we knew 30 years later we'd be asked these questions," he said laughing, "we'd have paid more attention" (Schwartz, "Dawn of the Silver Age," *Comics Scene Spectacular* No. 6).

226 **AMONG MILLIONS:** Wolfman said his rule was "not to kill any hero who was created before I was born" (Wolfman, *Crisis on Infinite Earths,* 7).

227 **"WHATEVER HAPPENED":** Moore, *Whatever Happened to the Man of Tomorrow.*

227 **SCHWARTZ'S GOODBYE:** Julie was on the cover of *Whatever Happened*—with Batman, Wonder Women, and others—waving goodbye to his Man of Tomorrow.

227 **"GENIUS":** It was safe to call Jerry that in the 1980s, with Jack Liebowitz no longer in charge, but wouldn't have been in the 1960s. Author interview with Mark Evanier.

227 **KRYPTONIAN PAST:** *Superman: The Man of Steel,* Vol. 1.

228 **BIRTHING MATRIX:** One could even argue (and fans did) that, having been hatched in outer space or upon arriving on Earth, Superman wasn't an alien at all but an Earthling, an American, and a Kansan.

228 **MARGOT KIDDER:** She says her role model for a strong-willed Lois was feminist Gloria Steinem. Author interview with Kidder.

228 **"IT'S A COLLECTIVE":** Author interview with Levitz.

229 **GOT INTO TROUBLE:** Author interviews with Waid, Elliot Maggin, and Len Wein.

230 **"I ADMIRE":** Mamet, *Some Freaks,* 179.

230 **BIRTHDAY PARTIES:** www.capedwonder.com/dc-70. Superman's birthday, we were told as far back as 1968, was February 29. That device—having a birthday on a leap day that occurs once in four years—also was used by Orphan Annie's handlers to playfully explain why the cartoon character aged so slowly (Wells emails).

230 **BOOK OF ESSAYS:** Dooley and Engle, *Superman at Fifty!* 12, 115, 170.

232 **CLARK KISSED LOIS:** Leslie Newman says she and her writing partner and husband, David, "snuck in our own love story there. When we

wrote the scene we both had tears going down our faces." Author interview with Newman.

232 **"MY FEELING":** Author interview with Donner.

232 **"DICK DONNER SAID":** Author interview with Ilya Salkind.

232 **"THE MIND BOGGLES":** Mann, "'Superman' Sequel: Flying in the Soup," *Los Angeles Times.*

232 **"IF I THINK":** "Margot Lois Lane Kidder," *People.*

232 **"TO MAKE [DONNER]":** Soderbergh and Lester, *Getting Away with It,* 124–25.

233 **PAID TWICE:** Yule, *The Man Who "Framed" the Beatles,* 305. Ilya Salkind says Warner Bros. kicked in only on the third film, but Spengler says the studio boosted Lester's salary for the second and third (author interview with Ilya Salkind and Spengler emails).

233 **"DECIDED NOT":** Soderbergh and Lester, *Getting Away with It,* 125. It would have cost them $1 million to use any of the Brando footage for *Superman II,* a cost no one wanted to pay.

233 **"UNCONTROLLABLE DESPAIR":** Soderbergh and Lester, *Getting Away with It,* 130–31.

233 **VILLAINESS URSA:** Author interview with Sarah Douglas.

233 **MEMORABLE LINES:** Leslie Newman says, "We never wrote that and there's no way on Earth that line would have gotten by DC Comics."

234 **COSTS COULD MOUNT:** Schoell, *Comic Book Heroes of the Screen,* 45.

234 **MARKETING STRATEGY:** Harmetz, "The Marketing of Superman and His Paraphernalia," *New York Times.*

235 **"BARELY BROKE":** Author interview with Ilya Salkind.

235 **"CRITICS WERE SPLIT":** Schickel, "Flying High," *Time;* Maslin, "'Superman II' Is Full of Tricks," *New York Times;* Boyum, "One-Dimensional Flights of Fancy," *Wall Street Journal;* Arnold, "'Superman II': The Plot Weakens," *Washington Post;* and Gasser, "Superman, What Happened to You?" *Los Angeles Times.*

236 **"IT WAS MAINLY":** Author interview with Ilya Salkind.

236 **"THE WHOLE GOOD":** Author interview with Newman.

237 *SUPERMAN III* **AS A WHOLE:** Maslin, "'Superman III'; Reeve Joined by Pryor," *New York Times;* Kempley, "Number III Is Not So Super, Man," *Washington Post;* Reeve, *Still Me,* 192; and Pryor, *Pryor Convictions and Other Life Sentences,* 205.

237 **ADDED $1 MILLION:** Author interview with Ilya Salkind.

237 **"MAKING MONEY":** Author interview with Ilya Salkind. Pollock, Alex Salkind's lawyer, says that "overall, Alex made a lot of money. . . . None of us know the real numbers. I doubt that anyone but Alex knew the real numbers" (Pollock emails).

237 **"I'M JUST OPTIMIST":** Reagan, *The Reagan Diaries,* 158–59. Ilya Salkind says President Reagan told him the movie "was 'very nice.' I don't know if he even saw the film" (author interview with Ilya Salkind).

238 **NUCLEAR WEAPONS:** Reeve's mother, real-world journalist Barbara Johnson, helped found the Coalition for Nuclear Disarmament.

238 **"I THOUGHT":** Reeve, *Still Me,* 218.

238 **"ONE OF THE":** Kempley, "It's Recurred! It's a Pain!" *Washington Post.*

238 **"CHINTZY":** Maslin, "'Superman IV: Quest for Peace,'" *New York Times.*

239 **"*SUPERGIRL* WAS HUGE":** Author interview with Ilya Salkind.

239 **"I JUST WANTED":** Author interview with John Haymes Newton. Newton was replaced after the first season for what the media said was at least one, and perhaps all, of these reasons: The producers weren't taken with his performance, he asked for a pay raise his bosses didn't think he deserved, and he was facing a charge of drunk driving. Newton says he disputed the drunk driving charge and got it dropped, and he regrets that he left the show.

239 **"HE WAS":** Author interview with Stacy Haiduk.

239 **BERKOWITZ'S MIND:** Author interview with Stan Berkowitz.

240 **FOR PRODUCER JULIA:** Author interview with Julia Pistor.

240 **"THIS IS A":** Brennan, "A Family Feud," *Los Angeles Times.*

240 **LOOKING BACK:** Author interview with Ilya Salkind.

241 **HE HAD A:** Author interview with Gae Exton.

241 **HAIRLINE YOUTHFUL:** His problem was less age-related and more a result of his alopecia areata, which caused the loss of clumps of otherwise healthy hair. He also suffered from mastocytosis, a skin disease that produces lesions and intense itching (email to author from Benjamin Reeve).

241 **"BY THE TIME":** Author interview with Benjamin Reeve.

241 **"MOSTLY A":** Reeve, *Still Me,* 199.

241 **HIS FATHER:** Frank Reeve emails.

241 **"WHEN I WAS":** Author interview with Smolinski.

242 **"WHAT I'M SUGGESTING":** Letter from Joanne Siegel to Steven J. Ross, February 16, 1988.

10. TILL DEATH DO US PART

243 **IT STARTED:** Recollections of the summit and its aftermath were based on author interviews with and emails from Cary Bates, Jon Bogdanove, Mike Carlin, K. C. Carlson, Chris Duffy, Dan Jurgens, Jenette Kahn, Karl Kesel, Jerry Ordway, Frank Pittarese, Louise Simonson, and Martha Thomases.

243 **COULD TAKE YEARS:** Some Superman writers worried that, given the quick turnover rate in the comic book business, they would be gone by the time the momentous wedding happened.

245 **"NEVER SAY":** McTernan, "Superman to Die Saving Metropolis," Cleveland *Plain Dealer.*

245 **"HOW DARE":** Author interview with Kahn.

245 **DURACELL BATTERIES:** Elliott, "Always a Place for Superman," *New York Times.*

246 **KILLING HIM:** Jurgens, Ordway, et al., *The Death of Superman.*

247 **THE CLIMAX:** The average number of panels per page was six, although Marvel artists had been making a splash with fewer pages and more single panels (Wells emails).

248 **"COPIES IN":** "Superman Death Issue to Go to Second Printing," *Wall Street Journal*.

248 **"GO ON THE":** "Look! It's a Bird! It's a Plane! It's Curtains for the Man of Steel," *New York Times*.

248 **"SUPERMAN," HE:** Rich, "Term Limit for the Man of Steel," *New York Times*.

248 **MORE HEADS OF STATE:** Stern, *The Death and Life of Superman*, 174.

249 **"GOD? 'S ME":** *World Without a Superman*, 46.

249 **MONTHS OFF:** To satisfy fans and DC bean counters, the company published a series of other comics during that downtime, including *Legacy of Superman* No. 1.

249 **"IF THIS MANY":** Carlin email.

250 **"NOW," HE:** Zinn, "It's a Bird, It's a Plane—It's a Resurrection," *Business Week*.

251 **"THAT BECAME":** Author interview with Kahn.

252 **"HE SAID":** Sangiacomo, "Superman Creator, Siegel, 81, Is Dead," Cleveland *Plain Dealer*.

252 **INTERESTED IN LOIS:** Jenette Kahn, the power behind the scenes, says her first treatment for the TV show was entitled "Lois Lane's *Daily Planet*." She also says she decided not to have her hero fly because the limited special effects available back then would have made it look "cheesy."

252 **"I DIDN'T WANT":** Author interview with Deborah Joy LeVine.

254 **ADVERTISING MONEY:** Gordon, "Superman on the Set," *Quality Popular Television*, 149.

254 **NETWORK PURPOSEFULLY:** Gordon, "Superman on the Set," 151.

256 **EARTH-2:** In his 1985 *Crisis on Infinite Earths*, Marv Wolfman carried this Earth-2 couple to an alternate dimension, where they could carry on without getting in the way of the Earth-1 couple and the newly simplified DC universe.

256 **ISSUE CALLED:** Superman writers and artists past and present, "The Wedding Album," *Superman: The Wedding Album* No. 1.

257 *MOONLIGHTING* **EFFECT:** Gordon, "Superman on the Set," 149–50; Flint and Snierson, "'Clark' Canned," *Entertainment Weekly;* and author interview with Kahn.

257 **"I WAS THAT":** Hatcher, *Burnt Toast and Other Philosophies of Life*, 191.

257 **CAIN HAD LESS:** "Dean Cain," *People;* Perigard, "Raising Cain," *Boston Herald;* and Jacobs, "Citizen Cain," *Entertainment Weekly*.

258 **"SUPERMAN: THE ESCAPE":** Wharton, "'Superman' Ride Still Grounded," *Los Angeles Times*. The Escape tied for the world's fastest ride with Tower of Terror II at Dreamworld Theme Park in Australia.

259 **"IN VIRTUAL":** Herz, "It's a Bird! It's a Plane! (And It Wobbles?)," *New York Times*.

259 **GUEST STARRING:** Dooley and Engle, *Superman at Fifty!* 182; www .seinfeldscripts.com; and "Seinfeld Meets a Really 'Super' Salesman," *New*

York Times. The American Express commercials—"A Uniform Used to Mean Something" and "Hindsight Is 20/20"—each lasted four minutes.

260 **"HE IS A CITIZEN":** "To the Rescue: Superman's Big Mission in Bosnia," *Time for Kids*.

261 **THE FIRST BOOK:** Levitz, *75 Years of DC Comics*, 574.

261 **"COMIC ART" AUCTIONS:** Lyne, "The Executive Life," *New York Times;* and "2 Comic Books Auctioned for $100,000," *New York Times*.

262 **"A BATTLER FOR":** *Kingdom Come*, 210.

262 **THE REAL AIM:** Author interviews with Waid and Maggin.

263 **FOR HIM, THOUGH:** Author interview with Jeph Loeb.

263 **"I DON'T WANT":** Email to author from Chris Clow.

264 **JO JO KAMINSKI:** Author interview with Ordway.

264 **NAMES OF GIRLS:** Author interview with Maggin.

264 **SUCH STORIES WERE:** Wells emails.

264 **WHITE AND:** Around this time, DC was collaborating with the new Milestone Media to distribute multicultural comic books featuring black superheroes like Hardware and Static.

265 **"STEEL WAS":** Author interviews with and emails from Simonson, Christopher Priest, and Kahn.

265 **"USED TO WATCH":** Gates, "A Big Brother from Another Planet," *New York Times*.

265 **"THERE WAS SOMETHING":** Author interview with Al Roker.

265 **SHAQUILLE O'NEAL:** Mead, "A Man-Child in Lotusland," *The New Yorker*.

266 **THREE-PART SERIES:** *Superman: The Man of Steel* No. 81; and author interview with Bogdanove.

266 **MIXED BALANCE SHEET:** Jensen, "Dead Superman May Revive DC Comics," *Advertising Age;* Lev, "Reaching Beyond the Ghouls and Gore for Major Payoffs," *New York Times;* Rhoades, *A Complete History of American Comic Books*, 129; Gabilliet, *Of Comics and Men*, 151; and Chang, "SPLAAAAAAAT!," *Los Angeles Times*.

267 **GALLUP POLL:** Hugick, "Public to DC Comics: Resurrect Superman!" The Gallup Poll News Service.

267 **IT WASN'T JUST:** Emails to author from Bill Necessary, Wurzelbacher, and Ken Cholette.

269 **JOE HAD BEEN:** Mietkiewicz, "Great Krypton!" *Toronto Star*.

269 **"I WAS SHOCKED":** Letter from Jean Shuster Peavy to Marty Payson, August 21, 1992.

270 **"THIS IS CALLED":** Reeve, *Still Me*, 15.

270 **"'WHAT IS A HERO?'":** Reeve, *Still Me*, 267.

271 **"SHE WAS FRIGHTENED":** "Margot Kidder Is Hospitalized for Psychiatric Observation," *New York Times*.

271 **"IT'S THE FIRST":** Author interview with Kidder.

272 **"THE FACT THAT":** Ordway emails.

272 **"THERE WAS AN":** Author interview with Levitz.

272 **"MORT WEISINGER":** Author interview with Evanier.

273 **KEPT A SEAT:** Nash, "Jack Liebowitz, Comics Publisher, Dies at 100," *New York Times.*

11. TIGHTS AND FIGHTS

275 **"WE MADE NO":** Author interview with Al Gough.

276 **"WE WERE VERY":** Author interview with Ken Horton.

277 **"JUST THE RIGHT":** Carson, "Small Comforts," *Esquire.*

277 **"I LOVE IT":** Hiatt, "Lex-Man," *Entertainment Weekly.*

277 **JONES LEFT:** He was arrested in 2009 by the Drug Enforcement Administration on trafficking charges, pled guilty in 2010, and the next year was sentenced to a year in prison.

278 **BROADER AND DEEPER:** Scivally, *Superman on Film,* 151–52.

279 **"WE WERE WINKING":** Author interview with Gough.

279 **"'SMALLVILLE' IS ONE":** Hinson, "Getting to the Heart of a Hero," *New York Times.*

280 **"SEEING THE SUPERMAN":** Carson, "Small Comforts."

280 **"FINALLY, CLARK":** Jensen, "Shows of Strength," *Entertainment Weekly.*

282 **A RECORD:** The cost would have been even higher if the studio hadn't received nearly $20 million in tax credits in Australia, where most of the filming was done, and if it hadn't canceled plans for a $20 million construction of Metropolis intended to be used afterward as a theme park. It reportedly cost $50 just to grow an ear of corn for the film. Jensen, "Greatest American Hero?" *Entertainment Weekly.*

282 **"A MODERN BLENDING":** Lewellen expert testimony, *Siegel and Larson v. Warner Bros. Entertainment.*

282 **REMAINS OF KRYPTON:** The next year, real-life scientists in Serbia found a new mineral whose chemistry matched the material described in the movie (Gustines, "Bad News for Superman," *New York Times*).

283 **"I GAVE MYSELF":** Swanson, "Super Troupers," *Premiere.*

283 **"I CAN'T TELL":** Bowles, "'Superman' Torch Is Passed," *USA Today.*

283 **"OUR GEORGE":** Rhodes, "The Continuing Adventures," *New York Times.*

284 **WATCH HIM FLY:** Grove, "Singer Was Man of Steel," *Hollywood Reporter.*

284 **AT A COST:** Swanson, "Super Troupers."

284 **"WRITING A STORY":** Author interview with Michael Dougherty.

284 **"MY GRANDMOTHER":** Singer, Dougherty, and Harris, *Superman Returns: The Complete Shooting Script,* 23.

284 **"IT'S INDESCRIBABLE":** Author interview with Dougherty.

284 **"I WAS PRACTICALLY":** Author interview with John Ottman.

285 **"SUPERHEROES—LET'S":** Duralde, "How Gay Is Superman?" *Advocate.*

285 **"MOST HETEROSEXUAL":** Jensen, "Greatest American Hero?"

285 **TOO GLOBAL:** That debate over whether Superman is all-American or all-world has surfaced repeatedly over the decades. Superman himself an-

swered it best in 1961 when, in response to being enrolled as an honorary citizen of all the member countries of the United Nations, he said: "What an honor! But of course my main loyalty will always be to the United States, where I grew up!" (*Superman* No. 146).

285 **"WARNER BROTHERS":** "Superman and the Culture War," bill oreilly.com.

285 **"THERE'S NO REASON":** Lundegaard, "Truth, Justice and (Fill in the Blank)," *New York Times.*

286 **MISHAPS:** Swanson, "Super Troupers."

286 **"AT ONE POINT":** Author interview with Bryan Singer.

286 **"THEY'RE VERY IMPORTANT":** Singer, Dougherty, and Harris, *Superman Returns: The Complete Shooting Script,* 10, 13.

286 **"*SUPERMAN RETURNS*":** Author interview with Singer.

286 **"EARLIER VERSIONS":** Corliss, "The Gospel of Superman," *Time.*

287 **"STAYED VERY MUCH":** Author interview with Donner.

287 **"OFFERS NOT SO":** Lane, "Kryptology," *The New Yorker.*

287 **"FIDELITY IS ONE":** D'Angelo, "Man, Yes; Super, Not Really," *Las Vegas Weekly.*

287 **"LEADEN":** Dargis, "Superman Is Back," *New York Times.*

287 **PRODUCTION COSTS:** Warner Bros. said it suffered a net loss of $81 million on *Superman Returns* (*Siegel and Larson v. Warner Bros. Entertainment*).

287 **"WAS A VERY":** Eller, "Picture This," *Los Angeles Times.*

288 **CASHED IN:** Johannes, "Superman Soars," *Promo Magazine;* Rossen, *Superman vs. Hollywood,* 290; and Holson, "More Than Ever, Hollywood Studios Are Relying on the Foreign Box Office," *New York Times.*

289 **"WE WERE STABBED":** Joanne Siegel letter to Richard D. Parsons, May 9, 2002.

290 **LEGAL FILING:** *DC Comics v. Pacific Pictures Corporation,* 2010 (complaint, response, counter-complaint and response, press release); Cieply and Barnes, "Warner Brothers Sues 'Superman' Lawyer," *New York Times;* and Cieply, "Lawyer Battles Back Against DC Comics in Superman Dispute," *New York Times.*

291 **CEASE-AND-DESIST:** The letter, from a Florida attorney claiming he represented Joanne and Laura, told Lois Amster to stop claiming she was the model for Lois Lane. But "she never claimed that," says Amster's son, Paul Rothschild. "After my brother sent him a lawyer's letter, we haven't heard from him since," Rothschild adds. "We don't know what his point was unless it was related to their suit against DC Comics" (author interview with and emails from Rothschild).

291 **PRELIMINARY RULINGS:** *Siegel and Larson v. Warner Bros. Entertainment.*

292 **EVEN AS:** *Siegel and Larson v. Warner Bros. Entertainment.*

292 **"THE WHOLE PURPOSE":** Author interview with Marc Toberoff.

292 **END THE SUPERMAN:** The concern is that once the Shuster heirs enter the case, DC and Warner Bros. would face such uncertainty over

their rights and their profits that they would no longer produce Superman movies, TV shows, or even comic books. Arguing against that is the presumption that Toberoff and his clients, short of trying to produce their own movies or other products—and worrying whether that would violate Warner's remaining rights to the character, scaring off any other studios or publishers that might have been interested—would want to reach a settlement to ensure that the Superman franchise they were getting a share of continues to earn money. The problem would come if both sides presume they can either stare down the other or win in a knock-down, drag-out battle through the courts.

292 **"THE NOTION THAT":** Author interview with Toberoff.

293 **TOBEROFF ALSO TRIED:** *Siegel and Larson v. Warner Bros. Entertainment;* and email from Don Bulson, Michael Siegel's lawyer in Cleveland. "Michael was interested in settlement, but the settlement discussions with DC Comics/Time Warner were controlled by Joanne and Laura as they owned a 75% interest," Bulson wrote. "This remained the same after the settlement discussions with DC Comics/Time Warner stalled."

293 **STOPPED PAYING:** Bella filed suit in Cleveland for nonpayment of child support, and the judge agreed that Jerry should pay up. Because Jerry was living in New York, the Ohio judge sent the petition on to the authorities in New York State (*Bella Siegel vs. Jerome Siegel,* "Judge's Journal Entry"). Michael Siegel said Jerry never did pay the child support he and Bella were due and that Jerry "broke all contact with me" after he and Bella were divorced (Michael Siegel emails to Mark Waid, 2005).

293 **MICHAEL BECAME:** Michael told Waid that he owned a business, apparently plumbing supply, got a college education, and had lived in places other than greater Cleveland. He sent Waid parts of Jerry's will showing that Jerry left everything to his wife, Joanne, and if she wasn't alive to his daughter, Laura, and her offspring. "If they all die and anything is left," Michael wrote, "I can have that if I am still alive." Michael added that it was ironic that Jerry, who made his living from comic books sold to children, treated his own son so poorly. "Why," Michael asked, "did he ignore me for almost my entire life?" (Michael Siegel emails to Waid).

293 **NATIVE SON:** Joe also got a commemorative plaque designating the street where he lived Joe Shuster Lane, with Lois Lane connecting Jerry's street to Joe's. Joanne never was able to get the permanent memorial for Jerry that she wanted in Cleveland and to which she promised to donate his typewriter, scripts, glasses, and half of his ashes. Cleveland fans are working on a Superman exhibit for the airport there and hoping to unveil Superman license plates. They and others also raised $110,000 to restore Jerry's house, and they set up a Siegel and Shuster Society (Sangiacomo, "Superman Creator's Widow Seeks Memorial," Cleveland *Plain Dealer;* Sangiacomo, "Joanne Siegel Dies," Cleveland *Plain Dealer;* author interview with Jamie Reigle).

293 **JERRY'S WILL:** The irony of Michael Siegel's death is that his half sister, Laura—someone he never had any relationship with and was jealous of—

inherits his estate, because he had no will and she is his closest living relative (Probate Court documents, Cuyahoga County, Ohio, 2006). The estate was valued at $250,000—but that didn't include Michael's share of whatever settlement there is in the lawsuit against DC Comics, which would likely be worth millions.

294 **WARREN PEARY WILL:** Warren is the executor of Joe Shuster's estate, and it is in that capacity that he is trying to reclaim the copyright to Superman. The sole beneficiary of that estate, however, is Warren's mother, Jean Shuster Peavy, who suffered a severe stroke in recent years and has other health issues.

294 **CONTINUED TO SAG:** "DC Comics Month-to-Month Sales," www.comicsbeat.com; and "*Superman* Sales Figures."

294 **REMAINING AUDIENCE:** Gabilliet, *Of Comics and Men,* 208, 357. Just how much a part of the culture comic books have been is suggested by the fact that, over the last seventy years, more than 150,000 individual issues have been published in America.

295 **IN THE PHILIPPINES:** Gayle, "Obsessed Superman Fan Has Cosmetic Surgery to Look Like His Hero," dailymail.co.uk.

295 **COLLECTORS STILL:** Sanchez, "Superman Comic Saves Family Home from Foreclosure," abcnews.go.com; and "Rare Superman Comic Sells for Record $2.16M US," cbc.ca.

295 **FAT PRICES:** Hake, *Official Price Guide to Pop Culture Memorabilia.*

296 **WORLD AND OURSELVES:** It was easier to contemplate Superman as a Russian after we had won the Cold War.

297 **CENTRAL PARK AND:** This is a paraphrase of Denny O'Neil's quip that Gotham is Manhattan below 14th Street at 3 A.M., November 28, in a cold year. Metropolis is Manhattan between 14th and 110th streets on the brightest, sunniest July day of the year.

Actor Michael Caine says Superman is how America sees itself, Batman is how the rest of the world sees us.

297 **CARY BATES:** At twenty years, Bates is the longest-serving Superman writer, versus seventeen for Jerry Siegel and sixteen for Alvin Schwartz. Bates actually reached twenty-two years if we count his earliest year selling DC story ideas for Superman, and his most recent Superman story—"The Last Family of Krypton"—in 2010. The longest-lasting artist, hands-down, was Curt Swan, at thirty-eight years.

297 **RENOUNCE HIS AMERICAN:** *Action* 900, which unleashed a firestorm of criticism when Superman said he planned to renounce his citizenship, was actually a story about his affirming his global connections, the way he had been almost since the beginning. It also was about his standing shoulder-to-shoulder with human rights demonstrators in a repressive Iran and, by extension, the rest of the Middle East and the planet. And while he might have been distancing himself from the American government, it is unlikely he would ever move away from the American people ("The Incident," *Action Comics* No. 900). Goyer, the writer of this comic book, also is the screenwriter for the new Superman movie due out in 2013.

297 **"HOLD FAST TO":** Hughes, *Collected Poems,* 32.

298 **COMICS WAS SUBSUMED:** Familiar figures remain in charge of key divisions, with chief creative officer Geoff Johns running the comic-books-to-movies operation, and co-publishers Dan DiDio and Jim Lee in charge of comic books. Here is what today's corporate ladder looks like: Time Warner, Inc., is up top. Warner Bros. Entertainment is one of its divisions, along with Time, Turner Broadcasting, and Home Box Office. Under Warner is DC Entertainment, under that is DC Comics, and helping hold it (and everything else) up is Superman.

Bibliography

INTERVIEWS, CORRESPONDENCE, AND UNPUBLISHED DOCUMENTS

From 2008 to 2011, the author interviewed or exchanged emails with the following Superman writers, artists, editors, scriptwriters, actors, directors, producers, biographers, bloggers, collectors, marketers, fans, and others: Jack Adams, Neal Adams, Jack Adler, Jim Amash, Lois Amster, Bob Andelman, Murphy Anderson, Luis Augusto, Roger Austin, Dick Ayers, Cary Bates, Bart Beaty, Jim Beaver, Robert Beerbohm, Douglas Belkin, Robert Benton, Ofer Berenstein, Stan Berkowitz, Murray Bishoff, Bill Blackbeard, Jon Bogdanove, Judy Bogdanove, Kal-El Bogdanove, Bobby Bonilla, Celine Bonnin, Rick Bowers, Chris Brockow, Nicky Wheeler-Nicholson Brown, Michael Bryan, Peggy A. Bulger, Don Bulson, Kurt Busiek, John Byrne, K. Callan, Mike Carlin, K.C. Carlson, David Chantler, Roberto Chavarria, Ellen Chesler, Ken Cholette, Nick Cirignano, Joshua Clark, Chris Clow, Phyllis Coates, Neil Cole, Chuck Colleta, Toni Collins, Justin Cousson, Rennie Cowan, John Cush, Bob Daly, Les Daniels, Geoff Darrow, Eric Lief Davin, Dwight Decker, J. M. De-Matteis, Sylvain Despretz, Bruce Dettman, Carole Donenfeld, Sonia "Peachy" Donenfeld, Richard Donner, Michael Dougherty, Robert Dougherty, Sarah Douglas, Chris Duffy, Randy Duncan, Jeff East, Jay Emmett, Mark Evanier, Gae Exton, Rob Falcone, Ruth Fine Farber, Jules Feiffer, Michael Feldman, Al Feldstein, Irv Fine, Jerry Fine, Andy Fogelson, Rob Friedman, Jim Galton, Bert Gibbs, Jackson Gillis, Dick Giordano, Robert Goldstein, Al Gough, Michael Green, Robert Greenberger, Larry Greenfield, Phil Grom, Gary Grossman, Jack Guidera, Kevin Gunn, Stacy Haiduk, David Hajdu, Carole Handler, Chuck Harter, Craig Harvey, Irwin Hasen, Michael Hayde, Dennis Hays, Jan Alan

Henderson, Dan Hirschfeld, Jane Hitchcock, Bob Holiday, Ken Horton, Rita Huber, Bob Hughes, Ellen Roney Hughes, Stuart Immonen, Carmine Infantino, Al Jaffee, Geoff Johns, Barbara Johnson, Gerard Jones, Dan Jurgens, Joyce Kaffel, Jenette Kahn, Truman Frederick Keefer, Stetson Kennedy, Karl Kesel, Margot Kidder, Orion Kidder, Rose Kirsh, Denis Kitchen, Sidney Kiwitt, Austin Knill, Lisa Kraemer, Joe Kubert, Eric Landriault, Jack Larson, Gene LeBell, Stan Lee, Deborah Joy LeVine, Paul Levitz, Joan Levy, Jeph Loeb, Edward Lozzi, Janet Luez, Dusty Luker, Richard Lupoff, Peter Lupus, Ernesto Machado, Elliot Maggin, Russ Maheras, Eugene Maletta, Tom Mankiewicz, Joe Mararinno, Mo Marcus, Eugene Mark, Ron Massengill, Harry Matetsky, Vincent Maulandi, Scott McCloud, Marc McClure, Shawn McGaughey, Brian McKernan, Daniel Meerkamper, Brad Meltzer, Todd Michney, John Jackson Miller, Erol Molnar, Kevin Moriarity, Will Murray, Carl Murway, Bill Necessary, Noel Neill, Jerry Newingham, Leslie Newman, John Haymes Newton, Jim Nolt, Paul Oddi, Luke Oldfield, Denny O'Neal, Bob O'Neil, Keith O'Neil, Jerry Ordway, John Ottman, Stephanie Shayne Parkin, Derrick Patry, Mark Warren Peary, Dawn Peavy, Jean Shuster Peavy, Zoran Perisic, Brian Peterson, Julia Pistor, Frank Pittarese, Sophie Plageman, Al Plastino, Jeanette Pollack, Tom Pollock, Christopher Priest, Hal Prince, Dave Prowse, Karen Pryor, Emilio Ramos, Jr., William Raymer, Gene Reed, Benjamin Reeve, Frank Reeve, Jamie Reigle, Trina Robbins, Mike Roberts, Jerry Robinson, Al Roker, John Romita, Conor Rooney, Bud Rosenthal, Paul Rothschild, Bob Rozakis, Jacob Rubinstein, Ilya Salkind, Michael Sangiacomo, Lee Saylor, Bill Schelly, Mary Schrank, Alvin Schwartz, Lew Sayre Schwartz, Terry Semel, Fred Shay, Jim Shooter, Rosie Shuster, Craig Shutt, Dave Siegel, Louise Simonson, Thol Simonson, Walt Simonson, Bryan Singer, Aaron Smolinski, Kelly Souders, Merrill Sparks, Pierre Spengler, Lynn Stallmaster, Benjamin Stevens, Robert Strankman, Sidney Strauss, Charles Strouse, Mike Stumbo, Trina Swuff, Craig Tenney, John Tenuto, Mary Jo Tenuto, Roy Thomas, Martha Thomases, Marc Toberoff, Anthony Tollin, Jeff Trexler, Michael Uslan, Mark Waid, Maya Warburg, Len Wein, John Wells, Ted White, Margery Wieder, Bart Williams, Bill Williams, John Williams, Tony Wilson, Norma Wolcov, Marv Wolfman, Donald Wurzelbacher, Alice Wyner, Craig Yoe, and Steve Younis.

Unless otherwise noted, the documents below are part of the public record of court cases filed by Jerry Siegel and his heirs against National Comics Publications and its successors, or were provided privately to the author.

Donenfeld, Harry. Letter to Jerry Siegel and Joe Shuster, September 22, 1938.
Ellsworth, Whitney. Letter to DC Staff. "Editorial Policy for Superman-DC Publications," Undated.
———. Letter to Jerry Siegel, January 22, 1940.
———. Letter to Jerry Siegel, February 21, 1940.
———. Letter to Jerry Siegel, November 4, 1940.
———. Letter to Jerry Siegel, February 19, 1941.

Fingeroth, Danny, Gerard Jones, Paul Levitz, and Nicky Wheeler-Nicholson Brown. "Grandchildren of the Golden Age." Panel discussion at the New York Comic Con. October 9, 2010.

Greenberg, Marc H. "Comics, Courts & Controversy: The Cases of the Comic Book Legal Defense Fund & the Superman Copyright Litigation." Paper presented at the annual Comic Arts Conference Comic-Con, San Diego, California, July 22, 2009.

Grossman, Gary. Transcripts of undated interviews with Whitney Ellsworth, based on recordings provided to author by Gary Grossman.

Hitchcock, Jane. Unpublished eulogy for her mother, Joan Alexander. 2009. Courtesy of Jane Hitchcock.

Kidder, Orion. "Telling Stories About Storytelling: The Metacomics of Alan Moore, Neil Gaiman, and Warren Ellis." Ph.D. diss., University of Alberta, 2010.

Lewis, Dorothy. Letter to Josette Frank. November 13, 1947. Child Study Association of America Files. Elmer L. Andersen Library, University of Minnesota.

Liebowitz, Jack S. Letter to Jerry Siegel, March 1, 1938.
———. Letter to Jerry Siegel, September 28, 1938.
———. Letter to Jerry Siegel, January 23, 1940.
———. Letter to Jerry Siegel, January 29, 1940.
———. Letter to Jerry Siegel, July 13, 1946.
———. Letter to Jerry Siegel, February 3, 1947.
———. Unpublished memoir. 1993. Courtesy of Joan Levy.

Maxwell, Robert. Letter to George Zachary, Office of War Information. April 12, 1943. Child Study Association of America Files. Elmer L. Andersen Library, University of Minnesota.

National Periodical Publications. Agreement with Alex and Ilya Salkind. November 6, 1974.

Peavy, Jean Shuster. Letter to Marty Payson, August 21, 1992.

Puzo, Mario and Carmine Infantino. Script Conference on *Superman: The Movie*. July 16, 1975.

Rosen, Leo. Letter to Gabriel Kaslow, April 15, 1952.

Salkind, Ilya, Mark Jones, and Cary Bates. "Superman Reborn." August 3, 1992. Unpublished screenplay.

Saylor, Lee. Transcript of 1989 interview with Leonore Lemmon, based on recording provided to author by Lee Saylor.

Shuster, Joe. Letter to Neal Adams, November 24, 1975.
———. Letter to Jay Emmett, November 23, 1975.

Siegel, Jerry. *Creation of a Superhero*. Unpublished memoir. 1978.
———. Letter to Harry Donenfeld, March 29, 1946.
———. Letter to Russell Keaton, July 12, 1934.
———. Letter to Jack Liebowitz, December 6, 1937.
———. Letter to Jack Liebowitz, February 1, 1940.
———. Letter to Jack Liebowitz, January 1, 1944.
———. Letter to Jack Liebowitz, July 13, 1946.

————. Letter to Jack Liebowitz, September 18, 1946.

————. Letter to Jack Liebowitz, November 11, 1946.

————. Letter to the President of Heilbrunn Associates. December 2, 1967.

————. Letter to Joe Shuster, September 18, 1946.

————. Letter to Laura Siegel. November 21, 1976.

————. *The Life and Times of Jerry Siegel.* Unpublished memoir.

————. *The Story Behind Superman No. 1.* Unpublished memoir.

Siegel, Jerry, and Joe Shuster. Letter to *Detective Comics,* March 1, 1938.

————. Letter to Harry Donenfeld, May 8, 1940.

Siegel, Joanne. Letter to Richard D. Parsons, AOL Time Warner, May 9, 2002.

————. Letter to Steven J. Ross, February 16, 1988.

————. Letter to unknown recipient. May 25, 1992.

Siegel, Michael. Correspondence with Mark Waid. 2005. Courtesy of Mark Waid.

Straus, Mrs. Hugh Grant. Letter to Editor. *PM.* May 20, 1946. Child Study Association of American Files. Elmer L. Andersen Library, University of Minnesota.

Wheeler-Nicholson, Malcolm. Agreements with Donny Press, Inc., World Color Printing Co., and Photochrome, Inc. November 15, 1937.

————. Letter to Donny Press, November 15, 1937.

————. Letter to Jerry Siegel, October 4, 1935.

————. Letter to Jerry Siegel, May 13, 1936.

Wylie, Philip. Letter to J. Randolph Cox, January 28, 1970. Courtesy of Truman Frederick Keefer.

Yanes, Nicholas. "Graphic Imagery: Jewish American Comic Book Creators' Depictions of Class, Race, and Patriotism." Master's thesis. Florida State University, 2008.

Zachary, George. Letter to Allen Ducovny, April 3, 1943. Child Study Association of America Files. Elmer L. Andersen Library, University of Minnesota.

COURT CASES

City of New York v. Kingsley Books, Inc. Supreme Court of New York. June 13, 1955.

In Re. Estate of Michael Siegel. Probate Court documents, Cuyahoga County (Ohio). March 13, 2006, March 16, 2006, and May 12, 2006.

DC Comics v. Pacific Pictures Corporation et al. United States District Court, Central District of California. May 14, 2010.

Detective Comics, Inc., vs. Bruns Publications, Inc. United States Court of Appeals for the Second Circuit. November 10, 1939.

National Comics Publications, Inc., v. Fawcett Publications, Inc., U.S. Court of Appeals Second Circuit. September 5, 1952.

Joseph Michael Shuster vs. Judith Ray Calpini. Request and Declaration for Final Judgment of Dissolution of Marriage. Superior Court of California, County of Los Angeles. April 15, 1981.

Bella Siegel vs. Jerome Siegel. Petition for Divorce, July 14, 1948.

Bella Siegel vs. Jerome Siegel. Petition for Support. "Judge's Journal Entry," June 9, 1953.

Jerome Siegel and Joseph Shuster v. National Comics Publications, Inc., et al. Supreme Court of New York, Westchester County. Final Judgment. May 21, 1948.

Jerome Siegel and Joseph Shuster v. National Comics Publications, Inc., et al. U.S. District Court, Southern District of New York. October 18, 1973.

Joanne Siegel and Laura Siegel Larson v. Warner Bros. Entertainment, Inc., et. al. United States District Court, Central District of California. October 8, 2004.

GOVERNMENT DOCUMENTS

City of Cleveland. Department of Health. "Certificate of Death, Michel Siegel." June 4, 1932.
———. Department of Public Health. "Birth Certificate for Jalon Kovacs." December 5, 1917.
———. Police Department. "Casualty Report for Michael Siegel." June 3, 1932.
Cuyahoga County (Ohio). Application for Marriage License. Jerome Siegel and Jolan Kovacs. October 13, 1948.
———. Application for Marriage License. Jerome Siegel and Jolan Kovacs. November 3, 1948.
———. Coroner's Office. "Coroner's Report for Michael Siegel." June 3, 1932.
City of Los Angeles. Police Department. Investigation Report. June 16, 1959.
County of Los Angeles. Archive Autopsy Report for George Reeves. Case Number 1959—45426.
———. Department of Chief Medical Examiner-Coroner. Medical Report. June 23, 1959.
———. Office of County Coroner. Autopsy Report. June 24, 1959.
State of Ohio. Department of Health. "Certificate of Death for Michael Siegel." June 4, 1932.
County of San Diego. Certificate of Registry of Marriage. "Joseph Michael Shuster and Judith Ray Calpini." December 29, 1976.
United States Bureau of the Census. Julius Schuster (1930).
United States Bureau of the Census. Moses Sigel (1910). Michael Siegel (1920). Michael Sigel (1930).
United States Immigration and Naturalization Service. Naturalization form, Michel Siegel. February 16, 1922.
United States Postal Service. Press release. "The Man of Steel and Other Super Heroes Take Flight as Stamps and Stamped Postcards." San Diego, Calif. July 20, 2006.

COMICS

Unless otherwise noted, the comic books below were published by National Periodical Publications and its successors.

Action Comics No. 1 (June 1938). Written by Jerry Siegel.

"The Amazing Story of Superman-Red and Superman-Blue," *Superman* No. 162 (July 1963). Written by Leo Dorfman.

"The Archer." *Superman* No. 13 (November–December 1941). Written by Jerry Siegel.

The Battle of the Century: Superman vs. the Amazing Spider-Man (1976). Published by National Periodical Publications and Marvel Comics Group. Written by Gerry Conway.

"The Bizarro Invasion of Earth!" *Superman* No. 169 (May 1964). Written by Jerry Siegel.

Detective Comics No. 38 (April 1940). Written by Jerry Siegel.

"Doctor Occult." *More Fun Comics* No. 16 (December 1936). Written by Jerry Siegel.

"Europe at War." *Action Comics* No. 23 (April 1940). Written by Jerry Siegel.

"Fury of the Energy-Eater." *Superman* No. 258 (November 1972). Written by Len Wein.

"I Am Curious (Black)!" *Superman's Girl Friend Lois Lane* No. 106 (November 1970). Written by Robert Kanigher.

"The Incident." *Action Comics* No. 900 (June 2011). Written by David S. Goyer.

Just Imagine Stan Lee's Superman (2001). Written by Stan Lee.

"King of the Comic Books." *Superman* No. 25 (November–December 1943). Written by Jerry Siegel.

"The Last Earth-Prime Story." *Superman* No. 411 (September 1985). Written by Elliot S. Maggin.

"The Master Mesmerizer of Metropolis!" *Superman* No. 330 (December 1978). Written by Martin Pasko.

"The Million-Dollar Marathon." *Action Comics* No. 65 (October 1943). Written by Don Cameron.

"Mr. and Mrs. Clark (SUPERMAN) Kent!" *Superman's Girl Friend Lois Lane* No. 19 (August 1960).

"Murder Plunge." *More Fun Comics* No. 68 (June 1941). Written by Jerry Siegel.

"The Mxyztplk-Susie Alliance." *Superman* No. 40 (May–June 1946). Written by Don Cameron.

"The Origin of Stuporman." *Not Brand Echh* No. 7 (April 1968). Published by Marvel Comics.

"The Origin of Superman." *Superman* No. 53 (July–August 1948). Written by Bill Finger.

"The Satanic Schemes of S.K.U.L." *Superman's Girl Friend Lois Lane* No. 63 (February 1966). Written by Leo Dorfman.

"The Soldier of Steel!" *Superman* No. 216 (May 1969). Written by Robert Kanigher.

"The Super-Family of Steel." *Superman's Girl Friend Lois Lane* No. 15 (February 1960). Written by Edmond Hamilton.

Superman No. 1 (Summer 1939). Written by Jerry Siegel.

"Superman and His Friends Around the World!" *Superman's Pal Jimmy Olsen* No. 113 (August/September 1968). Written by Mort Weisinger.

"Superman Breaks the Wall!" *Superman: The Man of Steel* No. 82 (August 1998). Written by Louise Simonson and Jon Bogdanove.

"Superman, Champion of the Oppressed." *Action Comics* No. 1 (June 1938). Written by Jerry Siegel.

"Superman Goes to Prison." *Action Comics* No. 10 (March 1939). Written by Jerry Siegel.

"Superman in the Ghetto!" *Superman: The Man of Steel* No. 81 (July 1998). Written by Louise Simonson and Jon Bogdanove.

"Superman in the Slums," *Action Comics* No. 8 (January 1939). Written by Jerry Siegel.

"Superman Joins the Circus." *Action Comics* No. 7 (December 1938). Written by Jerry Siegel.

"Superman Meets Al Capone." *Superman* No. 142 (January 1961). Written by Otto Binder.

"Superman Returns to Krypton." *Superman* No. 61 (November–December 1949). Written by Bill Finger.

"Superman Scores Again." Undated comic strip. Written by Jerry Siegel.

"Superman Takes a Wife." *Action Comics* No. 484 (June 1978). Written by Cary Bates.

"Superman: The Computers That Saved Metropolis." *Action Comics* No. 509 (July 1980). Written by Cary Bates.

Superman: The Wedding Album No. 1 (December 1996). By Superman writers and artists past and present.

"The Superman vs. The Atomic Skull!" *Superman: The Man of Steel* No. 80 (June 1998). Written by Louise Simonson and Jon Bogdanove.

"Superman's Mission for President Kennedy." *Superman* No. 170 (July 1964). Written by Bill Finger and E. Nelson Bridwell.

"Superman's Return to Krypton!" *Superman* No. 141 (November 1960). Written by Jerry Siegel.

"War in San Monte." *Action Comics* No. 2 (July 1938). Written by Jerry Siegel.

COMIC ANTHOLOGIES AND GRAPHIC NOVELS

Binder, Otto, et al. *Showcase Presents: Superman,* Vol. 1. New York: DC Comics, 2005.

Byrne, John. *Superman: The Earth Stealers.* New York: DC Comics, 1988.

———. *Superman: The Man of Steel,* Vol. 1. New York: DC Comics, 1991.

———. *The World of Smallville.* New York: DC Comics, 1987.

DC's Greatest Imaginary Stories. New York: DC Comics, 2005.

Gold, Mike. *The Greatest Golden Age Stories Ever Told.* New York: DC Comics, 1990.

The Golden Age Spectre Archives, Vol. 1. New York: DC Comics, 2003.

Johns, Geoff, and Richard Donner. *Superman: Last Son.* New York: DC Comics, 2006.

Jurgens, Dan, Karl Kesel, et al. *World Without a Superman.* New York: DC Comics. 1993.

Jurgens, Dan, Jerry Ordway, et al. *The Death of Superman.* New York: DC Comics, 1993.

———. *The Return of Superman.* New York: DC Comics, 1993.

Jurgens, Dan, Louise Simonson, et al. *Superman: The Death of Clark Kent.* New York: DC Comics, 1997.

Kelly, Joe, Marv Wolfman, Geoff Johns, and Jeph Loeb. *Superman: Infinite Crisis.* New York: DC Comics, 2006.

Loeb, Jeph. *Superman for All Seasons.* New York: DC Comics, 1999.

———. *Superman/Batman, Volume One: Public Enemies.* New York: DC Comics, 2005.

Lois & Clark: The New Adventures of Superman. New York: DC Comics, 1994.

Millar, Mark. *Superman: Red Son.* New York: DC Comics, 2003.

Moore, Alan. *Superman: Whatever Happened to the Man of Tomorrow?* New York: DC Comics, 2009.

O'Neil, Dennis. *Superman: Kryptonite Nevermore.* New York: DC Comics, 2009.

Pasko, Martin. *The DC Vault.* New York: DC Comics, 2008.

Ross, Alex, and Paul Dini. *Superman: Peace on Earth.* New York: DC Comics, 1999.

The Superman Chronicles, Vol. 1. New York: DC Comics, 2006.

The Superman Chronicles, Vol. 6. New York: DC Comics, 2009.

Superman: From the Thirties to the Seventies. New York: National Periodical Publications, 1971.

Superman in the Forties. New York: DC Comics, 2005.

Superman in the Fifties. New York: DC Comics, 2002.

Superman in the Sixties. New York: DC Comics, 1999.

Superman in the Seventies. New York: DC Comics, 2000.

Superman in the Eighties. New York: DC Comics, 2006.

Superman: The Action Comics Archives, Vol. 1. New York: DC Comics, 1997.

Superman: The Action Comics Archives, Vol. 3. New York: DC Comics, 2001.

Superman: The Action Comics Archives, Vol. 4. New York: DC Comics, 2005.

Superman: The Dailies, 1939–1942. New York: Sterling Publishing Company, 1998.

Superman: The Greatest Stories Ever Told, Vol. 1. New York: DC Comics, 2004.

Superman: The Greatest Stories Ever Told, Vol. 2. New York: DC Comics, 2006.

Superman: The Sunday Classics, Strips 1–183, 1939–1943. New York: DC Comics: 1998.

Uslan, Michael. *America at War: The Best of DC War Comics.* New York: Simon and Schuster, 1979.

Waid, Mark. *Kingdom Come.* New York: DC Comics, 2008.

———. *Superman: Birthright.* New York: DC Comics, 2004.

Wolfman, Marv. *Crisis on Infinite Earths.* New York: DC Comics, 2000.

FILM, TV, RADIO, AND MUSICAL PRODUCTIONS

Adventures of Superman. Seasons 1–2. Warner Home Video Inc., 2005.

Allen, Fred. Transcript prepared by author of radio interview with Jerry Siegel and Harry Donenfeld. October 9, 1940.

"American Icons: Superman." *Studio 360.* WNYC Radio. July 7, 2006.

Atom Man vs. Superman: The Complete 15-Chapter Adventure! Warner Home Video, 1989. Written by George H. Plympton, Joseph F. Poland, and David Mathews.

"Clan of the Fiery Cross." *Adventures of Superman.* June–July 1946. Transcript prepared by author.

Comic Book Confidential. Toronto: Sphinx Productions, 1988. Written by Ron Mann.

"The Defeat of Superman." *Adventures of Superman.* Warner Home Video, 1953. Written by Jackson Gillis.

"Drums of Death." *Adventures of Superman.* Warner Home Video, 1953. Written by Dick Hamilton.

George Reeves Double Feature: Thunder in the Pines and Jungle Goddess. VCI Entertainment. 2006.

"George Reeves: The Perils of a Superhero." Transcript prepared by author. *Biography.* A&E. February 9, 2000.

Hollywoodland. Universal Studios, 2007. Written by Paul Bernbaum.

Kill Bill: Vol. 2. Miramax Films, 2004. Written by Quentin Tarantino.

Lois & Clark: The New Adventures of Superman. Seasons 1–4. Warner Home Video, 2006.

It's a Bird . . . It's a Plane . . . It's Superman: The New Musical Comedy. Script. New York: Studio Duplicating Services, 1966. Written by Robert Benton and David Newman.

"The Panic in the Sky." *Adventures of Superman.* Warner Home Video, 1953. Written by Jackson Gillis.

The Paramount Cartoon Classics of Max & Dave Fleischer. Bosko Video, 1991.

Seinfeld. "The Cheever Letters" (1992). "The Chinese Woman" (1994). "The Face Painter" (1995). "The Heart Attack" (1991). "The Implant" (1993). "The Lip Reader" (1993). "The Marine Biologist" (1993). "The Race" (1994). "The Smelly Car" (1993). "The Stall" (1994). "The Stand-In" (1994). "The Stock Tip" (1990). "The Switch" (1995). "The Tape" (1991). "The Visa" (1993). Transcripts can be found at www.seinfeldscripts.com.

Smallville: The Complete First Season. Warner Home Video, 2002.

Smithsonian Historical Performances: Superman on Radio. Recordings of first 27 episodes. Schiller Park, Ill.: Radio Spirits, 1997.

Superman and the Mole Men. Warner Home Video, 1987. Written by Richard Fielding.

Superman: The Theatrical Serials Collection. Warner Home Video, 2006.

Superman: Ultimate Collector's Edition. Warner Bros. Entertainment, 2006.

Torchy Blane Collection. Warner Home Video, 2010.

WEBSITES

Bails, Jerry. "Who's Who of American Comic Books, 1928–1999." bailsprojects.com.

Borsellino, Mary. "The Changing Face of Supergirl." March 1, 2007. sequentialtart.com.

Brady, Matt. "Brad Meltzer on Pimpin' Comics in His Novels." April 26, 2007. bradmeltzer.com.

Butki, Scott. "Interview with Brad Meltzer, Author of the Book of Fate." October 6, 2006. blogcritics.org.

Chandler, Rick. "*An Unlikely Prophet* by Alvin Schwartz." December 7, 2008. superman.nu.

DC Comics Online Newsletter. "Post Office Announces Superman Stamp." September 1998. superman.nu.

"DC Timeline." dccomicsartists.com.

DialBForBlog.com. "Explosion and Implosion." dialbforblog.com.

———. "Superman's LLs." dialbforblog.com.

———. "Superman-Tim Comics!" dialbforblog.com.

Engblom, Mark. "Humble Beginnings: These Boots Are Made for Lacing." June 10, 2008. comiccoverage.typepad.com.

Frisch, Marc-Oliver. "DC Comics Month-to-Month Sales: January 2011." comicsbeat.com.

Gaiman, Neil, and Adam Rogers. "The Myth of Superman." June 2006. www.wired.com/wired/archive/14.06/myth.

Grost, Mike. "The Spectre: 1940's Comic Book Super Hero." mikegrost .com/spectre.

Harrington, Wallace. "Superman and the War Years: The Battle of Europe Within the Pages of Superman Comics." supermanhomepage.com.

Harrington, Wallace, Michael George O'Connor, Judy Thomas, and Joyce Kavitsky. "Superman IV: The Quest for Peace." chrisreevehomepage.com.

Hughes, David. "Who's Whose in DC Comics." supermanartists.comics .org.

Ingersoll, Bob. "The Law Is a Ass." October 24, 2000. worldfamouscomics.com.

"Jerry Siegel Attacks!" *Das Schwarze Korps.* April 25, 1940. Translation by Randall Bytwerk, 1998. www.calvin.edu/academic/cas/gpa/superman.

"Kirk Alyn: Superman Remembers." www.superman.nu/theages/kirk/ interview.php.

Kleefeld on Comics. "Paul Sampliner." June 8, 2007. kleefeldoncomics .blogspot.com.

Koza, Louis. "Relative Revelations." The Adventures Continue. January 9, 2007. jimnolt.com.

Lone Star College-Kingwood Library. "American Cultural History: The Twentieth Century." kclibrary.lonestar.edu/decades.html.

Magat, Rafael. "Mild Mannered Reviews—Classic Pre-Crisis Superman Comics: Superman Takes a Wife." supermanhomepage.com.

Mautner, Michael E. "From the Pit to the Peak: Superman and the Ascension of America." 1987. superman.nu.

McGorry, Ken. "Seinfeld and Superman Take on the Web." April 1, 2004. highbeam.com.

McMillan, Graeme. "Is Superman Really Damaged Goods?" July 2009. io9.com.

Mike's Amazing World of Comics. "The Database." dcindexes.com/database.

Miller, John Jackson. "*Superman* Sales." blog.comichron.com.

Nobleman, Marc Tyler. "Superman vs. Hitler." March 2, 2008. noblemania .blogspot.com.

———. "The Death of Jerry Siegel's Father: Part One." September 3, 2008. noblemania.blogspot.com.

O'Reilly, Bill. "Superman and the Culture War." July 6, 2006. billoreilly.com.

Reinhard, CarrieLynn D. "Making Sense of Superheroes: Awareness of Superhero Genre Conventions Around the World." Survey, Roskilde University, March 6, 2009. issuu.com.

Rogers, Vaneta. "Writer Cary Bates on His Return to Superman." May 19, 2010. newsarama.com.

Sanchez, Ray. "Superman Comic Saves Family Home from Foreclosure." abcnews.go.com. August 3, 2010.

Schwartz, Alvin. "After the Golden Age with Alvin Schwartz." worldfamouscomics.com.

Shi'an, Shen. "'Superman Returns' to His Bodhisattva Career." July 17, 2006. buddhistchannel.tv.

Siegel, Jerry. "Superman's Originator Puts 'Curse' on Superman Movie." Press release, October 1975. With introduction by Michael Catron. archives.tcj.com.

Siegel, Joanne. "The True Inspiration for Lois Lane." supermanhomepage .com.

"Superman on Radio." supermanhomepage.com.

"Superman: The Next Sequel." supermansupersite.com.

"Top Comic Books of the 2000s." comichron.com.

Trexler, Jeff. "Russell Keaton, Superman's Fifth Beatle." August 20, 2008. blog.newsarama.com.

Wallace, Amy. "Nastier Than a Speeding Bullet." September 17, 2007. portfolio.com.

Weisinger, Mort. "Here Comes Superman!" 1946. superman.nu.

Younis, Steve. "Superman and the Phone Booth." supermanhomepage.com.

Zacharek, Stephanie. "Superman Returns." June 28, 2006. salon.com.

NEWSPAPERS, MAGAZINES, AND JOURNALS

Akers, Paul E. "Bring Back the REAL Superman." *Washington Post.* December 31, 1988.

Albany Times Union. "Jerry Siegel, 81: Superman Co-Creator." January 31, 1996.

———. "Man of Steel Drops Cape in Wardrobe Makeover." January 4, 1997.

———. "Superman and Lois Finally Tying the Knot." September 8, 1996.

———. "Superman Fan Has Bond with Real-Life Hero Reeve." April 11, 1997.

———. "Time and Economics Prove Superman Mortal." September 4, 1992.

Albrecht, Brian E. "Superman Meets the Grim Reaper." Cleveland *Plain Dealer*. November 15, 1992.

Allen, Henry. "Superman & the Little Woman." *Washington Post*. October 26, 1990.

Altaner, David. "Sagging Superman Gets New Life." *Albany Times Union*. October 27, 1986.

Amash, Jim. "His Goal Was the Graphic Novel." *Alter Ego* No. 88 (August 2009).

———. "I Didn't Want to Know [What Other Companies Were Doing]!" *Alter Ego* no. 56 (February 2006).

———. "I've Always Been a Writer: Alvin Schwartz on His Long Career in Comic Books—and Elsewhere." *Alter Ego* No. 98 (December 2010).

———. "A Real Iconic, Quintessential American Figure." *Alter Ego* No. 88 (August 2009).

Ames, Walter. "Superman George Reeves and Producers Disagree on New Television Deal." *Los Angeles Times*. September 27, 1954.

———. "Video Actress Can't Convince Daughter; Palm Services Set." *Los Angeles Times*. March 29, 1953.

Anderson, Susan Heller. "It's a Bird! It's a Plane! It's a Movie!" *New York Times*. June 26, 1977.

Andrae, Thomas. "From Menace to Messiah: The Prehistory of the Superman in Science Fiction Literature." *Discourse* 2 (1980).

———. "Of Supermen and Kids with Dreams: An Interview with Jerry Siegel and Joe Shuster." *Nemo* No. 2 (1983).

Anti-Defamation League Bulletin. "Klan Sleuth Gives 'Superman' Secrets of Hooded Order." February 1947.

Arave, Lynn. "Man of Steel, King of the Seas in for Big Changes." *Deseret News*. January 6, 1997.

———. "Still Leaping Buildings in a Single Bound but in Brand-New Disguise." *Deseret News*. February 17, 1997.

———. "Superman No Longer a Man of Steel." *Deseret News*. June 2, 1997.

Arnold, Gary. "It's a Bird! It's a Pain!" *Washington Post*. June 17, 1983.

———. "'Superman II': The Plot Weakens." *Washington Post*. June 19, 1981.

Ascher-Walsh, Rebecca. "Cape Fear." *Entertainment Weekly*. May 29, 1998.

Associated Press. "Nicolas Cage and Wife Have Baby Boy." October 3, 2005.

———. "Rare Superman Comic Sells for Record $2.16M US." December 1, 2011. cbc.ca.

Atlanta Constitution. "Atlanta Boy Falls 3 Floors, Is Not Injured." June 7, 1941.

Aurthur, Kate. "The Past Catches Up with a Future Superman." *New York Times*. February 23, 2005.

———. "Young Male Viewers Boost 'Smallville.'" *New York Times*. May 20, 2006.

———. "Young–Superman Episode Delivers Clout for WB." *New York Times*. January 28, 2006.

Baker, Russell. "Geezer of Steel." *New York Times*. June 17, 1986.

———. "Sad Feet in the Sky." *New York Times*. September 25, 1973.

———. "The Heart of Superman." *New York Times*. December 17, 1978.

———. "Turn That Dial Back in Time: Superman & Co. Return!" *New York Times*. October 24, 1988.

Ballner-Bear, Lisa. "Golly, Miss Lane, Superman's 50." *Omni* 10 (March 1988).

Barnes, Brooks, and Michael Cieply. "A Custody Battle, Supersized." *New York Times*. March 21, 2010.

———. "Warner Brothers Sues 'Superman' Lawyer." *New York Times*. May 15, 2010.

Barr, Mike W. "The Madame and the Girls: How DC Got Rid of the Troublemakers." *Words & Pictures* No. 5 (August 1988).

Barron, James. "Boldface Names." *New York Times*. May 3, 2001.

———. "The Mystery of the Missing Man of Steel." *New York Times*. April 19, 2010.

Bart, Peter. "Advertising: Superman Faces New Hurdles." *New York Times*. September 23, 1962.

Bates, Cary, and Elliot Maggin. "The Men Behind the Super-Typewriter." *Amazing World of DC Comics* No. 2 (September 1974).

Bear, Greg. " 'Superman': Unable to Leap the Changing Decades?" *Los Angeles Times*. December 24, 1978.

Beaty, Bart. "The Recession and the American Comic Book Industry: From Inelastic Cultural Good to Economic Integration." *Popular Communication* 8, No. 3 (August 2010).

Beaver, Jim. Interview with Chuck Harter. *The Adventures Continue* No. 6 (1991).

Becattini, Alberto. "Jerry Siegel's European Comics." *Alter Ego* No. 59 (June 2006).

Beck, Marilyn. "$138 Mistake: Superman Creators Gave Him Away Cheaply." Cleveland *Plain Dealer*. January 7, 1979.

Belcher, Jerry. "Comic Characters Revised: At 48, Superman Has Slowed Down Just a Bit." *Los Angeles Times*. June 18, 1986.

Belkin, Douglas. "Superman Birthplace Is Restored." *Wall Street Journal*. July 11, 2009.

Beller, Miles. "Hollywood Is Banking on the Comics." *New York Times*. December 9, 1979.

Belloni, Matthew. "Siegels Win a Round in Epic Battle for Superman." *Hollywood Reporter*. December 21, 2010.

———. "Warners Wins Round in Superman Litigation." *Hollywood Reporter*. December 21, 2010.

Benchley, Peter. "The Story of Pop." *Newsweek*. April 25, 1966.

Bender, Lauretta. "The Psychology of Children's Reading and the Comics." *Journal of Educational Sociology* 18 (1944).

Bender, Lauretta, and Reginald S. Lourie. "The Effect of Comic Books on the Ideology of Children." *American Journal of Orthopsychiatry* 11 (1941).

Bianculli, David. "Jeepers! Jimmy to Superman's Rescue." *New York Daily News.* May 31, 1996.

Bierman, William. "Look What Flew Back Home." *Akron Beacon Journal.* July 31, 1988.

Billboard. "'Superman' vs. KKK." June 22, 1946.

Bishoff, Murray, and Alan Light. "'Superman' Grew out of Our Personal Feelings About Life." *Alter Ego* No. 56 (February 2006).

Blondheim, Earl. "Paging Superman." Letters to the Editor. *Washington Post.* December 20, 1941.

Blue, Carol, and Al Delugach. "'Superman': Rare Look at Film Finances." *Los Angeles Times.* April 3, 1980.

Blum, David J. "How Local Film Critics Meet the Man of Steel." *Wall Street Journal.* June 5, 1981.

Boldman, Craig. "Karl Kesel: A Superman Post-Mortem." *National Cartoonists Society Great Lakes Chapter Newsletter.* June 29, 2006.

Boston Globe. "Comic Book of Steel." February 23, 2010.

———. "Has Kryptonite Been Discovered?" January 26, 2009.

———. "Superman Comic Sold for $317,200." March 15, 2009.

Boucher, Geoff. "Undressed for Success?" *Los Angeles Times.* August 28, 2001.

Bowles, Guy Scott. "'Superman' Torch Is Passed." *USA Today.* March 16, 2006.

Boyer, Da Marie, and Patrick Daniel O'Neill. "David and Leslie Newman: Super-Screenwriters." *Starlog* No. 73 (August 1983).

Boyum, Joy Gould. "One-Dimensional Flights of Fancy." *Wall Street Journal.* June 19, 1981.

Brandon, Craig. "The Man of Steel Comics Fans Yawn as Superman Comes Back, Back, Back, Back." *Albany Times Union.* April 15, 1993.

Breasted, Mary. "Superman's Creators, Nearly Destitute, Invoke His Spirit." *New York Times.* November 22, 1975.

Brennan, Judy. "A Family Feud in Wake of 'Columbus' Movies." *Los Angeles Times.* November 24, 1993.

Brennan, Patricia. "Kirk Alyn: Man of Steel." *Washington Post.* February 28, 1988.

———. "This Week's Pics." *Washington Post.* February 28, 1988.

Broeske, Pat H. "Man of Steal?" *Los Angeles Times.* April 26, 1987.

Bronstad, Amanda. "Warner Bros. Sued over Liberal Usage of 'Superman' Footage." *Los Angeles Business Journal.* July 15, 2002.

Brown, Nicky Wheeler-Nicholson. "He Was Going to Go for the Big Idea." *Alter Ego* No. 88 (August 2009).

———. "Major Malcolm Wheeler-Nicholson, Cartoon Character or Real Life Hero?" *International Journal of Comic Art* 10, No. 2 (Fall 2008).

Brown, Slater. "The Coming of Superman." *New Republic.* September 2, 1940.

Brozan, Nadine. "Chronicle." *New York Times.* November 19, 1992.

———. "Superman Star Is Back Before the Public." *New York Times.* October 17, 1995.

Buchwald, Art. "The Miracle Worker: Super-K Tries Again." *Washington Post.* October 13, 1974.

———. "Henry, This Is a Job for Superman." *Washington Post.* April 20, 1975.

Buckley, Steve. "'Original' Superman Story Doesn't Fly." *Boston Herald.* January 10, 1997.

Buckley, Tom. "At the Movies." *New York Times.* May 26, 1978.

———. "The Writing of 'Superman': A Fantastic Story." *New York Times.* December 22, 1978.

Buhle, Paul. "Superbad: Joe Shuster's Seamy Scenes of Lois and Clark." *Forward.* August 7, 2009.

Burns, James H. "Sarah Douglas: The Human-Hating Kryptonian Super-Villainess from 'Superman II.'" *Starlog* No. 47 (June 1981): 22–24.

Burr, Ty. "Man and Superman." *Entertainment Weekly.* August 14, 1994.

BusinessWeek. "Superman Scores." April 18, 1942.

Canadian Press. "Lois Lane Just Fed Up, Dumping Man of Steel." February 9, 1996.

Canby, Vincent. "Nothing 'Went Wrong.'" *New York Times.* December 24, 1978.

———. "Screen: It's a Bird, It's a Plane, It's a Movie." *New York Times.* December 15, 1978.

Carlin, Mike. "Ask the Pros: Describe an Average Story Conference for DC's Superman Titles." *Comic Buyer's Guide* (September–October 1993).

Carlinsky, Dan. "On Krypton, Superman Might Have Been a Plumber." *New York Times.* December 10, 1978.

Carlson, Walter. "Advertising: TV Getting Superman in Color." *New York Times.* September 16, 1965.

Carr, Lisa. "Superman Started Here." *Glenville Torch.* April 1988.

Carr, Tommy. Interview with Chuck Harter. *The Adventures Continue* No. 9 (1993).

Carson, Tom. "Small Comforts." *Esquire* (February 2002): 48.

Caruso, David B. "Rare First Superman Comic Sold in Internet Auction." Associated Press. March 14, 2009.

Caulfield, Deborah. "Why Reeve Is Hanging Up His Cape." *Los Angeles Times.* June 20, 1983.

Cavander, Kenneth. "Hercules Lives!" *Horizon* 17, No. 3 (Summer 1976): 58–61.

Cerone, Daniel. "TV's 'Superman' Undergoing a Planetary Shift." *Los Angeles Times.* September 17, 1994.

Chang, Gordon H. "Superman Is About to Visit the Relocation Centers & the Limits of Wartime Liberalism." *Amerasia Journal* 19, No. 1 (1993).

Chang, Kenneth. "SPLAAAAAAAT! Comic Books No Longer Reaping Big Sales in Single Bound." *Los Angeles Times.* March 2, 1996.

Chernin, Donna. "Pow! Superman's Creators Take a Poke at Him." Cleveland *Plain Dealer*. October 26, 1975.

Chicago Daily Defender. "'Superman,' 11 Saved by Snowbank." December 7, 1964.

Chicago Tribune. "'Superman' Fan Injured." February 3, 1979.

Cieply, Michael. "Lawyer Battles Back Against DC Comics in Superman Dispute." *New York Times*. August 16, 2010.

———. "Ruling Gives Heirs a Share of Superman Copyright." *New York Times*. March 29, 2008.

Cieply, Michael, and Brooks Barnes. "Warner Brothers Sues 'Superman' Lawyer." *New York Times*. May 15, 2010.

Cinefantastique. "Superman '. . . Has Finally Been Brought Down to Earth.'" Summer 1979.

Clark, Delbert. "'Superman' for Peace." Letters to the Editor. *Washington Post*. February 26, 1940.

Cleveland Call and Post. "Memo to Parents: If Junior Imitates 'Tarzan' on Furniture, He May Make Better Man." June 25, 1949.

Cleveland Jewish Independent. "Deaths." June 10, 1932.

Cleveland Jewish Review and Observer. "Deaths." June 10, 1932.

Cleveland Magazine. "The Inspirations for Lois Lane." January 2009.

Cleveland *Plain Dealer*. "A Son Is Born to Superman Author." January 29, 1944.

———. "Death Notices." June 4, 1932.

———. "Half of Superman Drafted; Partner Awaits Army Call." June 30, 1943.

———. "Superman Creator Wed." October 15, 1948.

———. "'Superman' Is Coming to Plain Dealer Sunday." January 18, 1940.

———. "Superman Leaped Years, Too." February 2, 1988.

———. "Superman's Birthplace Is Now Historic Landmark." January 28, 1987.

———. "Superman's Creator Sued." July 15, 1948.

Cleveland Press. "Dies After Robbery." June 3, 1932.

Coe, Richard L. "Not Peter Pan, It's 'Superman.'" *Washington Post*. March 31, 1966.

Colmes, Alan. Interview with Noel Neill. *The Adventures Continue* No. 4 (1990).

Colton, David. "Superman's Story: Did a Fatal Robbery Forge the Man of Steel?" *USA Today*. August 25, 2008.

Colton, Michael. "Supersensitive 'Superman' Muffs Holocaust Story." *Washington Post*. June 27, 1998.

"The Continuing Study of Newspaper Reading: 138-Study Summary." Advertising Research Foundation. 1951.

Cook, Joan. "Faster Than a Speeding Bullet—Mayor Superman." *New York Times*. November 22, 1974.

Corliss, Richard. "The Gospel of Superman." *Time*. June 18, 2006.

Cornell, George W. "Superman/Jesus Similarities Examined." *Los Angeles Times.* February 24, 1979.

Cotton, Mike. "Brandon Routh Q&A." *Wizard.* No. 172. February 2006.

Crews, Chip. "The Role He Can't Escape." *Washington Post.* May 3, 1998.

Crist, Judith. "Horror in the Nursery." *Collier's.* March 27, 1948.

Dagnal, Cynthia. "It's a Bird, a Plane, a Movie: A Socially Relevant Superman?" *Los Angeles Times.* September 3, 1976.

Dalton, Joseph. "Death of First Superman Still a Supermystery." *Los Angeles Herald Examiner.* February 28, 1988.

Dangaard, Colin. "Reeve Flies to the Rescue of 'Superman.'" *Los Angeles Times.* July 31, 1977.

D'Angelo, Mike. "Man, Yes; Super, Not Really." *Las Vegas Weekly.* June 29, 2006.

Daniel, Clifton. "The Future of Elliot Richardson." *New York Times.* October 25, 1973.

Dargis, Manohla. "Superman Is Back to Save Mankind from Its Sins." *New York Times.* June 27, 2006.

———. "The Quiet Desperation of Superman." *New York Times.* September 8, 2006.

Davenport, Christian. "The Brother Might Be Made of Steel, but He Sure Ain't Super . . . Man." *Other Voices* 1, No. 2 (September 1998).

Davies, Patrick, and Julia Surridge, et al. "Superhero-Related Injuries in Paediatrics: A Case Series." *Archives of Disease in Childhood* 92 (2007).

Dean, Michael. "An Extraordinarily Marketable Man: The Ongoing Struggle for Ownership of Superman and Superboy." *Comics Journal* No. 263 (October 14, 2004).

Decker, Dwight R. "The Reich Strikes Back." *Alter Ego* No. 79 (July 2008).

Delugach, Al. "Cannon Bid as Major Studio Is Cliffhanger: Firm's Future at Risk in High-Stakes Gamble." *Los Angeles Times.* August 24, 1986.

———. "Salkinds Settle Brando, Puzo 'Superman' Suits." *Los Angeles Times.* April 6, 1982.

———. "'Superman' and the Sequel: The Lawsuits Continue." *Los Angeles Times.* September 13, 1981.

Deutschman, Alan. "Commercial Success: Traditional Advertising Is in Deep Trouble." *Fast Company.* January 1, 2005.

Dickholtz, Daniel. "Steel Dreams." *Starlog Yearbook* No. 16 (1998).

Docker, Philip. Interview with Chuck Harter. *The Adventures Continue* No. 15 (1998).

Dorrell, Larry D., Dan B. Curtis, and Kuldip R. Rampal. "Book-Works Without Books? Students Reading Comic Books in the School House." *Journal of Popular Culture* 29 (Fall 1995).

Dougherty, Philip H. "'Superman' Campaign Unwrapped." *New York Times.* December 1, 1978.

———. "Superman Product to B.&B." *New York Times.* June 4, 1982.

Downer, Mary Lou. "Small-Fry Supermen Leave Duds in Heap as They Leap." *Los Angeles Times.* August 30, 1954.

Doyle, Thomas F. "What's Wrong with the 'Comics'?" *Catholic World.* February 1943.

Dubner, Stephen J., and Steven D. Levitt. "Hoodwinked?" *New York Times.* January 8, 2006.

Duignan-Cabrera, Anthony, and Henry Cabot Beck. "Plan of Steel." *Entertainment Weekly.* September 20, 1996.

Duin, Steve. "Rewriting Comics History." *Oregonian.* August 26, 2008.

Duke, John. "Fathers of Superman, Tarzan, Renfrew Meet." *Midpacifican.* September 2, 1944.

Duralde, Alonso. "How Gay Is Superman?" *Advocate.* June 2, 2006.

Easton, Nina J. " 'Superman' Lawsuit Trial Date Set for April 16." *Los Angeles Times.* February 1, 1990.

Ebert, Roger. "Superman." *Chicago Sun-Times.* December 15, 1978.

Economist. "Middle Age Meets Superman." June 28, 1986.

Edmondson, Rolfe. "Superman Superior to Tarzan and Brothers Here Prove It." *Atlanta Constitution.* August 30, 1941.

Eichenwald, Kurt. "Grown-Ups Gather at the Comic Book Stand." *New York Times.* September 30, 1987.

Eller, Claudia. "Picture This: Warner Bros. Having a Rare Down Year." *Los Angeles Times.* August 18, 2006.

Elliott, Stuart. "Always a Place for Superman." *New York Times.* September 21, 1992.

———. "Seinfeld and Superman Join Forces Again in Spots for American Express, This Time on the Web." *New York Times.* March 30, 2004.

Ellison, Harlan. "It Ain't Toontown." *Playboy* (December 1988).

Ellsworth, Jane. Interview with Chuck Harter. *The Adventures Continue* No. 5 (1990).

Emmons, Josh. "Boy of Steel." *New York Times.* December 4, 2005.

Evanier, Mark, Robert Beerbohm, and Julie Schwartz. "There's a Lot of Myth Out There!" *Alter Ego* No. 26 (July 2003).

Falk, Ray. "Tokyo TV Report." *New York Times.* August 9, 1959.

Feiffer, Jules. "The Minsk Theory of Krypton." *New York Times Magazine.* December 29, 1996.

———. "Zowie! Comic Books Are Back." *Los Angeles Times.* January 23, 1966.

Fingeroth, Danny. "Mr. DC: The Paul Levitz Interview." *Write Now!* October 3, 2005.

Fleming, Victoria, and George L. Rafter. "For a Guy in His 40s He's Not Doing Half Bad as a Superhero." Cleveland *Plain Dealer.* December 3, 1978.

Flint, Joe, and Dan Snierson. " 'Clark' Canned." *Entertainment Weekly.* May 20, 1997.

Forman, Marilyn. "Superman Is Here Among Us." *New York Times.* August 30, 1981.

Frank, Leah D. "Superman Drops Comic-Strip Pose." *New York Times.* October 31, 1993.

Fremont-Smith, Eliot. "He's Coming . . . He's Almost Here." *New York Times*. March 27, 1966.

Friedrich, Otto, Beth Austin, and Janice C. Simpson. "Up, Up and Awaaay!!!" *Time*. March 14, 1988.

Gajewski, Josh. "Homegrown Hero." *USA Weekend*. June 16, 2006.

Garcia, Chris. "The Big Secret About 'Smallville.'" *Austin American-Statesman*. September 2003.

Gardner, Eriq. "The Man Hollywood Loves to Hate." *IP Law & Business*. October 9, 2008.

———. "Hollywood Heist: How a Burglary May Impact the Future of 'Superman.'" *Hollywood Reporter*. May 27, 2011.

Gardner, Eriq, and Matthew Belloni. "Warner Bros. Bulks Up for 'Superman' Litigation." *Hollywood Reporter*. March 1, 2010.

Gasser, Gay S. "Superman, What Happened to You?" *Los Angeles Times*. August 9, 1981.

Gates, Henry Louis, Jr. "A Big Brother from Another Planet." *New York Times*. September 12, 1993.

Gayle, Damien. "Obsessed Superman Fan Has Cosmetic Surgery to Look Like His Hero." dailymail.co.uk. October 8, 2011.

Gehman, Richard B. "Deadwood Dick to Superman." *Science Digest* 25 (1949).

Glenville Torch. "Senior B Student Publishes Science Fiction Magazine." October 6, 1932.

———. "Master Sleuth Solves Very Baffling Enigma." May 21, 1931.

Glueck, Michael Arnold. "Superman, Lois Lane and Me." *Jewish World Review*. July 7, 2006.

Goldman, Ed. "The Man Who Filled In for the Man of Steel." *Los Angeles Times*. April 8, 1979.

Goldstone, Patricia. "'Superman' and the Fear of Flying." *Los Angeles Times*. January 14, 1979.

Gootman, Elissa. "Superman Finds New Fans Among Reading Instructors." *New York Times*. December 26, 2007.

Gorman, Tim. "Cleveland-Born Hero Returns." Cleveland *Plain Dealer*. June 16, 1988.

Gould, Jack. "On the New Superman." *New York Times*. April 28, 1946.

Graham, Victoria. "As Jimmy Olsen He Turns Them On; As a Writer No." Associated Press. January 5, 1976.

Grant, Lee. "'Superman': At a Loss for Words." *Los Angeles Times*. January 1, 1979.

———. "Superstar Lineup for Superman." *Los Angeles Times*. January 15, 1977.

Grayling, A. C. "The Philosophy of Superman: A Short Course." *Spectator*. July 8, 2006.

Greenberger, Robert. "Superman III." *Starlog* No. 67 (February 1983).

Greenfield, Norma J. "Drawing on the Dark Side." *New York Times*. May 21, 1989.

Grobel, Lawrence. "The Good Times of Nicolas Cage." *Movieline* (June 1998).

Gross, Edward. "The Adventures of Superman When He Was an Actor." *Comics Scene* No. 6 (February 1989).

———. "John Haymes Newton: Boy of Steel." *Comics Scene* No. 6 (February 1989).

Gross, John. "Superman at Fifty." *New York Times.* December 15, 1987.

Gross, Michael Joseph. "It's a Bird! It's a Plane! It's the Man of . . . Feelings!" *New York Times.* June 4, 2006.

Grossman, Lev. "The Problem with Superman." *Time.* May 17, 2004.

Grove, Martin A. "Singer Was Man of Steel in Making 'Superman.'" *Hollywood Reporter.* June 7, 2006.

Gruenberg, Sidonie Matsner. "The Comics as a Social Force." *Journal of Educational Sociology* 18, No. 4 (December 1944).

Guenther, Wally. "Creator of Superman Character Dies." Cleveland *Plain Dealer.* August 3, 1992.

Gustines, George Gene. "Bad News for Superman." *New York Times.* April 25, 2007.

———. "Recalibrating DC Heroes for a Grittier Century." *New York Times.* October 12, 2005.

———. "Repairing a House with Superman Ties." *New York Times.* September 2, 2008.

Gustines, George Gene, and Adam W. Kepler. "So Far, Sales for New DC Comics Are Super." *New York Times.* October 1, 2011.

Gutis, Philip S. "Turning Superheroes into Super Sales." *New York Times.* January 6, 1985.

Hagen, Dan. "From Lassie to Superman: Jackson Gillis." *David Anthony Kraft's Comics Interview* No. 60 (1988).

Halloran, Robert. "Hero as Pitchman." *New York Times.* January 16, 1997.

Hamilton, Edmond. "Under the White Star." *Science Fiction* (March 1939).

Harden, Blaine. "'Nobody Groomed Me. I Groomed Myself,' Said the New Superman." *Washington Post.* March 13, 1977.

Harford, Margaret. "'Superman' on Strub Stage." *Los Angeles Times.* July 19, 1969.

Harmetz, Aljean. "Reeve Shaking Off His Superman Image." *New York Times.* August 20, 1979.

———. "'Star Trek II' Sets Mark for Sales at Opening." *New York Times.* June 8, 1981.

———. "'Superman' Breaks Record." *New York Times.* June 30, 1981.

———. "The Life and Exceedingly Hard Times of Superman." *New York Times.* June 14, 1981.

———. "The Marketing of Superman and His Paraphernalia." *New York Times.* June 21, 1981.

Harvey, Steve. "Ex-Superman Has Place of His Own to Hang Up Suit." *Los Angeles Times.* March 28, 1974.

Herz, J. C. "It's a Bird! It's a Plane! (And It Wobbles?)." *New York Times.* July 8, 1999.

Hiatt, Brian. "Empty Suit." *Entertainment Weekly*. March 18, 2003.

———. "Lex-Man." *Entertainment Weekly*. May 19, 2003.

Hill, Roger. "An Interview with Al Feldstein." *Squa Tront: The EC Comics Magazine* No. 10 (2002).

Hinson, Hal. "Getting to the Heart of a Hero." *New York Times*. January 27, 2002.

Holden, Stephen. "Superman as Dimwit in 1966 Parable." *New York Times*. June 20, 1992.

Holland-America Line. "Manifest List of Alien Immigrants." Rotterdam, 1900.

Holson, Laura M. "After Big Flops, Warner Hopes for 'Sleeper' Hit in Smaller Films." *New York Times*. October 9, 2006.

———. "In This 'Superman' Story, the Executives Do the Fighting." *New York Times*. September 15, 2002.

———. "More Than Ever, Hollywood Studios Are Relying on the Foreign Box Office." *New York Times*. August 7, 2006.

———. "Producing a 'Superman' Sequel Is Like Leaping Tall Buildings." *New York Times*. July 22, 2004.

Hoover, Penelope. "What Women See in Man of Steel." Letters to the Editor, *Los Angeles Times*. January 28, 1979.

Howe, Desson. "Superman's Back, with a Pot of Message." *Washington Post*. July 31, 1987.

Hugick, Larry. "Public to DC Comics: Resurrect Superman!" The Gallup Poll News Service. November 26, 1992.

Hutchinson, Katharine H. "An Experiment in the Use of Comics as Instructional Material." *Journal of Educational Sociology* 23, No. 4 (December 1949).

Hyams, Joe. "Haunts for Halloween." *Los Angeles Times*. October 29, 1967.

The Independent. "Bring Back Clark Kent." September 16, 2003.

Itzkoff, Dave. " 'Superman' Movie Series Is Up, Up and Away with a New Director." *New York Times*. October 4, 2010.

Ivor, Davis. "Marketing the Man of Steel!" *Maclean's*. December 11, 1978.

Jacobs, A. J. "Citizen Cain." *Entertainment Weekly*. February 16, 1996.

Jaffe, Robert David. " 'Superman' Director Lives Out His Dream." *Jewish Journal*. June 22, 2006.

Jefferson Daily Dispatch. " 'Superman' of Video Comes to Tragic End." June 17, 1959.

Jensen, Jeff. "Dead Superman May Revive DC Comics." *Advertising Age*. November 23, 1992.

———. "Greatest American Hero?" *Entertainment Weekly*. June 23, 2006.

———. "Shows of Strength: Giving the Superman Saga a Well-Needed Kick in the Tights." *Entertainment Weekly*. November 23, 2001.

———. "Super 5." *Entertainment Weekly*. June 24, 2005.

The Jewish Independent. "Deaths." June 10, 1932.

———. "Obituary." August 22, 1941.

———. "Wedding Notices." June 23, 1939.

The Jewish Review and Observer. "Deaths." June 10, 1932.

Johannes, Amy. "Superman Soars with Over $280 MM in Tie-Ins." *Promo.* June 1, 2006.

Johnson, Kim Howard. "Margot Kidder: Lois Lane's Last Headline." *Starlog* (July 1987).

Jordan, Gregory. "Mild-Mannered Comics Lover or Businessman of Steel?" *New York Times.* February 3, 1997.

Kael, Pauline. "The Current Cinema: The Package." *New Yorker.* January 1, 1979.

Kaffel, Joyce. "Digging Up Superman: A Daughter Remembers Mort Weisinger, Golden/Silver Age DC Editor." *Alter Ego* No. 98 (December 2010).

————. "Life with a Super Dad—'Superman Returns,' and So Do a Daughter's Memories." Newark *Star-Ledger.*

Kahn, E. J., Jr. "Why I Don't Believe in Superman." *New Yorker.* June 29, 1940.

Kauffmann, Stanley. "'It's a Bird . . . It's a Plane . . . It's Superman,' It's a Musical and It's Here." *New York Times.* March 30, 1966.

————. "Say It with Music, but Say It." *New York Times.* July 17, 1966.

Kealy, Jim, and Eddy Zeno. "My Attitude Was, They're Not Bosses, They're Editors." *Alter Ego* No. 59 (June 2006).

Keegan, Anne. "Superman's a Fizzle in a Clark Kent Town." *Los Angeles Times.* April 16, 1974.

Kehr, Dave. "The Adventures of Superman: The Complete First Season." *New York Times.* October 25, 2005.

Kempley, Rita. "It's Recurred! It's a Pain!" *Washington Post.* July 25, 1987.

————. "Number III Is Not So Super, Man." *Washington Post.* June 17, 1983.

————. "Superman: The Ramboization of the Comics' Man of Stale." *Washington Post.* November 2, 1985.

Kennedy, Stetson. "Response to 'Freakonomics: Hoodwinked?'" *New York Times Magazine.* January 8, 2006.

Kistler, Robert. "A Strange Life—A Tragic End." *Los Angeles Times.* October 1, 1970.

Klein, Alvin. "Another View of a Musical." *New York Times.* June 21, 1992.

Kleinfeld, N. R. "Superheroes' Creators Wrangle." *New York Times.* October 13, 1979.

Klemesrud, Judy. "'Superman' Road Show for the Special Olympics Rolls into New York." *New York Times.* December 12, 1978.

Kluger, Jeffrey. "He Never Gave Up." *Time.* October 25, 2004.

Knutzen, Eirik. "Man of Steel Splinters an American Dream." *Los Angeles Times.* February 25, 1979.

Kobler, John. "Up, Up and Awa-a-y!" *Saturday Evening Post.* June 21, 1941.

Kozlovic, Anton Karl. "Superman as Christ-Figure: The American Pop Culture Movie Messiah." *Journal of Religion and Film* 6, No. 1 (April 2002).

Krajicek, David J. "Truth, Justice and a Stickup." *New York Daily News.* August 30, 2008.

Kramer, Hilton. "Look! All Over! It's Esthetic . . . It's Business . . . It's Supersuccess!" *New York Times*. March 29, 1966.

Krebs, Albin. "Interview." *New York Times*. March 6, 1977.

Kroll, Jack. "Superman to the Rescue." *Newsweek*. January 1, 1979.

Kutner, C. Jerry. "Albert Zugsmith's Opium Dreams: Confessions of an Opium Eater." *Bright Lights Film Journal* 20 (1997).

Lambert, Bruce. "Joseph Shuster, Cartoonist, Dies." *New York Times*. August 3, 1992.

Lamken, Brian Saner. Interview with Bruce Timm. *Comicology* 2, No. 1 (Spring 2000).

Lane, Anthony. "Kryptology: 'Superman Returns.'" *New Yorker*. July 3, 2006.

Lansdale, John, Jr. "Superman and the Atom Bomb." *Harper's*. April 21, 1945.

Larsen, David. "Postscript: Even Superman Winds Up on Social Security." *Los Angeles Times*. December 17, 1976.

Larson, Jack. Interview with Noel Neill. *The Adventures Continue* No. 2 (1988).

Last, Jonathan V. "Damn! How! Take That, Evil-Doers Everywhere." *Wall Street Journal*. May 23, 2001.

Latino, Joe, Rich Morrissey, Ken Gale, and Tom Fagen. "Vin Sullivan—Present at the Creation." *Alter Ego* No. 27 (August 2003).

Lee, Patrick. "Without Tights or Flights, Smallville's Second Season Continues to Soar." *Science Fiction Weekly*. March 2003.

Lester, Peter. "Margot the Mom." *People*. August 24, 1981.

Lev, Michael. "Reaching Beyond the Ghouls and Gore for Major Payoffs." *New York Times*. February 17, 1991.

Levieros, Anthony. "Truman Ridicules General on Korea." *New York Times*. October 30, 1952.

Levin, Gary. "'Smallville' Is Super for WB." *USA Today*. November 25, 2002.

Levin, Myron. "'Protect Children Act' Aims to Ban Cigarette Deals in Films." *Los Angeles Times*. March 8, 1989.

Levitz, Paul. "DC Comics' Paul Levitz Talks 'Dark Knight.'" *Washington Post*. July 18, 2008.

Lewis, Randy. "Comics Convention to Focus on Life and Times of Superman." *Los Angeles Times*. November 11, 1983.

Liddick, Betty. "Superman Saves the Day at Swap Meet." *Los Angeles Times*. January 9, 1979.

Lillian, Guy H., III. "Mort Weisinger: The Man Who Wouldn't Be Superman." *Amazing World of DC Comics* (July 1975).

Little, Stuart W. "'Superman' Advance Sales Are Super, Too." *Los Angeles Times*. February 17, 1966.

Los Angeles Examiner. "Accusation by 'Superman' Bared." June 24, 1959.

Los Angeles Mirror News. "Superman Autopsy Ordered." June 23, 1959.

———. "TV Superman Kills Self in Home Here." June 16, 1959.

Los Angeles Times. "Actor Reeves' Mother Starts Death Inquiry." June 21, 1959.

———. "Alexander and Ilya Salkind's New 'Superboy' Is Perhaps the Worst." November 13, 1988.

———. "And Now . . . Mighty 'Superman IV' to the Rescue." January 2, 1987.

———. "Boy 'Superman,' 4, Dies of Fall Injuries." February 12, 1979.

———. "Brando Says Pact Was Broken, Sues 'Superman' Producers." December 15, 1978.

———. "Coroner Finds Shooting of Superman Suicide." June 24, 1959.

———. "'Death-Defying' Leap Kills Boy." July 6, 1941.

———. "Investigation Delays Burial of 'Superman.'" January 24, 1960.

———. "'King of Comics' Pays $1,801.26 for Superman Book." May 15, 1973.

———. "Metropolis Pins Hopes on Superman." August 15, 1979.

———. "Parents Move to Keep 'Superman' Son, 3, Grounded." August 9, 1966.

———. "Reeve Chosen After 2-Year Search." April 12, 1979.

———. "Reeves, Superman of TV, Kills Himself in His Home." June 17, 1959.

———. "Superman Fails to Save His 'Carmen.'" February 2, 1967.

———. "Superman Gives NY Newspaper a Light Story." July 14, 1977.

———. "Superman Leap Taken by Boy, 4, to Impress Girls." March 20, 1955.

———. "'Superman' Loses Out to Officer." November 1, 1975.

———. "'Superman' Receives Sci-Fi Society Awards." January 19, 1979.

———. "Superman's Estate Left to Wife of Friend." June 23, 1959.

———. "Superman's Mother and Atty. Giesler Confer." June 27, 1959.

———. "Superman's Mother, Who Fought Suicide Label, Dies in Pasadena." June 21, 1964.

———. "Superman's Town Could Use Its Hero." June 23, 1979.

———. "They're Lowering Their Sights at Cannon Films." January 15, 1987.

———. "TV Superman Hero Injured in Auto Crash." April 9, 1959.

———. "Two More Bullet Holes Deepen Reeves Mystery." June 26, 1959.

———. "Vintage Superman Collectibles Soar." July 7, 1983.

Lundegaard, Erik. "Truth, Justice, and (Fill in the Blank)." *New York Times*. June 30, 2006.

Luther, A. L. "Vigilantes Not Needed." Letters to the Editor. Cleveland *Plain Dealer*. June 3, 1932.

Lynch, Jason. "Chatter." *People*. October 9, 2000.

Lyne, Barbara. "The Executive Life: Beneath That Suit, Spider-Man Lurks." *New York Times*. May 23, 1993.

MacDonald, Heidi. "Inside the Superboy Copyright Decision." *Publishers Weekly*. April 11, 2006.

MacKenzie, Catherine. "Children and the Comics." *New York Times*. August 11, 1943.

———. "Movies—and Superman." *New York Times*. October 12, 1941.

————. "'Superman,' 'Dick Tracy' et al. Here to Stay." *New York Times*. December 15, 1944.

Malcolm, Andrew H. "Superman Rescues Metropolis Again." *New York Times*. August 8, 1972.

Mallozzi, Vincent M. "Hey Superman, Good Luck Finding a Place to Change." *New York Times*. February 19, 2006.

Mann, Jim. "'Superman' Shanghaied in Peking Screen Test." *Los Angeles Times*. January 25, 1986.

Mann, Roderick. "It's a Bird . . . It's a Plane . . . It's a Lawsuit," *Los Angeles Times*. December 7, 1980.

————. "She's Carrying 'Superman' on Her Shoulders." *Los Angeles Times*. July 18, 1978.

————. "'Superman 2' on Launching Pad." *Los Angeles Times*. October 9, 1979.

————. "'Superman': Leaping Tall Budgets." *Los Angeles Times*. April 6, 1978.

————. "Superman Makes the Leap to the Screen." *Los Angeles Times*. July 31, 1977.

————. "'Superman' Reeve a Born Flier," November 19, 1978.

————. "'Superman' Sequel: Flying in the Soup." *Los Angeles Times*. March 20, 1979.

————. "'Superman's' Battle of the Red Ink." *Los Angeles Times*. May 27, 1980.

Mansfield, Stephanie. "Superman Rusts in Legal Tussle." *Washington Post*. January 4, 1979.

Marston, William Moulton. "Why 100,000,000 Americans Read Comics." *American Scholar* 44 (Winter 1943).

Martin, Douglas. "Can Superman Be Superseded by a Capeless Wonder?" *New York Times*. January 12, 1997.

————. "Christopher Reeve, 52, Symbol of Courage, Dies." *New York Times*. October 11, 2004.

————. "Jackson Beck Dies at 92." *New York Times*. July 30, 2004.

Maslin, Janet. "Film: Animation Art of the Fleischers." *New York Times*. March 20, 1980.

————. "'Superman II' Is Full of Tricks." *New York Times*. June 19, 1981.

————. "'Superman III': Reeve Joined by Pryor." *New York Times*. June 17, 1983.

————. "Superman IV: Quest for Peace (1987)." *New York Times*. July 25, 1987.

Masters, Kim. "The Industry." *Esquire* (July 2003).

————. "Why Movies Are So Bad." *Esquire* (December 2002).

McKernan, Brian. Interview with Christopher Reeve. *Omni* (August 1983).

————. Interview with Gerard Christopher. *The Adventures Continue* No. 10 (1994).

————. Interview with Edward Langley, July 9, 1985. *The Adventures Continue* No. 11 (1995).

McMurran, Kristin. "It's Superman!" *People*. January 8, 1979.

McNary, Dave. "Super Snit in 'Smallville.'" *Variety*. April 4, 2006.

McTernan, William S. "DC Comics Is Plotting How to Bring Superman Back." *Newsday*. November 5, 1992.

———. "Superman to Die Saving Metropolis." Cleveland *Plain Dealer*. September 4, 1992.

Mead, Rebecca. "A Man-Child in Lotusland." *New Yorker*. May 20, 2002.

Melvin, Tessa. "Cartoonists Explain Superman's New Image to His Fans." *New York Times*. June 14, 1987.

Middletown Times Herald. "Company Formed." December 20, 1946.

Midpacifican. "Introducing 'SUPER GI.'" December 30, 1944.

Mietkiewicz, Henry. "Great Krypton! Superman Was The Star's Ace Reporter." *Toronto Star*. April 26, 1992.

Miller, William F. "Super Superman Collection in Town." Cleveland *Plain Dealer*. December 3, 1987.

Mitchell, John L. "Superman's Originators Warm Up After Long Freeze-Out." *Los Angeles Times*. June 18, 1981.

Mitchell, Lisa. "Superman Is Alive and Well and Living in North Hollywood." *Los Angeles Times*. August 12, 1977.

Moorman, Shelby. "At Home." *New York Times*. August 9, 1981.

Moraes, Lisa de. "Leaping over Four Tall Networks in a Single Bound!" *Washington Post*. October 17, 2002.

Moro, Eric. "All the Smallville Things." *Cinescape* (April 2003).

———. "The Hero . . . The Villain." *Cinescape* (February 2002).

Morrison, Patt. "Scholars Find Comic Lore a Portrayal of History." *Los Angeles Times*. February 9, 1979.

Murdock, Henry T. "'Superman' Lands in Town." *Philadelphia Daily News*. February 16, 1966.

Murphy, Mary. "Superman Film Set for Leap Year." *Los Angeles Times*. August 9, 1975.

Murray, Will. "DC's Tangled Roots." *Comic Book Marketplace* No. 53 (November 1997).

———. "The Driving Force That Really Made DC Great: Whitney Ellsworth and the Rise of National/DC Comics." *Alter Ego* No. 98 (December 2010).

———. "Gladiator of Iron, Man of Steel." *Alter Ego* No. 37 (June 2004).

———. Interview with Jack Schiff. August 1984.

———. "The Kryptonite Crisis: The Secret Origins of the 1940 'K-Metal' Story." *Alter Ego* No. 37 (June 2004).

———. "Mark of the Bat." *Comic Scene Yearbook* No. 1 (1992).

———. "The Pulp Connection: The Roots of the Superman!" *Comic Book Marketplace* No. 63 (October 1998).

Nadel, Norman. "'Superman,' Airy, Merry." *New York World-Telegram and Sun*. March 30, 1966.

Nash, Eric P. "Jack Liebowitz, Comics Publisher, Dies at 100." *New York Times*. December 13, 2000.

Newsweek. "Bust by Television." April 29, 1946.

———. "Comfort for Comics." January 9, 1950.

———. "Escapist Paydirt." December 27, 1943.

———. "It's Superflight." April 29, 1946.

———. "Superfans and Batmaniacs." February 15, 1965.

New York Times. "2 Comic Books Auctioned for $100,000." June 20, 1994.

———. "4-Year-Old Space Cadet Tries to Fly." March 17, 1954.

———. "A Sad Day at DC Comics as the Staff Mourns the World's Superhero." November 19, 2002.

———. "Admirer of Nasser; Rashid Karami." September 26, 1958.

———. "Advertising News and Notes." November 7, 1945.

———. "Alexander Salkind, 75; Produced 'Superman' Trio." March 20, 1997.

———. "Alfred E. Neuman Joining Superman." June 10, 1964.

———. "The Bell Tolls for Superman." September 5, 1992.

———. "Boy, 5, Causes Chills with Tricks on Ledge." March 18, 1953.

———. "Boy Who Tried to Fly 'Like Superman' Dies." February 12, 1979.

———. "Brando Sues on 'Superman' Film." December 16, 1978.

———. "Christopher Reeve, Thrown from Horse, Is Suffering Paralysis." June 1, 1995.

———. "Comic Books Can Prove Super Investment." January 1, 1973.

———. "'Comics' Blamed in Death." September 15, 1947.

———. "Conductor a Superman to Court After Arrest." January 17, 1957.

———. "Cult of Superman Decried by Visitor." August 1, 1955.

———. "Dear DC Comics." June 11, 1986.

———. "Escamillo as Superman Steps 'Carmen' in Italy." February 2, 1967.

———. "Follow-Up on the News." December 28, 1980.

———. "From Superman to Southern Gentleman." July 27, 1984.

———. "George Reeves, TV Superman, Commits Suicide at Coast Home." June 17, 1959.

———. "Has Superman Misplaced His Cloak?" March 21, 1972.

———. "In Seattle Superman Is No. 24." October 14, 1971.

———. "Kirk Alyn, 88, the Superman to Leap Tall Buildings First." March 20, 1999.

———. "Kissinger Quiet and Glum Day After His Statement." June 13, 1974.

———. "Look! It's a Bird! It's a Plane! It's Curtains for the Man of Steel." November 15, 1992.

———. "Los Angeles Station Bans 'Batman' and 'Superman.'" October 2, 1973.

———. "Man and Superman." November 8, 1952.

———. "Margot Kidder Is Hospitalized for Psychiatric Observation." April 25, 1996.

———. "Mechanical Man Guided by a Man Inside." June 16, 1964.

———. "Mort Weisinger, at 63, Editor of Comic Book." May 9, 1978.

———. "Notes on People." December 14, 1978.

————. "Notes on People." December 21, 1978.

————. "On the Mound: It's Superman Broberg!" August 1, 1971.

————. "Revealed: Why Superman Wears a Red Cape." December 14, 2003.

————. "Russian Says Comic Books 'Facisize' U.S. Children." October 16, 1949.

————. "Seinfeld Meets a Really 'Super' Salesman." January 8, 1998.

————. "'Superman II,' in First Weekend, Sets Records." June 22, 1981.

————. "Superman Adopted." May 31, 1948.

————. "Superman as Cyberman." January 14, 1997.

————. "Superman Discounted." April 12, 1955.

————. "Superman Leaps to the Big Board." May 27, 1965.

————. "Superman Meets Kennedy on Vigor." August 30, 1963.

————. "Superman Not as Fast as Police." August 26, 1950.

————. "'Superman' Plays Librarian as Comics Go Social-Minded." May 16, 1956.

————. "Superman Rescues Metropolis Again." August 8, 1972.

————. "Superman Struts in Macy Parade." November 19, 1940.

————. "Tomorrow May See End of 'Superman.'" July 16, 1966.

————. "TV Shows Scored by British Critics." March 10, 1957.

————. "When Superman Gets Boring." October 4, 1992.

————. "Whitney Ellsworth, 71, Producer of Superman Television Series." September 9, 1980.

North, Sterling. "A National Disgrace." *Chicago Daily News*. May 8, 1940.

O'Connor, John J. "TV Review: That Man in a Cape Is Still Flying." *New York Times*. April 9, 1995.

————. "TV Review: Superman at 50, A Special." *New York Times*. February 29, 1988.

O'Donnell, Patrick. "Novel's Superman Lore a Bit Weak on the Facts." Cleveland *Plain Dealer*. August 27, 2008.

Osth, Elizabeth H. Letters to the Editor. *Washington Post*. December 31, 1954.

O'Toole, Annette. "The New Woman in Superman's Life." *Starlog* No. 72 (July 1983).

Pachter, Richard. "A Rare Interview with Superman's Godfather." *Amazing Heroes* No. 41 (February 1984).

Paige, Connie. "Conn. Man Dies in Six Flags Coaster Accident." *Boston Globe*. May 2, 2004.

Parmenter, Ross. "Music World: 'Superman' Put Off." *New York Times*. March 11, 1962.

Parrott, Jennings. "For Clark Kent, Wimpery Is Out." *Los Angeles Times*. May 6, 1986.

————. "Superman to Honor a Moral Obligation." *Los Angeles Times*. November 25, 1975.

————. "Superman Turns into Santa for Two." *Los Angeles Times*. December 24, 1975.

Patton, Charlie. "Investigation of Stephen J. Dubner & Steven D. Levitt Article." *Florida Time-Union*. January 29, 2006.

Patton, Scott. "Superman, Fit and Almost 50." *Washington Post*. June 24, 1987.

Pearson, Rick. "Superman's Alive and Well in Metropolis." *Los Angeles Times*. May 22, 1983.

Peavy, Jean Shuster. "Look! Up in the Sky!" *Comics Journal* No. 184 (February 1996).

Peck, Seymour. "A Down-to-Earth Superman." *PM*. May 15, 1947.

People. "Dean Cain." May 9, 1994.

———. "Superman Christopher Reeve." July 6, 1981.

Perigard, Mark. "Raising Cain." *Boston Herald*. March 25, 1997.

Peterson, Franklynn. "Superman Goes Mod." *Indianapolis Star Magazine*. November 29, 1970.

PM. "Superman Broadcast Klan Secret, He Got 'Em from Stetson Kennedy." January 23, 1947.

Pollock, Dale. " 'Superman II' Baddies Pass the Good Word." *Los Angeles Times*. June 16, 1981.

Powers, Ron. "Penny Dreadfuls." *New York Times*. March 23, 2008.

Pyle, Richard. "Superman, Batman, Tarzan Still Have Some Punch at Auction." Associated Press. June 28, 1999.

Ramirez, Marc. "A Life-Changing Event Prompted a Mild-Mannered Auburn Man to Become a Superhero." *Seattle Times*. September 22, 2002.

Ravo, Nick. "A Happy Day of Heroes and Feasts." *New York Times*. November 28, 1986.

Reed, Walter. Interview with Boyd Magers. *The Adventures Continue* No. 16 (2001).

Reeves, Richard. "Parade to Draw 2 Million Today." *New York Times*. November 24, 1966.

Reynolds, Arthur W. "Comics, Radio, and Their Pretensions." *Clearing House* 26, No. 5 (January 1952).

Rhodes, Joe. "The Continuing Adventures and Movie Cameos of Jimmy Olsen and Lois Lane." *New York Times*. July 13, 2006.

Ricca, Brad. "I Was Just the Kid Sister Peeking Around the Corner." *Alter Ego* No. 79 (July 2008).

Rich, Frank. "Term Limit for the Man of Steel: Yes, It's Time for Him to Go." *New York Times*. November 22, 1992.

Richard, Paul. "Now Truth Is Out: Superman Helped." *Washington Post*. October 29, 1964.

Ridenour, Louis N. "Military, Security, & the Atomic Bomb." *Fortune*. November 1945.

Roberts, Michael D. "Scooped at Sea." *Cleveland Magazine*. July 2005.

Rohter, Larry. "Reinventing Superman: He'll Be Upwardly Mobile." *New York Times*. June 10, 1986.

Romano, Carlin. "Insights into the Man of Steel." *Philadelphia Inquirer*. January 17, 1988.

Rosenberg, Robert J. "Comic Geniuses." *BusinessWeek*. December 6, 2004.

Rosenblatt, Roger. "New Hopes, New Dreams." *Time*. August 26, 1996.

Rosett, Claudia. "TV: A Menu of Superheroes: World Series Has Them in Spades, but So, Too, Do Fox and WB." *Wall Street Journal.* November 5, 2001.

Ross, Alex. "It's a Bird! It's a Plane! It's a Symphony!" *New York Times.* January 12, 1994.

Rothenberg, Randall. "DC Comics in New Push to Sell Space." *New York Times.* December 22, 1988.

Routh, Brandon. Interview. *Wizard* No. 172 (February 2006).

Saft, Marcia. "Fairfield Artist Gives Superman a More Human Side." *New York Times.* October 12, 1986.

Salmans, Sandra. "The Salkind Heroes Wear Red and Fly High." *New York Times.* July 17, 1983.

Saltzman, Barbara. "Superman: From Phone Booth to Sound Booth." *Los Angeles Times.* January 26, 1975.

Saltzman, Joe. "Analyzing Clark Kent Out of His Superman Fantasy." *Los Angeles Times.* June 30, 1980.

Sangiacomo, Michael. "Author's X-Ray Vision Reveals Secrets Behind Superman." Cleveland *Plain Dealer.* October 24, 1998.

———. "Band of Gold for Man of Steel." Cleveland *Plain Dealer.* September 6, 1996.

———. "Finding a Tribute to Super Creator." Cleveland *Plain Dealer.* October 27, 1996.

———. "Flying High with Superman: Sixty Years of Getting the Bad Guy and the Girl." Cleveland *Plain Dealer.* January 18, 1998.

———. "Former Clevelander Was a Top Superman Artist in the Early Days." Cleveland *Plain Dealer.* May 26, 1996.

———. "It's a Bird, a Plane, It's Super Stamp." Cleveland *Plain Dealer.* July 15, 1988.

———. "Joanne Siegel Dies, Widow of Superman Co-Creator, Model for Lois Lane." Cleveland *Plain Dealer.* February 14, 2011.

———. "Journey into Comics: Superman's Silent Son." Cleveland *Plain Dealer.* October 26, 2005.

———. "Siegel & Schuster Relatives Unite at Siegel House." Cleveland *Plain Dealer.* July 13, 2009.

———. "Superman Creator Pondering Cameo Appearance on TV." Cleveland *Plain Dealer.* October 17, 1993.

———. "Superman Creator, Siegel, 81, Is Dead." Cleveland *Plain Dealer.* January 31, 1996.

———. " 'Superman' Creator's Son Lived and Died in Father's Shadow." Cleveland *Plain Dealer.* January 26, 2011.

———. "Superman Creator's Widow Seeks Memorial." Cleveland *Plain Dealer.* March 9, 1996.

———. "Superman Fans Mourn Artist's Death." Cleveland *Plain Dealer.* June 12, 1996.

———. "Superman's Resurrection Spurs Reader Interest Level." Cleveland *Plain Dealer.* October 28, 1992.

————. "'Superman' Writer an Old Fan." Cleveland *Plain Dealer*. August 8, 1998.

————. "Widow Wants Local Memorial for Late Superman Creator." Cleveland *Plain Dealer*. March 9, 1996.

Schickel, Richard. "Flying High." *Time*. June 8, 1981.

Schier, Ernest. "'Superman' Needs a Quick Course in Muscle Building." *Philadelphia Bulletin*. February 16, 1966.

Schwartz, Alvin. "The Real Secret of Superman's Identity." *Annual of the Modern Language Association Group on Children's Literature* 5 (1976).

Schwartz, Julius. "Dawn of the Silver Age." *Comics Scene Spectacular* No. 6. July 1992.

Seldes, Gilbert. "Preliminary Report on Superman." *Esquire*. November 1942.

Shabecoff, Phillip. "Look! Up in the Air! To Germans, It Could Be Ubermensch, Saubermann, or Superman." *New York Times*. November 7, 1967.

Shay, Don. "The Director of Steel Bends Producers in His Bare Hands." *Cinefantastique* 8, No. 4 (Summer 1979).

Sherwood, John. "Superman Still Makes Millions, but Not His Creators." *Washington Star*. October 29, 1975.

Shotz, Israel. "Superman a Sear?" Letters to the Editor. *Washington Post*. November 13, 1941.

Siegel, Jerry. "Detective Tries Composing." *Glenville Torch*. April 30, 1931.

————. "Five Men and a Corpse." *Glenville Torch*. January 14, 1932.

————. "Goober the Mighty Discovers Countless Foes in Wilderness." *Glenville Torch*. May 7, 1931.

————. "How Superman Would End the War." *Look*. February 27, 1940.

————. "Jerry Siegel Tells Why His Superman Won't End the War." *Midpacifican*. August 26, 1944.

————. "The Reign of the Super-Man." *Science Fiction: The Advance Guard of Future Civilization* No. 3 (January 1933). Written by Herbert S. Fine (Jerry Siegel).

————. "New Entertainment Company Puts on 'Shellsapoppin.'" *Midpacifican*. September 2, 1944.

Sisk, Richard. "'Superman' Creators Don't Want 'Pension.'" *Cleveland Press*. December 11, 1975.

Sloane, Leonard. "Advertising: Comics Go Up, Up, and Away." *New York Times*. July 20, 1967.

Smith, Cecil. "Broadway 'Superman': It's a Bird." *Los Angeles Times*. April 1, 1966.

Smith, Dinitia. "A Life with a Before and an After." *New York Times*. April 30, 1998.

Smith, Sean. "Steely Man." *Newsweek*. September 12, 2005.

Snook, Debbi. "Local Superman Boosters Face Bankruptcy." Cleveland *Plain Dealer*. July 21, 1988.

———. "Ordinary Mortals Not Up to the Superman Dream." Cleveland *Plain Dealer*. July 25, 1988.

Solnik, Claude. "Superman's Artist Feels Loss." *New York Times*. June 30, 1985.

Sones, W.W.D. "The Comics and Instructional Method." *Journal of Educational Sociology* 18, No. 4 (December 1944).

Spacey, Kevin. Interview. *Wizard* No. 172 (February 2006).

Stang, Joanne. "He Flies Higher Than Superman." *New York Times*. May 15, 1966.

Starlog. " 'Superman II' Movie Magazine." June 1981.

———. "Superman II Ready for Flight." July 1979.

Steinberg, Brian. "Comic Book's Superheroes Take Up the Cause for a Number of Advertisers." *Wall Street Journal*. November 10, 1998.

Stephens, William. "Film 'Superman' Flies on Wings of Nostalgia." *Los Angeles Times*. July 4, 1972.

Stevenson, Laura. "Superman's Creators Signed Away Their Baby 41 Years Ago, and Therein Lies a Sad, Sad Tale." *People*. February 12, 1979.

Strassmeyer, Mary. " 'Superman IV' to Premiere for Monument Aid." Cleveland *Plain Dealer*. May 26, 1987.

Stump, Al. "The Beautiful and the Dead: Hollywood's Unsolved Mysteries." *Los Angeles Herald Examiner*. December 23, 1979.

The Superman Radio Scripts, Vol. 1: *Superman vs. the Atom Man*. New York: Watson-Guptill Publications, 2001.

"Superman vs. Atom Man—the Prequel—and the Sequel!" *Alter Ego* No. 98 (December 2010).

Susman, Gary. "Achilles Heel." *Entertainment Weekly*. August 13, 2002.

———. "Bye Bye Brett." *Entertainment Weekly*. March 20, 2003.

———. "Cape Squad." *Entertainment Weekly*. July 9, 2002.

———. "McG Whiz." *Entertainment Weekly*. June 5, 2002.

———. "Tales from the Kryptonite." *Entertainment Weekly*. January 31, 2003.

Swanson, Tim. "Super Troupers." *Premiere: The Movie Magazine*. February 2006.

Tapley, Kristopher. "The (Tinsel) Town That Ate Superman." *New York Times*. August 20, 2006.

Taylor, Angela. "Discoveries." *New York Times*. January 31, 1979.

Taylor, Brad. "Murdering Superman." Letters to the Editor. *Los Angeles Times*. June 26, 1983.

Taylor, Charles. "Superman: The Christopher Reeve Collection." *New York Times*. September 10, 2006.

Teather, David. "After the 30-Year Struggle, a Heroic Victory." *The Guardian*. November 8, 2003.

Tepper, Ron. "A Job for Superman? He Lets George Do It." *Los Angeles Times*. May 10, 1959.

Thibodeaux, Keith. Interview with Louis Koza. *The Adventures Continue* No. 11 (1995).

Thomas, Margaret K. "Superman Teaches School in Lynn, Mass." *Magazine Digest*. April 1944.

Thomas, Robert McG., Jr. "Jerry Siegel, Superman's Creator, Dies at 81." *New York Times*. January 31, 1996.

Thomas, Roy. " 'K' Is for Krypton." *Alter Ego* No. 79 (July 2008).

———. "Super-Postscript." *Alter Ego* No. 37 (June 2004).

Thompson, Anne. "Risky Business: Fox Got Bigger Hit, but WB Happy with Singer." *Hollywood Reporter*. August 18–20, 2006.

Thompson, Dorothy. "What It Means to Be Neutral." *Look*. February 27, 1940.

Thorndike, Robert L. "Words and the Comics." *Journal of Experimental Education* 10, No. 2 (December 1941).

Time. "Americana." March 28, 1949.

———. "Are Comics Fascist?" October 22, 1945.

———. "Bang!" October 6, 1986.

———. "Cease Fire." September 3, 1945.

———. "Cliff-Hangers." May 31, 1948.

———. "Comic Culture." December 18, 1944.

———. "The Comics on the Couch." December 13, 1971.

———. "Good Grief." April 9, 1965.

———. "Here Comes Superman!!!" November 27, 1978.

———. "Jungle Sam." December 1, 1952.

———. "Man and Superman." January 5, 1976.

———. "Miscellany." August 10, 1942.

———. "Most Intimate Problem." October 24, 1949.

———. "Mystery of a Falling Star." May 6, 1996.

———. "Names Make News." June 11, 1956.

———. "The New Pictures." July 6, 1942.

———. "No Joke, Superman!" October 19, 1981.

———. "Not So Funny." October 4, 1948.

———. "Onward and Upward with the New Superman." August 1, 1977.

———. "Paperback Godfather." August 28, 1978.

———. "Paper Cutups." April 8, 1966.

———. "The Press: Superman Adopted." May 31, 1948.

———. "Radio: H–O Superman." February 26, 1940.

———. "Superman." September 11, 1939.

———. "Superman in the Flesh." September 14, 1942.

———. "Superman Jolted." August 20, 1945.

———. "Superman's Dilemma." April 13, 1942.

———. "Superman Stymied." March 11, 1940.

———. "Superman vs. Supersub." October 11, 1993.

Time for Kids. "To the Rescue: Superman's Big Mission in Bosnia." November 8, 1996.

Tollin, Anthony. *Smithsonian Historical Performances: Superman on Radio*. Schiller Park, Ill.: Radio Spirits, 1997.

————. *Smithsonian Historical Performances: Superman vs. Atom Man on Radio.* Schiller Park, Ill.: Radio Spirits, 1999.

————. *Smithsonian Historical Performances: Superman with Batman & Robin on Radio.* Schiller Park, Ill.: Radio Spirits, 1999.

TV Guide. "How They Make Superman Fly." September 25, 1953.

"Up in the Sky! Look! Jerry Siegel, Fred Allen, & Harry Donenfeld Celebrate Superman—in 1940!" *Alter Ego* No. 26 (July 2003).

Vacio, Alejandro. Interview with Chuck Harter. *The Adventures Continue* No. 15 (1998).

Vidal, David. "Mild-Mannered Cartoonists Go to Aid of Superman's Creators." *New York Times.* December 10, 1975.

————. "Superman's Creators Get Lifetime Pay." *New York Times.* December 24, 1975.

Wachter, Wall. "G.I. Hollywood Star Here." *Midpacifican.* August 26, 1944.

Waid, Mark. "K-Metal: The 'Lost' Superman Tale, the Most Important Superman Story Never Told." *Alter Ego* No. 26 (July 2003).

————. "Red Kryptonite." *Amazing Heroes* No. 41. February 15, 1984.

Waitman, Michael D. "Superman: Invulnerable to All but Kryptonite, Compassion, and Concupiscence." *Journal of Mental Imagery* 8, No. 3 (1984).

Wall Street Journal. "If 'Greatest Hero' Defeats Superman in Federal Court." March 19, 1981.

————. "'Superman II' Flies High, Setting Box-Office Record." June 22, 1981.

————. "Superman Death Issue to Go to Second Printing." November 20, 1992.

Warren, Jim. "Superman's Girl Friday." *TV People* (December 1953). Available at www.jimnolt.com/GirlFriday.htm.

Washington Post. "600 Pupils Hold Burial Rites for 2000 Comic Books." October 27, 1948.

————. "A High-Priced Comic Book." June 24, 1974.

————. "All's Well in Britain Now—Admiralty Enlists Superman." September 29, 1941.

————. "Boy Kills Self Showing Chum Gun Roulette." July 6, 1947.

————. "Bye-Bye 'Batman'." October 2, 1973.

————. "Children in Wartime." January 19, 1942.

————. "Deaths Elsewhere." March 17, 1999.

————. "He Says If Superman Can Do It Why Can't He?" April 14, 1940.

————. "It's a Bird, a Plane—a Happy Ending." December 27, 1975.

————. "Jury Blames Hanging of Boy on Comic Books." September 16, 1947.

————. "Reeves, 'Superman' on TV, Kills Self 3 Days Before Scheduled Marriage." June 17, 1959.

————. "Superman Emulation Puts Boy in Hospital." September 19, 1953.

————. "Superman Rescues His Creator from Florida Jail." December 31, 1940.

————. "Superman's Creator Now Pvt. Siegel." August 14, 1943.

————. "'Superman II' Smashes Records, 3-Day Gross Tops $14 Million." June 22, 1981.

————. "Tickets for 'Superman' Ranging High and Low." January 13, 1966.

————. "Tree Traps Boy." December 9, 1951.

————. "Window Leaper Finds He's Not Superman." April 23, 1954.

Weber, Bruce. "Joanne Siegel, the Model for Lois Lane, Dies at 93." *New York Times*. February 15, 2011.

Weinstein, Steve. "Done In by Low Ratings." *Los Angeles Times*. June 14, 1997.

Weisinger, Mort. "How They're Cleaning Up the Comic Books." *Better Homes and Gardens* (March 1955).

————. "I Flew with Superman." *Parade*. October 23, 1977.

Welkos, Robert W. "Who Shot TV's Superman?" *Los Angeles Times*. September 15, 2006.

Wharton, David. "'Superman' Ride Still Grounded." *Los Angeles Times*. August 17, 1996.

Whiteside, Thomas. "Up, Up, and Awa-a-y!" *New Republic*. March 3, 1947.

Whittlesey, Merrell W. "College Cage Chatter: 'Superman' a Must for Ex-Hoya Stretch Goedde." *Washington Post*. February 15, 1943.

Winchell, Walter. "'Superman' Artist Weds a Model." *Syracuse Herald-Journal*. October 18, 1948.

Winters, Rebecca. "It's a Bird! It's a Plane! It's . . . Who?" *Time*. November 1, 2004.

Worcester *Telegram & Gazette*. "22 Hurt in Six Flags Roller Coaster Accident." August 7, 2001.

Wysor, Michael S. "The Values of Superman Will Live On." Letters to the Editor. *New York Times*. October 22, 1992.

Yeh, Phil, and Randy Kosht. "Supersham!: The Men Who Created Superman Cannot Leap over Tall Buildings in a Single Bound." *Cobblestone* No. 12 (1975).

Yockey, Matt. "Somewhere in Time: Utopia and the Return of Superman." *The Velvet Light Trap: A Critical Journal of Film and Television* 61 (Spring 2008).

Zimmermann, Gereon. "Sean Connery on 007." *Look*. July 13, 1965.

Zinn, Laura. "It's a Bird, It's a Plane—It's a Resurrection." *BusinessWeek*. April 12, 1993.

Zoglin, Richard. "Superman vs. Supersub." *Time*. October 11, 1993.

Zolotow, Sam. "A Backstage Boss Wins as a Backer." *New York Times*. March 31, 1966.

————. "Superman Toils for Musical Role." *New York Times*. November 17, 1965.

BOOKS

Aichele, George, and Tina Pippin. *The Monstrous and the Unspeakable: The Bible as Fantastic Literature*. Sheffield, England: Sheffield Academic Press, 1997.

Alyn, Kirk. *A Job for Superman!* Self-published. 1971.

Amash, Jim. *Carmine Infantino: Penciler, Publisher, Provocateur.* Raleigh, N.C.: TwoMorrows Publishing, 2010.

Andelman, Bob. *Will Eisner: A Spirited Life.* Milwaukie, Ore.: M Press, 2005.

Andrae, Thomas. *Creators of the Superheroes.* Neshannock, Penn.: Hermes Press, 2011.

Andrae, Thomas, and Mel Gordon. *Siegel and Shuster's Funnyman: The First Jewish Superhero.* Port Townsend, Wash.: Feral House, 2010.

Anger, Kenneth. *Hollywood Babylon II.* New York: Dutton, 1984.

Austin, John. *Hollywood's Unsolved Mysteries.* New York: SPI Books, 1990.

Baetens, Jan, and Marc Lits. *Novelization: From Film to Novel.* Leuven, Belgium: Leuven University Press, 2004.

Beaty, Scott. *Superman: The Ultimate Guide to the Man of Steel.* New York: DK Publishing, 2002.

Becker, Stephen. *Comic Art in America.* New York: Simon & Schuster, 1959.

Benton, Mike. *Superhero Comics of the Golden Age: The Illustrated History.* Dallas: Taylor Publishing Company, 1992.

Berger, Arthur Asa. *The Comic-Stripped American.* Baltimore: Penguin Books, 1963.

Bifulco, Michael. *Superman on Television.* Grand Rapids, Mich.: Michael Bifulco, 1998.

Blanche, Tony, and Brad Shreiber. *Death in Paradise: An Illustrated History of the Los Angeles County Department of Coroner.* New York: Four Walls Eight Windows, 1998.

Bloom, Harold. *Modern Critical Interpretations: George Bernard Shaw's Man and Superman.* New York: Chelsea House, 1987.

Bradbury, Ray. *Fahrenheit 451.* New York: Ballantine Books, 1950.

Bradshaw, Douglas. *Shaquille O'Neal: Man of Steel.* New York: Grosset & Dunlap, 2001.

Brenner, Michael, and Gideon Reuveni. *Anticipation Through Muscles: Jews and Sports in Europe.* Lincoln: University of Nebraska Press, 2006.

Bruck, Connie. *Master of the Game.* New York: Simon & Schuster 1994.

Buhle, Paul. *From the Lower East Side to Hollywood: Jews in American Popular Culture.* New York: Verso, 2004.

———. *Jews and American Comics: An Illustrated History of an American Art Form.* New York: The New Press. 2008.

Burroughs, Edgar Rice. *A Princess of Mars.* New York: Grosset & Dunlap, 1917.

———. *John Carter of Mars,* Vol. 1. Seven Treasures Publications, 2008.

Buxton, Frank, and Bill Owen. *The Big Broadcast, 1920–1950.* New York: Avon Books, 1966.

Byrne, Craig. *Smallville: The Visual Guide.* New York: DC Comics, 2006.

Cabarga, Leslie. *The Fleischer Story.* New York: Da Capo Press, 1976.

Campbell, John W. *The Best of John W. Campbell.* New York: Doubleday, 1976.

Campbell, Joseph. *The Hero with a Thousand Faces.* California: New World Library, 1949.

Capp, Al. *The World of Li'l Abner*. New York: Ballantine Books, 1952.

Chabon, Michael. *The Amazing Adventures of Kavalier and Clay*. New York: Picador, 2000.

Coogan, Peter. *Superhero: The Secret Origin of a Genre*. Austin, Tex.: MonkeyBrain Books, 2006.

Couch, N. C. Christopher. *Jerry Robinson: Ambassador of Comics*. New York: Abrams, 2010.

Cramer, Richard Ben. *Joe DiMaggio: The Hero's Life*. New York: Simon & Schuster, 2000.

Curtis, Mike. *By George*. Greenbrier, Ark.: Shanda Fantasy Arts. March 2004.

Daniels, Les. *Comix: A History of Comic Books in America*. New York: Bonanza Books, 1988.

———. *DC Comics: Sixty Years of the World's Favorite Comic Book Heroes*. New York: Bullfinch Press, 1995.

———. *Superman: The Complete History*. San Francisco: Chronicle Books, 1998.

———. *Superman: The Golden Age*. San Francisco: Chronicle Books, 1999.

Davin, Eric Leif. *Pioneers of Wonder: Conversations with the Founders of Science Fiction*. New York: Prometheus Books, 1999.

De Haven, Tom. *It's Superman! A Novel*. New York: Ballantine Books, 2006.

———. *Our Hero: Superman on Earth*. New Haven, Conn.: Yale University Press, 2010.

Dent, Lester. Introduction to *The Man of Bronze plus The Land of Terror, Doc Savage: The Incredible Origin of the First Superhero*. Encinitas, Calif.: Nostalgia Ventures, 2008.

Dietrich, Brian D. *Krypton Nights: Poems*. Lincoln, Neb.: Zoo Press, 2002.

Dooley, Dennis, and Gary D. Engle, editors. *Superman at Fifty! The Persistence of a Legend!* Cleveland: Octavia Press, 1987.

Duin, Steve, and Mike Richardson. *Comics Between the Panels*. Milwaukie, Ore.: Dark Horse Comics, 1998.

Dunaway, Faye. *Looking for Gatsby*. New York: Simon & Schuster, 1995.

Duncan, Randy, and Matthew J. Smith. *The Power of Comics: History, Form & Culture*. New York: Continuum, 2009.

———. *Two Weeks in the Midday Sun: A Cannes Notebook*. Kansas City: Andrews and McMeel, 1987.

Eury, Michael, editor. *The Krypton Companion*. Raleigh, N.C.: TwoMorrows Publishing, 2006.

Evanier, Mark. *Superheroes in My Pants*. Raleigh, N.C.: TwoMorrows Publishing, 2004.

Feiffer, Jules. *Backing into Forward*. New York: Nan A. Talese/Doubleday, 2010.

———. *The Great Comic Book Heroes*. New York: Dial Press, 1965.

Fingeroth, Danny. *Disguised as Clark Kent: Jews, Comics, and the Creation of the Superhero*. New York: Continuum, 2007.

———. *Superman on the Couch: What Superheroes Really Tell Us About Ourselves and Our Society*. New York: Continuum, 2004.

———. *The Rough Guide to Graphic Novels*. New York: Rough Guides Ltd., 2008.

Fleischer, Richard. *Out of the Inkwell: Max Fleischer and the Animation Revolution*. Lexington: The University Press of Kentucky, 2005.

Fleisher, Michael L. *The Great Superman Book*. New York: Warner Books, 1978.

Friedrich, Otto. *City of Nets: A Portrait of Hollywood in the 1940's*. Berkeley: University of California Press, 1986.

Gabilliet, Jean-Paul. *Of Comics and Men: A Cultural History of American Comic Books*. Jackson: University Press of Mississippi, 2005.

Gaines, Jane M. *Contested Culture: The Image, the Voice, and the Law*. Chapel Hill: University of North Carolina Press, 1991.

Galloway, John T., Jr. *The Gospel According to Superman*. New York: A. J. Holman, 1973.

Gernsback, Hugo. *Hugo Gernsback Presents Science Fiction Stories*. California: Pulpville Press, 2009.

Gilbert, James. *A Cycle of Outrage: America's Reaction to the Juvenile Delinquent in the 1950s*. New York: Oxford University Press, 1986.

Glut, Donald F., and Jim Harmon. *The Great Television Heroes*. Garden City, N.Y.: Doubleday, 1975.

Goldsmith, Arnold L. *The Golem Remembered, 1909–1980: Variations of a Jewish Legend*. Detroit: Wayne State University Press, 1981.

Gordon, Ian. *Comic Strips and Consumer Culture, 1890–1945*. Washington, D.C.: Smithsonian Institution Press, 1998.

———. "Superman on the Set." *Quality Popular Television: Cult TV, the Industry, and Fans*. Edited by Marc Jancovich and Jamey Lyons. London: British Film Institute, 2003.

Gordon, Ian, Mark Jancovich, and Matthew P. McAllister. *Film and Comic Books*. Jackson: University Press of Mississippi, 2007.

Goulart, Ron. *Comic Book Encyclopedia: The Ultimate Guide to Characters, Graphic Novels, Writers, and Artists in the Comic Book Universe*. New York: It Books, 2004.

———. *Over 50 Years of American Comic Books*. Lincolnwood, Ill.: Publications International, 1991.

Granger, Stewart. *Sparks Fly Upward*. New York: G. P. Putnam's Sons, 1981.

Grant, Alan. *Last Sons*. New York: Warner Books, 2006.

Green, Michael, and Mike Johnson. *Superman/Batman: The Search for Kryptonite*. New York: DC Comics, 2008.

Greenberg, Martin H. *The Further Adventures of Superman*. New York: Bantam Books, 1993.

Greenberger, Robert, and Martin Pasko. *The Essential Superman Encyclopedia*. New York: Del Rey, 2010.

Griffin, Nancy, and Kim Masters. *Hit & Run: How Jon Peters and Peter Guber Took Sony for a Ride in Hollywood*. New York: Simon & Schuster, 1996.

Grossman, Gary. *Superman: Serial to Cereal*. New York: Popular Library, 1977.

Hajdu, David. *The Ten-Cent Plague: The Great Comic-Book Scare and How it Changed America*. New York: Picador, 2008.

Hake, Ted. *Official Price Guide to Pop Culture Memorabilia*. New York: Gemstone Publishing, 2008.

Harmon, Jim. *The Great Radio Heroes*. New York: Ace Books, 1967.

Harmon, Jim, and Donald F. Glut. *The Great Movie Serials: Their Sound and Fury*. New York: Doubleday, 1972.

Harris, Neil. *Cultural Excursions: Marketing Appetites and Cultural Tastes in Modern America*. Chicago: The University of Chicago Press, 1990.

Harter, Chuck. *Superboy & Superpup: The Lost Videos*. Hollywood, Calif.: Cult Movies, 1993.

Hatcher, Teri. *Burnt Toast and Other Philosophies of Life*. New York: Hyperion, 2006.

Havill, Adrian. *Man of Steel: The Career and Courage of Christopher Reeve*. New York: New American Library, 1996.

Hayde, Michael J. *Flights of Fantasy: The Unauthorized but True Story of Radio & TV's Adventures of Superman*. Albany, Ga.: BearManor Media, 2009.

Heer, Jeet, and Kent Worcester. *Arguing Comics: Literary Masters on a Popular Medium*. Jackson: University Press of Mississippi, 2004.

Henderson, Jan Alan. *Speeding Bullet: The Life and Bizarre Death of George Reeves*. Grand Rapids, Mich.: Michael Bifulco, 1999.

Holiday, Bob, and Chuck Harter. *Superman on Broadway*. Self-published. 2003.

Hughes, David. *The Greatest Sci-Fi Movies Never Made*. London: Titan Books, 2001.

Hughes, Langston. *The Collected Poems of Langston Hughes*. New York: Vintage Books, 1995.

Infantino, Carmine. *The Amazing World of Carmine Infantino*. Lebanon, N.J.: Vanguard Productions, 2000.

Jacobs, Will, and Gerard Jones. *The Comic Book Heroes: From the Silver Age to the Present*. New York: Crown Publishers, 1985.

Jones, Gerard. *Killing Monsters: Why Children Need Fantasy, Super Heroes, and Make-Believe Violence*. New York: Basic Books, 2002.

————. *Men of Tomorrow: Geeks, Gangsters and the Birth of the Comic Book*. New York: Basic Books, 2004.

Kahn, Jenette. *In Your Space: Personalizing Your Home Office*. New York: Abbeville Press, 2002.

Kakalios, James. *The Physics of Superheroes*. New York: Gotham Books, 2005.

Kane, Bob. *Batman & Me: An Autobiography*. Forestville, Calif.: Eclipse Books, 1989.

Kaplan, Arie. *From Krakow to Krypton: Jews and Comic Books*. Philadelphia: The Jewish Publication Society, 2008.

Kashner, Sam, and Nancy Schoenberger. *Hollywood Kryptonite*. New York: St. Martin's Press, 1996.

Keefer, Truman Frederick. *Philip Wylie*. Boston: Twayne Publishers, 1977.

Kennedy, Stetson. *The Klan Unmasked*. Gainesville: University Press of Florida, 1954.

Kisseloff, Jeff. *The Box: An Oral History of Television, 1929–1961*. New York: Penguin Books, 1995.

Knowles, Christopher. *Our Gods Wear Spandex: The Secret History of Comic Book Heroes*. San Francisco: Weiser Books, 2007.

Lawrence, John Shelton, and Robert Jewett. *The Myth of the American Superhero*. Grand Rapids, Mich.: Wm. B. Eerdmans, 2002.

LeBell, "Judo" Gene. *The Godfather of Grappling*. Santa Monica, Calif.: Gene LeBell Enterprises, 2004.

Lee, Stan, and George Mair. *Excelsior! The Amazing Life of Stan Lee*. New York: Fireside, 2002.

Legman, Gershon. *Love & Death*. New York: Breaking Point, 1949.

Lesser, Robert. *A Celebration of Comic Art and Memorabilia*. New York: Hawthorn Books, 1975.

Levitt, Steven D., and Stephen J. Dubner. *Freakonomics: A Rogue Economist Explores the Hidden Side of Everything*. New York: Harper Perennial, 2005.

Levitz, Paul. *75 Years of DC Comics: The Art of Modern Mythmaking*. Los Angeles: Taschen, 2010.

LoCicero, Don. *Superheroes and Gods: A Comparative Study from Babylonia to Batman*. Jefferson, N.C.: McFarland, 2008.

Longest, David. *Character Toys and Collectibles: Second Series*. Paducah, Ky.: Collector Books, 1987.

Lowther, George. *The Adventures of Superman*. Bedford, Mass.: Applewood Books, 1942.

Lupoff, Richard A. *Master of Adventure: The Worlds of Edgar Rice Burroughs*. Lincoln: University of Nebraska Press, 2005.

Lupoff, Richard A., and Don Thompson. *All in Color for a Dime*. New York: Ace Books, 1970.

The Mad Reader. New York: Ballantine Books, 1952.

Maggin, Elliot S. *Kingdom Come*. New York: Warner Books, 1998.

———. *Superman: Last Son of Krypton*. New York: National Periodical Publications, 1978.

Maltin, Leonard. *Of Mice and Magic: A History of American Animated Cartoons*. New York: Plume, 1980.

Mamet, David. *Some Freaks*. New York: Penguin Books, 1989.

Manso, Peter. *Brando: The Biography*. New York: Hyperion, 1994.

Mariotte, Jeff. *Trail of Time*. New York: Warner Books, 2007.

Marx, Samuel, and Joyce Vanderveen. *Deadly Illusion: Jean Harlow and the Murder of Paul Bern*. New York: Dell, 1990.

Matetsky, Amanda Murrah, and Harry Matetsky. *The Adventures of Superman Collecting*. West Plains, Mo.: Russ Cochran, Ltd., 1988.

McAllister, Matthew P., Edward H. Sewell, Jr., and Ian Gordon. *Comics and Ideology*. New York: Peter Lang Publishing, 2001.

McCloud, Scott. *Reinventing Comics: How Imagination and Technology Are Revolutionizing an Art Form*. New York: HarperCollins, 2000.

McIntyre, Ryk, and Melissa Guillet. *Look! Up in the Sky*. Providence, R.I.: Sacred Fools Press, 2006.

McLuhan, Marshall. *The Mechanical Bride: Folklore of Industrial Man*. Toronto: Copp Clark Company, 1951.

Medved, Michael. *Hollywood vs. America*. New York: Harper Perennial, 1992.

Meltzer, Brad. *The Book of Lies*. New York: Grand Central Publishing, 2008.

Menotti, Gian Carlo. *The Last Savage: An Opera in Three Acts*. New York: Franco Colombo, 1964.

Misiroglu, Gina. *The Superhero Book*. Detroit: Visible Ink, 2004.

Morris, Tom, and Matt Morris. *Superheroes and Philosophy: Truth, Justice, and the Socratic Way*. Chicago: Open Court, 2005.

Moskowitz, Sam. *Emperors of the Infinite: Shapers of Science Fiction*. New York: Meridian Books, 1963.

———. *Seekers of Tomorrow: Masters of Modern Science Fiction*. New York: Ballantine Books, 1967.

Murray, Will. "Superman's Editor Mort Weisinger." *The Krypton Companion*. Edited by Michael Eury. Raleigh, N.C.: TwoMorrows Publishing, 2006.

Nickson, Chris. *Superhero: An Unauthorized Biography of Christopher Reeve*. New York: St. Martin's Press, 1998.

Nietzsche, Friedrich. *Thus Spoke Zarathustra*. New York: Penguin Books, 1954.

Nobleman, Marc Tyler. *Boys of Steel: The Creators of Superman*. New York: Alfred A. Knopf, 2008.

Nyberg, Amy Kiste. *Seal of Approval: The History of the Comics Code*. Jackson: University Press of Mississippi, 1998.

Orwell, George. *A Collection of Essays*. Garden City, N.Y.: Doubleday, 1996.

Overstreet, Robert M. *The Comic Book Price Guide* No. 13. New York: Crown Publishers, 1983.

Paglia, Camille. *Sex, Art, and American Culture: Essays*. New York: Vintage Books, 1992.

Petrou, David Michael. *The Making of Superman the Movie*. New York: Warner Books, 1978.

Plowright, Frank. *The Slings and Arrows Comic Guide*. London: Aurum Press, 1997.

Prince, Harold. *Contradictions: Notes on Twenty-Six Years in the Theatre*. New York: Dodd, Mead, 1974.

Pryor, Richard. *Pryor Convictions and Other Life Sentences*. New York: Pantheon Books, 1995.

Reagan, Ronald. *The Reagan Diaries*. New York: HarperCollins, 2007.

Reeve, Christopher. *Nothing Is Impossible: Reflections on a New Life*. New York: Ballantine Books, 2002.

———. *Still Me*. New York: Ballantine Books, 1998.

Reynolds, Richard. *Super Heroes: A Modern Mythology*. Jackson: University Press of Mississippi, 1994.

Rhoades, Shirrel. *A Complete History of American Comic Books*. New York: Peter Lang, 2008.

Robeson, Kenneth. *Doc Savage: Murder Melody*. New York: Bantam Books, 1935.

Robinson, Jerry, Michael Chabon, and Jules Feiffer. *The Zap! Pow! Bam! Superhero: The Golden Age of Comic Books, 1938–1950*. Atlanta: The William Breman Jewish Heritage Museum, 2004.

Rose, William Ganson. *Cleveland: The Making of a City*. Cleveland: The World Publishing Company, 1950.

Rosenberg, Robin S. *The Psychology of Superheroes: An Unauthorized Exploration*. Dallas: Benbella Books, 2008.

Rossen, Jake. *Superman vs. Hollywood: How Fiendish Producers, Devious Directors, and Warring Writers Grounded an American Icon*. Chicago: Chicago Review Press, 2008.

Rubinstein, Judah, and Jane A. Avner. *Merging Traditions: Jewish Life in Cleveland*. London: The Kent State University Press, 2004.

Sadowski, Greg, ed. Introduction to *Supermen!: The First Wave of Comic Book Heroes 1936–1941*. Seattle: Fantagraphics Books, 2009.

Salisbury, Mark. *Burton on Burton*. London: Faber and Faber, 1995.

Savage, William W., Jr. *Commies, Cowboys, and Jungle Queens: Comic Books and America, 1945–1954*. Hanover, N.H.: Wesleyan University Press, 1990.

Schelly, Bill. *Words of Wonder: The Life and Times of Otto Binder*. Seattle: Hamster Press, 2003.

Schoell, William. *Comic Book Heroes of the Screen*. Secaucus, N.J.: Carol Publishing Group, 1991.

Schwartz, Alvin. *A Gathering of Selves*. Rochester, Vt.: Destiny Books, 2007.

———. *An Unlikely Prophet: A Metaphysical Memoir by the Legendary Writer of Superman and Batman*. Rochester, Vt.: Destiny Books, 1997.

Schwartz, Julius, and Brian M. Thomsen. *Man of Two Worlds: My Life in Science Fiction and Comics*. New York: HarperCollins, 2000.

Scivally, Bruce. *Superman on Film, Television, Radio and Broadway*. Jefferson, N.C.: McFarland, 2008.

Shapiro, Michael. *Jewish 100: A Ranking of the Most Influential Jews of All Time*. London: Simon & Schuster, 1994.

Shaw, George Bernard. *Man and Superman*. Baltimore: Penguin Books, 1903.

Sheridan, Martin. *Classic Comics and Their Creators: Life Stories of American Cartoonists from the Golden Age*. Arcadia, Calif.: Post-Era Books, 1973.

Siegel, Jerry, Ted Cowan, and Reg Bunn. *King of Crooks*. London: Titan Books, 2005.

Simon, Joe, and Jim Simon. *The Comic Book Makers*. Lebanon, N.J.: The Comic Book Makers, 2003.

Simonson, Louise. *Superman: Doomsday and Beyond* (novel). New York: Bantam Books, 1993.

Singer, Bryan, Michael Dougherty, and Dan Harris. *Superman Returns: The Complete Shooting Script*. London: Titan Books, 2006.

Skelton, Stephen. *The Gospel According to the World's Greatest Superhero*. Eugene, Ore.: Harvest House Publishers, 1973.

Soderbergh, Steven, and Richard Lester. *Getting Away with It: Or: The Further Adventures of the Luckiest Bastard You Ever Saw*. London: Faber and Faber, 1999.

Speriglio, Milo. *The Marilyn Conspiracy*. London: Transworld Publishers, 1986.

Stapledon, Olaf. *Odd John and Sirius*. New York: Dutton, 1936.

Steranko, Jim. *Steranko History of Comics,* Vol. 1. Reading, Penn.: Supergraphic Books, 1970.

———. *Steranko History of Comics,* Vol. 2. Reading, Penn.: Supergraphic Books, 1972.

Stern, Roger. *The Death and Life of Superman*. New York: Barnes & Noble Books, 1993.

———. *Smallville: Strange Visitors*. New York: Warner Books, 2002.

———. *Superman: The Never-Ending Battle*. New York: Pocket Star Books, 2004.

Stevens, Eric. *Superman: The Menace of Metallo*. Minneapolis: Stone Arch Books, 2009.

Strouse, Charles. *Put on a Happy Face: A Broadway Memoir*. New York: Union Square Press, 2008.

Tanakh: A New Translation of the Holy Scriptures. Philadelphia: The Jewish Publication Society, 1985.

Thomas, Evan. *The Man to See*. New York: Touchstone, 1991.

Vincent, Sidney Z. *Personal and Professional: Memoirs of a Life in Community Service*. Cleveland: Jewish Community Federation of Cleveland, 1982.

Ward, Larry Thomas. *Truth, Justice & the American Way: The Life and Times of Noel Neill, the Original Lois Lane*. Los Angeles: Nicholas Lawrence Books, 2003.

Waugh, Colton. *The Comics*. New York: Macmillan, 1947.

Weaver, Tom. *Science Fiction Stars and Horror Heroes*. Jefferson, N.C.: McFarland, 1991.

Weinstein, Simcha. *Up, Up, and Oy Vey! How Jewish History, Culture, and Values Shaped the Comic Book Superhero*. Baltimore: Leviathan Press, 2006.

Weisinger, Mort. *The Contest*. New York: New American Library, 1971.

Wertham, Frederic. *Dark Legend: A Study in Murder*. New York: Bantam Books, 1966.

———. *Seduction of the Innocent*. Laurel, N.Y.: Main Road Books, 1953.

White, David Manning, and Robert H. Abel. *The Funnies: An American Idiom*. New York: The Free Press of Glencoe, 1963.

Wolfman, Marv. *Crisis on Infinite Earths* (novel). New York: ibooks, 2005.

———. *Superman Returns*. New York: Warner Books, 2006.

Wolper, David L. *Producer: A Memoir*. New York: A Lisa Drew Book, 2003.

Wolverton, Mark. *The Science of Superman*. New York: iBooks, 2002.

Wright, Bradford W. *Comic Book Nation: The Transformation of Youth Culture in America*. Baltimore: The Johns Hopkins University Press, 2001.

Wylie, Philip. *Gladiator*. New York: Manor Books, 1976.

Wylie, Philip, and Edwin Balmer. *When Worlds Collide*. Lincoln: University of Nebraska Press, 1999.

Yeffeth, Glenn. *The Man from Krypton: A Closer Look at Superman*. Dallas: Benbella Books, 2005.

Yoe, Craig. *Secret Identity: The Fetish Art of Superman's Co-Creator Joe Shuster*. New York: Abrams ComicArts, 2008.

Young, William H., and Nancy K. Young, *The 1950s*. Westport, Conn.: Greenwood Press, 2004.

Yule, Andrew. *The Man Who "Framed" the Beatles: A Biography of Richard Lester*. New York: Donald I. Fine, 1994.

Zeno, Eddy. *Curt Swan: A Life in Comics*. Lebanon, N.J.: Vanguard Productions, 2002.

Index

Smallville: The Comic (comic book), 278
Smallville (TV show), xi, 197, 274–81, 284, 290
Smolinski, Aaron, xii, 241
Snyder, Zach, 298
Soviet Union (Russia), 9, 30, 58
Spacy, Kevin, 283, 288
Special Olympics, 213
Spectre (character), 116–17
Spengler, Pierre, 199, 232
Spider Lacy (character), 99
Spider-Man (character), 55, 72, 74–75, 167–68, 197, 212, 263, 267, 287
Spielberg, Steven, 193, 254
Spirit, The (comic strip), 74
"Spy" (Siegel and Shuster *New Fun* comic strip), 23, 48, 52
Squeezeblood, Rockwell P. (character), 120
Stalin, Joseph, x, 30, 58
Stallone, Sylvester, 195
Stalmaster, Lynn, 195–96
Star-Spangled Kid (character), 116–17
Star Trek (TV show), 169
Star Wars (movies), 210, 235
Steel (character), 250, 252, 264–65
Steel (movie), 265–66
"Sticky-Mitt Stimson" (comic book story), 36
St. John, J. Allen, 17–18
Straczynski, J. Michael, 297
Strange Suicides (magazine), 25
Streaky the Super-Cat (character), 170
Strouse, Charles, 175, 178–79
Stupor-Man (parody comic book), 180
Sugarhill Gang, 295–96
Sullivan, Chloe (character), 276–78
Sullivan, Vin, 29
Sunday Buffalo Times, 12
Superbaby (character), 161

Superboy (character), 186, 220–22, 225, 226
copyright and, 118–19
invention of, 63, 108–9, 111, 143
return of, in 1993 comics, 252
Smallville and, 274–75
Superman movies and, 193
TV cartoons and, 180
Superboy (comic book), 108, 111, 117–18, 173, 203, 239
Superboy (TV show), 239–40, 280
Super Friends (TV cartoon show), 212–13
Super G.I. (comic strip), 63
Supergirl (character), 161, 170–71, 175, 182, 186, 279. *See also* Zor-El, Kara; Lee, Linda
comic books, 249, 251
Earth-2 and, 226
Supergirl (movie), 238–39
Super-Man (early Siegel and Shuster character), 8, 16–17, 46–47, 205–6
Superman. *See also* Kal-El/L; Kent, Clark; Krypton; Shuster, Joe; Siegel, Jerry; superpowers; *and specific characters and titles of comic books, movies, radio shows, stories, and TV shows*
Action Comics introduces, 30–44
backstory developed, 18–19, 30–31, 40–44, 50, 88–89, 103–4, 107–8
Broadway musical, 175–70
catchphrases in, 96
changes in, over time, xiv, 68, 102–4, 109, 164
collectors and, 261–63, 295
·college courses on, 211–12, 295
comic books, of 1930s and 1940s, xi, xiv, 30–45, 47, 83, 103–4, 160
comic books, of 1950s, 127–32
comic books, of 1960s, and Weisinger remake, 158–88

ABOUT THE AUTHOR

Larry Tye was an award-winning journalist at *The Boston Globe* and a Nieman Fellow at Harvard University. Tye, who grew up with Superman on his night table and Clark Kent as a role model, now runs a Boston-based training program for medical journalists. He is the author of *The Father of Spin, Home Lands, Rising from the Rails,* and *Satchel,* and co-author, with Kitty Dukakis, of *Shock.* Tye is now writing a biography of Robert F. Kennedy.

ABOUT THE TYPE

This book was set in Bembo, a typeface based on an old-style Roman face that was used for Cardinal Bembo's tract *De Aetna* in 1495. Bembo was cut by Francisco Griffo in the early sixteenth century. The Lanston Monotype Machine Company of Philadelphia brought the well-proportioned letter forms of Bembo to the United States in the 1930s.